# WORKERS IN
# THE METROPOLIS

# WORKERS IN THE METROPOLIS

Class, Ethnicity, and Youth
in Antebellum New York City

RICHARD B. STOTT

Cornell University Press

ITHACA AND LONDON

Copyright © 1990 by Cornell University

All rights reserved. Except for brief quotations in a review, this book,
or parts thereof, must not be reproduced in any form without
permission in writing from the publisher. For information, address
Cornell University Press, 124 Roberts Place, Ithaca, New York 14850.

First published 1990 by Cornell University Press.

International Standard Book Number 0-8014-2067-9

Library of Congress Catalog Card Number 89-42890

Printed in the United States of America
*Librarians: Library of Congress cataloging information
appears on the last page of the book.*


♾ The paper used in this publication meets the minimum
    requirements of the American National Standard for Permanence
    of Paper for Printed Library Materials Z39.48-1984.

To my mother, Marian G. Stott,
and the memory of my father,
Richard B. Stott, Sr.

# Contents

# Tables

# Figures and Maps

# Acknowledgments

Writing history is not a solitary endeavor, and I am pleased to acknowledge those who have aided me in completing this manuscript. At Cornell University I thank Steven L. Kaplan and Gerd Korman, whose friendship and aid I deeply appreciate. I owe special thanks to Stuart Blumin, whose intellectual guidance and support have influenced both the questions I have asked in this book and the methodology I have used. His high standard of scholarship has made this a better work.

Several other historians have made helpful suggestions. Elliott Gorn and Roy Rosenzweig were tremendously helpful with their incisive comments and suggestions. I also owe grateful thanks to Christine Stansell, whose valuable comments did much to clarify my ideas and improve the manuscript, and Diane Lindstrom, who deserves thanks for her discerning criticism of the chapters on immigration and industrialization. The enthusiasm and encouragement of Peter Agree of Cornell University Press I deeply appreciate. The reference staff at Olin Library at Cornell was very helpful in obtaining material for the book.

I owe special thanks to Kerby Miller for bringing to my attention letters from Irish immigrants in New York. I also express my appreciation to Margaret Kassner for her help in copying these letters. I am especially grateful to Martin Bruegel for the translations from German. I also thank Kenneth Scherzer, for giving me permission to quote from his work, and Jane Torrey, for permission to quote the Henry Walter manuscript. To Roger Haydon of Cornell University Press I owe a dual debt. He not only copyedited the manuscript with skill and precision but provided me with a photocopy of the Walter manuscript and called my attention to other materials on English immigrants.

RICHARD B. STOTT

*Washington, D.C.*

# WORKERS IN
# THE METROPOLIS

# Introduction: The Metropolis and Working-Class History

New York is . . . composed of good and bad characters, sinners and saints, Frenchmen and English, Germans & Irish, and also a few Scotch. . . . & many mix altogether and get along the best way they can.
                                        —William Young, an Irish immigrant, 1850

American social history has advanced rapidly in the last twenty years, especially in the explosion of books and articles, collectively called the "new labor history," that has substantially increased our knowledge of workers' unions, political organizations, and lives. American historians now have a much clearer picture of how workers responded to the industrial revolution.

Most of these recent studies in social history have focused on specialized and not very large industrial cities: Paterson, Lynn, Lowell. The experience of workers in these cities is clearly essential to our understanding of the American working class. However, the experience of workers in New York, a metropolis of world importance, differed in a number of ways from that of workers in industrial cities.

There were wide variations among the industrial cities and towns of nineteenth-century America—between Lynn, with its relatively small shoe shops, and Lowell, with its huge, heavily capitalized factories. Yet despite this variety, industrial cities had some similarities. They were usually near a large port, and their workers were often concentrated in a single industry— shoes in Lynn, textiles in Lowell. Although virtually every industrial town had its share of small workshops, most were dominated by factories. Generally, the middle class in industrial towns seems to have been relatively small, and workers and bosses faced each other with hostility. Moreover, as Herbert Gutman has noted for Paterson, New Jersey, numerical dominance in these towns allowed workers to exercise considerable political power in the nineteenth century.[1]

1. Herbert Gutman, *Work, Culture and Society in Industrializing America: Essays in American Working-Class and Social History* (New York, 1977).

Other similarities characterized industrial cities. Although such cities were small enough to give residents a more intense communal experience, their size meant that workers had fewer amusements than their counterparts in major cities. Indeed, it may be that because of the tendency to focus on industrial cities, historians have not paid sufficient attention to working-class culture. New York, with its enormous number of saloons and theatres, provided a fertile ground for workers to create a dense recreational life off the job. Very likely it was in major cities, especially New York and Philadelphia, that a distinctive American working-class culture was first created.

Working-class life in the metropolis of New York, with an industry dominated by small shops, more complex class structure, and richer associational life, was quite different from that of Newark or Lowell. Optimistic historians sometimes assume that, despite complexity, there exists a "typical" historical experience. This does not seem to have been the case with antebellum workers—neither Lowell, nor Rockdale, Pennsylvania, nor New York City was "typical." The experiences of New York workers and those in surrounding towns were different, but those differences were not random. However, we can do more than emphasize the uniqueness of each locality.

Industrialization was an exceedingly complex phenomenon with variable effects not only from one industry to another but also from one community to another. Local studies of its social consequences should not fragment our understanding, however, but lead to a synthesis that contains the characteristic effects of industrial development in small factory towns, medium-sized industrial centers, and large cities. This book builds toward that synthesis by presenting a regional model of industrialization that helps explain certain of the significant differences between New York, a major port, and nearby Newark and Paterson. Previous studies of such industrial cities depict single locales within a metropolitan regional economy—locales whose industrial development was influenced by their place in the economic region. Examining industrial development in a regional context helps explain why industrialization was so complex and suggests that the progress of factories in Paterson and Newark, which seemed so startling to those involved, was heightened by peripheral location in a regional economy centered on New York City.

Two works of the new labor history deal with large port cities during the early industrial revolution: Bruce Laurie on Philadelphia and Sean Wilentz on New York. Both focus on the impact of industrialization on artisans, and both stress the diversity of urban industrial development in the 1830s and 1840s. Wilentz describes how New York's masters and journeymen believed that they, as skilled artisans standing between an elite corrupted by wealth and a dependent poor, were the guarantors of political virtue and freedom. Thus craftsmen in the first three decades of the nineteenth century believed it was their special duty to defend and extend the heritage of the American Revolution and preserve the common good. Wilentz calls this ideology "artisan republicanism," and he describes how it was strongly rooted both in the reality of the city's trades, mostly in artisans' shops, and in the symbol of the American Revolution.[2]

Wilentz then explains how artisan republicanism was threatened by industrialization, which began to replace the traditional artisan's workshop, with its master and skilled journeymen, by a debased "bastard workshop" using poorly trained "hands." Wilentz calls this process "metropolitan industrialization." By attacking the workshop and threatening to deprive journeymen of their "independence," industrialization created both an economic and an ideological crisis for urban artisans. "In their view," writes Wilentz, "resistance to capital, defense of the Republic, and preservation of their rights . . . were one and the same cause; above all the notion of independence, central to both republican politics and the order of the artisan system, propelled their critique of proletarianization." The protests of the city's workers in the 1830s are the main focus of *Chants Democratic,* and Wilentz shows how artisan republicanism continued to be a vital resource in the struggle against capital.[3]

Wilentz and Laurie are most interested in the reaction of artisans to the onset of industrialization, and they therefore deal mainly with the 1830s. "Yet," as Amy Bridges has pointed out, "in the most literal ways the American working classes did not have artisan origins, and surely not origins in Jacksonian workers. Of the wage workers of mid-century, a great majority were not American-born and a good number were not artisans before they emigrated. Whatever their initial cultural resources (about which we know precious little), they became the great majority of the American working classes." These workers are the focus of this book.[4]

The massive immigration of the 1840s began a transformation of the American working class. In New York by 1855, as Robert Ernst's pioneering work shows, over 80 percent of manual workers were foreign-born. If the city's working class was made in the 1830s, as Wilentz's research suggests, it was remade in the late 1840s and early 1850s. Immigrants were different in fundamental respects from the native journeymen of the 1830s who were proud of their trade and steeped in artisan republicanism. The artisan gave way to semiskilled and unskilled Irish and German workers to whom the language of "virtue" and "independence" had little meaning.[5]

---

2. Bruce Laurie, *Working People of Philadelphia, 1800–1850* (Philadelphia, 1980); Sean Wilentz, *Chants Democratic: New York City and the Rise of the American Working Class, 1788–1850* (New York, 1984).

3. Wilentz, *Chants Democratic,* 244–245. Laurie makes a similar argument in *Working People of Philadelphia,* 82.

4. Amy Bridges, "Becoming American: The Working Classes in the United States before the Civil War," in Ira Katznelson and Aristide R. Zolberg, eds., *Working-Class Formation: Nineteenth-Century Patterns in Western Europe and the United States* (Princeton, N.J., 1986), 194–195.

5. Robert Ernst, *Immigrant Life in New York City, 1825–1863* (1949; rpt. New York, 1979).

It was not just foreign birth that distinguished immigrants from other Americans, but also age. The immigrants were a peculiarly youthful group; the overwhelming majority were in their twenties and thirties. They gave New York City a very large population of young adults in the 1850s, which had a discernible effect on the city's remade working class. Indeed, the Bowery milieu of the 1850s, with its theatres, saloons, and lusty, brawling style, was to a large degree a youth culture. The preponderance of young adults in the nation's labor force may have affected the development of America's working class generally, and I shall suggest some ways demography may have influenced working-class formation.

The 1850s marked a watershed in the development of the nation's working class. As Herbert Gutman and Ira Berlin have noted, "the urban industrial working class formed in America prior to 1840 did not reproduce itself between 1840 and 1880. . . . In fact, with a few important exceptions, after 1840 most American workers were immigrants or the children of immigrants." Their research in the 1880 census shows that by that date, "native-born workers of native-born parents were . . . so few as to be nearly invisible." The late 1840s and 1850s were critical in the development of the American working class, for then immigrant domination of the workforce began, a process that shaped the class into the twentieth century. Although I use evidence from the 1820s to the 1860s to examine how the city's artisans were replaced by immigrant workers, mine is less a history of working men and women between those dates than an attempt to understand the remade working class of the 1850s. My focus, therefore, is mainly on the last two decades of the antebellum period. In this period the traditional artisan way of life was replaced by something new. I examine this change by analyzing such diverse aspects of working-class life as the rise of the saloon, the growth of prizefighting, and the beginning of vaudeville.[6]

Since the creation of an immigrant working class is the main theme of this book, immigrant workers, and especially Irish and British workers, are my focus. Ireland sent by far the largest number of immigrants to the city, and Irish influence was crucial in the transformation of the 1840s and 1850s. British immigrants came from an advanced industrial nation and often made interesting comparative comments on American industrialization, as well as providing a useful contrast to the Irish experience. German and native workers are not investigated as systematically as the Irish and British, but some evidence on these groups helps provide a more complete picture of the city's workforce at mid-century.

The remaking of New York's working class I explore mainly by examining

6. Herbert Gutman and Ira Berlin, "Class Composition and the Development of the American Working Class, 1840–1890," in Herbert Gutman, *Power and Culture: Essays on the American Working Class*, ed. Ira Berlin (New York, 1987), 382, 385, 386.

the everyday experience of the city's workers. One of the most difficult tasks facing social historians is to connect the experiences of ordinary people with large structural changes such as industrialization. I use quantitative evidence to study the impact of the industrial revolution on New York and the demographic transformation of the city's labor force. But if quantification provides much of the base on which this book rests, I also use diaries, letters, and reminiscences to examine the texture of urban working-class life. Social classes are aggregates of individuals with similar experiences, and the meaning of "working class" cannot be understood unless we understand those experiences. Too often, as Charles Joyner has warned, historians try "to analyze abstract wholes without having investigated concrete parts." Immigrant letters and diaries help us understand the concrete parts. Thus, while this book is about work, space, consumption, and demography in industrializing New York City, it is also about John Burke, an Irish shoemaker, Henry Price, who came to the city from an English workhouse and became a cabinetmaker, and Henry Walter, an immigrant manufacturing jeweler.[7]

Because of its focus on daily life, this book pays less attention to politics and unions than is customary. Neither is ignored—workers' political and labor organizations are described and analyzed. Workers, however, did not compartmentalize their lives, and unions and politics are treated as workers experienced them: a part of working-class life, not its essence.

I emphasize that the focus on daily existence does *not* mean I believe ideas and culture are unimportant. But I believe it is impossible to analyze workers' culture, and for that matter workers' politics, without understanding daily experience. A culture has to "make sense," and the material, even biological, realities of urban life in the mid-nineteenth century strongly influenced working-class culture. It is hardly surprising that when material conditions and the composition of New York's working class changed, culture changed as well.

This book is divided into two parts. The first three chapters provide context. Relying heavily on quantitative evidence, they trace the city's industrial development and changing demography. Chapters 1 and 2 examine the impact of industrialization on the city from 1820 to 1860 and note especially how the development of a New York–based regional economy influenced manufacturing in New York City. Chapter 3 looks at population changes in the 1840s and 1850s and describes the transition to an immigrant labor force. The second

7. Charles Joyner, *Down by the Riverside: A South Carolina Slave Community* (Urbana, Ill., 1984), xvii. On the perils and prospects for social historians trying to connect structural changes to the lives of ordinary people, see Charles Tilly, "Retrieving European Lives," and Olivier Zunz, "The Synthesis of Social Change: Reflections on American Social History," both in Zunz, ed., *Reliving the Past: The Worlds of Social History* (Chapel Hill, N.C., 1985).

part of the book—Chapters 4–9—examines working-class life in the city. Chapter 4 analyzes the interaction between the family and the labor market and examines the sharp difference in the experience of male and female workers in the city. Chapter 5 focuses on the workplace itself and tries to give some idea of New Yorkers' experience of manual work. Chapter 6 assesses the living standards of city workers and looks at the impact of the good American diet on the laboring population. Chapter 7 examines the spatial changes caused by industrialization, emphasizing the significance of the development of a working-class section of the city. Chapter 8 describes the leisure activities of city workers and how they changed during the 1840s and 1850s. Chapter 9 concludes the book by examining some aspects of the remade working-class culture that began to appear in the late 1840s and early 1850s.

CHAPTER I

# The City

"This is a great city, and is daily becoming greater," wrote English journalist Archibald Prentice about New York in 1848. Between 1820 and 1860 the growth of the city amazed observers. Even English and French visitors, accustomed to such major cities as London and Paris, were impressed with New York's expansion. To Americans, living in a country that was 80 percent rural in 1860, the increase in size seemed overwhelming. John Pintard, a merchant and banker, wrote in 1826, "We are rapidly becoming the London of America, I myself am astonished and this city is the wonder of every stranger." To Walt Whitman, New York City was nothing less than "the great place of the Western Continent, the heart, the brain, the focus, the main spring, the pinnacle, the extremity, the no more beyond of the new world."[1]

In 1820 New York was already a substantial city of 124,000 people and had spread as far north as Houston Street. Continued growth over the next forty years would create a metropolis that dwarfed the earlier city. By 1860 New York's population had grown to 814,000, and the city was built up almost to 42nd Street. The New York metropolitan area had 862,391 inhabitants in 1850, and 1,435,774 (including 267,000 in Brooklyn) in 1860. New York in 1800 had been the second-largest city in the United States, behind Philadelphia. In the 1820 census New York's population exceeded that of the Pennsylvania city for the first time, and its lead was rapidly widening. Some-

1. Prentice and Pimtard quoted in Bayrd Still, *Mirror for Gotham: New York as Seen by Contemporaries from Dutch Days to the Present* (New York, 1956), 125, 79. *Walt Whitman of the New York Aurora*, ed. Joseph Rubin and Charles Brown (State College, Pa., 1950), 19.

time in the 1830s New York surpassed Mexico City and became the largest city in the New World.[2]

How can we account for such an increase in population? Cities provide a variety of services to smaller towns in nearby areas, and one important reason for New York's growth was the rapid expansion of its hinterland in the early nineteenth century. The Hudson River is an unparalleled natural highway to inland areas, but the upstate region was relatively slow to develop. The power of the Indian tribes in the region and a restrictive land policy kept the population of upstate New York small; in 1780 New York State was estimated to be the fifth most populous state with 210,000 inhabitants—only 4,000 more than Connecticut. As the upstate region was opened to settlement, its population increased rapidly; by 1820 New York had become the second largest state in the union.[3]

COMMERCE

While the expansion of the hinterland explains much of the city's remarkable growth, it is only part of the story. New York's increase in population was part of the general urbanization of American society in the antebellum period. Between 1820 and 1860 the urban population of the United States (those living in places with more than 2,500 inhabitants) grew from 693,000 to 6,217,000 and, on a percentage basis, almost tripled from 7 percent to 20 percent.[4]

The development of transportation before the Civil War is central to an explanation of urbanization. New York's rise to the top of the nation's urban hierarchy was accomplished before the opening of the first section of the Erie Canal in 1820. Nonetheless, the state's canal system was important in sustain-

2. Robert Ernst, *Immigrant Life in New York City, 1825–1863* (1949; rpt. New York, 1979), 21. The metropolitan area is made up of the counties of New York, Kings, Richmond, and Westchester in New York; Bergen, Essex, Hudson, Passaic, and Union in New Jersey; and Fairfield County, Connecticut. Census Office, *Eleventh Census, 1890, Population* (Washington, 1895); George Rogers Taylor, "Comment," in David Gilchrist, ed., *The Growth of Seaport Cities, 1790–1825* (Charlottesville, Va., 1967), 39; Ira Rosenwaike, *Population History of New York City* (Syracuse, N.Y., 1972), 33–36. Mexico City regained the "championship" in the 1970s.

3. In 1790, according to Simeon Crowther, Philadelphia had 44,000 residents with an estimated hinterland population of 455,000 and New York City had 33,000 inhabitants and a hinterland of 393,000. By 1810 the totals for Philadelphia were 87,000 and 679,000; for New York City, a population of 101,000 and 695,000. Crowther, "Urban Growth in the Mid-Atlantic States, 1785–1850," *Journal of Economic History* 26 (1976), 629–630; see also Diane Lindstrom, *Economic Development in the Philadelphia Region, 1810–1850* (New York, 1978), 35, and Jeanne Chase, "L'organisation de l'espace économique dans le nord-est des Etats-Unis après la guerre d'Indépendance," *Annales ESC* 43 (1988), 997–1020.

4. Bureau of the Census, *Historical Statistics of the United States, Colonial Times to 1970* (Washington, D.C., 1975), 12; Eric Lampard, "The Evolving System of Cities in the United States," in Harvey Perloff and Lowdoun Wingo, eds., *Issues in Urban Economics* (Baltimore, Md., 1968), 108.

ing the city's growth; the Erie Canal opened up vast areas of the west to the city's trade and extended the city's commercial dominance over a much larger area. The canal not only increased the size of the city's hinterland but caused a redefinition within the hinterland region of the relationship between city and countryside.

The canal system dramatically reduced the cost of shipping. In 1817 the cost of transporting a ton of goods from New York to Buffalo was 19 cents a mile, but by the 1830s the price was 1.7 cents a mile. Increasingly, it made good economic sense for farmers to specialize in commercial agriculture. As they specialized, farm families began to purchase goods they had previously fabricated for themselves—home manufactures of textiles in upstate New York, largely by farm wives, dropped from 10.8 yards per capita in 1825 to 0.4 yards in 1855. The difference was made up by commercially produced textiles. The process by which farmers were drawn into the marketplace was of prime importance in the increased demand for manufactured consumer goods, especially after 1820 when this specialization began to replace hinterland growth as the motive force behind the city's development.[5]

The tremendous increase in trade obviously benefited the city. Agricultural products, particularly flour, were sent down the canal and the Hudson to New York for export to Europe. The return trade with the countryside, primarily manufactured goods and especially English textiles, was shipped up the Hudson to rural merchants. Between 1820 and 1860 about 33 percent of the entire country's exports from major ports, and 60 percent of the nation's imports, passed through New York: total imports and exports through the city increased from 338,000 tons in 1821 to 3,651,000 tons in 1860. This growing commercial sector, of course, required merchants, jobbers, clerks, and thousands of longshoremen.[6]

The city's position as commercial hub of a huge hinterland spurred the growth of financial institutions. The nation's trading center, New York naturally became the country's major banking center, and Wall Street became synonymous with America's financial community. By 1860 New York had, in Alfred Chandler's words, "one of the most sophisticated capital markets in the world." As the focal point of specialized business information and monetary services the city was able to capture a greater and greater share of the nation's trade.[7]

---

5. George Rogers Taylor, *The Transportation Revolution, 1815–1860* (1951; rpt. New York, 1968), 137; textile production figures compiled from Rolla Tyron, *Household Manufactures in the United States, 1640–1860* (Chicago, 1917), 304–305. Excellent on this process are Lindstrom, *Economic Development,* and Taylor, *Transportation Revolution.*

6. Robert Greenhalgh Albion, *The Rise of New York Port, 1815–1860* (New York, 1939), 76–94, 392–393, 411.

7. John Townsend, "Wall Street," in Chauncey Depew, ed., *One Hundred Years of American Commerce* (New York, 1895), 1:67–76; Alfred D. Chandler, Jr., *The Visible Hand: The Managerial Revolution in American Business* (Cambridge, Mass., 1977), 92. In the 1820s,

New York merchants used the city's centralized capital to capture trade that otherwise might have been carried on directly with Europe, and the Southern Trade became a major part of the city's commerce by the 1820s. Most European exports to the South were shipped through New York City, and in the 1820s and 1830s a substantial proportion of the South's cotton was sent to New York for transshipment to Europe. Between the 1820s and the 1840s the cotton trade was the most lucrative and important part of the city's commerce.[8]

## MANUFACTURING

The vast increase in commerce spurred not only the city's finance but its manufacturing as well. The goods that passed through the city often needed to be processed, and commerce itself demanded ships, barrels, and boxes; New York's manufacturing sector grew rapidly after 1820. Table 1 shows the percentage of the population (*not* of the workforce) engaged in manufacturing. The high 1850 figure makes it difficult to speak about trends with any certainty, especially since the census definition of manufacturing often changed. It is clear, however, that the manufacturing sector of the economy was large. By 1840, according to Diane Lindstrom's figures, $20,841,000 of the city's income originated in commerce and $12,504,000 in manufacturing.[9]

The next chapter discusses in detail the development of specific industries in the city. Here my main interest is in developing an overall picture of the importance of manufacturing in the city and in understanding the *types* of industries most likely to grow between 1820 and 1860. It is evident that a good deal of manufacturing was directly related to the city's role as a port and commercial center. Shipbuilding, sugar refining, and printing were all among the city's major industries. The Webb and Westervelt shipbuilding firm was one of the country's largest, and by the 1840s the East River was lined with foundries that specialized in building steam engines.[10]

However, in 1860 only 21 percent of manufacturing employees in the city were employed in industries ancillary to commerce. How can we account for a

---

27 percent of the nation's exports and 45 percent of its imports passed through the city; by the 1850s these proportions were 34 percent of exports and 64 percent of imports. Figures computed from Albion, *Rise of New York Port*, 390–391.

    8. Albion, *Rise of New York Port*, 95–121.

    9. Lindstrom, *Economic Development*, 52. The high 1850 total was probably due to the booming economy of the period; see Chapter 4.

    10. The foundries of New York City are discussed in Chapter 2. On the city's shipbuilding industry see John H. Morrison, *History of New York Ship Yards* (New York, 1909); Leander Bishop, *A History of American Manufactures from 1608 to 1860* (1868; rpt. New York, 1967), 3:136–144; and Albion, *Rise of New York Port*, 287–311.

TABLE I

Population of New York City and manufacturing employees, 1820–1880

| Year | City population | Manufacturing employees | Percent in manufacturing |
|------|-----------------|-------------------------|--------------------------|
| 1820 | 123,706 | | |
| 1830 | 202,589 | | |
| 1840 | 312,710 | 26,466 | 8.5% |
| 1850 | 515,547 | 84,580 | 16.4 |
| 1855 | 629,810 | 66,648 | 10.6 |
| 1860 | 813,669 | 90,204 | 11.1 |
| 1870 | 942,292 | 129,577 | 13.8 |
| 1880 | 1,206,299 | 217,974 | 18.1 |

*Note:* Because the 1840 Manufacturing Census does not list clothing workers, the total number of workers has been adjusted upward 32 percent (the percentage of clothing workers in the 1850 census).

*Sources:* Census Office, *Seventh, Eighth, Ninth, Tenth Census 1850, 1860, 1870, 1880, Manufactures;* Census Office, *Eleventh Census, 1890, Population,* 32; *Census of the State of New York, 1855.* The 1850 figures are compiled from manuscript returns of the *Census of Manufactures.*

large manufacturing sector unrelated to the city's commercial role? Demand for manufactured goods was growing as farmers were brought into the market, but there is no compelling reason why these goods should have been produced in the port and then shipped to the hinterland. Indeed, the majority of manufactured goods shipped inland from New York City were *not* produced there; most were imported from England or manufactured elsewhere in the United States. Of the ten largest American cities, however, the three Eastern ports of New York, Philadelphia, and Boston had a substantially higher percentage of the population engaged in manufacturing (13.4) than the seven others (7.3). Why?[11]

Manufacturing in cities has a number of advantages: access to capital, local markets, immediate information, good transport, and a large labor pool. In the case of port cities, labor may have been the most important advantage, as these cities were the debarkation points for the overwhelming majority of immigrants to the United States (see Appendix C). Although a wide range of industries, many of them commerce-related, flourished in port cities, the ports were especially attractive to manufacturers who needed a large, unskilled or

11. In 1860, of New York's 90,204 industrial employees, 21 percent were in entrepôt and commerce-serving manufacturing and 79 percent in what Lindstrom, *Economic Development,* calls "local"—a catchall category that includes all manufacturing not directly related to commerce. Of the nation's ten largest cities, Cincinnati had the largest percentage (18.2) of its population engaged in manufacturing. Next were the Eastern ports: Philadelphia (17.5 percent), New York (11.1 percent), and Boston (10.8 percent). The six other cities were Baltimore (8.0 percent), Buffalo (6.9 percent), St. Louis (5.8 percent), Chicago (4.9 percent), Brooklyn (4.8 percent), and New Orleans (3.0 percent). Census Office, *Eighth Census, 1860, Statistics* (Washington, 1866), xvii.

semiskilled labor force. The clothing industry was by 1820 already among the city's largest, and cigarmaking also became a major urban industry.[12]

By using an extensive division of labor, the city's industrialists were able to undercut rural and small-town manufacturers by hiring a few highly skilled workers to do the most difficult part of the manufacturing process and less skilled, cheaper workers to do the rest. In 1849 A COUNTRY TAILOR described this process in the *New York Tribune:*

> Do you know that the wholesale Clothing Establishments in your city are rapidly increasing their number and amount of business. . . . They are forcing their work into the villages along the rivers, canals and railroads, absorbing the business of the country; and thus casting many an honest and hardworking man out of employment, or drawing them to your city by taking their work there. . . . I know many pleasant and flourishing little villages which a few years ago sustained half a dozen tailors each, and are now giving a scanty support to less than half that number, because the merchants, and establishments devoted exclusively to the business are selling cheap ready-made clothing. . . . It is thus that the large cities swallow up the small towns.
>
> A man . . . rents a . . . story or two over some of your large downtown stores; . . . employs the necessary number of cutters; elevates one to the office of foreman . . . and then goes to work. . . . One cutter . . . will cut as many garments in one week as three hundred persons can make up in the same time. . . . The operatives in these establishments are, mostly if not all, poor people.[13]

The Panic of 1837 had been a severe setback, but New York's economy began to recover in the 1840s in a boom that continued until 1854. "Never before perhaps, in the history of the country, has there been so general a prosperity," boasted the *United States Economist and Dry Goods Reporter* in 1853. New York's manufacturing output, in what Edward Spann calls the city's Age of Gold, rose to new heights. In fact, however, the recovery from the Panic was a crucial turning point in the city's industrial history. Before the Panic a wide range of industries had flourished on Manhattan, but the economic recovery of the mid-1840s brought problems for certain types of manufacturing. Three factors—the city's lack of waterpower, its crowded streets, and the high value of real estate—combined to make it uneconomical for some industries to continue to do business there.[14]

12. Edward K. Muller, "Regional Urbanization and the Selective Growth of Towns in North America," *Journal of Historical Geography* 3, no. 1 (1977), 32–37, is a theoretical treatment of the growth of industry in port cities; see also Taylor, *Transportation Revolution*, 78–80; William Bromwell, *History of Immigration to the United States* (New York, 1856), 21–57. Chapter 2 below discusses the clothing industry.

13. *Tribune*, 16 June 1849.

14. *United States Economist and Dry Goods Reporter* 2 (1853), 294. The name of this publication changed several times. Edward Spann, *The New Metropolis: New York City, 1840–1857* (New York, 1981), chap. 11, "The Age of Gold."

New York, like most ports, had little usable waterpower, and growing firms that needed increasing amounts of energy found themselves at a disadvantage. Some industries had no alternative but to leave. In 1838, for example, John Howe moved his pin factory "from New York to Birmingham, Connecticut for its advantage of water power."[15]

The city's increasingly jammed streets and docks made it hard for many industries to operate efficiently. As early as 1835 one English businessman was complaining that when the Hudson River steamboats leave, "all the streets in the lower part of New York are blocked up." The situation became much worse. By 1857 a correspondent of the *Times* of London could write that "the throng and rush of traffic in the business part of New York is astonishing even for London. . . . There is a perpetual jam and lock of vehicles along the chief thoroughfare; the traffic is outgrowing the capacity of the streets to admit it." Before the 1850s Fulton Street was the only through street linking the Hudson and East River docks. To manufacturers, especially those dealing with large or bulky products, slow and difficult transport increased the cost of doing business.[16]

The most significant factor hindering the city's large industrial concerns was the rapid rise in real estate prices and rents. The Third Ward, to the west of City Hall Park, saw its assessed valuation grow from $12 million in 1841 to $32 million in 1856, as the city's warehouse district (which also contained a good deal of light industry) expanded into the area. Since this was a completely built-up area in 1841, the increase in assessments mainly reflected the rise in land values in the ward. The real estate boom also had a serious effect on property taxes—not only were tax bills growing as real estate values increased, but the property tax itself was increased from 89.5 cents per $100 of assessed valuation in 1845 to $1.55 in 1857.[17]

Many firms that needed power, dealt in large or heavy products, or used a large amount of land were finding it difficult to enlarge output so as to take advantage of the rapid expansion in demand. Those firms whose business was not booming found increased rent and operating costs were cutting into their profits. Manufacturers also discovered their opportunity costs were rising; many must have found they could make more money selling their land than remaining in business.[18]

15. Bishop, *History of American Manufactures*, 2:565.

16. *A Letter from a Tradesman Recently Arrived from America to His Brethren in Trade* (London, 1835), 16. *Times* quotation from Spann, *New Metropolis*, 284; see also Spann, 284–287, and Seymour Mandelbaum, *Boss Tweed's New York* (New York, 1965), 12–18.

17. Valuations from Moses Beach, ed., *Wealth and Pedigree of the Wealthy Citizens of New York* (New York, 1843), 24, and William Boyd, ed., *New York City Tax-Book* (New York, 1857), viii; see also Charles Lockwood, *Manhattan Moves Uptown: An Illustrated History* (Boston, 1976), 100. Tax rates are from Elizabeth Blackmar, "Housing and Property Relations in New York City, 1785–1850" (diss., Harvard University, 1980), 584. Most property was assessed at 60 percent of full value: Blackmar, 587–588.

18. The rapid rise in rents is discussed in "Rents," *United States Economist and Dry Goods Reporter* 13 (1853), 38, and *The Value of Real Estate in the City of New York Past, Present and*

The first reaction of the city's industrialists was to try to intensify production, especially through expanded overtime. But if that failed, they sought a new location, and an exodus began of transport-sensitive and land-extensive firms from the lower wards of the city. Some industries moved to the outskirts of Manhattan, either uptown or on the waterfront. In 1847, for example, the Higgins Carpet Manufactory moved from Pearl Street to the Hudson River at 43rd Street. The Delameter Iron Works moved from Vestry Street to the Hudson at 14th Street in 1850. By the late 1840s both the East and the Hudson rivers were lined with foundries and sugar refineries, in addition to the shipyards that had been there for decades. Isaac Kendall noted in 1865 that "the river borders are taken up for business purposes, for brick, stone and lumber yards, factories and machine shops." On the waterfront, transportation problems were eased because firms had less need to use the streets. However, the real estate problem worsened because waterfront property was becoming the most valuable in the city. Other firms built upward to stabilize real estate costs; by the 1860s, five- and six-story cast-iron industrial buildings were common in New York City (see Figure 1).[19]

Many manufacturing firms simply left Manhattan, usually for New Jersey (see Map 1). The towns and villages along falls on New Jersey rivers had long been the site of manufacturing. In 1791 the Society for Establishing Useful Manufactures, noting Paterson's "excellent water for . . . mill purposes [and] . . . its contingency to and easy communication with one of the first cities in the United States," decided to locate its factories there. The society was largely a failure, however, and as late as 1838 Paterson was regarded by New Yorkers as "an upcountry hamlet, chiefly noted for its fine waterfall and valuable waterpower." Newark, with its large leather industry, was a major industrial center before 1840, but early growth was only a prelude to the manufacturing expansion of the 1840s and 1850s.[20]

---

*Prospective* (New York, 1860). Rents for industrial firms are difficult to discover. One medium-sized printshop paid $600 yearly in the mid-1850s according to R. G. Dun's records. New York Vol. 194, 781, R. G. Dun & Co. Collection, Baker Library, Harvard University Graduate School of Business Administration. For the economic factors involved, see William Alonso, *Location and Land Use* (Cambridge, Mass., 1965), 45.

19. On increased intensity of production as rents rise see Edgar M. Hoover, *The Location of Economic Activity* (New York, 1948), 72, and M. T. Daly and M. J. Webber, "The Growth of the Firm within the City," *Urban Studies* 10 (1973), 307–308. On Higgins Carpet see Ortho Cartwright, *The Middle West Side* (New York, 1912), 34–35; on Delameter Iron see Bishop, *History of American Manufactures*, 3:128–129. Of the $22 million invested in 1855 in foundries, many of which were located along the city's rivers, $18 million was in real estate and only $4 million in machinery. New York Secretary of State, *Census of the State of New York, 1855* (Albany, 1857); Isaac Kendall [?], *The Growth of New York* (New York, 1865), 23; see also J. H. Baxter, "Along the Wharves," *Harper's Monthly Magazine* 25 (1862), 307–322.

20. Society quoted from the *National Gazette*, 14 July 1792, in William Goodwin, "The Middle Passaic Valley: Manufacturing Development in an Older Economic Region" (diss., Columbia University, 1957), 14–15. "Upcountry hamlet" quoted in Herbert Gutman, "Class,

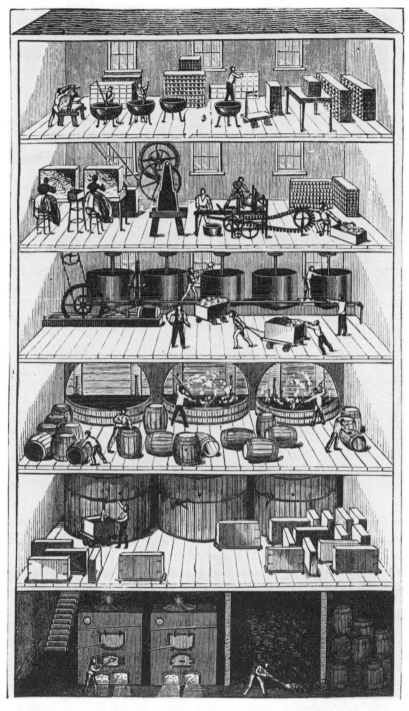

FIGURE 1. Multistory manufacturing firm. This is the Morgan Soap Factory on Bank Street. From Horace Greeley et al., *Great Industries of the United States* (Hartford, Conn., 1872), 678.

MAP 1. New York City region, 1860.

In New Jersey waterpower and better transport were available. Although railroads were slow to move onto Manhattan, eastern New Jersey had an extensive rail system by 1860. The cost of living in New Jersey was lower—in part because workers paid lower rents—and manufacturers could thus lower wages. New Jersey's greatest attraction, however, was cheap land. "In

Status and Community Power in Nineteenth-Century American Industrial Cities: Paterson, New Jersey: A Case Study," in Gutman, *Work, Culture and Society in Industrializing America: Essays in American Working-Class and Social History* (New York, 1977), 238. On Paterson's rural past see also "The Manufactures of Paterson, N.J.," *Scientific American* n.s. 1 (1859), 282. On Newark see Susan E. Hirsch, *The Roots of the American Working Class: The Industrialization of Crafts in Newark, 1800–1860* (Philadelphia, 1978), 18–19. Some idea of early manufacturing development in eastern New Jersey can be gained from *Documents Relative to Manufactures in the United States* ["The McLane Report"] (1833; rpt. New York, 1969), 2:134–194.

almost every case, where a manufacturing plant has left the City of New York,'' wrote Edward Pratt in 1911, "the removal was caused by the high land values.''[21]

J. L. Hewes and J. M. Phillips transferred their New York machine shop to Newark in 1846; Colgate Soap moved from the lower wards to Jersey City in 1847; and William Adams moved his looms in 1857 to Paterson, where the firm eventually became one of the nation's largest textile mills. Kreischer and Sons' brickmaking firm, finding their Delancey Street "property become too valuable for manufacturing purposes,'' transferred in 1873 "all tools and moulds, etc.'' to Staten Island (see Figure 2); "the buildings in New York were taken down and tenement houses erected in their stead.'' The Singer Sewing Machine Company moved twice: in 1857 from Centre Street to Mott Street, and in 1872 to Elizabethport, New Jersey. These are only a few of the dozens of industrial concerns that relocated outside the city. Many of these factories continued to maintain offices and warehouses in the city after moving their manufacturing operations out of town. In addition, New York capitalists backed firms on the periphery that engaged in the types of manufacturing with large power or real estate needs which were becoming unprofitable in the city. According to nineteenth-century economic historian Leander Bishop, "the manufactories of Newark are generally owned and operated by mercantile houses in New York,'' and the same was true of Paterson.[22]

Table 2 shows the growth of manufacturing between 1840 and 1855. Every industry listed showed a real increase in employment except lumber. (Unfortunately, the 1840 census did not include clothing, but there is little doubt that employment there also increased substantially.) The metals industry, machinery, and sugar refining posted the largest gains. The decline of the city's large,

21. For railroads see Carl Condit, *The Port of New York* (Chicago, 1980), 20; on lower wages see *The British Mechanic's and Labourer's Hand Book* (London, 1840), 215. (Although this is an immigrant guidebook, the writer clearly worked in New York City and wrote that "the observations apply more to the city and state of New York . . . than to other parts of the union,'' 284; see also Appendix A.) Edward Ewing Pratt, *Industrial Causes of Congestion of Population in New York City* (1911; rpt. New York, 1968), 109.

22. Hewes: William F. Ford, *The Industrial Interests of Newark, N.J.* (New York, 1874), 61–62. Colgate: Bishop, *History of American Manufactures,* 3:163. Adams: W. Woodford Clayton, *History of Bergen and Passaic Counties, New Jersey* (Philadelphia, 1882), 417–418. "E. Kreischer and Sons,'' undated manuscript in the New-York Historical Society (NYHS); "The Story of Singer,'' *Singer Light* 15, no. 4 (1941), 3–5; Ruth Brandon, *A Capitalist Romance: Singer and the Sewing Machine* (Philadelphia, 1977), 107. One geographer discovered that within a thirty-five-mile radius of New York City, "investment was significantly more oriented toward manufacturing than in the outlying urban places'': Crowther, "Urban Growth,'' 638; see also Bishop, 3:218. In Paterson, New York City silk merchants started or expanded most of the city's silk mills; L. R. Trumbull, *A History of Industrial Paterson* (Paterson, 1882), 176–193. Morris Ketchum and Jasper Grosvenor, "New York capitalists,'' backed the enlargement of Thomas Rogers's machine shop into the huge Rogers locomotive works; *Scientific American* n.s. 1 (1859), 298; see also Trumbull, 113–114.

18

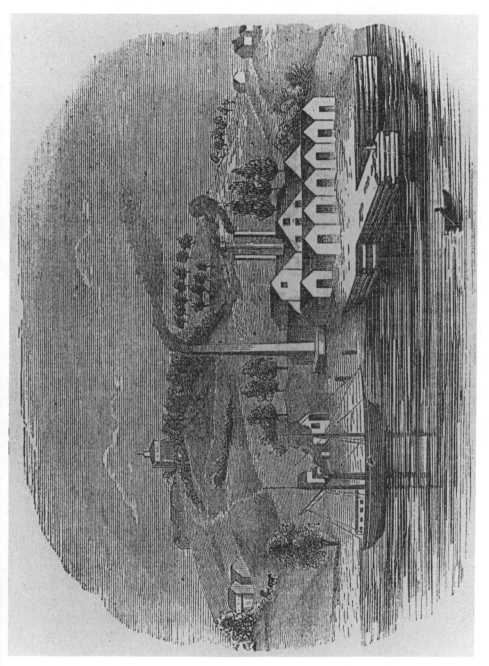

FIGURE 2. Kreischer and Sons' Brickmaking had both a Delancey Street (above) and a Staten Island (below) factory. All operations were transferred to Staten Island in 1873. From *Trow's New York City Directory, 1866,* and *Goulding's 1876 New York City Directory.*

TABLE 2

Changes in the workforce of major industries in New York City, 1840–1855

| Industry | 1840 | | 1855 | | Change (%) |
|---|---|---|---|---|---|
| | No. | % | No. | % | |
| Various metals | 798 | 6.0 | 5,218 | 20.6 | +14.6 |
| Machinery | 1,419 | 10.7 | 4,250 | 16.8 | +6.1 |
| Sugar refining | 327 | 2.5 | 1,628 | 6.4 | +3.9 |
| Precious metals | 542 | 4.1 | 1,705 | 6.7 | +2.6 |
| Musical instruments | 281 | 2.1 | 1,185 | 4.7 | +2.6 |
| Carriages | 297 | 2.2 | 1,094 | 4.3 | +2.1 |
| Furniture | 1,319 | 9.9 | 2,571 | 10.2 | +0.3 |
| Tobacco | 209 | 1.6 | 411 | 1.6 | 0 |
| Stonecutting | 472 | 3.6 | 888 | 3.5 | −0.1 |
| Glass and earthenware | 104 | 0.8 | 154 | 0.7 | −0.1 |
| Soap and candles | 229 | 1.7 | 355 | 1.4 | −0.3 |
| Liquor | 274 | 2.1 | 416 | 1.6 | −0.5 |
| Drugs and dye | 293 | 2.2 | 115 | 0.4 | −1.8 |
| Printing | 2,029 | 15.2 | 3,314 | 13.1 | −2.2 |
| Hats and caps | 1,361 | 10.2 | 1,577 | 6.2 | −4.0 |
| Leather | 724 | 5.5 | 143 | 0.6 | −4.9 |
| Lumber | 2,606 | 19.6 | 278 | 1.1 | −18.6 |
| TOTAL | 13,284 | 100.0 | 25,302 | 99.9 | |

*Note:* For illustrative purposes this table treats the industries listed as if they were the only ones in the city. Some census categories have been combined to facilitate comparison.

*Sources:* Census Office, *Sixth Census, 1840* (Washington, 1841); New York Secretary of State, *Census of the State of New York, 1855* (Albany, 1857).

land-extensive firms is illustrated in Table 3. The biggest 1840–1855 gainers—sugar refining, shipbuilding (not listed in 1840), machinery, and metals—were the biggest 1855–1870 losers. This decline was real, not just relative: in 1855 these four industries employed 13,423 workers, in 1870, 10,845. These firms initially located on the outskirts, usually the East or Hudson riverfront: by the 1850s, however, the industrial periphery had moved farther out, and they now faced many of the urban problems described earlier. In shipbuilding, for instance, "property became too valuable . . . for use as ship-yards."[23]

These land-extensive, often heavily capitalized, industries might all have departed for New Jersey were it not for strong inertial forces. Many of New York's sugar refiners and foundry owners had such huge fixed investments in the city that they found relocation costs unacceptably high. This factor does much to explain the persistence of sugar refining and some of the large steam-

23. Henry Hall, "Report on the Ship-Building Industry of the United States," in Census Office, *Tenth Census, 1880, Special Reports* (Washington, 1884), 118; see also Alan R. Pred, *The Spatial Dynamics of U.S. Urban Industrial Growth, 1800–1914* (Cambridge, Mass., 1966), 197–200.

TABLE 3

Changes in the workforce of major industries in New York City, 1855–1870

| Industry | 1855 No. | % | 1870 No. | % | Change (%) |
|----------|------|------|------|------|------|
| Tobacco | 411 | 0.9 | 3,525 | 5.2 | +4.3 |
| Furniture | 2,571 | 5.7 | 5,307 | 7.8 | +2.1 |
| Boots and shoes | 2,198 | 4.9 | 4,614 | 6.8 | +1.9 |
| Precious metals | 1,705 | 3.8 | 3,508 | 5.1 | +1.3 |
| Printing | 3,314 | 7.4 | 5,837 | 8.6 | +1.2 |
| Umbrellas | 270 | 0.6 | 1,121 | 1.6 | +1.0 |
| Leather | 143 | 0.3 | 732 | 1.1 | +0.8 |
| Hats and caps | 1,577 | 3.5 | 2,793 | 4.1 | +0.6 |
| Liquor | 416 | 0.9 | 1,045 | 1.5 | +0.6 |
| Clothing | 14,960 | 33.2 | 22,962 | 33.7 | +0.5 |
| Drugs and dye | 115 | 0.3 | 474 | 0.7 | +0.4 |
| Musical instruments | 1,185 | 2.6 | 2,018 | 3.0 | +0.4 |
| Soap and candles | 355 | 0.8 | 679 | 1.0 | +0.2 |
| Carriages | 1,094 | 2.4 | 1,768 | 2.6 | +0.2 |
| Lumber | 278 | 0.6 | 417 | 0.6 | 0 |
| Glass and earthenware | 154 | 0.3 | 194 | 0.3 | 0 |
| Stonecutting | 888 | 2.0 | 241 | 0.4 | −1.6 |
| Sugar refining | 1,628 | 3.6 | 1,120 | 1.6 | −2.0 |
| Various metals | 5,218 | 11.6 | 5,317 | 7.8 | −3.8 |
| Machinery | 4,250 | 9.4 | 3,819 | 5.6 | −3.8 |
| Shipbuilding | 2,327 | 5.2 | 589 | 0.9 | −4.3 |
| TOTAL | 45,057 | 100.0 | 68,080 | 100.0 | |

*Note:* For illustrative purposes this table treats the industries listed as if they were the only ones in the city. Some census categories have been combined to facilitate comparison.

*Sources:* New York Secretary of State, *Census of the State of New York, 1855* (Albany, 1857); Census Office, *Ninth Census, 1870, Industry* (Washington, 1872).

engine builders in the city. The fate of such industries is suggested by Edward Ewing Pratt: "At one time there were many foundries in Manhattan. . . . [Today, in 1911], however, . . . metal and machine industry is decadent. . . . The young, strong, virile concerns have left Manhattan, or perceiving the difficulties have located elsewhere."[24]

The decline in the proportion of workers employed in these large, land-extensive industries between 1855 and 1870 marked the start of New York City's decline as a manufacturing center. Despite the deterioration of the city's industrial base and its increasing importance as a commercial center, however, Table 3 shows that not all manufacturing employment declined. For

24. On inertial forces see Pratt, *Industrial Causes of Congestion*, 104–106, and Harold Carter, *The Study of Urban Geography* (London, 1972), 323. Some idea of the scale of the city's largest sugar refiners and foundries can be found in Bishop, *History of American Manufactures*, 3:150–153, and Jacob Abbott, "The Novelty Works," *Harper's Magazine* 2 (1851), 721–734. Pratt, *Industrial Causes of Congestion*, 52.

labor-intensive trades a Manhattan location proved no hindrance and was even an attraction—between 1855 and 1870 employment in cigars, furniture, boots and shoes, precious metals, printing, and the needle trades all grew faster than did urban manufacturing as a whole. What factors were behind the health of these industries? There is no one answer, but locational economists have long recognized the advantages of a central urban location for certain trades, and many of these advantages could be captured in nineteenth-century New York City.

First of all, these vigorous Manhattan industries were not transport-sensitive and used relatively little land. Employment in the needle trades, for example, mostly involved outworkers and in other industries was concentrated mainly in small shops. In addition, many of these industries (especially jewelry, furniture, carriages, and a growing segment of ready-made clothes) required specialized information, particularly about fashion. At Tiffany's "no cost . . . [is] spared to procure the freshest authorities in the way of theory or illustration," and in both furniture and jewelry the city's leading manufacturers regularly traveled to Europe to learn what was in vogue there. "The fact is," one city carriagemaker wrote, "that where rents are high to get up cheap work will not pay," and New York coachmakers relied on custom demand. The central urban location of these industries, therefore, facilitated access to crucial information about style.[25]

There were also "information economies" in printing. The need to deliver newspapers to the city's residents required printing on Manhattan. New York's increasing importance as the national center of intellectual life ensured that major magazine and book publishers located in the city. Most job printing, the third branch of the industry, was done for commercial purposes; it required consultation with the merchant and often had to be done on a tight schedule. Again a Manhattan location was necessary. In printing, as in the needle trades, the city's large pool of labor was also a major asset. According to an 1850 report by the Printer's Union, many printers "are 'only taken on for the job,' and when the job is completed they are discharged."[26]

Most significantly, many of Manhattan's industries were highly *seasonal*. Because of the harsh North American climate, seasonality was inherent in

25. Ready-made clothing began to undergo yearly style changes in the early 1850s; see *United States Economist and Dry Goods Reporter* 12 (1852), 62, and n.s. 11 (1857), 70. On Tiffany see Bishop, *History of American Manufactures*, 3:187. On trips to Europe by jewelers see Bishop, 3:183–184; by cabinetmakers see Elizabeth Ingerman, ed., "Personal Experiences of an Old New York Cabinetmaker," *Antiques* 84 (1963), 577–578. "Coach-Making Historically Considered and Incidentally Illustrated," *New York Coach-Maker's Magazine* 2 (1860), 227.

26. For book publishing see Frank Luther Mott, *The Golden Multitudes: The Story of Best Sellers in the United States* (New York, 1947), 76–79. Evidence on job printing is given in Chapter 2. Report of 1850 quoted in George A. Stevens, *New York Typographical Union No. 6* (Albany, 1913), 209. The importance of central location for "communication economy" industries is stressed in Alan R. Pred, "The Intrametropolitan Location of American Manufacturing," *Annals of the Association of American Geographers* 54 (1964), 175–176.

mid-nineteenth-century industry, and although almost all work was variable, Manhattan attracted the most seasonal segment of manufacturing demand. It is far more costly to idle capital than labor when business is slow; only when demand is relatively constant is it profitable to invest in machinery. Economist Michael Piore argues that industrialization thus creates a "segmented" manufacturing economy, with a "primary" sector meeting steady demand through investment in machinery and a "secondary" sector using labor-intensive techniques and low invested capital to meet variable and seasonable demand. To apply Piore's model to New York requires one revision: firms that wanted access to the city's labor market were forced to spend a substantial amount on land and rent. It is, however, clear that industrialization on Manhattan was typified not by the factory but by what Sean Wilentz calls the "bastard workshop." A labor-intensive, "sweating" strategy could be pursued only when there was a large pool of available workers. The clearest example was the city's clothing trades, which routinely hired thousands of sewers in the busy season and laid them off when work was slow. For such manufacturers, a Manhattan location was essential.[27]

Even within industries a labor-intensive sector met variable demand and a capital-intensive sector met steady demand. For example, tiny, hand-powered job printshops coexisted with the immense cylinder presses of the city's dailies. In addition, the city's manufacturing was becoming more reliant on repairs than on fabrication. In the 1860 manuscript Census of Manufactures many small shops list revenues from repairs under "Value of Product." As powered manufactories outside the city used their superior efficiency to capture the more constant mass production demand, city shops had to rely increasingly on repair demand. Furniture shops of the 1860s often made "a scanty living by repair," according to Ernest Hagen, a boss cabinetmaker; in the metals industry, shops were, in Pratt's words, turning to "repair work and the various odds and ends of work in the great city."[28]

27. The impact of seasonality on the labor market is discussed in Chapter 4 below. On the link between seasonality and labor-intensive manufacturing see Michael Piore, "The Technological Foundations of Dualism and Discontinuity," in Suzanne Berger and Piore, eds., *Dualism and Discontinuity in Industrial Societies* (Cambridge, England, 1980), 55–81, especially 61–62, and Piore, *Birds of Passage: Migrant Labor and Industrial Society* (Cambridge, England, 1979), 35–43. However, I doubt that these terms are completely applicable to the mid-nineteenth century, when so much demand was seasonal. Piore's theory is applied to the post–World War II garment industry in the city by Roger Waldinger in *Through the Eye of the Needle: Immigrants and Enterprise in New York City's Garment Trades* (New York, 1986). Philip Scranton explains that Philadelphia's small textile manufacturers avoided competition with the factories of Lowell by filling specialized and temporary demand that the Massachusetts firms, with their emphasis on a standardized product, could not meet; see Scranton, *Proprietary Capitalism: The Textile Manufacture at Philadelphia, 1800–1885* (Cambridge, Mass., 1983). On bastard workshops see Sean Wilentz, *Chants Democratic: New York City and the Rise of the American Working Class, 1788–1850* (New York, 1984), 107–142.

28. Hagen quoted from Ingerman, "Personal Experiences," 582; Pratt, *Industrial Causes of Congestions*, 32. Bruce Laurie also notes repair revenues, in *Working People of Philadelphia, 1800–1850* (Philadelphia, 1980), 215.

Centralization in the city created "external economies" that helped such industries function profitably. Nor was this true only on Manhattan. The development of specialized industry in satellite cities allowed capital-intensive manufactures to benefit from such economies: hats in Danbury, for example, and silk weaving in Paterson. But small manufacturers, as a rule, depend more than larger ones on outside agencies and by concentrating in the city had easier access to them. Thus subcontractors in the needle trades, such as artificial flower makers and dress trimmers, gave clothiers greater flexibility in their operations. The city's pianoforte makers relied on a number of small action and key-making shops. And small cabinetmaking firms in the 1840s sometimes combined to rent a warehouse where they could store furniture and display it to jobbers.[29]

Manufacturing that needed specialized information or was seasonal, therefore, found a core location attractive. While some industries were driven out of the city, others were drawn to Manhattan. Although labor-intensive industries such as clothing had long flourished in the city, before the 1840s a wide range of manufacturing, both labor- and capital-intensive, thrived on Manhattan. In the 1840s, however, the distribution of industry within the metropolitan region began to take on a different pattern. The evidence suggests that a *geographically segmented* metropolitan regional economy had begun to develop. Not only was secondary manufacturing centralizing on Manhattan, but primary manufacturing was concentrating in an industrial belt around the city, especially in New Jersey. Table 4 shows that industries with a city affinity were mostly labor-intensive, though two heavy industries—sugar refining and shipbuilding—were rooted on Manhattan by inertia. A number of types of manufacturing were not disproportionately represented in either locale, and industries needing land or power, such as cotton textiles or locomotive repair, located in the belt. Not only was the region's industry becoming split, but each type of manufacturing was gravitating to the geographical part of the region where it could be carried on most profitably.

## THE GEOGRAPHY OF THE NEW YORK
## METROPOLITAN REGION

By the 1850s a spatially bifurcated New York metropolitan region was developing. Manufacturing in the core was typically seasonal, labor-intensive, unmechanized, and carried on in the home or small shop (see Figure 3). In the

---

29. Daniel Spillane, *History of the Pianoforte* (New York, 1890). See also Pred, *Spatial Dynamics*, 202–204; and Waldinger, *Through the Eye*, 97–103. On furniture see "The Diary of Henry Edward Price," *British Records Relating to America in Microform* (East Ardsley, England, 1963), 30.

TABLE 4

Percentage of employees in major industries in the city and the industrial belt, 1870

| Industry | Employees | | Percentage in city |
| --- | --- | --- | --- |
| | City | Belt | |
| Sugar refining | 1,120 | 0 | 100.0 |
| Printing | 5,837 | 202 | 96.7 |
| Musical instruments | 2,018 | 98 | 95.4 |
| Shipbuilding | 589 | 33 | 94.7 |
| Furniture | 5,307 | 538 | 90.8 |
| Clothing | 22,962 | 2,720 | 89.1 |
| Tobacco | 3,525 | 732 | 82.8 |
| Jewelry | 3,508 | 1,408 | 71.4 |
| ALL MANUFACTURING | 129,577 | 64,573 | 66.7 |
| Boots and shoes | 4,614 | 2,564 | 64.3 |
| Soap and candles | 679 | 365 | 65.0 |
| Metalwork | 5,317 | 2,941 | 64.4 |
| Machinery | 3,819 | 2,445 | 61.0 |
| Liquor | 1,045 | 713 | 59.4 |
| Lumber | 417 | 371 | 52.9 |
| Carriages | 1,768 | 1,631 | 52.0 |
| Leather | 732 | 1,290 | 36.2 |
| Hats and caps | 2,793 | 6,107 | 31.4 |
| Stonecutting | 241 | 646 | 27.2 |
| Cotton goods | 107 | 1,937 | 5.2 |
| Locomotive building | 0 | 2,537 | 0.0 |

*Note:* The industrial belt consists of five New Jersey counties: Bergen, Essex, Hudson, Passaic, and Union; Fairfield County in Connecticut; and Westchester County in New York.
*Source:* Census Office, *Ninth Census, 1870, Industry* (Washington, 1871).

belt areas outside the city, industry was less seasonal, more mechanized, and carried on, after 1860, in somewhat larger settings (see Figure 4). Only 23 percent of a sample of Manhattan workers in 1860 labored in workshops that used steam power. In 1870 (the first census to give figures on power), 17 percent of Manhattan's industries were powered compared to 34 percent in the industrial belt.[30]

30. The 23 percent figure comes from a sample of the 1850 and 1860 manuscript *Census of Manufactures*. (The 1870 figures from *Ninth Census, 1870, Industry*.) The sample was taken from Ward Two east of William Street, a random sample of Ward Seven east of Jefferson Street, and all of Ward Sixteen. There were 516 firms in the sample in 1850 and 550 in 1860. In the 1890 census, which breaks down the components of capital investment, the average city firm had $7,145 invested in land and $4,168 in machinery; on the belt only $2,795 was in land, $6,432 in machinery. The high capital investments of the waterfront manufacturers boosted city figures: the inclusion of the city's fourteen sugar refineries alone boosted average capitalization for the city's 4,375 industrial firms $860 in 1860. There is little doubt that capital invested in firms not on the Hudson and East rivers was substantially lower than the citywide average. The citywide capital average in 1860 was $13,991; without the refiners it was $13,131. Census Office, *Eleventh Census, 1890, Manufacturing; Eighth Census, 1860, Manufactures.*

FIGURE 3. Manhattan manufactory, 1853. Warshaw Collection of Business Americana Archives Center, National Museum of American History, Smithsonian Institution.

FIGURE 4. New Jersey factory, 1874. From William Ford, *The Industrial Interests of Newark, N.J.* (New York, 1874).

27

TABLE 5

Average number of employees per workplace in New York City and the industrial belt, 1820–1890

|  | *1820* | *1850* | *1860* | *1870* | *1880* | *1890* |
|---|---|---|---|---|---|---|
| City | 14.7 | 25.0 | 20.6 | 17.0 | 20.0 | 13.9 |
| Industrial belt | | | 20.0 | 18.1 | 24.2 | 23.8 |
| Difference | | | +0.6 | −1.1 | −4.2 | −9.9 |

*Sources:* Census Office, *Eighth, Ninth, Tenth, Eleventh, Census, Manufactures, 1860, 1870, 1880, 1890;* Census Office, *Fourth Census, 1820, Manufacturing,* Manuscript; Census Office, *Seventh Census, Manufacturing, 1850,* Manuscript.

Table 5 suggests the magnitude of the change the region's industries underwent beginning in the 1840s. The average size of shop in the city grew between 1820 and 1850, and as late as 1860 average shop size was actually slightly larger in the city than in the industrial belt. The city figure is inflated by outworkers, so the true size of the working environment was somewhat smaller. Nevertheless, the trend is clear. By 1890 the average manufacturing firm was substantially smaller in Manhattan than in areas outside the city. Shop size outside Manhattan grew rather slowly in this period. This slowness may have been the beginning of an even larger spatial pattern, noted by Jean Gottmann for the twentieth century, in which the entire New York metropolitan region served as a specialized light manufacturing area for the Eastern seaboard.[31]

An emphasis on labor-intensive manufacturing might seem to suggest that the average New York City shop should have become larger, but it did not. An employer with a large workforce lacked the flexibility to compete in seasonal and fashionable trades. Jesse Pope, writing about the early-twentieth-century clothing trade, noted "the immense superiority which the small shop possesses over the larger." The growth in demand for ready-made clothes after the 1850s was met by a proliferation of small subcontractors.[32]

Because industries in the core were dependent on information, they clustered together near the commercial center of the city. These "agglomeration economies" made Ward Two the center of the city's labor-intensive industry (see Map 2). This area had originally been the city's warehouse district. Before the 1850s the more sheltered East River was the port area, and most

31. Jean Gottmann, *Megalopolis: The Urbanized Northeastern Seaboard of the United States* (New York, 1961), 491–496.
32. Jesse Eliphalet Pope, *The Clothing Industry in New York* (New York, 1905), 64. According to Waldinger, *Through the Eye,* 91, "in a market so prone to change as is apparel's, large firm size is more of a liability than an advantage." See also Roy B. Helfgott, "Women's and Children's Apparel," in Max Hall, ed., *Made in New York: Case Studies in Metropolitan Manufacturing* (Cambridge, Mass., 1959), 36.

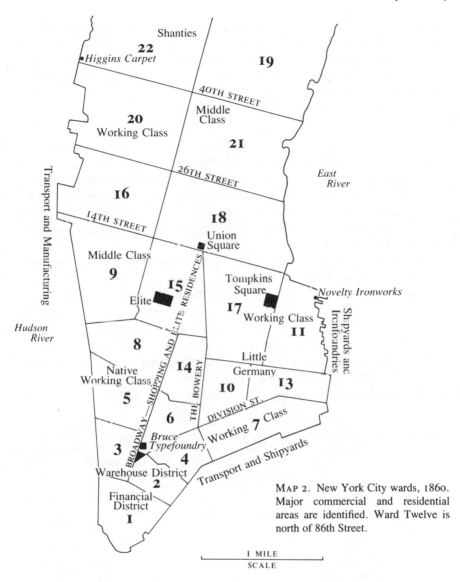

Shanties

**22**

•Higgins Carpet

**19**

40TH STREET

Middle
Class

**20**
Working Class

**21**

26TH STREET

East
River

**16**

14TH STREET

**18**

Union
■Square

Middle Class

**9**

**15**

Elite ■

Tompkins
Square ■

**17**
Working Class

*Novelty Ironworks*

ELITE RESIDENCES

*Hudson
River*

SHOPPING AND

THE BOWERY

Shipyards and
Ironfoundries

*Transport and Manufacturing*

**8**

Native
Working Class

**5**

**14**

Little
Germany

**10**

**13**

**11**

BROADWAY

**6**

DIVISION ST.

Working **7** Class

*Bruce
Typefoundry* ■

**3**

**4**

Transport and Shipyards

Warehouse District
**2**

Financial
District
**I**

MAP 2. New York City wards, 1860.
Major commercial and residential
areas are identified. Ward Twelve is
north of 86th Street.

I MILE
SCALE

merchants' offices and warehouses were located near the docks on Pearl Street
in the eastern part of Wards One and Two. When some of these merchants
turned to manufacturing in response to increased demand, they used empty
areas of their warehouses to carry on labor-intensive industry. "Manufacturing operations of various kinds are carried on throughout the district," the
city's sanitary inspector noted of Ward Two in 1865. In 1850 no fewer than
37,000 of the city's 83,000 manufacturing employees—44 percent of all
manufacturing jobs in the city—were located in the Second Ward, which

according to the *Herald* "may be called truly, the great workshop of the metropolis." (Ward manufacturing statistics for 1850 and 1860 are given in Appendix B.) The ward included many of the largest employers in the city, such as Lewis and Hanford Clothiers and James Gordon Bennett's printing house, whereas the district's lofts and attics contained hundreds of small printshops, manufacturing jewelers, and clothiers.[33]

By locating in Ward Two, employers hoped to gain quick access to relevant information about style and business conditions. Indeed, many industries concentrated on specific streets: in the 1820s and 1830s, for example, the city's artificial flower makers on William Street, the umbrella makers on Pearl Street. In the 1840s and 1850s manufacturing jewelers were on Reade Street, and milliners lined Division Street. This concentration also made it possible for buyers to contact the bulk of wholesale manufacturers rapidly in these seasonal trades.[34]

Outside Manhattan were most of the region's large, mechanized factories. A majority of these industrial satellite cities were in New Jersey, but West Farms and Mott Haven (in the present-day Bronx), Yonkers, Williamsburg, Bridgeport, and Danbury all contained large New York–owned factories. By 1860 the former "upcountry hamlet" of Paterson was a city of 19,000. Other eastern New Jersey cities such as Newark, Orange, and Passaic saw similar increases. The percentage of the population engaged in manufacturing in Newark was 26.2, and in Paterson 24.1.[35]

This geographically segmented industrial structure allowed industries to

33. For a theoretical discussion that influenced this description of the development of manufacturing in the warehouse district, see David Ward, *Cities and Immigrants* (New York, 1971), 89–93. Council of Hygiene and Public Health, *Report upon the Sanitary Conditions of the City* (New York, 1865), 16; *Seventh Census, Manufactures, 1850*, Manuscript; *Herald*, 14 July 1861. Many of the workers listed in the totals for the Second Ward were outworkers. Lewis and Hanford, in Pearl Street, listed 4,000 employees in the 1850 manufacturing census. However, only 75 worked on the premises in the inside shop; the other 3,925 employees were sewers in the outside shop, who worked at home in other wards. Nevertheless, inspection of the Manuscript returns of the *Census of Manufactures* shows that a substantial proportion of the city's workers labored in manufactories in Wards Two and Three. The Lewis and Hanford statistics are from *Seventh Census, 1850, Manufactures*, Manuscript, Ward Two, and Andrews & Company, *Stranger's Guide in the City of New-York* (New York, 1849), 24; see also *Hunt's Merchants' Magazine* 20 (1849), 348. A physical description of the warehouse district is "New York Daguerreotyped; Business Streets, Mercantile Blocks, Store and Banks," *Putnam's Magazine* 1 (1853), 125; see also Lockwood, *Manhattan Moves Uptown*, 15–18, 100–102.

34. Henry Fearon, *Sketches of America* (London, 1819), 24. John Doggett, ed., *New York City Business Directory* (New York, 1841); *Wilson's Business Directory* (New York, 1848 and 1857); Virginia Penny, *How Women Can Make Money* (1863; rpt. New York, 1971), 342.

35. The periphery had, on a percentage basis, even faster population growth than the city—between 1840 and 1870 the industrial belt counties grew from 195,018 to 617,927, a 317 percent increase, while Manhattan grew from 312,710 to 942,292, 301 percent. On Yonkers see David B. Sicilia, "Steam Power and the Progress of Industry in the Late Nineteenth Century," *Theory and Society* 15 (1986), 287–299. Population figures taken from Census Office, *Eleventh Census, 1890, Population* (Washington, 1895).

locate where they could be most efficient. The sensitivity of the region's manufacturers to the differences between the core and the belt is exemplified by McNab and Harlin's brass foundry, which moved from Mercer Street to Paterson in 1858, returned operations to Manhattan when business slumped at the start of the Civil War, and moved permanently to Paterson in 1870. In addition, segmentation increased productivity because industries could separate mechanized and labor-intensive parts of the fabrication and carry on each where it was most profitable. Hats made in Danbury were sent to the city to be finished and trimmed; the P. J. Lorillard Company cut and cured its tobacco in a Bronx plant and packed it in Manhattan; and in the booming hoop skirt industry of the 1850s it was common for manufacturers to make the iron frames outside New York, where they could use water power, and then ship the frames to the city to have the skirts sewed onto them.[36]

There were, of course, many exceptions to this primary-belt, secondary-core typology. Inertia kept many large firms on the city's waterfront. The Novelty Iron Works along the East River had 950 employees in 1860, making it, apparently, the largest workplace in the region. The Rogers Locomotive Works in Paterson, in contrast, had 604 employees. Also undermining any rigid typology were thousands of wives of New Jersey workers who labored as outside sewers for Manhattan clothing firms. In addition, hundreds of small machine shops in the industrial belt serviced and repaired the steam engines, looms, and other machinery the factories needed.[37]

Also throughout the region was what might be called "neighborhood" industry. As Appendix B shows, there were manufacturing firms in every city ward, even in those which were primarily residential. The manuscript manufacturing returns record hundreds of small tailors, shoemakers, and jewelers throughout Manhattan, and the returns for Paterson and Newark show a similar pattern. Though these local firms employed less than 10 percent of the city's manufacturing employees, and were far smaller than the sweatshops and factories that produced goods to ship outside the city, they were also a part of the economy of the metropolitan region and softened core-periphery differences.[38]

36. McNab and Harlin: Clayton, *History of Bergen and Passaic Counties*, 451. Hats: Edwin Williams, ed., *The New-York Annual Register for 1831* (New York, 1831), 112, and W. H. Francis, *History of the Hatting Trade in Danbury, Conn.* (Danbury, 1860), 6. Lorillard: Bishop, *History of American Manufactures*, 3:528–529. Hoop skirts: *New York Tribune*, 20 January 1858. The sewing of hoop skirts is illustrated in Figure 19.

37. *Eighth Census, 1860, Manufactures*, Manuscript, New York City, Ward Eleven. The Rogers works was the largest factory in eastern New Jersey: *Eighth Census, 1860, Manufactures*, Manuscript, New Jersey, Passaic County, Township of Paterson. William Ford, *Industrial Interests of Newark*, 196, estimated there were two thousand "sewing women" employed by Manhattan firms in Newark.

38. The less than 10 percent estimate is based on my sample of the 1850 and 1860 returns from Ward Sixteen, and a comparison of that sample with the returns for the entire city.

Despite many exceptions, however, the differences between the work environments of the core and the industrial belt were real, and they call attention to two differing manufacturing strategies—mechanized and labor-intensive—and to the spatial divergence between them. The process began in the 1840s and continued into the twentieth century. In the 1950s manufacturing firms were leaving New York for New Jersey at the rate of forty-five a year, the most common reason being "No room for expansion." Twentieth-century students of manufacturing in the New York region have been aware of the differences between Manhattan and New Jersey industry, and the 1928 *Regional Survey of New York and Its Environs* often made reference to it. In printing, for example, the report explained, "quantity work which can be standardized . . . will tend to disappear from the center of the metropolis." The *New York Metropolitan Region Study* in the late 1950s noted similar tendencies: one of its reports pointed out that "even within a given industry establishments in New York have wider fluctuations in employment than establishments elsewhere" in the region. The development of this regional pattern meant that the impact of industrialization differed from locale to locale. Manhattan entrepreneurs were more likely to try to increase output through increased labor; in New Jersey, through increased machinery. There was no *single* path to greater profits.[39]

This geographic specialization of industry is part of an even broader geographic pattern involving almost every aspect of urban life. Manhattan was the region's commercial and financial center. There was a specialized residential area developing in Brooklyn, which had one of the lowest percentages of population in manufacturing of any major city. There was even a transport center in Jersey City. Indeed, the rapid progress of this specialization not only reflected the region's growth, it probably helped cause it. The division of labor among the area's cities and towns spurred efficiency and gave New York manufacturers an advantage over less specialized urban areas. Manhattan entrepreneurs were especially lucky to have New Jersey's excellent water-power nearby. By 1860 express companies, ferries, and railroads—eighty trains a day left Newark for Manhattan in 1874—linked together this vast, intricate organism.[40]

Though I make frequent reference to areas outside Manhattan, the focus in this book is mostly on the city itself. The experience of Manhattan workers

39. On firms leaving the city see John I. Griffin, *Industrial Location in the New York Area* (New York, 1956), 95–97; A. F. Hinrichs, "The Printing Industry," in Robert Murray Haig and Roswell McCrea, eds., *Regional Survey of New York and Its Environs* (New York, 1928), 1A, 43; Helfgott, "Women's and Children's Apparel," 41–42.

40. On Brooklyn see note 11 above; also, Douglas V. Shaw, *The Making of an Immigrant City: Ethnic and Cultural Conflict in Jersey City, New Jersey, 1850–1877* (New York, 1976). Eighty trains: Ford, *Industrial Interests of Newark*, 249.

reflects only one aspect of metropolitan industrialization; in New Jersey the process proceeded differently. Though exceptions to the typology were many, the trend toward dichotomization did exist. Neither New York nor New Jersey was any more "typical" than the other—they were both part of the single process of industrialization.

# CHAPTER 2

# A Short History of
# the Trades of New York

The idea of the "segmentation" of the regional economy explains some, but not all, of the variation in the work experiences of New York's native and immigrant workers. The genesis of a Manhattan core and a New Jersey industrial belt, significant though it was, hardly explains fully the enormous complexity of the city's industrial development. Only by examining specific industries in detail can we understand how workers were affected by industrialization. This chapter focuses on four industries—clothing, metals, printing, and furniture—which were among the city's largest and which illustrate the diversity of New York manufacturing. Segmentation provides a useful general guide, but each of the trades discussed had unique features.

Approximately half of the city's manual workers were not involved in manufacturing (see Table 11), so two of the city's largest nonindustrial manual occupations—laboring and domestic servitude—are also discussed. To help clarify what occurred, I use manufacturing in 1820, as revealed in the manuscript census of that year, as a baseline to measure the changes of the next forty years.

## MANUFACTURING IN 1820

The manuscript *1820 Census of Manufactures,* which though incomplete is very useful, and other evidence from the period illuminate how production was organized. The city's manufacturing in 1820 was not preindustrial; Thomas Cochran has argued persuasively that the first stage of American industrialization was almost over by 1825, and this generalization is supported by the evidence from New York.[1]

The expansion of markets had caused a substantial reorganization of artisanal production before 1820. Before the regional bifurcation of manufacturing began, a wide range of products was made in the city for shipment to the South and the West Indies. In response to a question in the *1820 Census of Manufactures* asking about the "demand for, and sale of" manufactures, owners often mentioned exports to the South and, occasionally, upstate. "Southern States are the principal market" responded Isaac Minard, a cordwainer. John Leafield was pleased with the demand for his cast and sheet iron in the South, and Gilbert Haight, a Water Street saddler, seemed happy to report that "demand for our articles is increasing now in this state." Furniture, hats, and candles also were reported in the census as being made to be shipped to buyers outside Manhattan. Already in 1820 some New York artisans were involved in a substantial way in manufacturing for nonlocal markets.[2]

Adam Smith's famous axiom that "the division of labor is limited by the extent of the market" held true, and market expansion was accompanied by manufacturers who broke down work. These exporting firms had abandoned the traditional organization of production with a master working beside two or three journeymen in the shop. Shoemaking had become especially systematized in the drive to produce cheap export goods, and there were some quite large manufactories in the city. Isaac Minard employed sixteen men and two women (to sew the uppers, presumably) in his shoe manufactory. Law and Butler of 127 Broadway employed thirty men and five women (with an investment of $8,000). Firms in other industries that exported goods to the South or upstate were almost as large. Gilbert Haight's saddlery had ten men, two women (employed as sewers), and $50,000 in capital; Abraham King's hat company had seventy-five employees and did $90,000 worth of business in the South; Peter and George Lorillard employed "28 to 30" men and "15 to 16" children in their tobacco and snuff manufactory; and the Bruce Typecasting firm had a $50,000 investment and employed eighteen men, six women, and eight children.[3]

1. Thomas C. Cochran, *Frontiers of Change* (New York, 1981), 77.

2. Expansion of markets: Howard Rock, *Artisans of the New Republic: The Tradesmen of New York City in the Age of Jefferson* (New York, 1979), 238–242. Census Office, *Fourth Census, 1820, Manufactures,* Manuscript, First and Sixth Ward. The 1820 manufacturing census is incomplete. The definition of manufacturing was essentially limited to basic industries, so clothing, printing, and shoemaking were not counted in the printed totals. By mistake, however, some nonbasic firms *were* included in the manuscript returns. There are no returns from Wards Four and Eight, and in several other wards only a handful of firms are reported; there are only 101 returns for the entire city. Although the census contains a number of returns from small shops, it is obvious that smaller firms were very often not counted.

3. Adam Smith, *An Inquiry into the Nature and Causes of the Wealth of Nations,* ed. Edwin Cannan (1776; rpt. Chicago, 1976), 21–25; *Fourth Census, 1820, Manufactures,* Manuscript,

Even in smaller shops, the capital invested was substantial. Henry Fearon, who was "deputed" by a group of potential English emigrants to investigate America, listed the amount of capital needed in various city trades—cabinet-making, carpentry, masonry, $500; shoemaking, $500–$1,000; dyeing, $800–$2,000; "A Merchant Taylor," $2,500–$10,000; gilders and carvers, $4,000–$10,000; and distillers, $5,000. The *1820 Census of Manufactures* shows most small shops capitalized at between $800 and $4,000. Since the average journeyman's yearly wages in the Manufacturing Census were $312, it was surely difficult for most journeymen to become masters. Only in cabinetmaking, where Fearon found "small concerns, apparently owned by journeymen who had just commenced on their own," and the construction trades were capital requirements low enough to allow "jours," as they were often called in the nineteenth century, to routinely achieve master status. Large, heavily capitalized manufactories that divided labor were part of the city's industrial structure by 1820.[4]

Despite this evidence of divergence from traditional artisanal production, the small shop employing skilled workers remained the focus of New York's industrial economy. Although the 1820 census seems to have included only the larger shops, 68 of 101 firms enumerated had ten or fewer workers, and the average was 14.7 employees. Though women were employed, their numbers were small—only 6.1 percent of the adult workforce was female, well below the 12 percent found in 1850 and 1860 in the city's nonclothing trades. Only four firms had steam power, apparently, and most used only the simplest of machinery. Few manufacturers were very specialized. Daniel Morrison, a nailer, employed three journeymen and used a horse-powered cutting machine; Abraham Gargill had three journeymen and made "Tin Ware of all Descriptions, . . . and generally all Useful articles of Sheet Iron"; John Van Boskirk had four journeymen and three apprentices in his shop and made "Mahogany Furniture of every description" using "one turning lathe" and tools. Most shops, indeed, had only "tools appertaining to the trade," with lathes, molds, and boilers the most elaborate machinery found.[5]

---

Wards One, Three, Six. Some of the addresses are taken from *Longworth's New York Directory of the Year 1820* (New York, 1820).

4. Henry Fearon, *Sketches of America* (London, 1819), 25, 30–33. The $312 is total wages paid in shops with only male employees. *Fourth Census, 1820, Manufactures*, Manuscript; Fearon, 24.

5. *Fourth Census, 1820, Manufactures*, Manuscript, Wards One, Six. I qualify the statement about steam because the census asks about machinery, not power, so there are a few questionable cases. Carol Pernicone's sample from the 1819 jury lists shows 8 percent of industrial workers were women in the poor Sixth Ward. Pernicone, "The 'Bloody Ould Sixth': A Social Analysis of a New York City Working-Class Community in the Mid-Nineteenth Century" (diss., University of Rochester, 1973), 30. In 1820, 91 of 1,483 employees listed were female; in 1850, 30,752 of 83,900 were women. Of these, my sample indicates, two-thirds were in the clothing industry, hence the estimated 12 percent in nonclothing trades. In 1860 we can subtract clothing from the printed totals: there were 61,888 total nonclothing workers of whom 7,934 were women: about 13 percent.

These shops were internally undifferentiated. The master or "boss" such as Peter Cooper, the gluemaker and future industrialist, usually "labored side by side with the men." Foremen were virtually unknown. Even on construction sites where subcontracting was the rule, the boss, according to Henry Fearon, was no more than a head workman. Division of labor was widely used but remained limited: John Petheram, an English druggist, was stunned on his arrival in 1830 to discover that his employer expected him to wash bottles. And in the 1820s, John H. Morrison notes, "the skilled mechanic in the shipyard performed work of any character that was necessary to building the vessel," including hewing the planks out of wood, fastening them in place, and caulking them.[6]

This brief sketch suggests the nature of urban manufacturing around 1820. Already a number of relatively large, heavily capitalized firms used division of labor to make goods to be sold in the South or upstate, but most of the city's workers still labored by hand in small shops. The completion of the Erie Canal in 1825 gave the city's manufacturers extremely cheap transport to western markets, and the city's industries, already exporting to the South, were generally quick to take advantage of increased opportunities in the West. Cochran dates the second stage of the industrial revolution—"the industrial upsurge"—from 1825 and suggests that it was largely a response to the growing demand for manufactured goods created by improved transport. The following four sketches of trades indicate that in New York City, at least, the response of industries to the opportunities created by cheap transport was extremely varied.[7]

## THE CLOTHING INDUSTRY

Clothing manufacturers responded to increasing demand by hiring more workers and further dividing labor. This is the clearest example of the *labor-intensive* or *"sweated"* reaction, so characteristic of Manhattan manufacturing, to the possibilities opened up by cheap transportation. Clothing was by far the city's largest industry, employing 35 percent of all manufacturing employees in 1855 (see Table 11). Generally, labor-intensive industries had a competitive advantage in New York, as the growth of the clothing industry clearly shows.[8]

6. Edward Mack, *Peter Cooper—Citizen of New York* (New York, 1949), 74, 83. Fearon, *Sketches of America*, 22; see also G. W. Sheldon, "The Old Ship-Builders of New York," *Harper's Magazine* 65 (1882), 232. John Petheram, "Sketches of My Life," 1830–1831, NYHS; John H. Morrison, *History of New York Ship Yards* (New York, 1909), 94.

7. Cochran, *Frontiers of Change*, 78–80.

8. The standard account of the city's clothing industry in the antebellum period is Egal Feldman, *Fit for Men* (Washington, 1960). Jesse Pope, *The Clothing Industry in New York* (1905; rpt. New York, 1970), has only limited information on the period before 1880. Claudia

Traditionally tailors in the city had measured each customer who placed an order and then "tailor-made" every garment. In the 1820s in New York, custom tailoring still seems to have comprised the bulk of the clothing trade, but in 1817 Henry Fearon had noted the existence of "ready-made clothes' shops, as in London, at which articles of a cheaper but inferior description are sold." There is, however, only scattered evidence of large shipments of ready-made clothes outside the city before the 1820s.[9]

In predominantly rural nineteenth-century America, men's clothing was usually made not by custom tailors but by farm wives. The coat would "be cut up by the country retailer" and the sewing done at home; pants and shirts were often made entirely at home. Any major increase in ready-made clothing would occur less at the expense of custom work than at that of home manufacture—estimated at two-thirds of the market in 1810. The first breakthrough involved the South. Capitalizing on existing links to the region, city merchants began in the 1820s to ship clothes, "mainly of lower and inferior grades" to slaves and backcountry farmers but also including some fashionable clothing for planters. Taking advantage of the canal, "the Western Country opened up new markets for sale" in the 1840s, and city merchants flooded rural areas with casks of cheap flannel shirts and dungarees. In the words of the *Tribune*'s COUNTRY TAILOR, "the wholesale Clothing establishments in your city [New York] . . . are forcing their work into the villages, along the rivers, canals and railroads, absorbing the business of the country." Country stores saw the sales of piece goods to be sewn into garments plummet as ready-made sales boomed. City clothiers were able, in the words of the *United States Economist and Dry Goods Reporter*, "to furnish the garments ready made at such prices, that the cost to the consumer is less than he was able to obtain them by the old method, of purchasing the material and getting it made up at home." In the early 1850s the California trade became significant, and the ready-made clothing business was national.[10]

To take advantage of this growing market, merchants altered productive methods to mass-produce cheap goods. Although some garments, especially vests and pantaloons, were put out to women, in 1820 most tailors in New

---

Kidwell and Margaret Christman, *Suiting Everyone: The Democratization of Clothing in America* (Washington, 1974), is helpful on the growth of ready-made clothing in America.

9. Fearon, *Sketches of America*, 34; see also Charles L. Flint et al., eds., *Eighty Years Progress* (New York, 1864), 309, and Horace Greeley, ed., *Great Industries of the United States* (Hartford, Conn., 1872), 568. Umbrellas were shipped South in 1820: see *Mercein's City Directory, New York Register and Almanac* (New York, 1820), 13.

10. *United States Economist and Dry Goods Reporter* 2 (1852), 44; this short article gives an excellent description of the development of the industry. South: Feldman, *Fit for Men*, 1, 35–52. "Western Country": *Harper's Weekly* 8 (1864), 141. *Tribune*, 16 June 1849; *United States Economist and Dry Goods Reporter* 2 (1853), 330. California trade: John C. Gobright, ed., *The New-York Sketch Book and Merchant's Guide* (New York, 1858), 18. National: Edwin T. Freedley, *Leading Pursuits and Leading Men* (Philadelphia, 1856), 126; see also Virginia Penny, *How Women Can Make Money* (1863; rpt. New York, 1971), 351, 356.

York City were retailers who sewed most clothes themselves, even ready-made ones. The rapid expansion of female employment beyond these traditional branches, beginning in the 1820s, was in Edwin Freedley's words "a most important and complete revolution." Some male tailors began to employ female sewers to do stitching on coats: "A women helps us in making some parts of the work," one journeyman explained in 1836. Increasingly merchants set up large and systematized operations involving a considerable number of workers and substantial division of labor. "A man . . . rents a story or two . . . employs the necessary number of cutters . . . and then goes to work. . . . One cutter . . . will cut as many garments in one week as three hundred persons can make up in the same time. . . . The operatives in these establishments are mostly . . . poor people," the COUNTRY TAILOR wrote in 1849. Former artisan tailors often became skilled cutters and worked in "the inside shop," whereas women and immigrant men were hired as cheaply paid sewers and worked at home in the "outside shop." "Such large facilities," the *United States Economist and Dry Goods Reporter* noted, "renders competition on a small scale entirely out of the question." By using the putting-out system extensively and exploiting the city's growing pool of cheap labor, large clothiers were able to respond to seasonal variations and changes in style. In addition, this sort of expansion did not require a large industrial plant and the high fixed capital costs that such a plant would entail.[11]

By the mid-1830s several wholesale firms in the city had three hundred or more employees. Most of the major clothing firms collapsed after the Panic of 1837, but when the city's economy began to recover, the clothing industry rose to even greater heights—the amount of wholesale clothing sold grew from $2.5 million in 1841 to almost $20 million in 1853. It slumped to $18.9 million in 1860, but the expansion in the twenty-plus years after the 1837 panic was remarkable. By the late 1840s immense ready-made clothing firms had emerged: Lewis and Hanford had 75 "insiders" (cutters) and 4,000 "outsiders" (sewers) in 1849, and Brooks Brothers had 78 insiders and 1,500 outsiders. One writer calculated in 1858 that the industry employed 900 cutters, 200 trimmers, and 40,000 "work hands." By 1850 the *average* number of employees per city clothing establishment, in a sample from the 1850 *Census of Manufactures*, was 137.[12]

11. Vests and pantaloons: *Post*, 13 July 1819. There is no claim in this article that men had formerly made vests and pantaloons; male tailors protested only that by "right" they should make them. See also Fearon, *Sketches of America*, 33–34. Freedley, *Leading Pursuits*, 125. "A woman": *Working Man's Advocate*, 12 March 1836. COUNTRY TAILOR: *Tribune*, 16 June 1849. *United States Economist and Dry Goods Reporter* 2 (1852), 44. Ready-made clothing underwent seasonal style changes in the 1850s, see the *United States Economist and Dry Goods Reporter* n.s. 11 (1857), 70.
12. 1837: Feldman, *Fit for Men*, 4. Amount of wholesale clothing: Freedley, *Leading Pursuits*, 125, and Census Office, *Eighth Census, 1860, Manufactures* (Washington, 1865), 380. Lewis and Hanford and Brooks Brothers: Andrews & Company, *Stranger's Guide in the*

Packed into city's Second Ward, which provided the clothiers with access to both warehouses and docks and put them in a position to react rapidly to changing conditions in a volatile trade, the largest clothing firms increasingly dominated the wholesale business. Division of labor advanced well beyond the simple cutter-sewer distinction. D. and J. Devlin, one of the city's largest firms, in 1849 had their cutters "classified into four departments: one department exclusively for coats; a second for pants; a third for vests; and a fourth for trimmings," each directed by a foreman. At Lewis and Hanford "every thing about the concern is reduced to a system, and that system carried out with a degree of precision that would astonish the negligent and careless observer," wrote *Hunt's Merchants' Magazine.* An elaborate system of tags was used at Lewis and Hanford to keep track of merchandise from uncut cloth to finished garment. The sewing became highly specialized, with shirt sewers, for example, subclassified "into body makers, stitchers, finishers, and embroiderers."[13]

This was a labor-intensive industry. Before the mid-1850s and the perfection of the sewing machine, the growth of ready-made clothes depended solely on hiring more workers and dividing labor. There was a sharp division between the skilled cutters, who could make as much as $15 a week in 1850, and the sewers, who averaged $1.60 for women and $3.50 for men (compared to $7.20 weekly for men who were not tailors). In 1860, 57 percent of the sewers were women; the large number of male workers is surprising. While some men were cutters, many more were sewers. Lewis and Hanford, for example, a firm with 75 cutters, had 2,000 males out of 4,000 total employees in 1850. Generally men worked on sewing coats, since the cloth used was deemed too heavy for women to work easily, and women usually made vests, shirts, and pants. For all sewers, male and female, wages were very low. It is likely that in many families both husband and wife worked as sewers, since together their wages would probably have been barely enough to live on.[14]

---

*City of New-York* (New York, 1849), 24–25, and *Hunt's Merchants' Magazine* 20 (1849), 348. Gobright, *New-York Sketch Book*, 18. The 137 average is from an augmented sample of clothing firms in 1850. The sample contains 104 firms with 14,281 employees.

13. The importance of agglomeration economies in the twentieth-century garment industry is emphasized by Roger Waldinger, *Through the Eye of the Needle: Immigrants and Enterprise in New York's Garment Trades* (New York, 1986), 97–103. Devlin: *Hunt's Merchants' Magazine* 20 (1849), 116. Lewis and Hanford: *Hunt's Merchants' Magazine* 20 (1849), 348; see also Freedley, *Leading Pursuits*, 129. *Herald*, 11 June 1853.

14. Cutters' wages: *Tribune*, 15 November 1845. Robert Ernst's figures show that 18,715 of 22,428 tailors and seamstresses in the city were foreign-born, see Ernst, *Immigrant Life in New York City, 1825–1863* (1949; rpt. New York, 1979), 215, Table 11. Fifty-seven percent: Census Office, *Eighth Census, 1860, Manufactures*, 360. In my 1850 sample from Wards Two, Seven, and Sixteen, 58 percent of 11,668 employees were female. In the 1850 sample the average male monthly wage was $13.60, for women $6.50. Men in the 1860 sample averaged $16.90, women $8.70. Lewis and Hanford: *Seventh Census, 1850, Manufactures*, Manuscript, Ward Two. On the male domination of coat-sewing see Penny, *How Women Can Make Money*, 345, and Feldman, *Fit for Men*, 95, 98–99.

The clothing business was highly competitive and failures were common. The R. G. Dun and Company credit ledgers listed Lewis and Hanford as shaky in both 1851 and 1854 before its collapse in 1857, and few firms seemed really solid. "It is a singular fact that practical tailors, however skilful in their trade . . . rarely succeed as wholesale manufacturers," wrote Edwin Freedley. Freedley did not believe lack of capital was the problem, but the evidence suggests otherwise. Although fixed capital costs could be quite low, the circulating capital was substantial. A tailor going into business for himself might obtain cloth on credit, but wages for the sewers (estimated at 45 percent of his outlays) had to be paid in cash. A "large capital is necessary to carry on an extensive business"—an average of $18,450 per firm in 1850—and those without it had little chance in such a cutthroat business. Ordinary tailors had few opportunities in the ready-made business—virtually all the wholesale firms discussed in R. G. Dun and Company's records were started by merchants or clerks.[15]

New York in the 1850s still had a number of small neighborhood shops that custom-made clothes. James Demarest, a native-born tailor, opened a shop in the late 1840s at 8th Avenue and 24th Street. He was on "shaky" ground at first, but by 1853 R. G. Dun and Company reported he had "a fair business, mostly custom work," and by 1860, aged forty-seven, he had fifteen employees. His capital in 1860 was only $1,000, far below that of the major firms and too low to carry on an extensive wholesale business. Such neighborhood shops, though numerous, employed only a small minority of the trade's skilled workers, most of whom now worked as cutters for the big firms.[16]

Although small tailors' shops no longer dominated the trade, the supremacy of the huge firms also proved transitory. The average size of clothing firms dropped from 137 in 1850, to 103 in 1855, to 71 in 1860. The reasons for this decline in size was the growth of subcontracting. Large wholesale clothiers such as Brooks Brothers discovered it was more profitable, and easier, to subcontract with smaller firms that could adjust more easily to changes in season and fashion. The city's clothiers had become uneconomically large except during eras as prosperous as the Age of Gold. When the boom began to wane in 1854, major wholesalers found it increasingly to their advantage to leave the manufacturing to smaller and more flexible producers. Only a few of the very large manufacturers survived the 1857 panic, Brooks Brothers being

15. New York vol. 198, 111, 116, R. G. Dun and Company Collection, Baker Library, Harvard Graduate School of Business Administration. Freedley, *Leading Pursuits*, 126–127. 45 percent: *United States Economist and Dry Goods Reporter* 21 (1857), 134. Freedley, 126. Sample, 1850. *Eighth Census, 1860, Manufactures,* 380.

16. Information about Demarest compiled from New York vol. 209, 48, R. G. Dun and Company Collection, Baker Library, Harvard Graduate School of Business Administration; *Eighth Census, 1860, Manufactures,* Manuscript, Sixteenth Ward; and Census Office, *Eighth Census, 1860, Population,* Manuscript, Sixteenth Ward. Numerous custom tailors are noted in New York, vol. 212, R. G. Dun and Company Collection.

a notable example. In the clothing industry, increasing specialization through the increased use of subcontracting diminished the average size of the unit of production.[17]

Clothing, then, illustrates the labor-intensive or sweated reaction to the opportunities of the 1820s. By dividing labor and hiring new workers, large clothiers were able to expand output enormously. The creation of an elite coterie of highly skilled cutters and a huge pool of poorly paid immigrant sewers enabled clothiers to produce immense quantities of ready-made clothes. This "most important and complete revolution" was accomplished without use of steam power or machinery. In 1850 none of the fifty-five clothing firms sampled used steam, in 1860 one of forty-one did. The sewing machine, which became widespread in the late 1850s, appeared after the huge, highly organized clothing manufacturers had risen to their greatest heights and had already begun to decline.[18]

THE METAL TRADES

Metalworking was one of the city's largest industries, and its history after 1820 contrasts with that of clothing. The nature of the product demanded that the metals industry respond to increased demand through a *capital-intensive* or *factory* response, involving the use of large plants and steam power. This response was generally more typical of New Jersey manufacturing after the 1840s, but the city's largest foundries could not be economically moved as the periphery widened, and they continued to employ thousands of workers.

New York's metals industry in the 1820s was mostly concentrated in small, unpowered shops—the average number of employees in metalworking shops in 1820, including apprentices, was 6.8. Output was relatively unspecialized, and the line between founding and metalworking sometimes blurred, as the listing of products of Benjamin Birdsall, a Sixth Ward brass founder, makes clear: "All kinds of iron work for Buildings, such as Iron Railing, anchors, Bolts, Cornish Irons, and Smith Work of every description, all kind of machinery, engine work etc.—Brass Fronts, fire Grates, Brass Fenders, and every article in the white Smith line—all kinds of Tin and sheet and Sheet Iron

17. On subcontracting see Feldman, *Fit for Men*, 104; Pope, *Clothing Industry*, 64; and the *Herald*, 17 June 1853. Waldinger, *Through the Eye*, 91–97, explains the "liabilities of size" in the twentieth-century garment industry. These manufacturing firms were much larger than twentieth-century clothing firms: in 1982 the average shop size in men's clothing in the city was 24 and the national average 49; *Census of Manufactures, 1982* (Washington, 1986), III, pt. 2, N.Y. 55; I, pt. I, 1–6.

18. Sample of the 1850 and 1860 manufacturing census. On the impact of the sewing machine on the clothing industry see Flint, et al., *Eighty Years Progress*, 426–431; Feldman, *Fit for Men*, 108–111; U.S. Congress, Senate, Committee on Education and Labor, *Report of the Senate Committee upon the Relations between Labor and Capital* (Washington, 1885), 1:413–414; Penny, *How Women Can Make Money*, 310–312.

work of all descriptions.'' A few of the city's major iron foundries were quite big—in 1820 Robert McQueen, a steam engine builder and protegé of Robert Fulton, employed seventy men and twelve boys and had $200,000 in capital. [19]

The demand for enormous steamship engines, some of them weighing thirty tons, required vast expansion of the city's foundries; even ironworks the size of McQueen's were too small to cast the gigantic ''bed-pieces'' needed for the engines of the 1830s. The Allaire Works was started in 1813 by another protegé of Fulton's, but no other major foundries opened until 1830, when the Novelty Works (named after the engine it built for the steamship *Novelty*) was established. It was followed by the Morgan Ironworks in 1838, the Cornell Works in 1847, and the Delameter Iron Works (builder of the *Monitor* during the Civil War) in 1850. By 1860 both the East and the Hudson rivers were lined with these and other large foundries. [20]

By 1830 the Allaire Works had two hundred employees. Like the other major foundries it was hurt by the 1837 panic, and by 1847 had grown only to two-hundred-fifty ''hands.'' But the prosperity of the 1840s caused a rapid expansion of the big foundries: by 1850 Allaire had 550 employees, Morgan 650, and the Novelty Works 938 employees and $450,000 in invested capital. These enterprises were recognized, because of their size and organization, as the epitome of industrial progress in the city. The Novelty Works spread over five acres along the East River and was highly systematized (see Figure 5). It had a ''front office'' (surely one of the first in the city) with a superintendent and eleven clerks to keep employment and sales records, and eighteen separate departments ''at the head of each of which is a foreman.'' Its ''complicated maze of buildings'' along the East River was, as Figure 6 shows, carefully arranged internally and literally centered around the steam engine. In the words of a *Harper's* article, ''the establishment forms, in fact, a regularly organized community, having, like any state or kingdom, its gradations of rank, its established usages, its written laws, its police, its finance, its records, its rewards, and its penalties.'' [21]

19. Total of twenty metalworking firms listed in the *Fourth Census, 1820, Manufactures,* Manuscript. On McQueen see Carroll Pursell, *Early Stationary Steam Engines in America* (Washington, 1969), 50–51. *Fourth Census, 1820, Manufactures,* Manuscript, Sixth Ward.

20. Robert Greenhalgh Albion, *The Rise of New York Port, 1815–1860* (New York, 1939), 114–115; Leander Bishop, *A History of American Manufactures* (1868; rpt. New York, 1967), 3:123–146; Victor Clark, *History of Manufactures in the United States* (Washington, 1916), 1:506–507.

21. *Documents Relative to Manufactures in the United States* [''The McLane Report''] (1833; rpt. New York, 1969), 2:115; *Hunt's Merchants' Magazine* 16 (1847), 93; *Seventh Census, 1850, Manufactures,* Manuscript, Wards Seven and Eleven. On the Novelty Works see Bishop, *History of American Manufactures,* 3:125–128; *Hunt's Merchants' Magazine* 23 (1850), 463–465; *New York Post,* 16 July 1850; Jacob Abbott, ''The Novelty Works,'' *Harper's Magazine* 2 (1851), 721–734; and Joel H. Ross, *What I Saw in New York* (Auburn, N.Y., 1852), 200–206. Quotation from Abbott, 724.

FIGURE 5. The Novelty Ironworks from the East River, c. 1848. Courtesy of The New-York Historical Society, New York City.

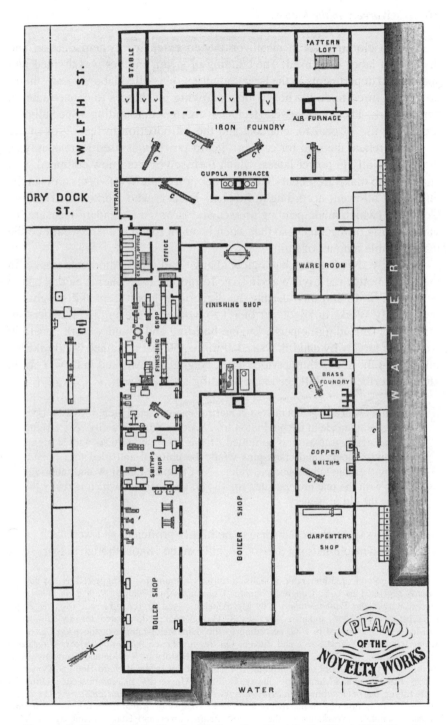

FIGURE 6. Floorplan of the Novelty Works, 1851. From Jacob Abbott, "The Novelty Works," *Harper's Magazine* 2 (1851), 723.

As with clothing, so in metalworking an extensive systematization and division of labor were used. The building of steam engines was divided into specialized departments in the large foundries. Unskilled laborers and "helpers" were hired to do the heavy jobs, allowing mechanics to concentrate on skilled work. There were several technical changes in founding, especially the increasing use of coal for charcoal and the introduction in the 1850s of the cupola to reheat the iron for casting. Steam power was used increasingly as well, especially to power lathes, which themselves were now equipped with slide rests to make preset cuts. The introduction of the Whitworth screw in the late 1840s allowed, according to Stephen Tucker, who worked for Hoe and Company (which made printing presses and saws), a "standard measure for various parts of machines, so that when brought together there would be the least possible amount of fitting."[22]

Generally, however, technological change had only a moderate impact in the period before the Civil War. In large foundries, each marine engine had to be custom-built, and this, despite the division of labor, kept skills high—at the Novelty Works in 1850, 711 of 1,170 workers were smiths, founders, or machinists (including helpers). Engine building and foundry work generally were done largely by hand. It was a laborious job that remained highly skilled throughout the antebellum period. A. F. Nagle, who worked in New York in 1861, described the skill needed in building such engines:

> I remember well a large double-crank marine-engine shaft belonging to the USS *Oneida*, being made in the old Fulton Iron Works, New York city. After being turned as nearly true as tools permitted, it was subjected to tests with straight-edges and calipers, and crank-pins would be chipped and filed to a greater accuracy than the lathe made possible. . . . Compare that slow and laborious process with the one now pursued [in 1893], and then ask which is really the wonder, the old or new.

Needless to say, such workers had to be highly proficient and were well paid. Molders and machinists got $10–12 weekly in the 1850s, though helpers were

22. The complicated hierarchy of skills in the city's foundries is suggested by the payroll records reprinted in U.S. Congress, Senate, Committee on Finance, *Report on Wholesale Prices, Wages and Transportation,* "by Mr. Aldrich," 52d Cong., 2d sess., 1893, S. Rept. 1394, pt. 3, 1169–1276, and pt. 4, 1277–1338. Though coal predominated, the city's foundries still used much charcoal in 1860 according to the manuscript returns of the *1860 Census of Manufactures* for Wards Seven and Eleven. On the cupola see *Wholesale Prices, Wages and Transportation,* Part Three, 1170. Stephen Tucker, "History of R. Hoe and Company, New York," 34–35, typescript of the original 1887 manuscript in the Richard Hoe and Company Papers, Rare Book and Manuscript Library, Columbia University; this reminiscence, edited by Rollo Silver, has been published in *Proceedings of the American Antiquarian Society* 82 (1972), 351–453. On technology in metalwork see Clark, *History of Manufactures,* 1:502–521, and Raphael Samuel, "Workshop of the World: Steam Power and Hand Technology in Mid-Victorian Britain," *History Workshop* 3 (1977), 39–44.

paid only about half that amount. The factory had done little to dilute workers' skills in the city's metalworking industry.[23]

The Age of Factories in New York City was brief; the soaring price of land soon forced large firms to leave the city or stagnate, and the most progressive sector of the marine engine business began to move south to the Delaware River. This process probably began as early as the mid-1840s, and the city's shipbuilding industry was further hurt by the 1857 panic: the Novelty Works declined from $1,105,000 business in 1850 to $1,005,000 in 1860, the Morgan Works from $836,000 to $600,000. The Civil War temporarily restored the industry, but in the long run the problems of a Manhattan location choked ship and steam engine building.[24]

As the largest factories were declining in Manhattan, however, hundreds of smaller foundries and metalworking firms prospered. The large number of small shops is clear in my sample from the *1860 Census of Manufactures*, which shows that only 14 of 58 firms in the metal trades had more than ten workers. Many small shops were in the Seventh Ward and did metal and maritime custom repair work. Another large segment of these small metalworking shops was ancillary to the construction trade; Richard Redfern, a Market Street tin roof maker with three employees, was typical. According to R. G. Dun's, Redfern "has no means of consequence but does not want much credit" with a capital of $500 and liabilities of only $25. A number of flourishing foundries of moderate size (50 to 150 employees) specialized in architectural and custom ironwork. Three relatively new areas of metal-

---

23. *Hunt's Merchants' Magazine* 23 (1850), 464. Nagle quoted in Robert Allison, "The Old and the New," *Transactions of the American Society of Mechanical Engineers* 16 (1893), 753; see also Charles H. Haswell, "Reminiscences of Early Marine Steam Engine Builders and Steam Navigation in the United States of America from 1807 to 1850," *Transactions of the Institution of Naval Architects* 40 (1898), 105. Further insight into 1850s' techniques in New York machine shops can be found in Charles T. Porter, *Engineering Reminiscences* (New York, 1908), esp. 31. Even in such allegedly mass production as the manufacture of sewing machines, the technology was primitive. In the 1850s in Singer's Nott Street Shop there were "no milling machines and no gang drillers. . . . The parts did not 'gage' at all . . . [and] parts were kept by themselves while the frame was being japanned, and afterwards put back on the same frame, as they were very far from interchangeable"; Henry Roland, "Six Examples of Successful Shop Management—Number Five," *Engineering Magazine* 12 (1897), 997. See also David A. Hounshell, *From the American System to Mass Production, 1800–1932: The Development of Manufacturing Technology in the United States* (London, 1984), 90–91. For wages see *Annual Report of the A.I.C.P. for the Year 1866*, 25, and *Wholesale Prices, Wages and Transportation*, pt. 3 and pt. 4.

24. *Seventh and Eighth Censuses, 1850 and 1860, Manufactures*, Manuscript, Wards Seven and Eleven. Dun's records also mention the Novelty Works' growing problems: see New York vol. 368, 401, R. G. Dun and Company Collection, Baker Library, Harvard Graduate School of Business Administration. On the decline of New York shipbuilding see Henry Hall, "Report on the Ship-Building Industry of the United States," Census Office, *Tenth Census, 1880, Special Reports* (Washington, 1884), 116–118; see also Albion, *Rise of New York Port*, 332, and Freedley, *Leading Pursuits*, 365–367.

work—plumbing (it was still common for plumbers to cast their own pipes), steamfitting, and gasfitting—emerged in this period as middle-class demand increased for the "modern conveniences" of indoor plumbing, central heating, and gaslight. These smaller firms, not the large foundries, were the most dynamic part of the metalworking trade in the city by the late 1850s.[25]

These smaller firms, even machinists' shops, were usually unpowered and had less than $1,000 in capital. Though it may seem unlikely that casting multi-ton steam engines equipped someone to make andirons, the proliferation of small shops did offer skilled metalworkers an alternative to being employees in large foundries. R. G. Dun's records contain numerous entries on small foundry and machinery shops started by "practical mechanics," almost invariably in partnership with a businessman who provided capital. Although there were many more small firms than large ones, most workers in the metals trades still worked for large foundries or machine shops; the Allaire, Novelty, and Morgan works alone account for one-third of all metalworking employees in the 1860 manufacturing census.[26]

In metalworking, then, the large factory emerged to meet the demand for large steam engines. Careful organization created large, capital-intensive firms. Because steam engines were customized, however, the work process itself, though thoroughly systematized, still depended on skilled and highly paid labor. The rise of these large firms did not cause the decline of small ones; indeed, smaller shops thrived and by 1860 seem to have been economically healthier than the city's largest foundries. Though factories flourished in outlying parts of the metropolitan region, they were not destined to dominate the city's metalworking trade in the second half of the nineteenth century.

## PRINTING

Printing was one of the fastest-growing trades in the antebellum city, and its history contrasts with that of its fellow commerce-serving trade of steam-engine building. The structure and development of printing between 1820 and 1860 were exceedingly complicated and serve to emphasize the complexity of New York's industrialization. The focus of our examination is the internal segmentation of this industry and the role of technology in fostering segmentation.

25. Sample of Wards Two, Seven, and Sixteen, from the 1860 *Census of Manufactures.* Information about small shops comes from the *Census of Manufactures,* which often goes into great detail about products, and New York vol. 316A, R. G. Dun and Company Collection, Baker Library, Harvard Graduate School of Business Administration. New York vol. 324, 294, Dun Collection. Ornamental ironwork: *Times,* 23 June 1865.

26. New York vol. 316A, R. G. Dun and Company Collection, Baker Library, Harvard Graduate School of Business Administration, contains entries on partnerships between "practical mechanics" and "capitalists."

TABLE 6
Employment in printing, 1860

|  | Number of firms | Average capital | Employees | Per capita monthly wages |
|---|---|---|---|---|
| Newspaper | 51 | $57,142 | 2,486 | $43 |
| Book | 17 | $183,588 | 2,153 | $27 |
| Job | 81 | $7,973 | 871 | $15 |

*Source: Eighth Census, 1860, Manufactures, 383.*

In 1818 there were approximately fifty printing offices in the city, employing five hundred journeymen. Small shops were the general rule, though some firms, such as David Bruce's, which had nine presses as early as 1809, were clearly substantial enterprises. Even in this era of small shops, however, the skilled printer enjoyed no golden age. Master printers hired boys who had served only a short apprenticeship as "half-way" journeymen and paid them low wages. Apprenticeship was never particularly well-established, and most branches of the trade required little strength. Country boys aged twelve to fifteen, who had learned a little composing, could come to the city and find work. Henry Fearon in 1817 found "a great portion of the work is done by boys," a practice that seriously hurt the city's journeyman printers. The process of skill dilution in printing began in the shop stage when the journeymen proved unable to control the labor market, which helps explain the early organization of employees in this industry.[27]

In the 1830s the printing industry began to divide into three parts—book, newspaper, and job or commercial printing. Although as early as 1810, according to master printer David Bruce, printshops in the city "all more or less assumed separate specialities," the tripartite division emerged when differences between the three branches became great enough to seriously weaken the printers' union. Book printing at first predominated: 70 percent of all printers in 1845 worked in this branch. The growth of newspapers in the 1840s and 1850s narrowed the gap considerably until in 1860 newspapers employed a plurality of workers in the trades, as Table 6 shows.[28]

The rise in the city of mass circulation newspapers with national readerships—the *Sun,* founded in 1833, the *Herald* in 1835, and the *Tribune* in

27. C. S. Van Winkle, *The Printer's Guide* (New York, 1818), xi. David Bruce remembered about thirty print shops in New York in 1810; Bruce, "Autobiography of David Bruce," undated manuscript in the NYHS. Rollo G. Silver, *The American Printer, 1787–1825* (Charlottesville, Va., 1967), 67; George A. Stevens, *New York Typographical Union No. 6* (Albany, N.Y., 1913), 66–69; Fearon, *Sketches of America,* 37.

28. Bruce, "Autobiography." In the early period the line between job and book printing was sometimes blurred: see Stevens, *New York Typographical Union,* 54–55. On book-newspaper hostilities see Stevens, 132–133; *British Mechanic's and Labourer's Hand Book* (London, 1840), 234; and the *Tribune,* 11 September 1845.

1841—created an enormous increase in demand for cheap printed matter which was met largely through technological innovations in printing. The development of larger and more rapid presses was long and complex, but the key event was the adoption of the cylinder press, sometimes known as the Napier press (see Figure 7), in the mid-1830s and first made in the United States by R. Hoe and Company of New York City. The extensive use of stereotyping, in which the matter to be printed is cast in lead, was, according to printing historian Rollo G. Silver, "quickly adopted . . . for large editions, such as Bibles and textbooks, that had a large national market," beginning in the 1820s. Again a New York City firm, David Bruce and Company, led the way.[29]

Steam was needed to power these large cylinder and rotary presses, and huge, highly capitalized printing establishments soon dominated the business. In 1860 Harper Brothers had a capital of $1.5 million, James Gordon Bennett $600,000, Moses Beach $240,000, and Street and Smith $100,000. In book and newspaper printing the per firm average was $88,750 in invested capital, with 55 employees. These, the most highly systematized manufacturing firms in the city, used a sophisticated division of labor. A journeyman printer who asked New York master Hugh Gaine in an earlier era if he needed a foreman had been ridiculed with the reply, "A foreman! . . . What is a foreman? he who first stalks out of the office to dinner?" By the 1850s things had changed. The *Tribune* had two foremen and nine assistant foremen in 1853, each with his own area of supervision in the printing and composing rooms. Harper's in 1855 had numerous foremen and forewomen and a different department on each floor of its seven-story plant on Pearl Street, in the Fourth Ward.[30]

The development of these large printing factories was accompanied by a sustained attack on the skill of workers. The hiring of semitrained apprentices, known by the 1840s as "two-thirders" (from their pay compared to that of a regular journeyman), undercut wages. Although two-thirders preceded the use of high-speed presses, technological innovation helped accelerate division of labor. The cylinder press, according to the *Tribune*, "gave the first impulse to *cheap publications,* and these, *rushed* out as they were . . . made it incumbent to adopt the same rule generally, *viz.* a few good workmen to make

29. For growth in demand see Eugene Exman, *The House of Harper* (New York, 1967), 18; Frank Luther Mott, *The Golden Multitudes* (New York, 1947), 76–79; and James Crouthamel, "The Newspaper Revolution in New York, 1830–1860," *New York History* 65 (1964), 91–113. Robert Hoe, *A Short History of the Printing Press* (New York, 1902), 17–20, and James Moran, *Printing Presses: History and Development from the Fifteenth Century to Modern Times* (Berkeley, Calif., 1973), 123–141. Silver, *American Printer*, 61.

30. *Eighth Census, 1860, Manufactures,* Manuscript, Wards Two and Four; *Eighth Census, 1860, Manufactures,* 383. Gaine quoted in "William McCulloch's Additions to Thomas's History of Printing," *Proceedings of the American Antiquarian Society* n.s. 31 (1921), 96. *Tribune: Times,* 1 June 1853. Harper's: Jacob Abbott, *The Brothers Harper* (New York, 1855), 41–50.

FIGURE 7. Hoe's ten-cylinder rotary press, c. 1857. From Robert Hoe, *A Short History of the Printing Press* (New York, 1902), 35.

up and impose, while the rest set up copy.'' With the printing nearly auto-
matic, printers were expected to be able to undertake both case- and presswork
only in the smallest shops. The main demand was for workers who were, in
the *Tribune*'s words, ''mere type-setters, and not printers . . . in the strict
sense of the word.'' It took only six months to learn to become a ''mere''
typesetter. The *Tribune* itself listed no printers among its employees in 1853,
only ''compositors'' and ''feeders.''[31]

The tremendous cost of a cylinder press made it virtually impossible for
journeymen to become book or newspaper printers. Monthly wages in printing, though still above average, were below those of several other urban trades
(see Table 7). But monthly wages obscure the very different experiences of
newspaper, book, and job printers (see Table 6). Newspaper printers were one
of the very few groups of workers in the city who could count on year-round
employment: a daily newspaper, after all, is published six days a week, fifty-
two weeks a year. Although *weekly* wages in newspaper printing were usually
only a dollar higher than those in book printing ($12 versus $11 in the late
1850s), *monthly* wages for newspaper printers, as Table 6 shows, were 60
percent higher. In antebellum New York City, high wages per se were less
significant than regularity of employment, which made newspaper printers the
elite of city workers.[32]

As in metalworking, however, the growth of large, powered establishments
in printing did not destroy the small shop. The trade became segmented, and
job printing emerged to fill seasonal and sporadic demand for printed matter.
Concentrated in the Second Ward, near both the commercial and the financial
areas of the city, job printing was the bastion of the independent printer. The
seasonal nature of much of the city's manufacturing and trade made commercial printing unavoidably seasonal. ''In the book and job offices there were,
from day to day as well as from season to season, great variations in the
amount of work to be done,'' economist George Barnett noted in his history of
the printer's union. W. Eric Gustafson studied the city's printing industry in
the 1950s; as he explained, ''large shops are possible only if demand comes in
large pieces or the work is of highly routine nature.'' Because job demand was
mostly for small runs and items less than a page in size, cylinder presses, with
their high set-up costs and energy expenses, were uneconomic for job work.
Job printing therefore relied on the small shop (10.8 employees was the 1860
average) and hand- or foot-powered presses such as the popular Gordon jobber

31. Stevens, *New York Typographical Union,* 213–214. For an account of life as a ''two-
thirder'' in the 1850s, see J. B. Graham, *Handset Reminiscences* (Salt Lake City, Utah, 1915),
57–66. *Tribune,* 15 September 1845. Even in colonial times, many journeymen specialized in
casework or presswork; see *The Journals of Hugh Gaine Printer,* ed. Paul Ford (New York,
1902). *British Mechanic's and Labourer's Hand Book,* 235; see also Penny, *How Women Can
Make Money,* 382. ''Feeders'': *Times,* 1 June 1853.

32. On the difficulty of journeymen becoming bosses, see the *Tribune,* 11 September 1845.
Weekly printers' wages: Penny, *How Women Can Make Money,* 383.

TABLE 7
Monthly wages in selected industries in New York, 1850 and 1860, in dollars

| Trade | Year | No. of firms | Male wage | Female wage |
|---|---|---|---|---|
| Clothing | 1850 | 55 | 13.6 | 6.5 |
|  | 1860 | 41 | 16.9 | 8.7 |
| Building | 1850 | 36 | 32.0 | — |
|  | 1860 | 38 | 49.0 | — |
| Printing | 1850 | 41 | 32.3 | 13.1 |
|  | 1860 | 97 | 37.1 | 12.4 |
| Metals | 1850 | 60 | 30.2 | 14.8 |
|  | 1860 | 58 | 36.8 | 22.6 |
| Shoes | 1850 | 61 | 21.8 | 10.0 |
|  | 1860 | 61 | 38.4 | 18.0 |
| Furniture | 1850 | 15 | 28.4 | 10.0 |
|  | 1860 | 10 | 42.4 | — |
| Baking | 1850 | 22 | 25.8 | 12.0 |
|  | 1860 | 16 | 31.9 | 19.0 |
| Wood and lumber | 1850 | 21 | 33.1 | 3.6 |
|  | 1860 | 20 | 44.5 | 15.6 |
| Jewelry | 1850 | 9 | 29.8 | 10.5 |
|  | 1860 | 35 | 42.8 | 20.4 |
| Shipbuilding | 1850 | 10 | 33.5 | — |
|  | 1860 | 46 | 40.9 | — |
| Hats and caps | 1850 | 14 | 32.1 | 15.1 |
|  | 1860 | 7 | 40.8 | 20.0 |
| Chemicals | 1850 | 13 | 25.3 | 39.6 |
|  | 1860 | 18 | 12.2 | 18.8 |
| Butchering | 1850 | 10 | 35.8 | — |
|  | 1860 | 1 | 60.0 | — |
| All nonclothing | 1850 | 461 | 27.8 | 10.4 |
|  | 1860 | 509 | 32.5 | 15.4 |
| TOTALS | 1850 | 516 | 20.7 | 7.7 |
|  | 1860 | 550 | 29.0 | 10.7 |

*Note:* These are wages by *industry*. In printing, for example, they include everyone who worked in a printing establishment—bookbinders, laborers, etc.—not just printers.

*Sources:* Sample of 2nd, 7th and 16th Wards from the Census Office, *Seventh Census, 1850, Manufactures,* Manuscript; Census Office, *Eighth Census, 1860, Manufactures,* Manuscript.

(see Figure 8). These presses were much cheaper and allowed firms with only $2,000 or $3,000 in 1860 to find a niche in the competitive job printing business. That year, for example, Frank McElroy of Nassau Street, an "Irishman age 28 . . . formerly a journeyman printer," was able to become proprietor of a substantial job printing business with twenty-three workers.[33]

33. George E. Barnett, "The Printers: A Study in American Trade Unionism," *American Economic Association Quarterly* 10 (1909), 209; W. Eric Gustafson, "Printing and Publishing," in Max Hall, ed., *Made in New York: Case Studies in Metropolitan Manufacturing*

FIGURE 8.  The Gordon jobber, 1858. From *The Printer* 1 (1858), 40.

Printing was splitting into a heavily capitalized, mechanized sector, spe-cializing in predictable, standardized printing, and a less capitalized sector relying on variable and customized demand. Because some book and news-paper printers found they could do larger job runs cheaply and profitably, the job printers were left mostly with the most transient and seasonal part of the market. It was a fluctuating and highly competitive business; "the worst features of the trade are to be found in the smaller offices, holes and corners," according to an 1850 report based on a survey of printing offices by the New York local of the International Typographical Union. The report continues: "In the meaner kinds of book and job offices . . . [printers] are 'only taken on for the job,' and when the job is completed they are discharged, to be out of work perhaps longer than they were in." The report paints a dismal picture of the small master:

> Many of these small employers, after using any and every means to keep
> themselves afloat (and injuring the trade as much as they are able) go down; and

(Cambridge, Mass., 1959), 165. Gordon jobber: *The Printer* 1 (1858), 11; see also Moran, *Printing Presses*, 147–148. Capital: inspection of the Census Office, *Eighth Census, 1860, Manufactures*, Manuscript, Ward Two. McElroy: New York vol. 194, 794, R. G. Dun and Company Collection, Baker Library, Harvard Graduate School of Business Administration.

either return to the ranks or leave the city to try elsewhere; but there are many more who keep up and for many years hang about the skirts of the trade, picking up stray jobs here and there, taking them for any price they can get.

Typical of these small job printers was Lemuel Starr, whom R. G. Dun's described as thirty years old in 1858 and "hardly making more than a living." Starr continued on a shoestring in the city into the 1880s, when R. G. Dun's noted, "not believed to more than hold his own."[34]

Employers in the large firms that came to dominate the trade were able to use division of labor and faster presses together in a way that both cut costs and undermined highly skilled printers. Small print shops endured, but only "on the skirts of the trades," sustained by a demand too limited and sporadic to be profitable for larger firms.[35]

FURNITURE

The cabinetmakers of New York before 1830 were known throughout the nation for their skill and craftsmanship, and their history provides an interesting contrast to the other three trades. As in clothing, an emphasis on style helped keep manufacturing labor-intensive; but unlike in clothing, mass demand never overwhelmed the market for expensive custom-made products. The famous cabinetmakers of the city, of whom Duncan Phyfe was the most renowned, made furniture largely for an international elite market—cabinets and chairs were shipped to the West Indies as early as the last decade of the eighteenth century. In the early nineteenth century, furniture was sent to South America, and in 1817 John Budd advertised "orders for Southern ports immediately attended."[36]

Duncan Phyfe, whose firm had a hundred workers at its height, was a clear exception in a trade generally dominated by small shops. More typical was John Van Boskirk, who in 1820 made "Mahogany Furniture of every description," with "4 men sometimes more [and] 3 boys," and had $4,500 in

34. In advertisements the large publishing houses sometimes mention job printing. Quotations from the I.T.U. report in Stevens, *New York Typographical Union,* 209, 211, 212; see also Abbott, *The Brothers Harper,* 44–45. Starr: New York vol. 193, 635, R. G. Dun and Company Collection, Baker Library, Harvard Graduate School of Business Administration.

35. Although the region's printing was concentrated on Manhattan in 1860, like other capital-intensive manufacturing the large firms eventually left the city. Beginning around 1900, according to Gustafson, "Printing and Publishing," 150–152, the "standardized, large-lot printing" has moved to "the 'ring' of the Industrial Area [which] has gained much of the work which New York City has lost"; see also A. F. Hinrichs, "The Printing Industry," in Robert Murray Haig and Roswell McCrea, eds., *Regional Survey of New York and Its Environs* (New York, 1928), IA, 43.

36. Nancy McClelland, *Duncan Phyfe and the English Regency, 1795–1830* (New York, 1939), 195, 199; Albion, *Rise of New York Port,* 177.

capital. Henry Fearon, a British traveler who visited the small cabinetmaking shops on Greenwich Street, found most contained "a variety, but not a large stock." The cabinetmakers themselves were highly skilled (Fearon believed their work superior to that of the English) and well-paid since a union price-book was enforced.[37]

As early as 1820 there was manufacture and export of inexpensive furniture as well as expensive works for the elite market. Van Boskirk noted in 1820 that "a number of manufacturing establishments have opened in the last 5 years which sell cheap furniture." This market grew rapidly in the 1830s and 1840s as the auction system developed in which merchants bought furniture in lots for export and resale. This cheap production, often denigrated as "stick furniture," was originally sold largely to the South and South America and to rural areas in the East and Midwest. Before the opening of the Erie Canal, much farm furniture in the United States was made by farmers during the winter from rough, precut parts bought at the general store. But by 1843, 4,149 tons of furniture were shipped westward on the Erie Canal, and furniture was usually the value leader among manufactured goods transported on the canal. It is reasonable to assume that much of it was made in New York City and replaced furniture formerly manufactured at home.[38]

By the early 1850s a complex furniture industry had developed. The growth of the city's population made local demand for furniture significant, but in 1853 five-sixths of all production was shipped outside New York. "Much of it was sent out West," according to Ernest Hagen, a German cabinetmaker who worked as an apprentice and journeyman in the 1840s and 1850s in a "slaughter shop," as auction shops were sometimes called, "and a great deal went South to New Orleans and also the West India Islands." Because demand varied from mahogany dining tables, desks, and sideboards selling for hundreds of dollars to cheap cane chairs, the industry was highly stratified. The *Tribune* divided it into three classes in 1853—"first class" consisted of highly skilled cabinetmakers who worked on fashionable pieces and were well paid at $15 weekly; "second class" at $8 weekly; and the "third class," the slaughter shops, used poorly trained workers (called "botches" by more skilled cabinetmakers) at $5 to $6 weekly.[39]

37. Thomas Hamilton Ormsbee, *Early American Furniture Makers* (New York, 1930), 76; *Fourth Census, 1820, Manufactures,* Manuscript, First Ward; Fearon, *Sketches of America,* 24. Charles F. Montgomery gives a list of pricebooks in *American Furniture—The Federal Period* (New York, 1966), 488.

38. Van Boskirk: *Fourth Census, 1820, Manufactures,* Manuscript, Ward One. On the auction shops, see McClelland, *Duncan Phyfe,* 196. *Tribune,* 11 November 1845. On the domestic manufacture of furniture, see Ormsbee, *Early American Furniture Makers,* 110–112. Tons of furniture: *Hunt's Merchants' Magazine* 8 (1843), 526–529; see also Clark, *History of Manufactures,* 1:473.

39. Elizabeth Ingerman, ed., "Personal Experiences of an Old New York Cabinetmaker," *Antiques* 84 (1963), 577; *Herald,* 18 June 1853.

The first-class firms were distinguished from the rest of the industry in part by the bosses' training and knowledge of what was stylish. Charles Baudouine, one of the city's most fashionable cabinetmakers, took yearly trips to his native France in order to remain *au courant*. In addition, higher capital was needed to buy the woods for expensive products and hire first-class workmen. The skill of the workmen was also important because, even with division of labor, poorly trained workers were unable to execute the elaborate decoration of the Victorian Style. At the fashionable Hutchings manufactory, workers averaged about $45 monthly in 1860, compared to a $32 average in the Thirteenth Ward auction shops. Highly skilled cabinetmakers still were numerous in 1845 when the *Tribune* noted that "much of the fashionable work [is] . . . done [as] exquisitely as any where on the globe."[40]

To meet the growing demand for cheap furniture, auction shops specialized in a single item and extensively divided labor. English immigrant Henry Price discovered in 1845 that "my [new] employer call'd himself a Cabinet Maker but he made nothing but Chest of drawers." Richard Tweed (the father of William Marcy Tweed) manufactured cane chairs, at a Ridge Street shop jocularly known as "the old flea patch," which wholesaled at $2.14 apiece in 1860. These cheap, unpowered slaughter shops were often, like the one Price worked in, run by Germans and located in Little Germany—Kleindeutschland—in the Eleventh, Thirteenth, and Seventeenth Wards. The bosses in these shops believed that "men employed at one department of work can do more than when their attention is divided between two or three. Besides," the *Herald* continued, "every cabinet maker is not thoroughly skilled in all the branches of his trade." By using poorly trained, cheap workmen these small shops were able to turn out large quantities of simple, inexpensive furniture. Even cheap furniture underwent occasional style changes, however, and the manufacturing process itself was basically similar in the first-class and auction shops. Division of labor was universal in the cheap shops, but it was also used in fashionable shops. In all shops, Ernest Hagen recalled, "the work was all done by hand . . . the employers . . . having no machinery at all."[41]

There seem to have been few economies of scale in nineteenth-century furniture manufacturing. Because elite demand was international, the most

40. On Baudouine see Ingerman, "Personal Experiences," 577–578. *Eighth Census, 1860, Manufactures*, Manuscript, Wards Eight and Thirteen; *Tribune*, 11 November 1845.

41. Auction shops: *Tribune*, 11 November 1845. "The Diary of Henry Edward Price," in *British Records Relating to America in Microform* (East Ardsley, England, 1963), 34 (this "diary" is actually a reminiscence). See also Ernst, *Immigrant Life*, 80–81, and Thomas Mooney, *Nine Years in America* (Dublin, 1850), 150–151. Leo Herskowitz, *Tweed's New York* (Garden City, N.Y., 1977), 7; *Eighth Census, 1860, Manufactures*, Manuscript, Ward Thirteen. *Herald*, 18 June 1853; see also Ingerman, "Personal Experiences," 577. On the absence of machinery see also Polly Anne Earl, "Craftsmen and Machines: The Nineteenth-Century Furniture Industry," in Ian Quimby and Earl, eds., *Technical Innovation and the Decorative Arts* (Charlottesville, Va., 1974), 309–315.

expensive furniture shops in the city were among the largest. Edward Hutchings's Broome Street manufactory, which manufactured "the best class of furniture," had seventy-five workers in 1860, sales of $70,000 yearly, and a branch in Chicago. Alexander Roux, nearby on Mercer Street, had eighty employees and $200,000 in capital. He turned out "the finest styles of French furniture." Most of the auction shops, on the other hand, were quite small, with an average of fifteen employees in 1860. Capital in these shops was correspondingly small also—in 1860 often less than $1,000.[42]

The transportation revolution opened a market for cheap furniture, but because fashionable demand was so large, the trade was never overwhelmed by low-priced product as it was in clothing. Though shop size grew and a more intensive division of labor was used, skilled cabinetmakers continued to flourish, unthreatened by botches who catered to a different market.

UNSKILLED LABOR

Not all of the city's manual workers were in manufacturing. Two of the city's largest occupations—laboring and domestic servitude—were essentially unskilled, and any attempt to outline the impact of economic changes on New York's workers must deal with them. Generally, both occupations experienced considerably less change than did manufacturing.

In 1855 unskilled laborers were easily the single largest category of male employees with twenty thousand workers—virtually all of them Irish—listed in the census. There is, unfortunately, only limited evidence on which to base their history, and this section is, therefore, more general than the others.[43]

The term "unskilled labor" is a vague one and covered very diverse work. The British Mechanic in 1840 wrote of "a great variety of employ" in "building, quarrying, stone-work, excavation, levelling and laying out of streets, making docks, quays, jetties, piers or slips." Thomas Mooney explained in 1850 that "there is a great deal of labour work to be done in New York," and he noted "Irishmen . . . do almost all the rude and heavy work: they are generally employed in buildings . . . they are found portering on the quays, repairing, cleaning and watching the city; sawing wood," and doing many other types of work. Because of this diversity, it is difficult to determine where the jobs were at any one time. We can, however, detect a strong need for unskilled workers in three areas. The first was on the waterfront. As the

42. Hutchings: New York vol. 190, 398, 400, R. G. Dun and Company Collection, Baker Library, Harvard Graduate School of Business Administration, and *Eighth Census, 1860, Manufactures,* Manuscript, Ward Eight. Auction shops: ibid., Ward Thirteen. Roux: New York vol. 190, 397, R. G. Dun and Company Collection.

43. Ernst, *Immigrant Life,* 217, notes that the figure of 20,238 in the census is "obviously too small."

nation's largest port and one where trade was growing faster than population, New York, in the absence of technological developments in loading cargo, required a large and growing number of longshoremen. The second was in construction. The enormous growth of the city kept building at a high level and demanded thousands of hod carriers and other unskilled building laborers. The third resulted from the increasing division of labor. The work of crafts- men concentrated on the most highly skilled part of the manufacturing process and left less skilled work to lower-paid employees.[44]

There was little division of labor in the shipyards of the 1820s and 1830s, for example, heavy timbers were carried on the shoulders of skilled workers before the general "breaking up of the labor in the yards" in the late 1830s. Then laborers began to be hired to do the lugging. The machinist Stephen Tucker remembered that when he went to work for Hoe and Company in the early 1830s, "laborers were scarce in the factory and apprentices took their places." Though it is difficult from the evidence to gauge the timing and extent of the process, the extension of the market and increased division of labor caused manufacturing firms to hire more laborers in the 1830s. On the first two areas of unskilled work—the docks and the building industry—more information is available. Even in these cases, however, there is little evidence before the 1850s.[45]

"The shipowners in New York, and the other great cities, are continually employing job-porters and discharging them," wrote Mooney. The numbers of longshoremen were very substantial in the 1850s—5,000 to 6,000 might be working on any given day. Typically the shipowner would subcontract with a stevedore who would hire the laborers. The stevedore would supervise the loading or unloading of the ship, and once the goods were on the dock, other laborers, under a stevedore hired by the merchant who owned the goods, would load them on wagons to take them to the warehouses. The hiring seems to have been done mostly by the "shape up," though a few large mercantile houses such as Grinell and Minturn did employ a permanent crew of laborers. The longshoremen had to remit one shilling (eight cents) of their twelve shilling (one dollar) daily pay to the stevedore to get work, a practice laborers furiously resented.[46]

Although horse-powered winches had replaced manual winches by the

---

44. *British Mechanic's and Labourer's Hand Book*, 275; Mooney, *Nine Years in America*, 84.

45. Morrison, *History of the New York Ship Yards*, 94; Tucker, "History of R. Hoe," 2. Few of the city's leather tanners in the 1820s had unskilled employees, and "there were . . . only two stores that employed porters or laborers. It was usual for the clerks to do the menial work"; Frank W. Norcross, *A History of the New York Swamp* (New York, 1901), 109.

46. Mooney, *Nine Years in America*, 86; *Tribune*, 5 October 1852; Charles H. Farnham, "A Day on the Docks," *Scribner's Monthly* 18 (1879), 40. In 1852 the longshoremen struck over the remittance; see the *Tribune*, 13, 14, 15 October 1852.

1850s, loading and unloading in 1852 was work "of the most ardous kind," according to the *Tribune*. "Employment is irregular, two or three days frequently occurring when the stevedore will have nothing to do." Most work in the city was seasonal, but dockwork was by its nature extremely variable; there was a seasonal winter decline, and even in summer a fog or calm could prevent ships from docking. Some longshoremen were even paid by the hour rather than the day or half-day, so they could be discharged immediately when a job was finished. Not knowing whether a job would last "three hours or three days" was the most serious objection to dockwork.[47]

Most construction laborers in the 1820s were hired directly by the builder, but as early as 1840, with the growth of "lump-work" or subcontracting, many laborers were hired by gang bosses employed by the builder. Almost all the "rude and heavy work . . . in buildings," according to Mooney, was done by Irish laborers. Among longshoremen the "shape up" was usually the rule, but the building laborers' relationship with their employer was more personalized and regular. The work, however, was equally rigorous. According to the British Mechanic, "where labourers' work gets into the hands of the contracting employer, who constantly superintends the operations in order to enforce the speed . . . it is absolutely painful to witness their exertions." It was also extremely variable, with work usually impossible in the winter. In other seasons rain or excessive heat could slow work to a halt.[48]

The daily wages at both dockwork and construction labor were relatively high. "The wages of the mere labourer approach nearer to those of the finished artist than they do with you [in Scotland]," John Prentice wrote in 1834. The traditional dollar and sometimes $1.25 a day, which prevailed throughout much of the antebellum period, were wages comparable to those of lower-paid skilled workers. But employment and wages were highly variable. It was the prospect of being so frequently out of work, and the sharp variations in wages even when employed, that made laboring so distasteful to workers. Laboring was regarded not as a profession so much as a temporary expedient while the laborer tried to find a better job. Even workers who found laboring their only possible employment might eventually be forced to quit as increasing age deprived them of the strength and endurance the work demanded. Savings were the most obvious way out of unskilled labor and, in the 1840s, 40–50 percent of the city's new savings bank depositors were laborers, a very

47. Winches: *Reports of the New York Harbor Commission of 1856 and 1857* (New York, 1864), 118, 224–308. *Tribune*, 15 October 1852; see also Cliff Barnes, *The Longshoremen* (New York, 1915), 57–58. On winter decline see "Trade and Commerce of New York," *Hunt's Merchants' Magazine* 32 (1855), 275–304; see also Albion, *Rise of New York Port*, 31–33.

48. Contractor's journal, 1815–1820, Rare Books and Manuscripts Division, The New York Public Library, Astor, Lenox and Tilden Foundations; Fearon, *Sketches of America*, 22–23; *British Mechanic's and Labourer's Hand Book*, 278–282. Mooney, *Nine Years in America*, 84. *British Mechanic's and Labourer's Hand Book*, 279.

high figure that probably also reflects an attempt to counteract seasonal unemployment. ''By common thrift, they [Irish laborers] save a few dollars, . . . and, generally speaking, [go into] a way of business which is customary to them all.'' Construction laborers often saved to buy a horse and cart, and many longshoremen hoped to buy a saloon, according to the British Mechanic. Despite this universal desire to leave laboring, the reality was often different—in 1855 almost one-third of Sixth Ward laborers were over age forty.[49]

This analysis gives us little sense of change in laboring. Does it reflect true continuity or a lack of evidence? Surely in building the change from post-and-lintel construction to the balloon frame, and then to cast-iron architecture, must have affected unskilled construction labor. For longshoremen, on the other hand, the changeless impression may be more realistic. Iron-hulled ships made dockwork less seasonal, but laboring on the waterfront remained almost totally horse- and man-powered. We can find reasons why the number of unskilled workers was probably growing (though statistical evidence is lacking), but it is harder to generalize about the work itself.

## DOMESTIC SERVITUDE

There were 32,000 servants in the city in 1855, the vast majority of them women. Most were Irish because, as William Bobo, a Southerner who wrote an account of his 1852 visit to the city, pointed out, ''nothing but compulsion would ever induce a native-born American to assume the character of a servant.'' Even in the 1820s, when Irish immigration was low, an 1826 survey found 60 percent of the city's servants were Irish, a figure that rose to between 70 and 80 percent in the 1840s and 1850s. As the urban middle class and the number of boarding houses in New York grew, so did the demand for servants. Domestic servitude remained the largest single occupation in the city throughout the period.[50]

49. John Prentice, ''Letter to the Working Classes of the City of Edinburgh,'' *The Scotsman,* 16 April 1834. On the good health laborers needed see J. H. Baxter, ed., *Medical Statistics of the Provost Marshall's Bureau* (Washington, 1875), 85. Age: Barnes, *Longshoremen,* 24; see also Eugene P. Moehring, *Public Works and Patterns of Urban Real Estate Growth in Manhattan, 1835–1894* (New York, 1981), 274. Alan Olmstead, *New York City Mutual Savings Banks* (Chapel Hill, N.C., 1976), 50–52; *British Mechanic's and Labourer's Hand Book,* 267. The relationship between bartending and aging laborers is noted in Clyde Griffen and Sally Griffen, *Natives and Newcomers: The Ordering of Opportunity in Mid-Nineteenth Century Poughkeepsie* (Cambridge, Mass., 1978), 113. Sixth Ward: computed from figures in Pernicone, '' 'Bloody Ould Sixth,' '' 102.

50. William Bobo, *Glimpses of New-York City* (New York, 1852), 187; *Society for the Encouragement of Faithful Domestic Servants, First Annual Report* (New York, 1826), 13; *Tribune,* 6 November 1845; Table 11.

The great majority of servants lived with the family they worked for, causing a surplus of young women in the city's wealthiest wards. Households with more than one servant divided labor among cook, waiter, and chambermaid, but in most households one servant did all the work. It was semiskilled labor, and some knowledge and training was necessary; Irish peasant girls often found some of the tasks quite difficult. James Bogert, for example, a wealthy New Yorker who employed numerous servants, was constantly vexed by "very ignorant" servants who were "unacquainted with cooking."[51]

Although domestic service remained semiskilled between 1820 and 1860, it was not unchanging. The introduction to middle-class homes of indoor plumbing, gas, and stoves was beginning to make the job less physically strenuous. As Charles Haswell, a civil engineer who grew up in the city, explained in his reminiscences, in the 1820s and 1830s "all water required for the kitchen, or bedrooms, or for baths, was drawn from the nearest street-pump, and all refuse water and slops were carried out to the street and emptied into the gutter." The hours remained long, however, and whatever time was saved by the introduction of various urban amenities was probably taken up with increased washing, scrubbing, and sweeping as standards of cleanliness rose among middle-class women.[52]

Generally the servants were supervised by the lady of the house and were at her beck and call. "Help" was, in fact, quite different from other occupations in that the peculiarly personalized relationship between employer and employee could never be simply economic. "They are of the family, yet apart from it," the *Tribune* noted in 1845. Because the association was so personalized, ruptures could occur over issues unrelated to work, which perhaps helps explain why turnover among servants was extremely rapid. In the 1820s the Society for the Encouragement of Faithful Domestic Servants gave bonuses for a two-year tenure, which was considered exceptionally long. In addition, geographic concentration in the wealthy wards of the city and long hours isolated servants from other workers. Servants were not at home in the middle-class households where they worked, nor were they able to participate in working-class neighborhood life.[53]

Domestics were probably better off than most working women. Wages were always very low—Bogert paid his female servants $6 or $7 monthly in

51. Christine Stansell describes the city's servants in some detail in *City of Women: Sex and Class in New York, 1789–1860* (New York, 1986), chap. 8. On ignorant servants see the James Bogert servant account book, 1823–1857, Museum of the City of New York, and "The New York Labor Market—Female House Servants," *Harper's Weekly* 1 (1857), 418–419.

52. Charles Haswell, *Reminiscences of an Octogenarian* (New York, 1896), 69. See Chapter 6 for evidence on the growth of "modern conveniences." On cleanliness see Stansell, *City of Women*, 159–160.

53. *Tribune*, 6 November 1845; see also David Katzman, *Seven Days a Week* (Urbana, Ill., 1981), 146–183.

the 1830s and $7 in the 1840s, and these seem to have been near the prevailing rates. The large influx of immigrants kept wage rates steady in the 1850s. Housing and board were free, however, and although the servants' quarters were usually shabby and small, this was a substantial asset. The assurance of food and a place to stay allowed servants greater freedom of employment than other workers, since they had a place to live while looking for a new position before they decided to "give notice."[54]

Another important female occupation, prostitution, was always linked with servitude in the public imagination and, it seems, in reality as well. William Sanger, in his 1859 report to the city's almshouse, determined that almost half—933 out of 2,000—of the prostitutes he interviewed had formerly been servants, in a city where 15 percent of all women were servants. With New York's large population of single men, prostitution flourished. Estimates of the numbers of prostitutes in the city vary widely; Sanger's figure of six thousand seems the most reliable. Generally prostitution was not a full-time profession but a way for women to supplement their income. It was, as Christine Stansell has noted, intermittent and casual: 63 percent of the prostitutes in Sanger's study made $2 or less weekly.[55]

Most servants, of course, did not become prostitutes. Many worked for a few years, then married and quit. Like male unskilled workers, and like female workers generally, few servants wanted to make a career out of their occupation. But like laborers, many were forced to. Older servants were, however, comparatively rarer than laborers: the average servant's age in the Sixth Ward in 1855 was 28.5. Although becoming less physically arduous, domestic service remained between 1820 and 1860 an occupation characterized by long hours and limited autonomy.[56]

INDUSTRIAL GROWTH AND THE WORKING CLASS

Although manufacturing in New York had gone beyond the artisanal stage by 1820, small shops still dominated city manufacturing. Historians of industrialization often rely on a "shop breakdown" model, in which large factories, using new technology and semiskilled workers, undermine the shop's central role in production. In New York City, however, there was a diversity of responses to the opportunities offered by growing demand. Most manufactur-

54. James Bogert servant account book, and *Society for the Encouragement of Faithful Domestic Servants, Third Annual Report* (New York, 1828), 23, both mention $6 as the prevailing wage, the same figure Penny, *How Women Can Earn Money*, 426, lists for "good" servants thirty years later. *Tribune,* 6 November 1845.

55. Stansell gives an excellent account of the city's prostitutes in *City of Women*, chap. 9. William W. Sanger, *The History of Prostitution* (New York, 1859), 524, 575, 529.

56. Estimated from Pernicone, " 'Bloody Ould Sixth,' " 155.

ing was small, unpowered, and unspecialized in the 1820s, and industrialization did not necessarily change these three factors.

Between 1820 and 1850 the average shop size in New York grew from 16 to 25 workers. After 1850, however, shop size stagnated and then declined as the city realigned spatially and manufacturers used more subcontracting; by 1890 the average shop size was 14 (Table 5). Likewise the use of steam power was not inevitable—factories developed in metalwork and in printing, but in 1860 some 75 percent of the city's employees worked in an unpowered setting. Nor did the city's manufacturers become more specialized. Though subcontractors and specialty suppliers were among Manhattan's advantages, other city manufacturers broadened their output into new lines. R. Hoe and Company had made only printing presses before the late 1830s, but "as the new shop was large anything was taken in that was offered and seemed reasonably profitable." Indeed, only increased division of labor was universal; labor was more extensively divided in 1860 than in 1820 in virtually every trade.[57]

The overall pattern was, therefore, very complex. Geographical segmentation provides a helpful guide; in New Jersey, something closer to the classic pattern of industrialization was taking place, but even there small shops flourished. Manhattan's peculiar conditions favored the shop, but the different characteristics of trades made each industry's response unique. This diversity was not "uneven development," which suggests different industries moving at different rates toward complete mechanization. In antebellum New York, rather, the differences *within* trades were as large as the differences *between* trades. Moreover, firms meeting seasonal or fashionable demand, or engaged in repair or custom work, *never* evolve into large factories. Clearly the decline in seasonal production that accompanied the development of the nation's railway network allowed more constant and mechanized production, but there could never be a River Rouge or Sparrows Point in the garment industry. Manhattan's small shops of the 1850s were not atavisms; they were created by regional industrialization.[58]

As small shops dominated in both 1820 and 1860, it might seem there was substantial continuity in Manhattan's industrial structure. Such continuity is illusory. The small shops of 1820 were the focus of production, those of 1860 were not. In industries with relatively constant demand, industrialization was quite rapid, and factories in New Jersey and elsewhere in the East came to meet the consistent portions of demand, leaving the city with the variable work. Increasingly the city's shops, like the job printers, found themselves at "the fringes of the trade." The city's shops were left with what Edward Pratt

57. Tucker, "History of R. Hoe," 13.
58. For "uneven development" applied to the metropolitan region see Susan Hirsch, *The Roots of the American Working Class: The Industrialization of Crafts in Newark, 1800–1860* (Philadelphia, 1978), 21–36.

calls the "repair work and the various odds and ends of work in a great city."[59]

How did these industrial changes affect the city's workers? Clearly the diversity of industrialization is significant. The different responses of industries to opportunities to increase output made the various trades quite diverse. The core–industrial belt division was significant—"along with dualism in the industrial structure," economists Michael Reich, David Gordon, and Richard Edwards have noted, "there developed a corresponding dualism of working conditions, skill and social mobility." A New Jersey worker might face relatively steady work as a machine tender in a factory, with only a modest chance to raise enough capital to become a factory owner; a Manhattan worker more often found seasonal employment in an unpowered workshop, with the possibility of becoming a subcontractor.[60]

It seems probable that the city workforce was as a whole less skilled in 1860 than it had been in 1820. Industrialization did create new skilled trades. There were, for example, two hundred plumbers in New York in 1850. Twelve years earlier, the *Tribune* noted, "there were not a dozen plumbers . . . ; the introduction of Croton water has caused the increase." Many of these thriving skilled trades reflected the growing market for "modern conveniences," as trades such as stovebuilding and gasfitting emerged in the 1830s and 1840s.[61]

The trend was not, however, toward unskilled labor (though that did increase) but toward semiskilled work. Even "semiskilled" is misleading, since most workers continued to have a craft, albeit one demanding a less thoroughgoing knowledge of the trade. Even the botches in furniture, "merc" typesetters in printing, and outside tailors had skills. The artisan declined as the shop lost its centrality, but Manhattan's role as the region's center for seasonable and fashionable demand ensured the persistence of manual dexterity. However, a term such as "cabinetmaker" or "tailor" meant something less in 1860 than it had in 1820.

From the point of view of the city's industrial development, the overall level of skill had probably diminished. From the point of view of the city's workers, however, the significance of these changes was bounded by the tremendous growth of the city's industry and population. The workforce *as a whole* was somewhat less skilled in 1860 than in 1820, but it was approximately 6.5 times larger. There were wide variations between the skills of the best-paid and worst-paid employees in most trades, and the number of highly skilled jobs was, therefore, almost certainly much greater in 1860. There were

59. Edward Ewing Pratt, *Industrial Causes of Congestion of Population in New York City* (1911; rpt. New York, 1968), 52.
60. Michael Reich, David M. Gordon, and Richard C. Edwards, "A Theory of Labor Market Segmentation," *American Economic Review* 63, Supplement (1973), 363. Chapter 5 below deals with working conditions in detail.
61. *Tribune*, 15 May 1850.

about 200 cabinetmakers in the city in 1805–6, for example, almost all of whom were highly skilled. In 1853 there were 4,000, of whom about 800 were highly skilled. Similarly, the 1,110 cutters and trimmers in 1858, combined with the remaining custom tailors, far exceeded the number of skilled tailors in the city in 1820. Even repairing required a high degree of skill, and some who used their skills fixing and refurbishing found it quite remunerative; in the city's shipyards, for instance, repair work paid $1.50 more per week than did the actual building. From this perspective, manufacturing and repair work far outstripped population growth, and in most trades more new jobs, even well-paying skilled jobs, were created than were eliminated. Because of the growth of the market for cheap goods, the victim of the expansion of semiskilled work was not the highly trained urban craftsman but the rural artisan and the farm wife—it was their work New Yorkers were taking.[62]

It is unlikely that workers saw their chance for proprietorship diminish; it probably increased. In 1820 capital requirements were too high to allow journeymen to routinely gain master status. Manhattan's emergence in the 1840s as a center of shop production and subcontracting made entry costs in some trades relatively low. John Burke, an Irish immigrant shoemaker, described how, when he was refused a wage increase in 1852, "I left and went to start on my own." Although, as one analyst of the city's twentieth-century seasonal industries has noted, "exit is just as easy as entry," the large number of small shops gave employees in some trades a realistic hope of becoming a boss. Jean Gottmann has described the city as "an incubator" for the region's industry; small firms could get started there and then move to New Jersey if they proved profitable.[63]

In addition, the influx of young immigrants aged twenty to thirty, described in the next chapter, made it necessary to hire supervisers to oversee an inexperienced workforce. Skilled workers who remained in the city long enough to move into an older age cohort might often find jobs as foremen. With the expansion of the city's economy, therefore, the number of skilled workers who saw their opportunities narrowed by industrialization was probably small.

But what of the tens of thousands of semiskilled employees—the helpers in foundries, the mere typesetters, the botches in the furniture industry—the

62. Cabinetmakers estimated from Rock, *Artisans of the New Republic*, 12–13, and the *Herald*, 18 June 1853. Shipyards: *Annual Report of the A.I.C.P. for the Year 1866*, 25. In shoemaking "the menders . . . make, on average, more than the man who works for a shop"; *Tribune*, 27 May 1853.

63. "John Burke Reminiscences," 1891 manuscript, NYHS. Burke eventually created a good custom shoe firm: see New York vol. 189, 281, R. G. Dun and Company Collection, Baker Library, Harvard Graduate School of Business Administration. "Exit": Raymond Vernon, *Metropolis 1985: An Interpretation of the Findings of the New York Metropolitan Region Study* (Cambridge, Mass., 1960), 73. Jean Gottmann, *Megalopolis: The Urbanized Northeastern Seaboard of the United States* (New York, 1961), 494.

division of labor in the city demanded? These were not deskilled artisans but immigrants. To immigrants, the substantial increase in industrial employment was far more salient than any long-term decline in skill caused by divided labor. Division of labor may have actually expanded the probability of remunerative work by dovetailing the immigrant's modest skills with the requirements of the city's occupational structure. Henry Price, for example, lacked the training to be a skilled cabinetmaker but found in New York City he was able to work for a boss who made "nothing but Chest of drawers."[64]

Trade union leaders in the 1850s who spoke of a decline in the status of "the working class" were correct, but the decline in skill for the working class *as a whole* does not translate into a decline for individual workers. In many trades the typical artisan was more skilled and independent than his industrial descendant, but that artisan, if he remained in the city, often became part of the highly skilled minority that continued to exist in many trades. The majority of industrial workers entering the city's workforce were semiskilled immigrants.

64. Price diary, 34.

CHAPTER 3

# The People

Who were the people who made up the growing industrial workforce of New York, and where did they come from? By the 1850s the overwhelming majority of workers in the city were immigrants, and so the way most workers evaluated their experience in the city's workshops and neighborhoods was strongly influenced by their European background. At the same time the influx of immigrants created a very youthful population, itself influencing working-class life in the city. This chapter briefly looks at the population of New York in 1820 and then examines its growth and the background and motives of the immigrants.

THE CITY'S POPULATION IN 1820

Evidence on the city's population in 1820 is comparatively meager. The census did not register place of birth, and ages were broken down only into five categories. It asked about "foreigners not naturalized"—that is, aliens—which, of course, measures only a fraction of the foreign-born population. Howard Rock concludes from a sample of mechanics from the 1819 jury lists that less than 10 percent of the city's artisans were immigrants—in other words, more than 90 percent were native-born Americans. Since his sample excludes laborers, however, it almost certainly understates the immigrant presence in the workforce as a whole. It is possible to make a rough estimate of total foreign-born in the city from the alien total in the census, by adding unnaturalized women—who, since they could not vote, do not seem to have been counted as aliens—to total aliens in the census and then adding the naturalized population. The resulting estimate of total foreign-born is very rough: 10–25 percent of the city's population was born overseas in the period 1820–1830. For comparative purposes even such a rough estimate is useful; even if the foreign-born percentage was as high as 25 percent, it was much smaller than in the 1850s.[1]

On age structure in the city's population we are on firmer ground, though the small number of age categories in the printed census makes comparisons with later decades somewhat difficult. It is clear there were a very large number of children in the city—42 percent of the 1820 population was under age ten, only 12 percent over age forty-five. Carol Pernicone's sample of 1819 jury lists for the Sixth Ward also suggests that the working population was youthful—34 percent of workers were under thirty years of age.[2]

New York City would add almost seven hundred thousand residents to its population in the forty years after 1820. This growth could have been because of natural increase (an excess of births over deaths) or migration (an excess of in-migrants over out-migrants) or a combination of both.

1. Howard Rock, *Artisans of the New Republic: The Tradesmen of New York City in the Age of Jefferson* (New York, 1979), 243. The 1855 state census notes how erratic the alien percentage had been in the city: see the *Census of the State of New York, 1855* (Albany, 1857), xliii. Some of this variation probably stems from inconsistency in counting women. Aliens in the 1810, 1820, and 1830 censuses are between 5 and 10 percent of the totals. If we add women, aliens are 10–20 percent of the population. Later censuses list both alien status and place of birth, and the percentage of immigrants is usually about 5 percent higher than aliens. Adding this 5 percent to the earlier estimate yields the 5 to 25 percent estimate of total foreign-born. See also Carol Pernicone, "The 'Bloody Ould Sixth': A Social Analysis of a New York City Working Class Community in the Mid-Nineteenth Century" (diss., University of Rochester, 1973), 24, 35, and Ira Rosenwaike, *Population History of New York City* (Syracuse, N.Y., 1972), 39. *Migrants* here refers to all those, native and foreign, who moved to the city from elsewhere. *Immigrants* refers to those who came from Europe. Figures refer to *whites* only; the age breakdown for blacks in the census is less detailed.

2. Census Office, *Fourth Census, 1820* (Washington, 1821); Pernicone, " 'Bloody Ould Sixth,' " 28. New York in this period had a relatively high birthrate for a city: the child/woman ratio, 1830–1860, compiled from the population censuses, is given below (children under five to women 15–40, free whites only).

|      | Children | Women   | Children per thousand women |
|------|----------|---------|------------------------------|
| 1830 | 23,535   | 41,155  | 571                          |
| 1840 | 45,959   | 79,586  | 577                          |
| 1850 | 64,824   | 133,657 | 485                          |
| 1860 | 117,418  | 205,390 | 572                          |

*Sources:* Census Office, *Fifth, Sixth, Seventh, and Eighth Censuses of the United States, 1830, 1840, 1850, 1860, Population.*

MIGRATION

To determine how much of the city's population growth after 1820 was due to natural increase and how much to migration, it is crucial to know the number of births. The city's birthrate is difficult to discover, however, because no accurate statistics were compiled.[3]

Diane Lindstrom has estimated the role of natural increase of the city's population growth by comparing age cohorts in the censuses. Table 8 shows that after 1820, the vast majority of the city's population were migrants. My own estimate for the 1850s confirms a number in the range of 80 percent for that decade. The great bulk of the city's population growth came, therefore, from migration to New York City. The population history of antebellum New York is the history of migration to the city.[4]

Before 1820 native-born migrants to New York predominated, but even before the massive upsurge in immigration from overseas in the mid-1840s, large numbers of Europeans found their way to the city. After 1820 New York became the port of entry of a growing percentage of immigrants to the United

3. In 1854 a regulation required that city physicians and midwives record births. The law, however, was not strictly enforced, the city inspector reporting in 1856 that "not more than one-third" of the births were recorded; *Annual Report of the City Inspector for the Year 1856* (New York, 1857), 157. The census also lists births but clearly understates true totals. For what it is worth, the censuses give the city's annual birthrate per thousand as follows: 1825—27.3, 1835—33.1, 1845—35.6, 1850—28.2, 1855—35.1, 1860—30.4. Compiled from James Hardie, *Description of the City of New York* (New York, 1827), 154, and the *Census of the State of New York, 1865* (Albany, 1867), lxiii. On the inaccuracy of such figures see Hardie, 157.

4. If the city had 10,000 10–20-year-olds in 1820, for example, Lindstrom subtracted estimated deaths and compared the figure with the 20–30-year-old group in 1830; Diane Lindstrom, "Economic Structure, Demographic Change and Income Inequality: Antebellum New York," in *New York City: Essays in Time, Culture, and Space* (New York, forthcoming). The procedure I used, which is possible only for the 1850s, was to take the population listed as under age one in the federal census and add it to the deaths under age one listed in the city's mortality statistics. By this technique, I calculate 18,903 births in 1850 and 31,631 births in 1860. The crude city birthrate for those years, per thousand inhabitants, was 36.7 in 1850 and 39.2 in 1860; these are high figures, due probably to the selective migration of young women to the city. Because New York, like all major ports, was frequently visited by infectious disease, the deathrate, unlike the birthrate, was carefully recorded and analyzed by city authorities. If the 1850 and 1860 estimates of the number of births are averaged and multiplied by ten (for the number of years in the decade) we get 252,670 births in the city in the decade. Deaths numbered 212,046, so the estimated natural increase in the city's population was 40,624. Since the population of New York increased 298,115 between 1850 and 1860, estimated natural increase accounts for only 14 percent of the growth while an in-migration of 257,491 accounts for 86 percent, slightly higher than Lindstrom's estimate. Census Office, *Seventh Census, 1850, Statistics* (Washington, 1853); Census Office, *Eighth Census, 1860, Population* (Washington, 1864). Deaths for children under one year are taken from the *Annual Report of the City Inspector* for the years 1849, 1850, 1859, and 1860. To compensate for the different census "year" (the census was taken in the summer), the year of the census and the preceding year were averaged. On immigrant mortality see John Duffy, *A History of Public Health in New York City, 1825–1866* (New York, 1968), 537, 578, 580–581; Edward Spann, *The New Metropolis: New York City, 1840–1857* (New York, 1981), 462.

TABLE 8

Percentage of the population increase of New York County attributable to net migration, 1810–1860

|  | *1810–20* | *1820–30* | *1830–40* | *1840–50* | *1850–60* |
|---|---|---|---|---|---|
| Male | 28.9% | 72.0% | 72.5% | 84.9% | 78.7% |
| Female | 22.3 | 62.9 | 66.4 | 75.9 | 73.4 |
| Average | 25.2 | 67.2 | 69.3 | 80.6 | 75.8 |

*Source:* Diane Lindstrom, "Economic Structure, Demographic Change and Income Inequality: Antebellum New York," in *New York City: Essays in Time, Culture, and Space* (New York, forthcoming). I thank Professor Lindstrom for permission to reproduce this table.

States, not because immigrants were especially eager to come to New York City but because immigration before the 1850s followed ocean trade routes. The immigrants made their way to the great commercial ports of Europe— Bremen, Hamburg, Le Havre, London, and Liverpool—and sailed aboard commercial vessels to the New World. As the greatest American port, New York received the bulk of those coming to America. Indeed, the increasing numbers of immigrants landing in the city provide further evidence of New York's rise to the pinnacle of the nation's urban hierarchy. In the years of greatest immigration in the 1840s and 1850s, more than two-thirds of all immigrants to the United States landed in New York (see Appendix C). As early as the mid-1820s Irish immigrants came to predominate, and the Irish continued to be the largest single national group among immigrants until the early 1850s, when Germans achieved a plurality. The famine of the 1840s brought immigration to record levels, and numbers stayed high until the 1854 recession. In the late 1840s and early 1850s, between 200,000 and 400,000 immigrants landed in New York City every year.[5]

Letters and guidebooks often warned immigrants against staying in New York, where they would face dishonest boardinghouse keepers and a glutted labor market. The evidence indicates that the vast majority of immigrants— many of whom wanted to farm and had no interest in staying in the city anyway—took the advice of the writers. In 1860 the city inspector estimated that only 14 percent of all immigrants landing in the city planned to remain there.[6]

5. Marcus Hansen, *The Atlantic Migration, 1607–1860* (1940; rpt. New York, 1961), 178– 193; Philip Taylor, *The Distant Magnet: European Emigration to the U.S.A.* (New York, 1971), 92, 127–128. There are no complete figures on immigration. Some evidence suggests that the totals in Appendix C are too low, though by how much is not certain; see Charlotte Erickson, "Emigration from the British Isles to the U.S.A. in 1831," *Population Studies* 35 (1981), 180– 181.

6. Thomas Mooney's emigrant guidebook *Nine Years in America* (Dublin, 1850), 79–94, gives the standard argument for leaving New York. *Annual Report of the City Inspector for the Year 1860* (New York, 1861), 30; for a similar estimate see Richard J. Purcell, "The Irish

Although the percentage remaining was small, so many immigrants landed in the city that the foreign-born population overwhelmed the native. In 1845, 36 percent of the city's residents were foreign-born; in 1850, 46 percent; and in 1855, 51 percent. Irish and German immigrants alone made up 43 percent of New York's inhabitants in 1855, as shown in Table 9, and only 11 percent of the city's population were native in-migrants (compared to 75 percent in Rock's 1819 jury list sample). Some of the 37 percent of New York's population born in the city were lifelong adult residents, but as 147,884 city residents were under age ten, it is clear that most of the "city-born" were children. If the native-born were disproportionately young, those born outside the United States were disproportionately adult. Immigrants were thus found in even greater numbers in the labor force than in the population as a whole. Robert Ernst has calculated than in 1855, 75 percent of the workforce in the city was foreign-born. My own calculations from Ernst's statistics put the proportion of immigrants in the manual workforce even higher, at 84 percent (see Table 11). The story of the city's working class in the 1840s and 1850s is, therefore, the story of immigrants. In the words of Carl Degler, in New York City "labor and the immigrant were often indistinguishable."[7]

## IMMIGRATION: BACKGROUND AND MOTIVES

Immigration is crucial to any understanding of the city's working class. Although immigration was a complex process, we can make five general points about immigrants to the New World in the antebellum period.

First, the immigrants were usually *young adults* (see Table 10). In 1850, 29 percent of the nation's population was aged fifteen to thirty, but 50 percent of those who landed in America that year were between these ages. In every year between 1820 and 1860 the 25-to-30 age group among landing immigrants exceeded in number those over age thirty-five. And those immigrants who stayed in New York were, according to Walter Kamphoefner, even more likely to be "young, single and mobile" than the general population of

Immigrant Society of New York," *Studies: An Irish Quarterly Review* 27 (1938), 593. For figures comparing immigration and population growth see Kate Claghorn, "The Foreign Immigrant in New York City," *Reports of the Industrial Commission*, 25 (Washington, 1901), 464.

7. Rock, *Artisans of the New Republic*, 243. *Census of the State of New York, 1855* (Albany, 1857). The figure on the workforce is compiled from Robert Ernst, *Immigrant Life in New York City, 1825–1863* (1949; rpt. New York, 1979), 214–217. David Ward's sample from the 1860 manuscript census estimates 85 percent of manual workers were foreign-born; Ward, "The Internal Spatial Differentiation of Immigrant Residential Districts," *Special Publication* no. 3, Dept. of Geography, Northwestern University (Evanston, Ill., 1970), 32. Ward's figures come from a 20 percent sample of household heads. Carl Degler, "Labor in the Economy and Politics of New York City, 1850–1860: A Study of the Impact of Early Industrialism" (diss., Columbia University, 1952), 132.

TABLE 9
Origin of New York City's population, 1855

| In-migrants from | No. | % of migrants | % of the population |
|---|---|---|---|
| New York State | 30,001 | 7.6 | 4.8 |
| New Jersey | 12,259 | 3.1 | 1.9 |
| Connecticut | 7,239 | 1.8 | 1.1 |
| Massachusetts | 6,205 | 1.6 | 1.0 |
| All native | 71,566 | 18.2 | 11.4 |
| Ireland | 175,735 | 44.5 | 27.9 |
| Germany | 95,968 | 24.3 | 15.1 |
| England | 22,713 | 5.7 | 3.6 |
| Scotland | 8,474 | 2.1 | 1.3 |
| France | 6,321 | 1.6 | 1.0 |
| All foreign | 322,129 | 81.8 | 51.2 |
| Total | 394,129 | | 62.6 |
| Born in New York City | 232,155 | | 36.8 |
| Unknown | 3,620 | | .6 |
| TOTAL | 629,904 | | 100.0 |

*Source: Census of the State of New York, 1855 (Albany, 1857).*

TABLE 10
Sex and age of all immigrants, 1820–1860

| Age | No. | % | Males | % Male |
|---|---|---|---|---|
| Under 5 | 419,093 | 7.9 | 218,417 | 52.1 |
| 5–10 | 380,310 | 7.2 | 199,704 | 52.5 |
| 10–15 | 361,413 | 6.9 | 194,508 | 53.8 |
| 15–20 | 754,093 | 14.3 | 404,338 | 53.6 |
| 20–25 | 1,098,827 | 20.8 | 669,853 | 60.9 |
| 25–30 | 846,376 | 16.1 | 576,822 | 68.1 |
| 30–35 | 516,397 | 9.8 | 352,619 | 68.3 |
| 35–40 | 353,633 | 6.7 | 239,468 | 67.7 |
| 40+ | 542,334 | 10.3 | 342,022 | 63.1 |
| TOTAL | 5,272,484 | | 3,197,823 | 60.6 |

*Source: Friedrich Kapp, Immigration and the Commissioners of Emigration (1870; rpt. New York, 1969), 228.*

arriving immigrants. It seems clear that the unmarried were disproportionately represented: the fertility ratio (children under five per thousand women aged 15–40) for immigrants was only 277 in 1850, far below the national figure of 612 for that year.[8]

8. Bureau of the Census, *Historical Statistics of the United States, Colonial Times to 1970* (Washington, 1975), 15; William Bromwell, *History of Immigration to the United States* (New York, 1856). Walter Kamphoefner found that Westfalian immigrants who stayed in New York

"Young America" was literally true in New York, as Figure 9 shows. In 1820, 47 percent of the city's population was aged sixteen to forty-five; by 1850 an estimated 57 percent was in that age group. The laboring population was younger still: an astonishing 45 percent of a sample of Sixth Ward Irish workers were under age thirty, in Kleindeutschland 48 percent of the adult population was younger than thirty. As the Anonymous Cabinetmaker remarked of New York City life: "Another peculiarity observable by a stranger is the youthfulness of the population. The appearance of the busy throngs that pass up and down the streets would lead one to deduct a third from the chance of life as compared with Britain. Young men from twenty to twenty-five are there seen in positions which in older countries are filled by men of twice that age."[9]

Second, most immigrants were *male*. Among migrants over age 25, two-thirds were men (see Table 10). A marked change occurred between 1820 and 1860: men were always in the majority, but the percentage of female immigrants steadily increased. In the 1821–1825 period, only 23 percent of all immigrants were women. The number of women grew until by the 1855–1860 period 43 percent of immigrants were female. The growing demand for servants in American cities, as the next chapter explains, is the most plausible explanation for this increase in female immigration.[10]

The third generalization is that immigrants, though poor by American standards, were from the middling ranks of the peasantry. Even with remittances sent by relatives in America, the very poor were unable to afford the journey, whereas those who were well-off had little incentive to leave. One

---

and Philadelphia were five years younger, on average, than those who went to the Midwest; Kamphoefner, *The Westfalians: From Germany to Missouri* (Princeton, N.J., 1987), 84. Figures compiled by New York State do not list married status, so more general figures on this subject are not available. Cormac Ó Gráda's evidence, from a sample of ships' passenger lists, that 48 percent of Irish immigrants traveled alone in the period 1820–46 suggests that the unmarried were heavily represented among those coming to America; Ó Gráda, "Across the Briny Ocean: Some Thoughts on Irish Emigration to America, 1800–1850," in T. M. Devine and David Dickson, eds., *Ireland and Scotland, 1600–1850: Parallels and Contrasts in Economic and Social Development* (Edinburgh, 1983), 124. However, traveling alone does not necessarily mean immigrants were unmarried. Many husbands left their wives in Europe and eventually sent for their families, thereby making up this deficit of children over time. *Seventh Census, 1850, Population.*

9. *Fourth Census, 1820; Seventh Census, 1850, Population;* Pernicone, " 'Bloody Ould Sixth,' " 28, 102–109; Stanley Nadel, "Kleindeutschland: New York City's Germans, 1845–1880" (diss., Columbia University, 1981), 83. Pernicone's sample is from the 1855 census, Nadel's from 1850. Cabinetmaker: "A Working Man's Recollections of America," *Knight's Penny Magazine* 1 (1846), 105.

10. Cormac Ó Gráda's figures indicate that 40 percent of Irish female migration was unaccompanied, and thus an increase in this group was primarily responsible for the change in the sex ratio. Unfortunately, yearly breakdowns of age by sex are not available. Ó Gráda, "Across the Briny Ocean," 124.

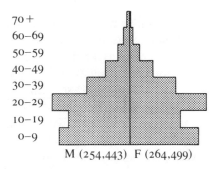

M (254,443)  F (264,499)

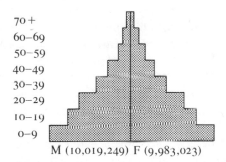

M (10,019,249)  F (9,983,023)

FIGURE 9. New York City and national population, 1850.

English parliamentary commission concluded that from Ireland in the early 1840s, "the industrious and well-conducted are almost the only emigrants."[11]

Most immigrants were peasants who were farmers or belonged to the large and growing rural, nonagricultural sector created by European industrialization. Some had no skills except as agriculturalists. For many, however, plots in Europe were too small for self-sufficiency, and peasants had to make ends meet through a wide range of "informal" rural work—for example, brewing, brushmaking, and other "trifling occupations." Only among the English— coming from a country that was predominantly urban by 1851—were immigrants from cities or towns common. In most years no more than 25 percent of all immigrants arriving in America listed an occupation other than farmer. However, artisans were overrepresented among immigrants choosing to remain in New York City.[12]

11. John Bodnar, *The Transplanted: A History of Immigrants in Urban America* (Bloomington, Ind., 1985), 13–23. Parliamentary commission quoted in Kerby Miller, "Emigrants and Exiles: The Irish Exodus to North America, from Colonial Times to the First World War" (diss., University of California, Berkeley, 1976), 232.

12. Evidence on the background of immigrants is given in Bodnar, *The Transplanted*, 1–56; Kerby Miller, *Emigrants and Exiles: Ireland and the Irish Exodus to North America* (New York,

What motives did these middling people have for immigrating? Europe in the eighteenth and nineteenth centuries experienced a population growth which could reasonably be described as rapid by any earlier standards, according to E. A. Wrigley. The European population (excluding Russia) grew from 125 million in 1750 to 208 million in 1850. This growth put increasing pressure on the land as each acre in production had to feed more people, and in some regions living standards, poor to begin with, declined.[13]

Conditions of life for most European peasants were very low at mid-century. In Derry—a very poor county and an area of high emigration—the Devon Commission Report of 1845 (just before the famine) found that 66 percent of all residences were one-room mud huts. One German immigrant later recalled his home in Hannover: "As you entered the house you became acquainted with the whole of it. One big hall, the floor of which was stamped earth. . . . We lived, cooked, and occasionally had the animals there." Logs and stones were used as seats; straw and rags were the only bedding many Irish and German peasants had. "Furniture indeed, drawers and chairs, eh! such things would look odd enough in our places," was the amused response by one Irishman to a question about furniture. Many peasants literally wore rags. American traveler Henry Colman described Irish laborers in 1844 as "ragged and dirty beyond all description, with the tatters hanging about them like a few remaining feathers upon a plucked goose." The diet was at best monotonous; "every meal centered around a grain dish," according to Jerome Blum, and in Ireland even bread was a luxury. As poor and unvaried as this diet was, peasants often felt lucky to get it, since major dearths occurred in 1817, 1832, and 1846. The situation became even worse with the potato famine that began in 1846 and struck Ireland, Scotland, Wales, and Germany. William Bennett described the interior of an Irish peasant hut in 1847:

> Furniture, properly so called, I believe may be stated at *nil*. I would not speak with certainty, and not wish to with exaggeration—we were too much over-come to note specifically—but as far as memory serves, we saw neither bed,

1985), 193–240; Ó Gráda, "Across the Briny Ocean," 125–127; Oliver MacDonagh, "The Irish Famine Emigration to the United States," *Perspectives in American History* 10 (1976); Maldwyn Jones, "The Background to Emigration from Great Britain in the Nineteenth Century," ibid. 7 (1973); Dallas L. Jones III, "The Background and Motives of Scottish Emigration to the United States of America in the Period 1815–1861, with Special Reference to Emigrant Correspondence" (diss., University of Edinburgh, 1970); Mack Walker, *Germany and the Emigration, 1816–1885* (Cambridge, Mass., 1964); Kamphoefner, *Westfalians*, 40–69; and Wolfgang Köllmann and Peter Marshalck, "German Emigration to the United States," *Perspectives in American History* 7 (1973). On "trifling occupations" see House of Commons, *Parliamentary Papers* (1836), XXXII, Poor Inquiry (Ireland), Appendix D; the quotation is on page 104.

13. E. A. Wrigley, *Population and History* (1969; rpt. New York, 1973), 205; see also Jerome Blum, *The End of the Old Order in Rural Europe* (Princeton, N.J., 1978), 255–256.

chair nor table, at all. A chest, a few iron or earthern vessels, a stool or two, the dirty rags and night coverings, formed the sum total of the *best* furnished.[14]

Living standards in England were substantially above those on the Continent or in Ireland, but in both town and village conditions were poor. Friedrich Engels depicts a population sunk in misery, living in hovels, too poor for women to afford shoes. Although Engels focused on the very poorest parts of Manchester, it is clear that average standards were not high. In Keighley, Yorkshire, in 1855, for example, one-half of the workers were too poor to afford any meat at all. In rural areas, concluded Colman, "The bulk of agricultural labourers in the country are, *at the best,* just able to struggle on from hand to mouth. . . . Any suspension of employment, rise in the price of provisions, or unforseen casualty, must, of necessity, compel them . . . to descend to a coarser diet, and exchange [their] . . . habits for those of an Irish peasant." This, it must be emphasized, is a description not of the most impoverished minority but of much of the European population.[15]

Upswings in population and attendant dearths and famines had happened before in European history, but in the nineteenth century emigration was available as an alternative. Clearly the motive for most immigrants was economic: they came to America to try to find something better than a life of poverty. This is the fourth of our generalizations and the most significant. Many were frank about their motives. America is a "much better place for a poor man than Ireland. It's a money-making country," wrote John Doyle, a New York City printer, in 1818. James and Mary Toal wrote their nephew in 1845: "I Prefer this Country for good Employment and good living than there is in Ireland yet I allways respect the land of my birth More than I Do this Country." William Darnley, a housepainter from Stockport, England, put the matter bluntly in an 1857 letter to his wife: "You wish to know how I like the

14. Devon Report quoted in Redcliffe Salaman, *History and Social Influence of the Potato* (Cambridge, England, 1949), 278. German: Charles Heartman, ed., *An Immigrant of a Hundred Years Ago* (Hattiesburg, Miss., 1941), 5. "Furniture": House of Commons, *Parliamentary Papers* (1836), XXXII, Poor Inquiry (Ireland), Appendix E, 71 (this is the best source on the living conditions of the Irish peasantry). Henry Colman, *European Agriculture and Rural Economy* (Boston, 1846), 1:50. Colman visited Europe before the famine. Blum, *End of the Old Order,* 183. On the condition of the peasantry, see Blum, *End of the Old Order,* 178–193; E. J. Hobsbawm, *The Age of Revolution, 1789–1848* (New York, 1962), 238–257; and Miller, *Emigrants and Exiles,* 204–221. On the Irish famine see Cecil Woodham Smith, *The Great Hunger* (New York, 1962). Scotland: Michael Flinn, *Scottish Population History* (Cambridge, England, 1977), 431–438. Germany: Walker, *Germany and the Emigration,* 71–74. William Bennett quoted in Diarmaid O. Muirithe, ed., *A Seat behind the Coachman: Travelers in Ireland, 1800–1900* (Dublin, 1972), 124, emphasis added to "best"; see also Miller, *Emigrants and Exiles,* 221–222. European living standards are also discussed in Chapter 6 below.

15. Friedrich Engels, *The Condition of the Working Class in England* (1844), trans. W. O. Henderson and W. H. Chaloner (New York, 1958), 30–87; E. J. Hobsbawm, "The British Standard of Living, 1790–1850," in his *Labouring Men* (Garden City, N.Y., 1964), 64. Colman, *European Agriculture,* 1:69; pp. 40–74 give a detailed account of English living standards.

country. I don't like it as well as our own, their is verry few people that do the[y] like the money."[16]

The degree to which people were "pushed" out of Europe or "pulled" into the United States is not particularly helpful in understanding immigration to the New World. Conditions were worsening in parts of rural Europe, but the sharp decline in immigration during the 1837 and 1857 depressions in the United States makes it clear that a prosperous American economy was a precondition for large-scale immigration. Both Old and New World conditions played their part; it was the difference in living standards that was crucial. The common people of Europe, albeit by making a complete break with their past life, could now improve their standard of living. Even during the famine, only a minority of the Irish population left; those who did emigrate thus made a conscious decision to improve the material conditions of their existence. Henry Price, a cabinetmaker, recalled in his diary his reasons for leaving England: "I never had enough to spend on to supply what I conceve to be sufficient for the supply of the legitimate Wants of My family." The Scottish woman who wrote to a friend in America in 1847 illustrates the motivation of most emigrants: "We are maken it no wors but we can not mak it much better. All that we can duo is if you Could give us any encourgesment [is] to ama[grate?] to your Country."[17]

Immigrants were primarily interested in escaping poverty, and most did not come to America hoping to make a fortune; usually their economic goals were modest. There were exceptions: many Ulster immigrants and very highly skilled English artisans did hope to become affluent. But most were far less optimistic about what they hoped to achieve. Few seemed interested in becoming bosses or finding nonmanual work—comments in letters are about manual wages not chances for upward mobility. Surely many dreamed of great fortunes, but most seem realistic, accepting that they would probably not "strike it rich" in the New World.[18]

16. "Letter of John Doyle," 25 January 1818, in *Journal of the American Irish Historical Society* 12 (1913), 204; James and Mary Toal, letter to Edward Toal, 1845, Public Record Office of Northern Ireland (PRONI); William Darnley, letter to his wife, 6 September 1857, Darnley Family Letters, Rare Books and Manuscripts Division, The New York Public Library, Astor, Lenox and Tilden Foundations. The significance of economic motives is emphasized in Charlotte Erickson, *Invisible Immigrants: The Adaptation of English and Scottish Immigrants in Nineteenth-Century America* (1972; rpt. Ithaca, N.Y., 1990).

17. On the decline in immigration during depressions, see note 20 below. "Diary of Henry Edward Price," in *British Records Relating to America in Microform* (East Ardsley, England, 1963), 18; Mary Millhill, letter to Jane Robertson, 28 April 1847, quoted in Jones, "Background and Motives," 40.

18. James Carlisle, an Ulster Protestant who came to the city in 1851, expected more than a living from America. Carlisle had a good job but wrote his sister, "I look forward to something better to come . . . I feel it my duty honestly and uprightly in the eyes of God to endeavour for the improvement of my circumstances." James Carlisle, letter to his sister, 30 January 1851, Carlisle Correspondence, PRONI; see also E. R. R. Green, "Ulster Emigrants' Letters," in Green, ed., *Essays in Scotch-Irish History* (London, 1969), 94. Skilled artisans: Erickson, *Invisible Immigrants*, 237, 239.

It was the prospect of an immediately better material life that most immigrants came for and that most interested those to whom America letters were sent—food and wages caused most comment in letters. Few immigrants seemed affected by British radicalism, and there is little evidence that political motives played a major part in encouraging emigration. Usually immigrants spoke only of hopes for a "decent" or a "comfortable" life. Such modest expectations recur frequently: "A man who keeps from drink & bad company by industry can acquire a comfortable living," wrote Irish sawyer William McLurg in 1833. In 1847 John Kerr wrote to his cousin urging him to emigrate but warning that "the most you can do is by industry and economy make livelihood."[19]

Indeed, immigrant letters rarely contained overly optimistic (or pessimistic) accounts of life in America. Most were, instead, cautious, even circumspect, in their assessments. Of Irish letters Arnold Schrier concludes that "romantic illusions [of America] were belied by the realism and general truthfulness which characterized . . . these direct reports. America, they made clear, was no idle paradise." There was too much at stake to risk boasting in the letters; a distortedly cheerful description might encourage others to immigrate, with disastrous results. William McLurg was noncommital in an 1833 letter to his parents in County Tyrone: "I have seen a great many old Country folks some have done very well & some have not." So was German immigrant Pankratz Settele in 1854: "Not everything goes well and not everything goes badly." When American conditions were bad, letters forcefully conveyed the news to the Old World, and emigration shrank rapidly. If economic conditions as described in the letters seemed better in the New World than in the Old, it was simply because most immigrants found a higher standard of living in America.[20]

European living standards were so low that it did not take much of an increase to convince the poor that America was a "land of plenty." Margaret

19. William McClurg, letter to his father David McClurg, 5 July 1833, McClorg Correspondence, PRONI; John Kerr, letter to James Graham, 5 June 1847, Kerr Letters, PRONI.

20. Labor recruitment by American employers was rare in this period, and potential emigrants had few other sources of information. Guidebooks were available, and some emigrants certainly used them, but most migrants, including the overwhelming majority of the Irish, probably never saw one. On the lack of labor recruitment see Erickson, *Invisible Immigrants,* 32, and Jones, "Background and Motives," 228–229. On the limited significance of guidebooks see Erickson, 34–35, and Jones, 110. Arnold Schrier, *Ireland and the American Emigration, 1850–1900* (Minneapolis, 1958), 20; see also Erickson, *Invisible Immigrants,* 5; Walker, *Germany and the Emigration,* 63; and Jones, 247. William McClurg, letter to his father David McClurg, 5 July 1833; Pankratz Settele, letter to his brother Franz, 20 November 1854, in Wolfgang Helbich, ed., *"Amerika ist ein freies Land . . . :" Auswanderer schreiben nach Deutschland* (Darmstadt, 1985), 52. The effectiveness with which information was conveyed from the New World to the Old is strikingly illustrated by the sharp drop in immigration during American depressions. In 1837, 84,959 immigrants came to America, but in 1838 only 45,159, as Appendix C shows. The recession of 1854, which has escaped the attention of some historians, was well-known to immigrants. In 1854, 460,474 came, but in 1855 only 230,476 arrived. By 1858, in the depths of the 1857 recession, the number was down to 123,126.

MCarthy, an Irish servant, urged her parents in 1850 to come to New York, "where no man or woman ever Hungerd or ever will and where you will not be Seen Naked . . . where you would never want or be at a loss for a good Breakfast and Dinner." Indeed, the prospect of improved diet seems to have been the most important factor in encouraging immigration. "Hunger brought me . . . here [and] hunger is the cause of European immigration to this country," wrote Henry Brokmeyer, a German immigrant who worked in New York in the 1850s as a tanner and shoemaker. Ole Helland wrote back to Norway in 1836, "I have such good service with board and bed that you would not believe it. Yes, I often think of you when I go to a prepared table with much expensive food before me." In 1844 Robert Williams wrote, "the chief farmers of Wales would be amazed to see the tables of the poor spread with five- to ten-course dishes at every meal."[21]

Immigrants came largely for economic reasons, but they were not a random cross-section of the European population. Males and the young predominated, which leads to our fifth generalization. Obviously many immigrants came to America for strictly personal reasons, but more often the decision to emigrate was made not solely by the individual but as part of a *family* decision. "The first fundamental characteristic of the farm economy of the peasant is that it is a family economy," notes A. V. Chayanov, and children were expected to help bolster the family's welfare. Both the young John Gough and Henry Price, before they emigrated to New York City, had helped their parents glean the fields after the harvest. Major decisions such as emigration were made with the family economy in mind. James Burn and his wife and children decided to come to the New World after holding a "family consultation." The emigration of Robert Bonner, later a famous New York editor, is characteristic: "The coming hither [to America] of an elder brother being under consideration in the family circle one evening, and doubts as to his ability to make his way being entertained, it was finally suggested that . . . [Robert] should be sent with him." The hope of parents for the upward mobility of their children, though surely a factor, is not salient in immigrant letters; the immediate welfare of the entire family mattered most in the decision to emigrate.[22]

21. Margaret MCarthy, letter to Alexander MCarthy, 22 September 1850, reprinted in Eilish Ellis, "State-Aided Emigration Schemes from Crown Estates in Ireland c. 1850," *Analecta Hibernica* 22 (1960), 390–391; Henry C. Brokmeyer, *A Mechanic's Diary* (Washington, 1910), 12, 11; Helland letter quoted in A. N. Rygg, *Norwegians in New York, 1825–1895* (Brooklyn, 1946), 5; Robert Williams letter, 22 May 1844, in Alan Conway, ed., *The Welsh in America: Letters from the Immigrants* (Minneapolis, 1961), 25.

22. Chayanov quoted in Eric R. Wolf, *Peasants* (Englewood Cliffs, N.J., 1966), 14; see also Hasia R. Diner, *Erin's Daughters in America: Irish Immigrant Women in the Nineteenth Century* (Baltimore, Md., 1983), 13–16, and Bodnar, *The Transplanted*, 48–52. John Gough, *Autobiography and Personal Recollections* (Springfield, Mass., 1870), 42; Price Diary, 16; James Burn, *James Burn; The "Beggar Boy"* (London, 1882), 253; Oliver Dyer, "Robert Bonner and the New York Ledger," *Packard's Monthly* 1 (1868), 17. Some Scottish immigrants were exceptions to the view that children's chances for upward mobility in America were not a crucial factor encouraging immigration; see Jones, "Background and Motives," 38.

After weighing information about America, the "family circle" often made the decision for the entire family to emigrate or for one or more family members to leave for America. This second strategy explains the disproportionate number of young, male emigrants. A young man with strength and endurance had, it was felt, the best chance to succeed in America. "I wish Mick Hay was here," wrote immigrant servant Eliza Quin, "or all the younghsters if they would take care of themself but let the old People stop at home." As the demand for servants increased, younger daughters often made the journey. William Sanger's 1857 survey of immigrant prostitutes (most of whom were former servants) illustrates the nonindividualistic context of immigration from Europe. Of the women who answered the question "What induced you to emigrate to the United States?" 711 answered either "Came with relatives" or "Sent out by Parents," the other 400 "Came to improve their condition." John Francis Maguire described the process in 1866: "Resolving to do something to better the circumstances of her family, the young Irish girl leaves home for America. There she goes into service, or engages in some kind of feminine employment. The object she has in view—the same for which she left her home and ventured to a strange country —. . . is the welfare of her family." It is doubtful that many were as selfless as Maguire suggests, but it is clear that, in Oliver MacDonagh's words, immigration was " 'communal' rather than . . . solitary."[23]

This family orientation helps explain the extraordinary amount of money remitted from America to Europe. Jacob Harvey, who investigated the subject in 1847, estimated that $2.2 million was sent back in that year to Ireland from New York, Boston, Philadelphia, and Baltimore. Letters from New York City to parents or wives across the Atlantic often note the remittances sent through exchange agencies. "Dear Parents," Eliza Quin wrote in 1848, "I am sending ye two pounds . . . I had no oppirtunity to Sending ye no more but I will not forget to send ye some assistance as soon as I can." Margaret MCarthy wrote in 1850, "This my Dr. Father Induces me to Remit to you in this Letter 20 Dollars that is four Pounds thinking it might be Some Acquisition to you untill you might Be Clearing away from that place all together and the Sooner the Better."[24]

These remittances helped out the family in one of two ways. Most often the

23. Erickson, *Invisible Immigrants,* 242; Eliza Quin, letter to her parents, 28 March 1848, in House of Commons, *Parliamentary Papers* XI (1849), "Appendix to the Minutes of Evidence before the Select Committee on Colonization from Ireland—Appendix Ten: Letters from Irish Immigrants and Others," 129. William Sanger, *The History of Prostitution* (New York, 1859), 465; John Francis Maguire, *The Irish in America* (London, 1868), 319; MacDonagh, "Irish Famine Emigration," 429.

24. Schrier, *Ireland,* 105, has estimated that between 1848 and 1900, $260 million was sent from the United States to Ireland and England. Harvey estimates cited in M. Wilson Gray, *Self Paying Colonization in North America* (Dublin, 1848), 7. Eliza Quin, letter to her parents, 28 March 1848, in House of Commons, *Parliamentary Papers* XI (1849), "Appendix Ten," 129. Margaret MCarthy letter, in Ellis, "State-Aided Emigration," 390.

money was used to raise the standard of living of those remaining in the Old World—Schrier estimates that 60 percent of all money sent from America was used to aid those remaining in Ireland. The other 40 percent was sent back to pay for passages of family members to America. Since few immigrants were sufficiently well-off to remit more than a single passage at a time, families often migrated sequentially. ''The most enterprising of a family goes first, he sends home for part of his family, and then in some time longer for more of them, until the whole are brought out,'' a Liverpool agent explained in 1834. Such systematic emigration was probably rather rare, but it is clear that thousands of emigrants to America had their passages paid by others who had arrived earlier. ''I will be able to pay yours passage withe the help of God on the First of August next,'' wrote Thomas Garry from ''Beekskeel'' to his wife in 1848. Kate Kennedy and her sister emigrated from Ireland in 1849 and worked for four years in the city sewing cloaks to remit sufficient money to bring over the rest of the family. In this sense emigration to the United States had a momentum of its own—the more who came over and the harder they worked, the more money was sent back to Europe to bring others to America.[25]

The decision to emigrate, then, was made with fairly realistic information about American conditions and with the family's welfare in mind. This is not to suggest that immigrants found the decision to leave easy; very few people who could make a decent living in Britain or Ireland emigrated. Nor is it to suggest that immigrants were completely prepared for what they found in America. Some wanted to believe America was the promised land and read accounts of living conditions in the New World, cautious though they usually were, as confirming that view. Many failed to recognize that a letter writer might have endured several years of poverty in America before finding a satisfactory position. A few, indeed, were woefully ignorant: Coventry ribbon weaver Benjamin Tilt arrived in New York City in 1830 to learn that ''there is not a Ribon being made in America.'' Many immigrants were shocked by their own first months in the New World.[26]

Virtually all left with feelings of sadness. An anonymous English cabinet-maker wrote an account in 1846 of his experience as an immigrant in America; he expressed the uncertainty and final acceptance of the necessity of leaving

25. Schrier, *Ireland,* 110. Liverpool agent quoted in MacDonagh, ''Irish Famine Emigration,'' 395; see also Gray, *Self Paying Colonization,* 6. Thomas Garry, letter from Peekskill to his wife, 8 March 1848, in House of Commons, *Parliamentary Papers* XI (1849), ''Appendix Ten,'' 130. Kennedy: Merriam Allen de Ford, *They Were San Franciscans* (Caldwell, Idaho, 1947), 145–146.

26. Benjamin Tilt, letter to James Powney, 12 May 1830, Coventry City Record Office. My thanks to Roger Haydon for drawing this letter to my attention. Despite this inauspicious start, Tilt later became a successful weaver in the city, and, like many other bosses, moved his shop to Paterson; see L. R. Trumbull, *A History of Industrial Paterson* (Paterson, N.J., 1882), 213.

the Old World felt by most immigrants: "How many times is the resolution taken and given up; how eagerly is every means resorted to which may avert the painful necessity! The startling fact continually recurs, we have not enough to eat; the physical conquers the moral: *the mind succumbs to the stomach*—and the final decision is made."[27]

This is the profile of a typical immigrant. Indeed, this profile fits not only the period before the Civil War but much of American history, including the "new" immigrants of the late nineteenth century and the Mexican immigrants of the 1980s. These more recent immigrants are poor, mostly male, predominantly young, and in Michael Piore's words "probably the closest thing in real life to the *Homo economicus* of economic theory."[28]

There is, however, one significant difference. Unlike many immigrants of the late nineteenth century and the 1980s, few of the antebellum immigrants intended returning to their native land. "On the 4th of June, 1829, I took—as I then supposed—a last view of my native village," remembered John Gough about his departure from Sandgate, England, to come to America. Most antebellum immigrants had come to America to live permanently. The expense and rigors of an ocean voyage under sail made the prospect of multiple crossings of the Atlantic uninviting, and for the Irish, of course, the collapse of agriculture in their homeland made return an unlikely prospect. Indeed, "American wakes" were commonly held in Ireland, since "the departure for

27. "A Working Man's Recollections," 97, emphasis added.
28. Even during the Irish emigration of the late 1840s, which was largely a flight from famine conditions, this profile held true. A greater number of complete families left during the famine, but a comparison of the five years before the famine with the famine emigration shows little change in age structure. There were many more emigrants in the 1840s and 1850s, and they seem to have been somewhat poorer and less skilled, according to Cormac Ó Gráda and Kerby Miller, but demographically they were the same *type* of immigrant as before (Miller, *Emigrants and Exiles*, 293–300; Ó Gráda, "Across the Briny Ocean," 123), as a comparison of prefamine and famine immigration to the United States makes clear.

| Years | 0–10 | 10–20 | 20–25 | 25–30 | 30–35 | 35+ | %M |
|-------|------|-------|-------|-------|-------|-----|-----|
| 1841–1845 | 16.6 | 20.3 | 20.6 | 16.5 | 9.2 | 16.8 | 58.9 |
| 1846–1850 | 15.5 | 20.8 | 22.0 | 15.4 | 10.0 | 16.2 | 59.8 |

N = 1841–45, 425,887; 1846–50, 1,118,385

*Source:* Bromwell, *History of Immigration*, 109–152.

Continuity is illustrated in a 1983 *Time* magazine article on Los Angeles immigrants. According to the article, "the international hordes now streaming in . . . [have] no-nonsense ideas about what they want: to work hard and make money. . . . Many have left such misery that their dreams are extremely modest." "Hun Yum . . . speaks barely passable English. Yum has not refused to become fluent. He is just too busy. 'Money is our first priority. . . . We have to work first, and then we will have time to learn the language.'" Kurt Andersen, "The New Ellis Island," *Time*, 13 June 1983, 18–25. Michael Piore, *Birds of Passage: Migrant Labor and Industrial Societies* (Cambridge, England, 1979), 54.

North America of a relative or neighbor," according to Kerby Miller, "represented as final a parting as a descent into the grave." When Scottish emigrants left Inverness in the 1840s they were saluted with the bagpipe *pibroch "Cha till ma tuille"*—"We shall return no more."[29]

Although they were not "target earners," hoping to make a sum of money and return to Europe, antebellum immigrants came to America for economic reasons. It is in this broader sense that they can be considered similar to postbellum and contemporary immigrants. Yet to argue for a "typical immigrant" does not, of course, mean that immigrants were all alike. There were wide differences in both motivation and expectation between an immigrant English mechanic and an Irish peasant, and the divergence between the fortunes of German and Irish immigrants to New York testifies to the importance of national differences. The success of Ulster immigrants in comparison with those from the rest of Ireland illustrates that regional diversity was significant as well. Nevertheless, the "immigrant profile" is more than demographic coincidence. It indicates a significant similarity among immigrants throughout the period and offers a clue to their objectives. Most came from a rural European society that, although containing sharp differences between countries and provinces, had enough homogeneity to allow historians to characterize it as "peasant." My argument here is that the backgrounds and motives of most of the groups coming to America coincided sufficiently to make the term "immigrant" a useful generalization.

Immigration is the key theme in the history of New York City's population. By the 1850s immigrants made up the majority of all inhabitants and three-quarters of the city's labor force. To the question Who made up the city's population, there is an answer: the vast majority were migrants from Europe.

OUT-MIGRATION

The high *net* migration to the city obscures a substantial out-migration from New York. About 80 percent of the city's growth was due to in-migration, but this estimate, while correct about the in-migrant component of urban growth,

29. On return immigration in the late nineteenth and twentieth centuries, see Taylor, *Distant Magnet,* 105–106, and Miller, *Emigrants and Exiles,* 427. Gough, *Autobiography,* 47. Some antebellum immigrants did return. Only scanty records have been kept, but they do show a countermovement, albeit a weak one. For English immigrants evidence from the depressed years of 1858–1861 shows a significant return, about 20,000 yearly, one-third of the total coming to America. A surprising number of the English immigrants whose letters and diaries I examined returned, though usually just for a visit. For Germans and Irish, the number going back was much smaller. During the 1854–1855 recession, those returning to Germany equaled only 5 percent of the total arriving in the United States. The 1871 census of County Clare, an area of heavy emigration, showed only 100 foreign citizens, mostly Americans, in a population of 150,000. See Maldwyn Jones, "Background to Emigration," 24; Walker, *Germany and the Emigration,* 173; Schrier, *Ireland,* 130. American Wakes: Miller, *Emigrants and Exiles,* 556–561, quote 557. *Pibroch:* Jones, "Background and Motives," 137.

offers a decidedly simplified view of the process. My earlier estimate was that 257,000 in-migrants settled in New York City between 1850 and 1860, but this figure represents only the *total* increase in the immigrant population. Between these two censuses thousands of native and foreign migrants had resided in the city and then left, their places taken by other migrants.[30]

The vast majority of immigrants landing at Castle Garden did not stay in the city but continued on to other locations. Thousands of others stayed in the city for a few months or years before moving on; Timothy Coffee "got work . . . the same day he landed" and stayed in the city until his sister wrote him with information about conditions in Detroit. Thomas Mooney—an Irish immigrant who published a guidebook in the form of letters to his Cousin Patrick, "a farmer in Ireland"—wrote, "You may possibly desire to stay some time in New York, to 'try your luck,' as the saying is," though Mooney himself recommended against it.[31]

Contemporary observers were well aware of the rapid turnover of the city's population: descriptions of the packed streets on "Moving Day"—May First, when leases expired—were standard fare in the metropolitan literature of the day. According to the *Herald*, a person who stayed put "was regarded either as eccentric or very stupid." During the Civil War the draft enrollment procedures were seriously hindered by the city's constantly changing population.[32]

Evidence compiled by Jay Dolan from parish registers and directories in the city suggests that about 40 percent of the city's 1850 population had left by 1860. This nonpersisting sector of the population was, as the research of

30. Urban population turnover attracted a good deal of attention from American historians in the 1970s—in attempting to trace social mobility in the nineteenth century, these historians were surprised at the large proportion of their samples who left the communities under study between the decadal censuses. Numerous studies attest to the attention this subject has received; see especially Michael Katz, *The People of Hamilton, Canada West* (Cambridge, Mass., 1975), 94–175; Stephan Thernstrom, *The Other Bostonians: Poverty and Progress in the American Metropolis* (Cambridge, Mass., 1973), 221–232; and Thernstrom and Peter R. Knights, "Men in Motion: Some Data and Speculations about Urban Population Mobility in Nineteenth-Century America," *Journal of Interdisciplinary History* 1 (1970), 7–35. The net in-migration figure is from note 4.

31. Lindstrom's estimate is calculated to determine net migration and must therefore assume "that no one who lived there in the previous decade left the city"; Lindstrom, "Economic Structure." Coffee: "An Irish Immigrant's Letter," *Living Age* 32 (1852), 422. Mooney, *Nine Years in America*, 83. Jay Dolan, in his study of immigrant Irish and German Catholics, discovered that about one-fifth of his sample of communicants stayed in New York for several months and then went elsewhere; Dolan, *The Immigrant Church, New York's Irish and German Catholics, 1815–1865* (Baltimore, Md., 1975), 38; see also William Chambers, *An Emigrant's Five Years in the Free States of America* (London, 1860), 204.

32. *Herald*, 1 May 1850. On turnover of the city's population see Lydia Maria Child, *Letters from New York* (New York, 1845), 17, and Burn, *Beggar Boy*, 270. Draft: J. H. Baxter, ed., *Medical Statistics of the Provost Marshall's Bureau* (Washington, 1875), 1:243, 245. Dolan, *Immigrant Church*, 39–41; see also Kenneth Alan Sherzer, "The Unbounded Community: Neighborhood Life and Social Structure in New York City, 1830–1875" (diss., Harvard University, 1982), 65–83.

Stephan Thernstrom and Peter R. Knights suggests, very volatile, composed of people who would enter the city, stay a year or two, leave, and be replaced by other in-migrants. Their study of Boston (a city with net turnover similar to that of New York) estimates that gross migration to the city might have been as high as *eight times* that of net in-migration. Net in-migration to New York in the 1850s of 257,000 could have been the result of 1,650,000 people moving into the city and 1,415,000 leaving. Since New York directories did not list yearly drops and adds (the method used by Thernstrom and Knights), it is impossible to estimate actual totals. The main point is that rapid in- and out-migration existed in New York, and to emphasize net migration to the city does little to alert us to the extraordinary fluidity of the urban population. The rapid turnover of population was a major factor in working-class life in the antebellum period.[33]

This discussion of out-migration completes our analysis of the city's population. The most important conclusion is the growing significance of European immigrants in the city's population—by 1855 approximately 84 percent of the manual workforce was foreign-born. Any attempt to understand the history of the city's workers in the antebellum period must start with the fact that a large proportion, and by the 1850s an overwhelming majority, of them had been born in Europe and emigrated to the United States.

33. Dolan, *Immigrant Church*, 40. Thernstrom and Knights, "Men in Motion," 22, conclude that, while Boston's population grew by 387,000 between 1830 and 1860, 3,325,000 immigrants entered the city in that period.

# CHAPTER 4

# The Labor Market and
# the Family Economy

Both immigrant and native workers had to find work if they planned to stay in New York. Most of the city's migrants came to New York to find high wages, and so the job situation strongly influenced their behavior. Their entrance into the labor market, like the decision to emigrate itself, was shaped by familial considerations.

Many immigrants were not certain where they were going and decided to "try their luck" before moving on. Others were too poor to go beyond the city and were forced to take whatever work they could find. A large number of immigrants, however, remained in New York City because, despite the huge influx of workers and constant warnings of a glutted job market, the city offered them a good chance of employment. *Wiley and Putnam's Emigrant's Guide* recounted the story of a British plumber who arrived in New York in 1842, followed some dubious advice, and went upstate seeking employment. He virtually starved before "he found that in the City of New-York there was a great demand for such labor." When another English immigrant, a cabinet-maker, announced his intention to go to the West when he failed to find a job in New York, he was told, "Don't do any such thing; if you can't get a living in New York, you can't in any part of the Union; I have tried both, and know it." Demand for workers in New York, both in printing and in some construction trades, was as strong as anywhere in the country. In addition, there was work for tens of thousands of unskilled laborers on the city's docks and in the building trades. Generally, however, the demand for unskilled labor, in this boom period for massive canal and railroad building, was stronger outside the city.[1]

1. *Wiley and Putnam's Emigrant's Guide* (London, 1845), 72–73; "A Working Man's Recollections of America," *Knight's Penny Magazine* I (1846), 102; *British Mechanic's and Labourer's Hand Book* (London, 1840), 236–237, 244–245.

Few immigrants arrived in New York without the name of a relative or fellow townsman they could contact to help them find employment. Among the Irish especially, because of chain migration, immigrants arriving in the city were rarely without a brother, cousin, or uncle who could help the neophyte city dweller find a place to work. David Kerr was met by his brother John Kerr when he arrived in 1847; Jane Fleming wrote to a friend in Donegal in 1853 that she "came a stranger to all here but my sister and they are all very kind to me"; and Mary Brown's aunt and two friends "met me with all sort of kindness" on her arrival in the city in 1857. Those who landed completely without contacts could visit one of the city's unofficial information centers for immigrants, such as Frederick Wang's saloon, which served as a gathering place for New York's small Norwegian community, or Grant Thorburn's seed store, which served a similar purpose for Scots. Having relatives in the city, or even finding a saloon patronized by one's compatriots, did much to ease the shock of the transition to urban life as well as provide information about lodging and the labor market. Native migrants seem, curiously, to have been more often on their own than were foreigners, though evidence on this point is limited.[2]

Immediate information about jobs was crucial since few of the migrants, native or foreign, arrived with much money. In 1832 Henry Walter, an immigrant manufacturing jeweler, disembarked with ten dollars, the same amount Brown Thurston, a printer from northern New York State, arrived in 1834 with. Although immigrants were usually not poor by the standards of their native countries, by American standards they were poor, and what little money they had they usually expended on the voyage. Alfred Green, a London brushmaker, had only twenty-six shillings left when he landed in 1857. In 1844, the New York Immigrant Aid Society calculated, the average Irish immigrant arrived with $20 in his pocket, enough for two months' room and board.[3]

2. John Kerr, letter to David Graham, 29 September 1847, Kerr letters, Public Record Office of Northern Ireland (PRONI); Jane Fleming, letter to Mr. McVitty, 3 May 1853, PRONI; Mary Brown, letter to Mary ?, 11 March 1858, Schrier Collection. My thanks to Prof. Arnold Schrier for permission to quote from this letter. A. Y. Rygg, *Norwegians in New York, 1825–1895* (Brooklyn, 1946), 6. Thorburn: Peter Carter, *Peter Carter, 1825–1900* (New York, 1901), 8–9. On native workers, see the Robert Taylor diary, 5 February 1846, Rare Books and Manuscripts Division, The New York Public Library, Astor, Lenox and Tilden Foundations, and Horace Greeley, *Recollections of a Busy Life* (New York, 1868), 84–85.

3. Henry Walter, "Autobiography of an English Tramp from 1812 to 1880 inclusive," 23. I thank Prof. Jane W. Torrey for permission to quote from this document. Brown Thurston, "Reminiscences of the Early Life of Brown Thurston," in the Brown Thurston journal, 1834–1893, American Antiquarian Society; Alfred Green, letter to his mother, 28 July 1857, British Library of Political and Economic Science, London School of Economics. $20: Kerby Miller, "Emigrants and Exiles: The Irish Exodus to North America, from Colonial Times to the First World War" (diss., University of California, Berkeley, 1976), 726. *British Mechanic's and Labourer's Hand Book,* 48, gives typical boardinghouse prices.

Few of the immigrants were very highly skilled. Generally there seems to have been a stronger demand in Europe for luxury items, and most accomplished artisans saw little reason to emigrate. "A man who can make a living at home has no business to come to the United States," printer John Doyle wrote to his wife in 1818. However, European protoindustrialization had created a large rural population that was nonagricultural or that supplemented farming with various manufacturing activities, and so many immigrants had rudimentary knowledge of a craft. Most immigrants were young, and those who knew a craft usually had been apprenticed to masters who were not highly skilled. Thomas Chamberlain was hired as a printer in 1835 even though his employer, William Dean, had to teach him composing. The eighteen-year-old Henry Price had learned little in England "about the [carpentry] Trade . . . beyond planing up a few boards" when he was hired by a German cabinetmaker. Margaret MCarthy's comment to her father that "Dan Keliher Tells me that you Knew more of the House Carpentery than he did himself and he can earn from twelve to fourteen Shiling a day" reflected the situation for many workers. The extensive division of labor in the city and the emphasis on speed rather than quality generally meant that mediocre skill was not a serious handicap. The difference in the manner of working in America (discussed in Chapter 5) required many immigrants to relearn much of their trade anyway, so the lack of complete training may even have been something of an advantage.[4]

The labor market they entered was *regional*. The city's newspapers ran advertisements for jobs in nearby areas, and labor unions in the city were often organized on a regional basis. The hatters' union, for example, included New York City, Danbury, Williamsburg, Yonkers, Port Chester, and Newark and insisted on a uniform bill of prices for all these cities. Immigrants commonly lumped together the city and nearby areas in their discussion of the job market in guidebooks and letters, and workers seem to have moved around the metropolitan area rather freely. The Anonymous Cabinetmaker went from working in New York to Poughkeepsie and back again; Robert Taylor, a cooper, worked in the city, Brooklyn, and Middletown, Connecticut; Samuel Gompers worked in Hackensack as well as in New York. One New York

4. The relative weakness of American luxury demand is discussed in Chapter 5 below. "Letter of John Doyle," 25 January 1818, in *Journal of the American Irish Historical Society* 12 (1913), 204; Thomas Chamberlain diary, 13 June 1835, Rare Books and Manuscripts Division, The New York Public Library, Astor, Lenox and Tilden Foundations. On the creation of a European, rural, nonagricultural population, see Jan de Vries, *European Urbanization, 1500–1800* (Berkeley, Calif., 1985), 237–249. "The Diary of Henry Edward Price," in *British Records Relating to America in Microform* (East Ardsley, England, 1963), 48. Margaret MCarthy, letter to Alexander MCarthy, 22 September 1850, in Eilish Ellis, "State-Aided Emigration Schemes from Crown Estates in Ireland c. 1850," *Analecta Hibernica* 22 (1960), 391. See also Charlotte Erickson, *Invisible Immigrants: The Adaptation of English and Scottish Immigrants in Nineteenth-Century America* (1972; rpt. Ithaca, N.Y., 1990), 230–232.

carpenter worked for a time at Yorkville and returned to the city only on weekends, and James Burn worked as a hatter in Newark, Brooklyn, and New York City.[5]

Many single immigrants labored in the New World in order to earn money to remit to Europe, and so they came to America enmeshed in the family economy. When the entire family came, labor force participation was, as a number of studies have shown, similarly regulated by family influences. In most parts of Europe it was simply assumed that women and children would help out. "Every member of the family" in America, according to Thomas Mooney, "will do something to contribute to the family commonwealth." The father, of course, always worked when he could, but the timing of the entry of wives and children into the job market depended on the family's life cycle and economic situation and on the state of the urban economy. Workers were well aware that members of the family other than the chief wage-earner could bring in substantial sums of money, and a large family was sometimes mentioned in letters as an inducement to emigrate. Because the familial economy decreed differing roles for men, women, and children, I discuss each group's relation to the labor market separately.[6]

ADULT MEN

Eager to earn money, adult males usually wasted no time in looking for a job. That adult men would labor from their first job until their death was a given in the nineteenth-century city; single men were completely reliant on their own earnings, and married men's earnings were the backbone of the family economy. How did a typical male worker try to find a job in the antebellum urban economy?

It helped if the worker had brought with him a letter of recommendation. The British Mechanic described such letters as of "essential importance to the

5. Hatters: *Working Man's Advocate*, 21 September 1844. The *Working Man's Advocate* commonly reported labor news from neighboring towns, especially Newark. On guidebooks see, for example, Thomas Mooney, *Nine Years in America* (Dublin, 1850), 92–93. Further evidence on regional union organization is given in Lawrence Costello, "The New York City Labor Movement, 1861–1873" (diss., Columbia University, 1967), 186–205. "A Working Man's Recollections of America"; Robert Taylor diary, 5 February 1846; Samuel Gompers, *Seventy Years of Life and Labor* (1925; rpt. New York, 1967), 1:37–41; John Morrow, *A Voice from the Newsboys* (New York, 1860), 33; James Burn, *Three Years among the Working-Classes in the United States during the War* (1865; rpt. New York, 1982).

6. The importance of the family economy among immigrants is emphasized in John Bodnar, *The Transplanted: A History of Immigrants in Urban America* (Bloomington, Ind., 1985). Mooney, *Nine Years in America*, 16. This analysis is similar to Michael Haines, "Poverty, Economic Stress and the Family in a Late Nineteenth-Century American City: Whites in Philadelphia, 1880," in Theodore Hershberg, ed., *Philadelphia: Work, Space, Family and Group Experience in the 19th Century* (New York, 1981), 240–275.

mechanic or working-man . . . speaking to the qualities of sobriety, ability, honesty and industry.'' For example, James McBeath, a native worker from Bath, New York, brought this letter with him: "The bearer of this James McBeath of Bath, [is] a bookbinder by trade. He wishes to obtain employment in this city. I know the family well & know them to be worthy of all confidence. His father [an Ulsterman] is a book binder. . . . Yours etc Wm Hosmer, May 24, 1851.'' The first thing was to ask relatives and friends if they knew of openings. Few of the city's workshops had formal hiring procedures, and most workers found jobs by word of mouth. According to Virginia Penny, the female labor reformer who studied work in the city in 1859 and 1860, "much depends on the kind of friends a lady has to secure her a place. It is the same case with a young man.'' Horace Greeley found a job in the city as printer when some Irishmen he met in a tavern in 1831 (Greeley insists he was not drinking with them) directed him to a shop where there was an opening. John Burke and his brother were hired as bootmakers at Kimball and Rogers, "the largest first-Class Shoe Establishment in New York,'' in 1847, through a friend. A townsman could also be of help. Benjamin Tilt, Coventry ribbon weaver, was unable to get work until by "accident found M. M. Roy [?] a Coventry man and he promised us employment.''[7]

An informal network of information helped certain immigrant groups dominate particular trades. Table 11 illustrates the ethnic division of labor in the city. Perhaps its most striking aspect is the overwhelming domination of immigrants in every manual trade. Eighty-four percent of all manual workers were foreign-born, and in none of the listed manual trades were native-born workers a majority. Nevertheless, there were marked variations among national groups. Some obviously reflected differences in Old World experience: for example, the huge Irish majorities in unskilled work, the scarcity of German printers, the large number of English and Scottish machinists. Other variations are harder to explain. Why were the Irish so dominant in bricklaying, whereas a plurality of carpenters were American-born? Why so many German cigarmakers and so few Irish? Why was housepainting popular with British immigrants and cabinetmaking unpopular? It is hard to find logical answers, just as it is hard to explain why, in the 1980s, Koreans in New York City dominate the produce trade whereas Pakistanis often operate newstands.

7. *British Mechanic's and Labourer's Hand Book*, 20. Letter of recommendation for James McBeath's son, 24 May 1851, James McBeath and Family Papers, Minnesota Historical Society; for another example see Robert Crowe, *Reminiscences of Robert Crowe the Octogenarian Tailor* (New York, 1901), 20. John Petheram, an English druggist, brought letters of introduction with him; see Petheram, "Sketches of My Life" 1830–1831, New-York Historical Society (NYHS). Virginia Penny, *How Women Can Make Money* (1863; rpt. New York, 1971), 40, see also 370; Greeley, *Recollections*, 85; John Burke, "Reminiscences," NYHS; Benjamin Tilt, letter to James Powney, 12 May 1830, Coventry City Record Office.

TABLE 11
Ethnic division of labor, New York City, 1855

| Occupation | No. | % Foreign-born | % Native-born | % Irish | % German | % English & Scot | % Black |
|---|---|---|---|---|---|---|---|
| *Manual* | | | | | | | |
| Servant | 31,749 | 93 | 7 | 74 | 14 | 3 | 3 |
| Laborer | 20,238 | 98 | 2 | 86 | 9 | 2 | 3 |
| Tailor | 12,609 | 96 | 4 | 33 | 53 | 5 | 0 |
| Seamstress | 9,819 | 67 | 33 | 46 | 10 | 7 | 1 |
| Carpenter | 7,531 | 64 | 35 | 30 | 22 | 9 | 0 |
| Shoemaker | 6,745 | 96 | 4 | 31 | 55 | 5 | 0 |
| Carter | 5,498 | 58 | 41 | 46 | 7 | 4 | 1 |
| Baker | 3,692 | 90 | 10 | 23 | 54 | 8 | 0 |
| Bricklayer | 3,634 | 79 | 21 | 61 | 9 | 9 | 0 |
| Cabinetmaker | 3,517 | 83 | 17 | 12 | 61 | 4 | 0 |
| Painter | 3,485 | 77 | 23 | 31 | 26 | 15 | 0 |
| Porter | 3,052 | 64 | 36 | 48 | 11 | 3 | 6 |
| Blacksmith | 2,642 | 82 | 18 | 51 | 20 | 9 | 0 |
| Laundress | 2,563 | 79 | 21 | 69 | 6 | 2 | 14 |
| Shipbuilder | 2,287 | 57 | 43 | 29 | 7 | 13 | 0 |
| Printer | 2,077 | 55 | 45 | 25 | 11 | 14 | 0 |
| Cigarmaker | 1,996 | 77 | 23 | 5 | 61 | 4 | 0 |
| Peddler | 1,915 | 98 | 2 | 39 | 49 | 3 | 1 |
| Stonecutter | 1,914 | 96 | 4 | 65 | 11 | 17 | 0 |
| Driver | 1,741 | 56 | 44 | 46 | 3 | 5 | 6 |
| Machinist | 1,714 | 72 | 28 | 23 | 21 | 22 | 0 |
| Manufacturing jeweler | 1,705 | 61 | 39 | 10 | 28 | 10 | 0 |
| Hatter | 1,422 | 63 | 37 | 20 | 30 | 5 | 0 |
| Leatherworker | 1,386 | 71 | 29 | 30 | 28 | 9 | 0 |
| Total, manual occupations | 156,610 | 84 | 16 | 51 | 23 | 7 | 2 |
| Percentage of all workers in manual occupations = 77 | | | | | | | |
| Total, in manufacturing = 75,248 | | | | | | | |
| Percentage of all workers in manufacturing = 37 | | | | | | | |
| *Nonmanual* | | | | | | | |
| Clerk | 13,929 | 43 | 56 | 15 | 16 | 7 | 0 |
| Food dealer | 8,300 | 63 | 37 | 22 | 37 | 3 | 0 |
| Merchant | 6,299 | 27 | 72 | 4 | 10 | 7 | 0 |
| Shopkeeper | 2,641 | 69 | 31 | 35 | 17 | 12 | 0 |
| Boardinghouse keeper | 1,723 | 44 | 56 | 17 | 14 | 7 | 1 |
| Physician | 1,469 | 38 | 62 | 8 | 16 | 8 | 0 |
| Total, nonmanual occupations | 44,734 | 49 | 51 | 17 | 20 | 7 | 1 |
| Percentage of all workers in nonmanual occupations = 23 | | | | | | | |
| TOTAL, All | 204,344 | 76 | 24 | 43 | 23 | 7 | 2 |

*Note:* Ernst's statistics on immigrant workers are taken from the manuscript schedules, totals for all workers in an occupation from the printed census. As Ernst notes, some of the printed totals are undercounts, so these figures may exaggerate the foreign-born percentage in some trades.

*Source:* Robert Ernst, *Immigrant Life in New York City, 1825–1863* (1949; rpt. New York, 1979), 214–217.

Nothing in the immigrant background provides an explanation. These seemingly random variations may stem from a few immigrants of a single nationality becoming established in a particular occupation and then helping their fellow countrymen by employing them. The 1850s even saw regional concentrations in the New York labor market, such as Corkonians in the city's gasworks. Despite this ethnic division of labor, however, virtually every trade had a range of nationalities, and immigrants were a majority in every major manual occupation.[8]

If an immigrant was without friends or relatives, or those he had were unable to get him work, his next recourse was to go from shop to shop. Jobs were never easy to get in New York; even in good times, workers often lacked information about openings, and many had to resort to the time-consuming method of visiting shops in their trade. Horace Greeley "climbed into upper stories, came down again, ascended other heights, descended, dived into basements." James Burn was inquiring for work at a hat factory on 24th Street when he heard the voice "of a countryman, a broad Northumbrian," from his home village of Bexham, who recommended him to the boss. (Burn was hired.) The flood of immigrants in the late 1840s and early 1850s made finding a job even more difficult. Nevertheless, when the economy was healthy, most immigrants, according to *Wiley and Putnam's Emigrant's Guide* "are pretty sure to find employment, . . . though they often experience some delay in finding it."[9]

All of the above-mentioned hirees were skilled though not, for the most part, highly skilled workers. What of the unskilled, the 23,000 laborers and porters revealed by the 1855 state census? How were they hired? Evidence here is less clear, but since unskilled labor was casual, the job search was nearly continuous. Longshoremen would often congregate in a waterfront saloon or "lounge about a ship for several days while waiting to discharge, or 'waiting for a freight,' " according to Thomas Mooney. So central was the need for information that many laborers seem to have lived close to the waterfront so as to act quickly when the opportunity for work presented itself.[10]

8. Robert Ernst, *Immigrant Life in New York City, 1825–1863* (1949; rpt. New York, 1979), 214–217. On the ethnic division of labor see also David Ward, "The Internal Spatial Differentiation of Immigrant Residential Districts," *Special Publications* no. 3, Dept. of Geography, Northwestern University (Evanston, Ill., 1970), 28, and Kenneth Alan Scherzer, "The Unbounded Community: Neighborhood Life and Social Structure in New York, 1830–1875" (diss., Harvard University, 1982), 175. Gasworks: Jeremiah O'Donovan, *Irish Immigration in the United States* (1864; rpt. New York, 1969), 92–93.

9. James Parton, *The Life of Horace Greeley* (Boston, 1872), 87; James Burn, *James Burn; The "Beggar Boy"* (London, 1882), 264; *Wiley and Putnam's Emigrant's Guide*, 86, 88.

10. On laborers see Mooney, *Nine Years in America*, 86; Thomas Gunn, *The Physiology of New York Boarding-Houses* (New York, 1857), 112; see also *British Mechanic's and Labourer's Hand Book*, 265–283, and *Annual Report of the New York Association for Improving the Condition of the Poor for the Year 1852* (New York, 1853), 26. On laborers' residences see Table 20.

Was there a male *labor scarcity* in many city trades? Marked differences characterized job markets for different trades, skilled and unskilled workers, busy and slack seasons, and good and bad years. Indeed, the term "labor scarcity" is itself rather misleading—only in busy seasons in good years was there an actual scarcity. It is clear that European immigrants found the labor market in the New World much tighter than in the Old.[11]

"In Europe work is often wanting for hands, here in America hands are wanting for work," wrote Michel Chevalier in 1839, and many guidebooks and immigrant accounts speak of labor scarcity in general terms. "In the United Kingdom," Burn wrote, "there are five men to do the work of three, and lately in America there were two to do the work of five." In 1829 Benjamin Smith, editor of a collection of letters from emigrants, claimed with a good deal of exaggeration that "the demand for labour at New York and Philadelphia is so great, that the emigrants . . . are certain to obtain immediate employment." The British Mechanic told his readers, "There is a certainty of ready employment." "WHO SHOULD GO? First, the Working man *who wishes to find the best market for his labour,*" announced an 1843 emigrant's guidebook. The flood of famine immigrants and the depressions of the 1850s seem to have resulted in a much more cautious view of American labor conditions, but as late as 1865 James Burn could speak of "the unlimited demand there is in the country for industry."[12]

Some workers, especially in the 1830s and 1840s, were hired at the first place they applied. Henry Walter had been apprenticed to a retail jeweler in England and was skeptical he would be hired as a manufacturing jeweler in America. But in the first shop in Reade Street he entered, he was told by the boss, " 'Come in the morning . . . and I will see what you can do. . . .' I fully expected I should have to serve an apprenticeship of a year or two. But there was no such thing as holding back," and Walter worked at the shop for five years. Even though he came to the city during the August slack season, Greeley searched for work for only two days. The Anonymous Cabinetmaker who wrote an account of his work in the United States in the 1830s had to look for over a week before getting a job, which was considered a very long time. Unlike in England it was rarely necessary to "mug" (that is, bribe) the boss;

---

11. On the great surplus of labor in some English trades see Charles Manby Smith, *The Working-Man's Way in the World* (New York, 1854), esp. 28–34.

12. Michel Chevalier, *Society, Manners and Politics in the United States* (1839; rpt. Ithaca, N.Y., 1961), 143; James Dawson Burn, *A Glimpse at the Social Condition of the Working Classes during the Early Part of the Present Century* (London, n.d.), 150; Benjamin Smith, *Twenty-Four Letters from Labourers in America to Their Friends in England* (London, 1829), 1; *British Mechanic's and Labourer's Hand Book*, 201; *Emigration—Who Should Go; Where to Go; How to Get There; and What to Take* (London, 1843), 3. Immigrant letters became noticeably more pessimistic in the 1850s: see Miller, "Emigrants and Exiles," 391–392. Burn, *Three Years*, 19.

indeed, American workers in the 1820s and 1830s often demanded, and were given, an advance when hired. Workers understood the existence of a labor scarcity and seem to have regarded it as commonplace. One English worker told Thomas Gunn the reason he decided to emigrate: "The old country . . . , though the comfortablest in the world—*if you had money*—was rather crowded."[13]

The availability of work varied from one trade to another. Both immigrant letters and guidebooks existed in part to help potential immigrants evaluate specific labor markets, and the guidebooks often contained lists of trades and the need for workers in them. In the 1850s and 1860s the Association for Improving the Condition of the Poor and the New York Chamber of Commerce both published lists of trades in the city and the prospects for finding a job in them. The evidence is sometimes contradictory, but patterns do emerge. Generally, in a city experiencing rapid growth, the building trades had a very strong demand for workers—in 1820 the construction trades were in "greatest request," "exceedingly good" in 1840, and in 1859 in the midst of a recession they were still in "moderate demand." Although the printing trade was divided into book, newspaper and job work, each with its own labor market, we find a fairly steady demand for most types of print work. Among the city's poorer trades were shoemaking, forced to compete with Massachusetts factories, and tailoring, where the use of female seamstresses made the labor market increasingly crowded after 1840.[14]

13. Walter, "Autobiography," 22, 23. Robert Brownlee, a Scots stonecutter, was hired at the first place he applied in New York in 1836; Robert Brownlee, *An American Odyssey: The Autobiography of a 19th-Century Scotsman*, ed. Patricia A. Etter (Fayetteville, Ark., 1986), 19. The tailor husband of German immigrant Angela Heck was hired before he even got off the boat; Angela Heck letter, 1 July 1854, quoted in Walter Kamphoefner, *The Westfailians: From Germany to Missouri* (Princeton, N.J., 1987), 155. "A Working Man's Recollections of America," 102. Advance: "Chips," *Fincher's Trades' Review*, 3 March 1866. Gunn, *Physiology*, 243.

14. The best sources on the city labor market are the *British Mechanic's and Labourer's Hand Book*, 203–283, and Penny, *How Women Can Make Money*. Virtually all emigrant guidebooks have some information, and Henry Fearon, *Sketches of America* (London, 1819), 22–37, and Mooney, *Nine Years in America*, 129–154, are especially good. Though not geared specifically to New York City, C. L. Fleischmann, *Erwerbszweige, Fabrikwesen und Handel der Vereinigten Staaten von Nordamerika* (Stuttgart, 1850), contains much detailed information. *The Annual Report of the Chamber of Commerce of the State of New York for the Year 1858* (New York, 1859), 158, and Thomas D. Shipman, "Report of the State of the Labor Market in New York," *Canada Agriculture Department, Annual Report of the Minister, 1865* (Ottawa, 1866), 8–10, both give lists of trades in the city with the demand there for labor and wages. The city's newspapers often ran stories on the state of the labor market—the *Tribune*, 31 March 1860, is especially detailed. Construction: Daniel Blowe, ed., *A Geographical, Historical, Commercial, and Agricultural View of the United States* (London and Liverpool, 1820), 371; *British Mechanic's and Labourer's Hand Book*, 203–208, and *Chamber of Commerce Report, 1858*, 158. On printing, see *British Mechanic's and Labourer's Hand Book*, 234–245; *Tribune*, 22 August, 11 and 15 September 1845; *Chamber of Commerce Report, 1858*, 158; George A. Stevens, *History of Typographical Union No. 6* (Albany, N.Y., 1913), 210–216. On tailoring, see Fearon, 33–34; *Working Man's Advocate*, 5 March 1836; *Tribune*, 15 November 1845.

The most striking aspect of the labor market for unskilled workers is how well demand seems to have held up in the face of a massive immigration to the city. The city's role as a great port and the construction boom kept demand high in summer. "Labourers . . . are always sure of work and wages," according to the city's Shamrock Society in 1817. The British Mechanic in 1840 spoke of a "great demand [in] the eastern Atlantic cities [for] ship and wharf labourers." The 1857 depression left the "market glutted." However, the decline in immigration with the Civil War seems to have partially revived demand, and James Burn, who was looking for work as a hatter in 1862, discovered he could easily find work as a laborer if he desired.[15]

To discuss skilled trades in this way only begins to unravel the complexity of the situation. A highly skilled worker could usually find a job, even in a crowded craft such as cabinetmaking, whereas employers in some other trades preferred less skilled and hence cheaper workers. Also, some industries waxed after 1840 in the city, others waned. In addition, the time of year and the state of the national economy had a strong impact on employment. Skilled workers had to weigh all of these factors in assessing their prospects.[16]

Whether the adult male was single or married with children, it was on the breadwinner's success in obtaining a good job that the family's economic fate depended. If the husband lost his job, it was virtually impossible for other family members to make up the lost income. But other family members did make significant contributions to the family economy, contributions that both lessened the dangers of short-term unemployment of the breadwinner and raised the family's living standards.

## CHILDREN AND APPRENTICES

Children were expected to labor in Europe, and immigrants lost little time in finding employment for sons and daughters in America. The prospect of children laboring for wages was viewed not as an expedient forced upon workers by poverty but as a tremendous advantage. In Ireland, children could help with the weeding and such other mundane tasks but "are hardly ever employed for hire. . . . The earnings of children are absolutely nothing." Immigrants reacted with delight to the discovery that in America children could actually bring money into the family economy. The labor reformer John

---

15. *Hints to Emigrants from Europe* "by the Shamrock Society of New York" (New York, 1817), 12; *British Mechanic's and Labourer's Hand Book*, 275. "Glutted": *Chamber of Commerce Report, 1858*, 158. Burn, *Beggar Boy*, 262.

16. Emigrant guidebooks often mentioned the importance of skill in various trades; see especially *British Mechanic's and Labourer's Hand Book*, and Penny, *How Women Can Make Money*. See also *Annual Report of the A.I.C.P. for the Year 1855*, 17–18.

Prentice informed his fellow Scots that "men with families find no difficulty in getting them employed." The British Mechanic described the situation in the New World to his readers:

> In America, whatever be the extent of a man's family, and whether girls or boys, they will not be found the very heavy burthen they too frequently are in old countries. Except in the difficulty of getting them over there, number will be no disadvantage, owing to the constant demand there is for their services. It is the custom to send children out to employment at the early age of nine or ten years, and . . . fair renumeration may readily be obtained for them.

Indeed, the labor market may have been better for children than for men; one group of Sheffield cutlers in the city in the 1830s discovered they were able to find work for their children while they themselves remained unemployed. So important was children's income to the family that many workers took their children out of school when they came of working age. "If parents can derive the most trifling pecuniary advantages from their [children's] services," "Rev. Arnold" explained in 1834, "from the age of ten to sixteen years, in printing offices, bakeries, tobacco manufactorics, etc. or by sending them into the streets as hawkers . . . they keep them from school." No more than 50 to 60 percent of the school age population, Carl Kaestle has discovered, attended classes regularly in the period 1825–1850.[17]

Children mostly contributed to the family economy through various sorts of "informal work." In putting-out trades, where the family was the unit of production, children could help with the simpler parts of the manufacturing process. In tailoring, they could do the basting (the sewing of long, loose stitches in order to hold part of a garment, such as the lining, in place during final stitching), and in shoemaking "the fitting is . . . so simple a process that children can help work on it." When not involved in home manufacture children could help the family in other ways: "Girls from the age of eleven or twelve are sought after as day-helps, either to nurse children or attend about house" to earn money, and young boys could run errands or, in poor families, scavenge along the docks for coal in the winter.[18]

17. House of Commons, *Parliamentary Papers* XXXI (1836), Poor Inquiry (Ireland), Appendix D, 85–86. In England children were often able to get employment; see Michael Anderson, *Family Structure in Nineteenth Century Lancashire* (Cambridge, England, 1971), 74–78. John Prentice, "Letter to the Working Classes of Edinburgh," *Scotsman,* 16 April 1834; *British Mechanic's and Labourer's Hand Book,* 101. Cutlers: "A Working Man's Recollections of America," 101; see also *London v. New York* "by an English Workman" (London, 1859), 46, and John West letter in G. Poulett Scrope, *Extracts of Letters from Poor Persons* (London, 1832), 28. "Rev. Arnold" quoted in the *Man,* 4 August 1834; see also the 1832 Public School Society Report quoted in Carl Kaestle, *The Evolution of an Urban School System—New York City, 1750–1850* (Cambridge, Mass., 1973), 94. Kaestle, 89.

18. On tailoring see Penny, *How Women Can Make Money,* 111; Carl Wittke, *The Utopian Communist: A Biography of Wilhelm Weitling* (Baton Rouge, La., 1950), 310–311; U.S.

The most significant contribution children could make to the family economy was regular, paid employment. The wage labor of girls is discussed in the section on female labor, here our focus is on boys. Boys as young as age ten were paid lower wages, making such youthful workers attractive to employers. British workers were surprised at the ease with which skilled apprenticeships could be obtained in the New World. In Europe apprenticeships were hard to get, and a substantial bonus often had to be paid; Henry Walter's mother had paid forty pounds to have him apprenticed to a London jeweler. The increased division of labor meant that most boys received less training in New York city than their predecessors earlier in the century; but such considerations were of little concern to immigrants trying to make ends meet.[19]

Margaret MCarthy, an Irish immigrant, was exaggerating when she wrote her father in Ireland regarding her brother, "Michl can get a place Right off as you will not be In the Second day when you can Bind him to any Trade you wish." Nevertheless, even more cautious immigrant observers found apprenticeships substantially easier to obtain in New York than in England. The British Mechanic stated that the apprentice "will have none of the difficulties so common in his own country . . . in the way of providing premiums." "Frank Harley," a young upstate worker who came to the city in the 1830s, had offers of apprenticeships from four city shipbuilders. John Kerr had no doubt his brother David could easily find an apprenticeship in 1847, "I believe now the best trade he can learn is a Ship Carpenter, and he can become an apprentice to that here I think without much doubt. . . . If he does not choose to learn this trade he can take his choice."[20]

Because apprenticeships were easy to obtain, the formality that traditionally accompanied Old World apprenticeship was largely missing in the New. In labor-scarce America, apprenticeship had never been very strong, and it weakened even further as increasing division of labor made broad knowledge of a trade less necessary. As the *New York Herald* put it in 1853, "as a general

Congress, Senate, Committee on Education and Labor, *Report of the Senate Committee upon Relations between Labor and Capital* (Washington, 1885), 1:413–414, and Egal Feldman, *Fit for Men: A Study of New York's Clothing Trade* (Washington, 1960), 99, 104–105. Shoemaking: *Herald*, 5 September 1845, also 9 September 1845, and Penny, *How Women Can Make Money*, 332–333. "Girls": *British Mechanic's and Labourer's Hand Book*, 102. Errands: Penny, 444. Scavenging coal: *Children's Aid Society, Third Annual Report, 1856* (New York, 1857), 26, and Charles Farnham, "A Day on the Docks," *Scribner's Monthly* 18 (1879), 39.
19. Walter, "Autobiography," 16.
20. Margaret MCarthy, letter to Alexander MCarthy, 22 September 1850, in Ellis, "State-Aided Emigration," 390; *British Mechanic's and Labourer's Hand Book*, 106–107; "Chips," *Fincher's Trades' Review*, 27 January 1866. The author of this series of reminiscences on shipbuilding in the 1830s and 1840s calls himself Frank Harley, but no such name appears in the city directories. George E. McNeil in *The Labor Movement: The Problem of Today* (New York, 1892), 341, attributes this series to Richard Trevellick, but Trevellick came to America only in 1857. The term "chips" was slang for ship carpenters. John Kerr, letter to James Graham, 5 June 1847. The lack of hostility American apprentices faced is discussed in Chapter 5.

thing, the system of apprenticeship in every trade is not so strictly carried out as it was twenty or thirty years ago.'' Formal indentures, with a signed contract, were rare; most boys had their apprenticeships arranged by oral agreement between themselves or their fathers and the boss. ''I don't want any binding indentures,'' Boss Sneeden, a shipbuilder, told Frank Harley. ''When I don't like you, or you don't like me, or we mutually dislike each other, we'll quit and separate.'' The traditional five-year apprenticeship existed only in a few trades, such as pianomaking, and ''indoor apprenticeships'' where the boy actually lived with the master were unusual in New York. Typical was printing, where the five-year apprenticeship was defunct by 1810, if, indeed, it had ever existed. Generally, most boys served as apprentices only a ''short time'' or a ''few months.'' Since the wages for apprentices were well below those for men (often no more than a few dollars a month), bosses in New York, as in England, often used partially trained apprentices to undermine adult wages.[21]

Although arranging apprenticeships was simple in comparison to Britain, the training received was usually not very extensive. The *Herald*'s 1853 description seems typical of most city trades: ''It is almost impossible to obtain a complete practical knowledge in so short a time [two to four years], and the consequence is that a considerable number of workmen are incompetent for anything except the roughest and coarsest work.'' Nevertheless, apprenticeships before 1860 never completely degenerated into wage work; instruction, albeit shallow, continued to play a role.[22]

Because apprenticeships were easy to get, and involved an increasingly short period, many boys were apprenticed to more than one trade before they became journeymen. According to the anonymous English Workman who wrote an 1859 account of his experience in New York City, ''a boy, after he

21. The weakness of apprenticeship in the eighteenth century is noted in Samuel McKee, Jr., *Labor in Colonial New York, 1664–1776* (New York, 1935), 87–88. *Herald*, 18 June 1853; ''Chips,'' *Fincher's Trades' Review*, 27 January 1866. ''Boss Sneeden'' was probably Samuel Sneden, a shipbuilder in the city in the 1830s and 1840s. On short apprenticeships in most trades in 1859–1860, see Penny, *How Women Can Make Money*. Examples of informal apprenticeship are found in the discussion of Isadore Amaig's [?] becoming an apprentice machinist in the Robert Hoe letterbook, 25 November 1844, Richard Hoe and Company Papers, Rare Book and Manuscript Library, Columbia University, and Peter Cooper's apprenticeship as a coachmaker in Edward Mack, *Peter Cooper—Citizen of New York* (New York, 1949), 38. On apprenticeships in pianomaking see Daniel Spillane, *History of the Pianoforte* (New York, 1890), 201, and Penny, 462. In a few other trades such long apprenticeships were common into the 1820s; see, for example, the five-year contract for John Englis to become a shipwright (including the customary clause not to ''haunt ale-houses'') quoted in G. W. Sheldon, ''The Old Ship-Builders of New York,'' *Harper's Magazine* 65 (1882), 232. In some trades indoor apprenticeships continued: ''It was the custom in the German [cabinetmaking] Factories to Board and lodge in the House,'' the apprentice Henry Price wrote in 1842, Price diary, 25. On printing apprenticeships see Stevens, *History of Typographical Union*, 213. Undercutting wages: for tailoring, Fearon, *Sketches of America*, 33; for printers, Stevens, 213–214.

22. *Herald*, 18 June 1853; see also *British Mechanic's and Labourer's Hand Book*, 109.

left school, enters a workshop, and after a year of application to one branch of the trade, sets himself up as a journeyman; then perhaps he goes to sea for a year or two, and getting tired of that returns home and takes to some other trade; so that during the seven years that a boy is apprenticed in England the young American has gained a smattering of three or four occupations.'' Other British immigrants such as James Burn supported this view:

> Indeed, it is nothing unusual to find men with two or more trades on their finger ends. While in New York I worked shopmate with one genius who was a hatter, a watchmaker, a maker of *understandings,* and a quack M.D. This diversity of business knowledge is accounted for by the easy manner in which young men can obtain situations as learners in almost any branch of business. I have known men who had boxed the compass of almost every sort of employment in the country.[23]

Workers in Britain, who felt lucky to obtain a single apprenticeship, became highly specialized in, and devoted to, ''the trade.'' American workers, on the other hand, ''learn two trades, and that in half the time usually devoted to acquire trades in Ireland.'' In bookbinding, the *Tribune* explained, ''those educated in this country work at [both] Forwarding and Finishing; but the English workmen understand only a single branch.'' A young boarder described by Thomas Gunn had been a bartender, clerk, house painter, and glazier at various times. He was probably not uncommon and contributed, no doubt, to the rapid turnover of labor.[24]

If laid off in one trade, American workers could move comparatively easily into another branch or even an entirely different trade, since they had an ''insight,'' as the expression went, into more than one skill. Some shops actually had employees known as ''insight workers,'' who worked a short time to learn the rudiments of a trade. ''To many of the Americans,'' Burn explained, ''it is not a matter of any great consequence about the failure of the trade they are . . . engaged in, inasmuch as they are ready to apply themselves to some other.'' British immigrants, on the other hand, with their training in a single craft, remained wedded to their trade even when failure seemed probable. To succeed in America, John Prentice noted, ''Scotch proverbs are nearly falsified, 'Jack of all Trades, master of none'; it requires a 'master of all work' to be at home here.'' With a background that stressed the importance of ''the trade,'' however, many British workers were unwilling to change and faced, as Dallas L. Jones puts it, ''unemployment which was literally of their own making.'' Frederick Lockley, who had apprenticed as a

23. *London v. New York,* 10; Burn, *Beggar Boy,* 270–271.
24. Mooney, *Nine Years in America,* 15; see also House of Commons, *Parliamentary Papers* XXXVI (1854), ''Special Report of Mr. George Wallis,'' 13. Bookbinding: *Tribune,* 22 August 1845. Gunn, *Physiology,* 228.

butcher in England, arrived in New York in 1848. He wanted to visit Greeley and see if there was a job available on one of the city newspapers but eventually decided to stay a butcher. "I had a weak and foolish dread of abandoning my trade, a feeling . . . instilled by my parents," Lockley later ruefully wrote. Christoph Vetter in an 1849 book describes his work as a teacher, tobacconist, and painter. Such job changes, Vetter noted, would raise eyebrows in Germany where "a man is judged by his occupation." But, he added, "the immigrant is better off if he discards his notion because otherwise he won't get far." Labor scarcity combined with a high degree of division of labor gave American workers a very different, and much looser, attachment to "the trade" than Europeans had.[25]

Part of the reason apprenticeships were easy to obtain was that the training was not thorough. Because multiple apprenticeships were common, however, an apprentice, by the time he became a journeyman, often had a broader instruction in various trades than his Old World counterpart. "Caleb Snug," an apprentice coachmaker in Saugatuck, Connecticut, learned woodworking, painting, and smithing and was sent by his boss to the trimming room *"as a recreation."* The boy himself, despite the limited instruction he received, probably benefited from a diverse, shallow training and was on the way to becoming the versatile and inventive workman admired by visitors to America.[26]

Within the family economy, enthusiasm for apprenticeships had to do less with training for a son's future than with immediate income. Apprentices got one to three dollars a week in the 1840s and 1850s, which was, of course, turned over to their parents. Boys, according to the British Mechanic, "are fully able to provide for themselves and thereby assist the parent." Thomas Gunn told of one twenty-one-year-old journeyman watchmaker "suspected of having money in a Savings Bank, and of concealing his book, that his mother

25. "Insight workers": *The Coach-Maker's Illustrated Hand-Book* (Philadelphia, 1872), 352. Burn, *Beggar Boy*, 270; Prentice, "Letter," *Scotsman*, 16 April 1834; see also Thomas L. Nichols, *Forty Years of American Life* (London, 1864), 1:378. Dallas L. Jones III, "The Background and Motives of Scottish Emigration to the United States of America in the Period 1815–1861, with Special Reference to Emigrant Correspondence" (diss., University of Edinburgh, 1970), 238; Frederick Lockley, "Memoirs," NYHS, 212; Christoph Vetter, *Zwei Jahre in New-York* (Hof, 1849), 158–159. Wilbur Shepperson's analysis of published accounts by British immigrants determined that only 8 of 34 workers "undertook careers in America outside their primary area of interest or competence. . . . The immigrants' reluctance to attempt a new occupation was one of the most significant factors in prompting return"; Shepperson, *Emigration and Disenchantment* (Norman, Okla., 1965), 186.

26. "The Autobiography of Caleb Snug, of Snugtown, Carriage-Maker," *New York Coach-Maker's Magazine* 2 (1859), 162. On the versatile American worker as he appeared to English parliamentary investigators, see "Wallis Report," 13–16, and House of Commons, *Parliamentary Papers* L, (1854–1855), "Report of the Committee on the Machinery of the United States," 630–631; see also H. J. Habakkuk, *American and British Technology in the Nineteenth Century* (Cambridge, England, 1967).

may n't get it.'' Children's earnings in America were important supplements to the family income.[27]

## WOMEN

The third major group contributing to the family economy was wives and daughters. Their involvement in the labor market was complex and differed markedly from that of men. In the early part of the century women's chances to earn wages in the city were limited. But two factors, urban growth (which sharply increased the demand for servants) and expanded production of ready-made clothes (which enlarged the demand for sewers), raised female employment. By 1850, 36 percent of all the city's manufacturing workers were women.[28]

Throughout the period 1820 to 1860 men made up a substantial majority of immigrants landing in the city, as Chapter 2 pointed out, yet throughout that same period (as Table 12 shows) women made up a small but consistent majority in the city's population. Why? One possibility is that male mortality was higher than female, but the age pattern of the surplus makes it plain this is not the explanation. Mortality was indeed somewhat greater for males, but almost the entire female surplus was in the 15-to-25 age group, and males actually predominated after age thirty-five. In addition, the largest majority of women was found in the city's richest wards. The evidence clearly points to the labor market as an explanation for the city's female majority.[29]

Male immigrants, and men generally, found a substantial range of employment in America's rural and western areas. They could become farm laborers or work on the nation's canal and railway systems. Irish immigrants were especially numerous in these types of employment—in the words of a popular song, ''Paddy Works on the Railroad.'' Women who wanted to work, on the other hand, had little choice but to stay in a city where there was a demand for servants and seamstresses.[30]

27. *British Mechanic's and Labourer's Hand Book*, 106; Gunn, *Physiology*, 228. For a later period, see David Nasaw, *Children of the City: At Work and at Play* (New York, 1986), 130–137.

28. Census Office, *Seventh Census, 1850, Manufactures*, Manuscript.

29. In 1860 the male deathrate was 30.0 per thousand and the female rate 25.9, according to the figures given in the *Annual Report of the City Inspector for the Year 1860*, 63, and Census Office, *Eighth Census, 1860, Population*. The Fifteenth and Eighteenth Wards (the two richest residential wards) had the largest majorities of women—57.4 percent and 55.9 percent respectively. In both wards in the age 15–25 category, women outnumber men *two to one*. The excess is servants. Compiled from the *Census of the State of New York, 1855* (Albany, 1857), 38–39, and William Boyd, ed., *Boyd's New York City Tax Book* (New York, 1857), viii.

30. The male majority in developing areas is noted in George Blackburn and Sherman L. Ricards, Jr., ''A Demographic History of the West: Manistee County, Michigan,'' *Journal of American History* 67 (1970), 604; see also Chapter 9 below.

TABLE 12

Sex of New York City residents, 1820–1860

|      | Male    | Female  | % Female |
|------|---------|---------|----------|
| 1820 | 61,824  | 64,023  | 50.9     |
| 1830 | 95,014  | 102,098 | 51.8     |
| 1840 | 149,654 | 163,056 | 52.1     |
| 1850 | 254,108 | 261,459 | 50.7     |
| 1855 | 302,986 | 326,918 | 51.9     |
| 1860 | 396,990 | 416,679 | 51.2     |

*Source:* Population censuses.

Immigrants were disproportionately young, and Figure 10 shows that the female surplus was concentrated in the age 15-to-30 group. As immigrants landed in New York, the men found the pull of employment outside the city greater than women did, and a substantially higher proportion of female immigrants remained in the city. This pattern was especially true for Irish women who, because they spoke English, could find jobs as servants more easily than could other immigrants—the Irish-born population in the city in 1850 was 58 percent female. The "bulge" for both sexes around ages 15 to 40 in Figure 10 reflects the age structure of immigrants to the city discussed in Chapter 2. This bulge was larger for women than for men because urban employment opportunities for the sexes differed.[31]

The large excess of young women in the city is significant in another way. Women, in both nineteenth-century America and Europe, tended to work for wages only part of their lives. Men were expected to work until death, but regular female employment usually ended when women had children. For women wage labor was part of their life-cycle, and most women, unless they were widows (quite a large category, it should be noted), expected employment to be transitory.[32]

Carol's Pernicone's sample from the 1855 state census of Ward Six shows 48 percent of women age 15 to 19 working but only 19 percent of women over thirty as wage laborers. Employers often complained about the temporary nature of female workers' labor. "The female," one ruled-paper manufac-

31. There were 86,580 Irish-born men in New York City and 117,120 women in 1850; Census Office, *Seventh Census, 1850, Population,* 609. The sex ratio in other immigrant groups was equal or slightly pro-male. Even here, however, the percentage of males was lower than among all immigrants entering the country. Lynn Lees discovered a similar phenomenon in London: Lees, *Exiles of Erin: Irish Migrants in Victorian London* (Ithaca, N.Y., 1979), 89.

32. On this point see Louise Tilly and Joan Scott, *Women, Work, and Family* (New York, 1978), 126–136, and Laurence Glasco, "The Life Cycles and Household Structures of American Ethnic Groups," *Journal of Urban History* 1 (1975), 339–364. For the familial context of women's work in New York in a later period, see John Sharpless and John Rury, "The Political Economy of Women's Work, 1900–1920," *Social Science History* 4 (1980), 317–346.

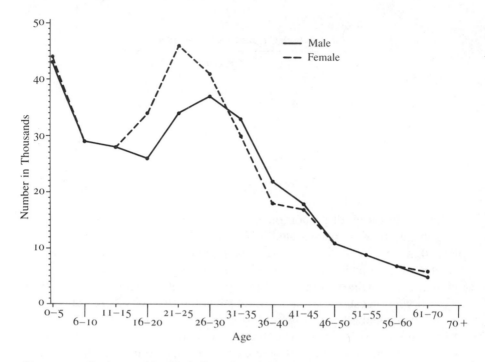

FIGURE 10. Sex by age, New York City, 1855. From Census of the State of New York, 1855. Ages 50–55 and 55–60 are estimates.

turer told Virginia Penny, "when she marries, bids farewell to the shop and her trade." The demographic balance of men and women in the city after age thirty attests to this life-cycle involvement of women. After marriage, women found the nature of the labor market becoming largely irrelevant, and they drifted away from the city with their husbands. When the "working phase" of their life ended, women lost interest in New York's superior employment opportunities for female labor.[33]

Women's wage work in New York, then, was usually impermanent. This generalization obscures a sharp difference, however, between those women who were primary (albeit temporary) wage earners and those who were supplementary wage earners. By "primary" I mean women whose livelihood depended on their wage earnings. "Supplementary" refers to women working to supplement their families' income. The sizes of the two groups are difficult to ascertain, especially since they sharply varied both seasonally and cyclically. Virginia Penny believed half of the city's women workers lived with

33. Compiled from figures in Carol Pernicone, "The 'Bloody Ould Sixth': A Social Analysis of a New York City Working-Class Community in the Mid-Nineteenth Century" (diss., University of Rochester, 1973), 161–162. These statistics do not include taking boarders as wage labor. Penny, *How Women Can Make Money*, 380.

their families and half were on their own in the 1860s, the same estimate the *New York Tribune* had applied to the city's female bookfolders in 1845. Christine Stansell's sample of women in Wards Four and Seven puts the proportion of primary workers at 60 percent. This is much higher than the percentage of primary women workers in the city in the late nineteenth and early twentieth centuries, but it seems clear the *supplementary* workers gave the women's labor market its distinguishing characteristics.[34]

Supplementary female workers were mainly daughters of families in the city, although they also included wives. Contemporary observers of the 1840s and 1850s often portrayed these women as interested in earning "pin money" for themselves. William Hancock, for example, believed that in America "there is nothing degrading in 'going out to work,' and the daughters of many well-to-do people prefer this course to being limited in pocket-money at home." The *Tribune* claimed outwork in the clothing industry was done by "well-off women . . . to relieve the tedium of the absence of their husbands." However, the importance immigrants placed on the work of women makes it clear that supplementary earnings were a significant source of income to many families.[35]

Carol Perniconc found the work of wives and daughters vital to poor Sixth Ward Irish families in 1855, a view confirmed by the immigrants themselves. William Darnley wrote to his wife in England that a friend should "learn you to make caps when he knows you are comeing. I think it would be as well for you to learn before I send for you." Often the work was "informal": the British Mechanic in 1840 suggested wives or daughters do laundry or knit stockings, and in 1849 urban journalist George "Gaslight" Foster told his readers that a worker's "wife must . . . [be] ready to do a little odd job for a neighbor whenever she can make a shilling by it." Mary Van Kleek's conclusion for early-twentieth-century New York that the typical woman worker was a "girl whose home is comfortable but whose work is, nevertheless, necessary to maintain or improve the traditional family standard," is probably too optimistic for the mid-nineteenth century, but it does suggest that for many working-class families, female supplementary workers were, as the British Mechanic put it, "a most important advantage."[36]

34. Virginia Penny, *Think and Act* (1869; rpt. New York, 1971), 215; *Tribune*, 20 August 1845; Christine Stansell, "Women of the Laboring Poor in New York City, 1820–1860" (diss., Yale University, 1979), 66, 68. The census was usually taken during the summer slack season. Leslie Woodcock Tentler found only 10–25 percent of working women were primary workers in the early twentieth century: see Tentler, *Wage-Earning Women: Industrial Work and Family Life in the United States, 1900–1930* (1979; rpt. New York, 1982), 115.

35. Perniconc, " 'Bloody Ould Sixth,' " 157; William Hancock, *An Emigrant's Five Years in the Free States of America* (London, 1860), 212. *Tribune*, 8 June 1853.

36. Perniconc, " 'Bloody Ould Sixth,' " 152–162; William Darnley, letter to his wife, 22 May 1859, Darnley Family Letters, Rare Books and Manuscripts Division, The New York Public Library, Astor, Lenox and Tilden Foundations. *British Mechanic's and Labourer's Hand*

With so many supplementary workers, there was no labor scarcity for women, but immigrants were often surprised that their wives and daughters could make money. One witness from County Sligo explained the Irish situation to an English committee investigating the poor law: "Where there are so many men out of work it cannot be expected that women should be often employed." Jobs may have been difficult for women to get in New York, but immigrant families seemed pleasantly surprised to find that any work was available. "However large his family may be, there are certain prospects of ready and remunerative employ for the female branch of it," wrote the British Mechanic. Women, like men, were usually hired through friends or, because "women's work" was so seasonal, through help wanted advertisements in newspapers. Wages were very low: in the 1840s one to two dollars was the weekly norm for experienced sewers; in the 1850s, $1.50 to $2.50 was the typical range for women's wages.[37]

Such wages were small but represented a significant supplement to a family's income. Indeed, because the board and room of supplementary workers was largely paid for by the father's wages, competition for jobs forced wages *below* the subsistence level in the needle trades. Supplementary workers essentially defined the market for "women's work," with disastrous consequences for primary workers trying to earn a living by their own labor. The *Herald* noted the primary-supplementary divergence among the city's straw sewers: "Some [women] who live with their parents, and are not wholly dependent upon their work for a subsistence, are enabled to dress better and indulge in some of the luxuries of life, but a large number, who have no other means of support but their needle, and whose health is their only capital, seldom vary the dull monotony of their lives with amusements of any kind." Penny explained the unfortunate consequence of supplementary workers for the market for female labor: "Those girls that live at home can afford to do work cheaper generally than others. Such girls are drawbacks to those who pay their board." Primary women found the labor market glutted and wages driven down so low as to make it difficult for them to obtain the "necessaries of life."[38]

Most primary female workers were servants. Usually servants, or "help"

*Book,* 104–105; George Foster, *New York in Slices* (New York, 1849), 97; Mary Van Kleek, *A Seasonal Industry—A Study of the Millinery Trade in New York* (New York, 1917), 61. Such informal work would almost certainly not be reflected in the census returns. *British Mechanic's and Labourer's Hand Book,* 104.

37. Poor Inquiry (Ireland), Appendix D, 85. On women's labor in England, see Anderson, *Family Structure,* 71. *British Mechanic's and Labourer's Hand Book,* 104; see also Mooney, *Nine Years in America,* 16–17. Wages: *Working Man's Advocate,* 11 September 1845; *Tribune,* 14 August 1845. See Table 7.

38. *Herald,* 7 June 1853; see also *Tribune,* 20 August 1845. Penny, *How Women Can Make Money,* 316, see also 326.

as they preferred to be called, were live-in help, although "going out to day-work" and working as "house-cleaners" were common by the 1840s and 1850s. Live-in jobs were not attractive to wives or daughters who already had a place to live, serving to insulate to some degree the labor market from competition from supplementary workers. The labor market was further restricted because, in an oft-repeated comment, "nothing but compulsion" would induce native-born Americans to become servants. Before the 1840s there was a shortage of servants. The great increase in immigration in that decade changed the situation considerably and, although middle-class complaints about the shortage of "good help" continued to be heard, working women knew better. Virginia Penny pointed to the large number of "situations wanted" by domestics in the *Herald* as evidence of "what a surplus there is of domestics in cities." Hired through intelligence agencies organized to facilitate domestic employment, the thirty thousand help in the city made service the largest female occupation.[39]

Women could earn a living as servants but not in the needle trades, the second-largest female occupation in New York. A labor market that looked inviting to immigrants like Darnley, who looked to supplement his family's income, was almost hopeless for women who tried to live on their own labor. The Brooks Brothers spokesman who told Penny in 1860 that in the sewing trades "there is a surplus of hands in New York" was putting it mildly. As Penny pointed out, "in New York city there is always a surplus of girls seeking labor; they are daughters of the poorer classes. . . . I am told by manufacturers, in New York, that daily applications of girls for employment . . . is a source of annoyance, and that they are obliged to paste placards on their door to avoid them." One clothier boasted to a journalist that "if any girl . . . wants to stop working at those prices, she's *perfectly* welcome to stop; there's a dozen wants it, where one gets it." For primary workers, the difficulty of employment and low wages made what the *Tribune* called the "wretchedness of the needlewomen" proverbial. Only by rooming together could widows and single young women make enough to live on, and then only barely enough. Thirty percent of the city's needlewomen were aided by the New York Association for Improving the Conditions of the Poor in 1858, a group probably coterminous with primary workers in the trade.[40]

Women's work, as Chapter 2 noted, was a part of the traditional European peasant family economy. Women in New York continued to work within a

39. *British Mechanic's and Labourer's Hand Book,* 104; *Annual Report of the A.I.C.P. for the Year 1852,* 26; Penny, *How Women Can Make Money,* 425; see also *Report of the Chamber of Commerce, 1859,* 158. Robert Ernst, *Immigrant Life in New York City, 1825–1863* (1949; rpt. New York, 1979), 215.

40. Penny, *How Women Can Make Money,* 113, 303–304; Wirt Sikes, "Among the Poor Girls," *Putnam's Magazine* n.s. 1 (1868), 435; *Tribune,* 8 June 1853; *Annual Report of the A.I.C.P. for the Year 1858,* 30.

family context, but in the New World in their late teens and early twenties they labored for wages. Women who desired to supplement family income were delighted that wage work was available in the city. But the large number of supplementary wages earners kept wages for all women, even those who were independent, below the subsistence level.

## FLUCTUATION IN DEMAND FOR LABOR

In describing the labor market in general terms, I made only brief mention of one factor that powerfully influenced the demand for labor, namely the very strong cyclical and seasonal variations in the nineteenth-century urban economy. All workers, male and female, young and old, skilled and unskilled, found that their employment chances diminished and increased seasonally. A segmented labor market had begun to develop in the New York City region in the nineteenth century, with a mechanized sector and an intermittently employed labor-intensive sector. This segmentation, however, was only beginning, and almost all work in the antebellum city was highly cyclical and seasonally sensitive.[41]

The period between 1820 and 1860 saw marked fluctuations in the nation's economy which had, of course, an impact on the city's workers. There were four major *cyclical* downturns—1828, 1837, 1854, and 1857—and those of 1837 and 1857 were extraordinarily severe. Between these downturns were periods of varying economic health, ranging from mediocre in the mid-1820s to the boom of the late 1840s and early 1850s. Depressions, although common, were looked on as aberrations by most workers, and good times were considered the norm. I have followed this contemporary attitude, and the preceding section on the labor market refers to nonrecessionary periods.[42]

Because a large number of small firms in the city depended on outside agencies, business collapsed very rapidly when panics began and an immediate decline in the demand for labor occurred in most trades. New York, whose imports had risen to $118 million in 1836, found them reduced to $68 million by 1838. The *New York New Era* described the employment situation in 1837:

> At no period of its history has there been so great a degree of general distress in this city as there is at this day. Of its mechanics and other working men, at least ten thousand are now without employment: and the wives and families of these, which amount . . . to ten thousand persons more, are suffering want. . . . Of

41. In Massachusetts cyclical and seasonal unemployment continued to be widespread until World War I; see Alexander Keyssar, *Out of Work: The First Century of Unemployment in Massachusetts* (Cambridge, England, 1986).
42. On the business cycle in this period see Stanley Lebergott, *Manpower in Economic Growth* (New York, 1964), 172–178.

seamstresses, book folders, bonnet makers and other industrious females, . . .
three thousand are at this moment in pining destitution, and exposed to heartless
temptation.

Henry Walter remembered his experience: "Business was at a stand still. . . .
I had nothing to do. There was no call for Jewellry. Bread and butter was the
need of most folks in those trying times. . . . I had been brought to a similar
position as regards finances. As I was in when I first landed in America. . . .
Such a time of distress has never been experienced since that time in this
Country."[43]

In the 1857 downturn, demand for labor melted away with extraordinary
rapidity. Layoffs averaged a thousand a day in November. The International
Typographical Union No. 6 lost two-thirds of its members by 1858; four-fifths
of the city's coopers lost their jobs within three weeks. Workers, like the
employees at Stephenson's Coachworks on East 27th Street who went on two-
thirds time in November 1857, considered themselves lucky to have any work
at all. Ernest Hagen, then a boss cabinetmaker, remembered the 1857 depression:

> The outlook was not very bright—we worked ourselves at the bench with 2 or 3
> hired men and could hardly make as much as our men, which was about one
> Dollar a day. . . . We economized where we could and held on, hoping for a
> good time to come. We worked mostly for the trade, suplying the furniture
> stores, who paid very poorly; and we had to wait a long time to get it and also
> lost some pretty large bills alltogether by failures.

Housepainter William Darnley's letter of 25 October 1857 to his wife in England describes what must have been typical experiences for many workers:

> The whole of the Banks have suspended payment with a verry Few exceptions.
> Machine Shops and all other Kind of establishments are turning their men off
> every week. The man I work for has turned 4–5 off within this last month. I
> have lost about 3 pounds 15 shillings in wages since I last wrote. He told me that
> I shall have a share of what work comes in but he says he dare [?] not think it will
> be much as things are so bad. Indeed their is a great deal of his work stopt and he
> cannot get money for the work he has done.[44]

43. Francis J. Grund, *The Americans in Their Moral, Social and Political Relations* (1837;
rpt. New York, 1968), 292; Robert Greenhalgh Albion, *The Rise of New York Port, 1815–1860*
(New York, 1939), 381. *New York New Era* quoted in *Nile's Weekly Register* 52 (1837), 227;
Walter autobiography, 29, 33, 32.

44. Carl Degler, "Labor in the Economy and Politics of New York City, 1850–1860; A Study
of Early Industrialization" (diss., Columbia University, 1952), esp. 81–82, 177–183; *Annual
Report of the A.I.C.P. for the Year 1857*, 21. The information about Stephenson is from New
York vol. 367, 400, R. G. Dun and Company Collection, Baker Library, Harvard Graduate
School of Business Administration. Elizabeth Ingerman, ed., "Personal Experiences of an Old
New York Cabinetmaker," *Antiques* 84 (1963), 580; William Darnley, letter to his wife,
25 October 1857.

These periodic recessions and depressions affected the skilled and the unskilled job markets almost equally; having a trade was no guarantee of work during hard times. The Association for Improving the Condition of the Poor (A.I.C.P.) remarked during the short but severe downturn in 1854 that "it was very trying to witness so large a number of our valuable fellow-citizens, including industrious mechanics, and energetic women who never before had needed charity, now asking aid to save themselves from suffering." Skilled workers would take any job, even an unskilled one, when conditions were bad. The A.I.C.P. noted the "eager willingness to accept of little jobs" in 1854, and in 1857 Darnley began "new work" (clearly some semiskilled construction job) because he thought "we had better do that than be idle. We should only make the same wages as we should at home but I can assure you that their is plenty that would be glad to get it as we have got it." The sharp decline in immigration during depressions (see Appendix C) did counteract, to a small degree, the contraction of the city's labor market, but even so very few workers were neither out of work nor feared losing their jobs.[45]

As important as cyclical fluctuations were to the city's economy, *seasonal* variations were even more critical. It would be hard to overstate the seasonal nature of most work in the city. "Nature and human institutions conspire to produce seasonal variation in industrial and trade activity," wrote Simon Kuznets in 1933. In the antebellum period, however, climatic variations were clearly more significant. Throughout the period 1820 to 1860, with a perceptible but limited trend toward regularization in the 1850s, New York's business was extremely variable.[46]

Sharp climatic changes in the New World affected both the *demand* for labor—by periodically increasing and decreasing the demand for products manufactured or shipped from the city—and the *supply* of labor—by making work, especially outdoor work, difficult. Although New York was especially sensitive to seasonal variation because of the concentration of labor-intensive industry in the city, seasonality was a common part of nineteenth-century economic life. The main reasons were endemic to the mid-nineteenth-century American economy.

The climate of the American northeast was far more severe than that of western Europe (see Figure 11), and before the effective integration of New York into the nation's rail network in the 1850s, the freezing of the Hudson—the city's great avenue of trade—drastically slowed demand for labor. Between 1844 and 1854 the Hudson was frozen between New York and Albany an average of eighty-nine days each winter. Usually it froze in December and melted in March; often the Erie Canal was shut six weeks longer than the Hudson. Every winter the city's hinterland was cut off for three or four

45. *Annual Report of the A.I.C.P. for the Year 1855*, 21, 22. William Darnley, letter to his wife, 29 November 1857.
46. Simon Kuznets, *Seasonal Variations in Industry and Trade* (New York, 1933), 9.

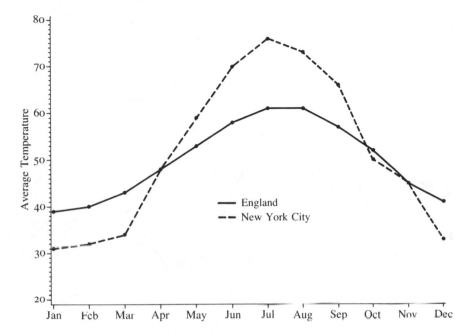

FIGURE II. Average monthly temperature, New York City 1850–1863 and England 1941–1970 (in degrees Fahrenheit).

months. This pattern was compounded by the seasonality of oceanic transport; most ships other than packets avoided winter crossings.[47]

Because trade was so dependent on climate, rural merchants carefully timed their purchases in the city. Frederick Wyse explained the process in 1846:

> The business season of New York, or rather when its intercourse with the interior is more frequent, . . . may be considered to commence in the month of April, or when the cold and winter season has disappeared, and given way to a warmer and more congenial climate, and continues during the month of May, a part of the month of June, and again in the Fall months of September, October and November following, and before that the winter can re-assert its influence, in closing up the varied channels of communication with the interior.

Country merchants came to the city, "prowling from countinghouse to countinghouse to find the best bargains . . . to fill their shelves," twice yearly— once to replenish their stocks after the winter was over and again in the fall to stock up before ice closed the Hudson.[48]

47. *Hunt's Merchant's Magazine* 34 (1856), 245; Carl Condit, *The Port of New York* (Chicago, 1980), 20; Albion, *Rise of New York Port,* 41.
48. Francis Wyse, *America, Its Realities and Resources* (London, 1846), 2:371; see also Carol Halpert Schwartz, "Retail Trade Development in New York State in the Nineteenth Century with Special Reference to the Country Store" (diss., Columbia University, 1963), 27–29, 145. Albion, *Rise of New York Port,* 280. Henry Southworth, a milliner, describes seasonal

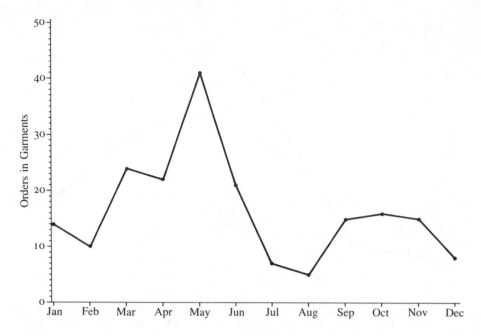

FIGURE 12. Orders of a clothing firm, 1844–1845. Ledger of an unidentified tailor, probably Hanford Reynolds, Montgomery Collection, Rare Book and Manuscript Library, Columbia University.

Most New York City trades therefore had two busy seasons—spring (the larger and more important) and fall—and two slack seasons—winter and summer (see Figures 12–15). Each trade had a slightly different season, and the season itself could be shortened or lengthened by the business cycle, as during the boom of 1850 when wholesale milliner Henry Southworth wrote in his diary on June 5, "extremely busy at the store, this season business had held out later than any former season." Nevertheless, the pattern of busy and slow seasons each year defined most industry in New York. A few highly capitalized trades such as typecasting (Figure 16) showed little seasonal variation, but those in the city's dominant "sweated trades" fluctuated markedly.[49]

Seasonality of demand for products does not in theory have to translate into seasonality in demand for labor. Indeed, at a few firms such as Brown and Bliss, cabinetmakers, "the works are run all the year round, the surplus piled up in dull seasons being sold at other seasons." For most manufacturers,

---

visits by retailers, mostly from upstate New York and Connecticut, to his wholesale shop, in Southworth diary, 1850–1851, NYHS.

49. Penny, *How Women Can Make Money*, is by far the best source on seasonality in the city. For earlier periods the *British Mechanic* and the *Tribune* articles in 1845 and 1853 offer good information. Southworth diary, 5 June 1850.

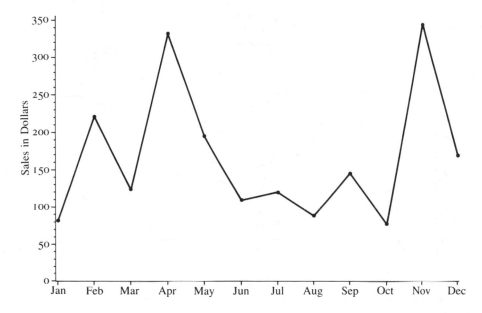

FIGURE 13. Sales of a soapmaker, 1815–1817. Smith and Colgate account books, Baker Library, Harvard Graduate School of Business Administration.

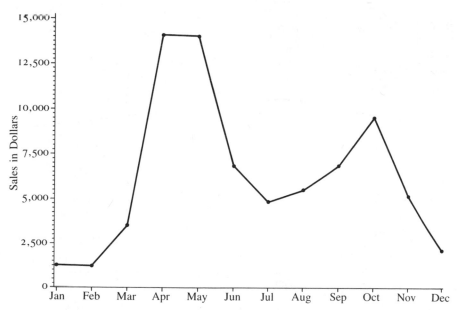

FIGURE 14. Sales of a carpetmaker, 1838–1839. Probably C. S. Higgins Co., New York. Bigelow-Sanford Carpet Papers, Baker Library, Harvard Graduate School of Business Administration.

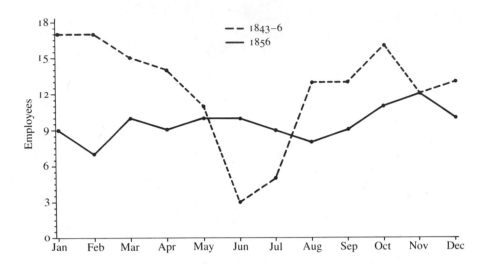

FIGURE 15. Employment in combmaking, 1843–1846 and 1856. Thomas Palmer account books, The New-York Historical Society, New York City.

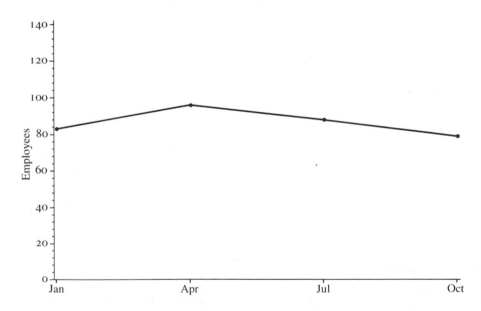

FIGURE 16. Employment in typecasting, 1859–1863. Day list of a New York City typecasting firm, probably Bruce and Co., Typographical Papers, Rare Book and Manuscript Library, Columbia University.

however, "stock work"—piling up a surplus—was not an option. Because of the city's high rents, few bosses could afford to store a large inventory. Clothiers were especially reluctant to engage in stock work; ready-made clothes were "the most unprofitable of all stocks to carry over," the *United States Economist and Dry Goods Reporter* explained, because a style change could reduce the value by half in a matter of months. Even when style was not a factor, a coachmaker's guide noted,

> it is by no means uncommon to hear carriage-builders regretting their lack of energy during the winter when the spring trade opens and finds them with but a small quantity of new work finished. . . . We are well aware that lack of capital prevents a good many firms from running a full force of hands during the winter when there are but few if any sales of work.[50]

Trades such as clothing and millinery experienced a weak off-season local demand—"the city trade"—but many, perhaps most, workers expected to be without work two or three months every year. For example, Thomas Palmer, a combmaker on Duane Street, employed an average of seventeen workers in January and February between 1843 and 1846 but only four in June and July (see Figure 15). Even those not laid off were likely to be underemployed. Among city saddlers, "in dull seasons and in winter chequers was a favorite game," and James Burn lamented that "there are few things more disagreeable . . . than that of hanging about a workshop . . . to get a share of any windfall that might come in the way." If the labor market deteriorated in slack seasons, then in busy season the reverse was true. "In busy seasons good hands are very scarce" in the needle trades, according to Penny. Time-and-a-half pay for overtime was the rule, and working all night not uncommon. Workers viewed this cycle, with periods of overwork followed by seasonal unemployment, not as a cause for protest but as a natural part of life. A winter without layoffs was as unimaginable as a winter without cold weather. One coachmaker's guide stated the commonplace contemporary view: "It is a well-known fact, that there is, and always will be, a surplus of hands in the winter season, or a deficiency in the spring and summer."[51]

The New York climate sharply limited the *supply* of workers. During winter it was often too cold to work outside, and both the building trades and

50. Brown and Bliss: Census Office, *Tenth Census, 1880, Wages in Manufacturing* (Washington, 1886), XX, 449; see also on stock work Van Kleek, *A Seasonal Industry*, 7, 9, and *Report of the Chamber of Commerce, 1859*, 225. *United States Economist and Dry Goods Reporter* n.s. 11 (1857), 70; *The Coach-Maker's Illustrated Hand-Book* (Philadelphia, 1872), 351–352.

51. Thomas Palmer account book, 1843–1846, NYHS; Frank W. Norcross, *A History of the New York Swamp* (New York, 1901), 66; Burn, *Beggar Boy*, 313; Penny, *How Women Can Make Money*, 297; *Times*, 2 March 1859; *Coach-Maker's Hand-Book*, 354.

shipbuilding slowed virtually to a halt (see Figure 17). William Darnley complained to his wife that, although he had a housepainting job in February 1861, "we could not get along with it in consequence of the frost." Even when work was available, laborers' wages in dockwork and construction were "reduced by reason of short hours" 25 cents a day. Because some shops were poorly heated, extremely cold weather often made it impossible to carry on even indoor work. "This [1852] being the severest winter that was here in twenty years . . . there was nothing doing . . . people could not get without doors," one boxmaker wrote to Ireland. When the winter was mild or a thaw occurred, "out-door work is resumed at intervals." The wages of workers in many trades, especially laborers, were closely dependent on the severity of the winter.[52]

In the summer, conversely, it was often too hot to work. Most of the city's workers came from a climate considerably milder than North America's. The summer temperature in England is almost fifteen degrees below that of New York (see Figure 11). Immigrants were accustomed to uncomfortably cold temperatures but not uncomfortably hot ones, and letters from immigrants invariably describe the summer heat as most dreadful. "It is unbearably hot here, sweat is dripping from me as I write this. People stay out of doors at night instead of going to bed—dozens are daily struck dead—yes! hundreds," wrote Welsh immigrant John Lloyd. James Burn dreaded hot weather and was so completely exhausted at the end of each hot day that he had no appetite.[53]

Torrid weather slowed indoor and outdoor work considerably. There were 260 deaths from heat stroke during the brutal summer of 1853, and the building trades sometimes suspended work between noon and four during heat waves. Even those working inside, though spared the danger faced by laborers in the sun, found the heat made work difficult. In July 1846 Richard M. Hoe, the printing press manufacturer, wrote a customer in Buffalo: "It is our

52. William Darnley, letter to his wife, 18 February 1861; see also *Annual Report of the A.I.C.P. for the Year 1868*, 36, and Mooney, *Nine Years in America*, 85–86. "Short hours": *Tribune*, 31 March 1860. Laborers' wages on the city's public works are given in U.S. Congress, Senate, Committee on Finance, *Report on Wholesale Prices, Wages and Transportation*, "by Mr. Aldrich," 52d Cong., 2d sess., 1893, S. Rept. 1394, pt. 2, 517–522; this report shows that wages were seasonally reduced $0.25. The "Contractor's journal, 1815–1820," Rare Books and Manuscripts Division, The New York Public Library, Astor, Lenox and Tilden Foundations, shows that laborers' wages were upped two shillings in March or April and reduced by the same amount in November. Anonymous New York boxmaker, letter to the Society of St. Vincent de Paul, 3 February 1852, reprinted in John Nicholas Murray, *Ireland: Industrial, Political and Social* (London, 1870), 178.

53. Franklin Hough, ed., *The Results of a Series of Meteorological Observations*, 2d ser. (Albany, N.Y., 1872), 79. John Lloyd, letter to his parents, 1 August 1868, in Alan Conway, ed., *The Welsh in America: Letters from the Immigrants* (Minneapolis, 1961), 47. On the reaction of Irish immigrants to the heat, see Miller, "Emigrants and Exiles," 779–780. Burn, *Three Years among the Working-Classes*, 304.

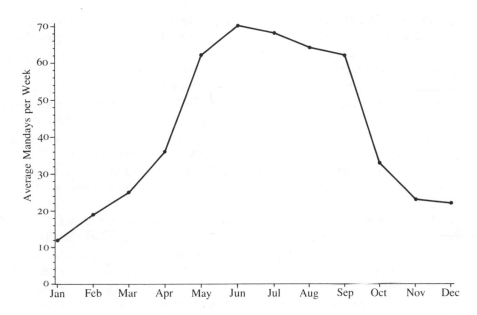

FIGURE 17   Employment in construction, 1815–1820. Contractor's journal, Rare Books and Manuscripts Division, The New York Public Library, Astor, Lenox and Tilden Foundations.

expectation to be able to ship your press next week but it may possibly be early in the following week if this *extremely* warm weather continues as we find that a number of our men are away from sickness and other causes.'' In summer as in winter, the climate served to limit severely the supply of labor.[54]

The completion of the Erie Railroad to near Buffalo and the Hudson River Railroad to Albany, both in 1851, largely freed the city from the seasonal restrictions imposed by the freezing of the Hudson. Horace Greeley, in comparing the 1830s to the 1860s, wrote that ''winter is relatively dull now, but not nearly so stagnant as it formerly was.'' Thomas Palmer's account book (Figure 15) suggests that in combmaking, the sharp seasonal pattern of the 1840s was giving way by the 1850s to more regular trade. However, the city's emergence as a center of labor-intensive manufacture ensured that seasonality would continue to be significant. In addition, the factors affecting labor supply—cold winters and hot summers—did not change. Laborers remained the group most prone to seasonal unemployment; those building Central Park averaged only 210 working days in 1862.[55]

54. *Annual Report of the City Inspector for the Year 1853* (New York, 1854), 199. ''A Working Man's Recollections of America,'' 104. R. Hoe, letter to E. R. Jewett, 11 July 1846, Hoe Papers; see also *United States Economist and Dry Goods Reporter* 24, no. 725, (1859), 2.

55. Condit, *Port of New York*, 33, 58. As late as 1865, however, the tonnage of goods carried by the state's railways only equaled that of the Erie Canal. David Ellis, ''Rivalry between the

Although laborers were clearly the male group most affected by seasonal unemployment, women workers were also subject to cyclical and seasonal influences. According to economist Jacob Mincer, "labor force sensitivity to employment conditions is a characteristic of the secondary labor force," and certainly this was the case in antebellum New York. Women, and to a lesser extent children, responded to increased employment opportunities during booms and busy seasons by moving into the job market. Supplementary women workers exchanged housework for wage work when jobs were easy to get and wages high. The process was obviously a tremendous advantage for labor-intensive industries such as clothing, because it gave them an extraordinarily flexible workforce and, no doubt, encouraged firms to locate in the city.[56]

The participation of women in the labor force was procyclical, as a comparison of the 1850 and 1860 *Census of Manufacturers* suggests. In 1850, during the Age of Gold, a high percentage of women worked in manufacturing. After 1857 and the near-collapse of the city's economy, female labor force participation returned to a lower level (see Table 13). The contrast between male and female workers is clear: manufacturing employment among men dropped less than 20 percent, among women almost 50 percent. Women were more sensitive than men to changes in the city's economy. Indeed, the female percentage of the labor force in 1850, during the Age of Gold, was 36.4 percent—the highest at any time during the century.[57]

Women workers, with the important exception of servants, were thus more liable than men to seasonal variation. The divergence between busy and slack seasons was so great it could be overcome only by recruiting women out of the home when business was brisk. In dress trimming, only one-quarter of those

New York Central and Erie Railroad," *New York History* 29 (1948), 269. Greeley, *Recollections,* 87; Eugene P. Moehring, *Public Works and Patterns of Urban Real Estate Growth in Manhattan, 1835–1894* (New York, 1981), 247.

56. Jacob Mincer, "Labor-Force Participation and Unemployment: A Review of Recent Evidence," in John F. Burton et al., eds., *Readings in Labor Market Analysis* (New York, 1971), 89; see also Glen G. Cain, "Unemployment and the Labor-Force Participation of Secondary Workers," *Industrial and Labor Relations Review* 20 (1967), 275–297, esp. 284. The central concern of both Mincer and Cain is cyclical variation, but the logic of their interpretations can be applied to seasonal variation as well.

57. The inaccuracy of the population censuses regarding female labor is well-known; see Pernicone, "'Bloody Ould Sixth,'" 169, and Douglas Shaw, *The Making of an Immigrant City: Ethnic and Cultural Conflict in Jersey City, New Jersey, 1850–1877* (New York, 1976), 36. The accuracy of the manufacturing censuses on this point is less clear; they may understate the true number of working women, at least in part because women's employment was so transitory, but they seem adequate for comparative purposes. The female percentage of the manufacturing labor force is: 1850—36.4, 1860—26.8, 1870—24.9, 1880—32.9, 1890—29.5, 1900—31.3. The 1850 and 1860 figures are from the manuscript returns. There is no solid evidence that children were drawn into the labor market in booms, though evidence on school attendance in the 1830s and 1840s cited by Kaestle, *Evolution of Urban School,* 95, suggests this may have been the case.

TABLE 13

Workers engaged in manufacturing in New York City, by sex, 1850 and 1860

|  | Total | No. in manufacturing | % |
|---|---|---|---|
| *Men* |  |  |  |
| 1850 | 254,108 | 53,781 | 21.2 |
| 1860 | 396,990 | 68,358 | 17.2 |
| *Women* |  |  |  |
| 1850 | 261,459 | 30,799 | 11.8 |
| 1860 | 416,679 | 25,163 | 6.0 |

*Sources:* Population censuses, 1850 and 1860. Manufacturing censuses, manuscript, 1850 and 1860.

employed in the busy season worked during the January-to-July slack season, and in straw sewing, "of the whole three thousand [sewers] there are not perhaps three hundred who are dependent on it." When the busy season began in 1852, an advertisement for five hundred sewing girls drew "an hour after the time for calling passes . . . hundreds of girls flocking upstairs to get the work." When the three-to-six-month busy season was over, "inferior hands are turned off without an hour's notice." One clothing manufacturer actually had no permanent employees. Some women might find other employment in the needle trades, but most were out of work. For primary women workers trying to live on their income as seamstresses, this pattern meant recurrent unemployment and poverty. Supplementary workers could return to the home, following the early-twentieth-century pattern described by John Commons for the clothing industry in which, during the busy season, "housewives, who formerly worked at the trade and abandoned it after marriage, are called into service for an increased price of a dollar or two a week." Indeed, the strict demarcation of home and work was a middle-class concept. In many trades work was done at home, and many housewives periodically reentered the labor market.[58]

Women and unemployed workers were especially prone to seasonal variations in the labor market, but almost all workers were subject to such fluctuations. The main method by which workers tried to counteract seasonal (and to a lesser extent cyclical) changes was by varying their saving and buying patterns in response to predictable slack periods (see Chapter 6). Another, but less common, response was to try to change jobs. The busy seasons in various

58. *Herald*, 7 June 1853; William Bobo, *Glimpses of New-York City* (New York, 1852), 105. This account is slightly fictionalized but Penny, *How Women Can Make Money*, 301–303, 309, 352, makes it clear it was grounded in reality. Sikes, "Among the Poor Girls," 436. John R. Commons, "The Sweating System in the Clothing Industry," in Commons, ed., *Trade Unionism and Labor Problems* (Boston, 1905), 318; see also Van Kleek, *A Seasonal Industry*, 59–60.

parts of the clothing industry did not completely coincide, so that when the straw-sewing season ended in June or July some women found work as seamstresses during the late summer and early fall. Multiple apprenticeships may have encouraged many men also to look for work in other trades. In general, however, seasons tended to overlap too much to make such a change a real possibility.[59]

For some male workers, "tramping" was a way to avoid winter unemployment. Some printers went to the South during the winter, often to help print state legislative proceedings, and so did workers in shipbuilding and construction. Emigrant guidebooks recommended such trips during the winter, but substantial funds were needed for such a journey. Tramping probably did mitigate the impact of seasonality to a limited degree, especially for single workers, but the difficulty and expense involved made it an ineffective solution for most laborers.[60]

WORK, POWER, AND THE FAMILY

The city's labor market was vitally important to the city's workers. Immigrants, who made up three-quarters of the city's labor force, had come to America for economic reasons, and their behavior was strongly influenced by employment conditions. In leaving native villages, friends, and relatives in the Old World, they had staked almost everything on obtaining a better living in America.

In the United States, unlike Europe, the supply of labor did not greatly exceed demand; sometimes labor was even scarce. But there was one catch: the American climate was much less temperate than most of western Europe, and the demand for labor, although fundamentally stronger, was more variable in the New World. British workers were not unused to seasonality in their homeland, but James Burn and other immigrants agreed that American work was *more* irregular than English—a novel and unpleasant prospect. Irish immigrants, though also dismayed at the severity of American weather, were more accustomed to the seasonal pattern of rural life and hence found the sharp ups and downs of the job market less dismaying.[61]

59. On changing jobs see *Herald*, 7 June 1853, and Penny, *How Women Can Make Money*.

60. On tramping see the *Tribune*, 11 September 1845; Wyse, *America*, 2:11, 18; and *British Mechanic's and Labourer's Hand Book*, 229, 275, 279–280.

61. P. J. McGuire called attention to seasonality later in the century: "The fluctuations in the labor market . . . do not occur to such a marked extent in Europe." U.S. Congress, Senate, Committee on Education and Labor, *Report of the Senate Committee upon Relations between Labor and Capital* (Washington, 1885), 1:337. Seasonality in London in the nineteenth century is described in Gareth Stedman Jones, *Outcast London: A Study in the Relationship between Classes in Victorian Society* (1971; rpt. Harmondsworth, England, 1976), 33–51, 376–384. Seasonal employment in Ireland: Poor Inquiry (Ireland), Supplement to Appendix D, 1–393. See also Chapter 6 below.

Though immigrants came to America's shores out of a desire for economic security, most were not profit-maximizing individualists. To the contrary, as many recent studies suggest, their frame of reference was not the individual but the family. The labor scarcity in America was significant not because all family members worked—immigrants were used to that—but because they all worked for *wages,* and most enthusiastically adapted to the new situation. Two factors, economic orientation and family orientation, together determined labor-market participation: because they were economically oriented, immigrants responded strongly to seasonal and cyclical variations in the urban economy; because they were family-oriented, their work was closely tied to the family life-cycle.

Not only did familial considerations influence labor-market entry, but the labor market, in turn, influenced the family. Because children and wives were such substantial assets to the working-class family economy, the labor market had an impact on power relationships within the family itself. The oft-noted independence of American children may have been one result. Thomas Dudgeon, a Scots immigrant to New York, noted in 1841 that "the facility with which boys and girls obtain board, clothing, and education, for their labour, is so considerable, that if a boy or girl is sharply rebuked for any misdemeanour, they view themselves quite entitled to controvert the matter." Severe tensions often developed between parents and working sons—"boys are men at sixteen . . . they all work for themselves," Thomas D'Arcy McGee complained. Many young males could find paying work with wages high enough to support themselves outside the family and hence were quite independent; they could always move out if parents were too demanding. American conditions thus posed a serious challenge to the strong relation of immigrant sons to the traditional family economy.[62]

Though wage work increased the autonomy of children of both sexes, its impact on girls was much smaller. Daughters were very helpful in supplementing family income, but they received lower wages and had much more difficulty sustaining themselves outside the family. They were thus more closely tied to the home and much less independent.

If single women found that working outside the home did not make them independent, for married women the situation was different. Conditions in the city allowed married women to find informal or seasonal work, which gave them an increased, though still much inferior, economic status in relation to

---

62. Thomas Dudgeon, *A Nine Years Residence, and a Nine Months Tour on Foot, in the States of New York and Pennsylvania, for the Use of Labourers, Farmers and Emigrants* (Edinburgh, 1841), 14; see also Robert Williams Letter, 22 May 1844, in Conway, *The Welsh,* 25. Thomas D'Arcy McGee, *A History of Irish Settlers in North America* (Boston, 1852), 236; see also Nasaw, *Children of the City,* 132. This is similar to the pattern Michael Anderson found in Preston, England where "children's high individual wages allowed them to enter into relational bargains on terms of more or less precise equality," Anderson, *Family Structure,* 131; see also Tentler, *Wage-Earning Women,* 107–112.

their husbands. By leaving the wife less time for housework, moreover, such paid work compelled the husband to assume some household responsibilities, and British immigrants were often startled by the way men in New York City helped their wives around the house. James Burn noted that men do "a considerable amount of the slip-slop work [housework]" in New York. The husband "lights the stove-fire, empties the slops, makes ready his own breakfast, and if his work lies at a distance he packs up his midday meal." When women worked for pay in the city, one result seems to have been a devolution of household responsibilities. Overall, the status of married working-class women was higher in the New World than in the Old. Burn explained to his readers:

> It is a common thing for matrons among the working-classes in England to call their husband by the title of "old masters." Were a married woman to do this within earshot in America, she would be held up to derision, and the idea of either husband or wife acknowledging one or the other to be "Boss" would be quite out of the question.[63]

Although the impact of the workplace involvement of women and children on familial power relations is largely conjectural, it does call attention to the commanding importance of the labor market in workers' lives. Immigrants, after all, had crossed the Atlantic in hopes of greater income. The tight labor market that was largely responsible for large-scale immigration to America continued to have a powerful effect after immigrants arrived in the New World. Not only did it influence family relations, but it also had a significant effect on workplace turnover, the pace of work, and employer-employee relationships.

---

63. Burn, *Three Years among the Working-Classes,* 77; see also "A Working Man's Recollections of America," 106; Gunn, *Physiology,* 33; Faye E. Dudden, *Serving Women: Household Service in Nineteenth Century America* (Middletown, Conn., 1983), 136–137. "In London, and probably elsewhere, when wives worked outside the home, their husbands more often worked inside it": Michael Young and Peter Willmott, *The Symmetrical Family* (Harmondsworth, England, 1973), 114. However, other studies have shown that husbands do not automatically contribute more to family tasks when their wives are employed; see Joseph H. Pleck, "The Work-Family Role System," in Rachel Kahn-Hut, Arlene Kaplan Daniels, and Richard Cloward, eds., *Women and Work: Problems and Perspectives* (New York, 1982), 103. Burn, *Beggar Boy,* 277. Even in the twentieth century, some working-class English women addressed their husband as "master," see Robert Roberts, *The Classic Slum: Salford Life in the First Quarter of the Century* (1971; rpt. Harmondsworth, England, 1983), 112.

# CHAPTER 5

# The Workplace

Workers left home each morning to go not to a labor market or an industry—for these are abstractions—but to specific workplaces. The city's workplaces varied greatly, but by examining them we may make more concrete the generalizations already discussed at a broader level and discover new ones as well. Three generalizations are especially significant: the fast pace of work, the extreme division of labor, and the high turnover of employees. These factors were almost universal, and this chapter analyzes how they exerted a pervasive influence on workers' relations with the "boss" and fellow employees.

## THE PHYSICAL SETTING

The great variation in responses of city manufacturers to expanding demand was reflected in the workplace. To understand the character and ambience of the city's workplaces, it is helpful to have some idea of the actual physical layout of the different types of workplace. To simplify, we can divide them into three types—home, shop, and factory. The line between shop and factory is hazy, but the use of power and the presence of supervisory personnel other than the proprietor characterize the latter.

The *home* was the work setting for thousands of New Yorkers, especially in the clothing industry as the "outside shop" expanded in the 1840s. In 1845 the *Tribune* described the city's seamstresses: "These women . . . rent a single room, or perhaps two small rooms, in the upper story of some poor, ill-constructed unventilated house in a filthy street. . . . In these rooms all the processes of cooking, eating, sleeping, washing, working and *living* are indiscriminately performed.'' Conrad Carl, a German immigrant tailor and labor leader, described outwork in the Tenth Ward in the late 1850s: ''Before we had sewing-machines we worked piece-work with our wives, and very often our children. We had no trouble then . . . because it was a very still business, very quiet. . . . We worked at home in our rooms. We had to buy fuel to heat the irons for pressing, and light in winter. . . . Piece-work, only piece-work in our own rooms.'' Work in homes that were small and crowded, hot in summer and cold in winter, seems to have changed little between 1820 and 1860.[1]

Most *workshops* in the 1820s and 1830s were located in frame houses or on the ground floor or courtyards of commercial or residential buildings. City cabinetmakers' shops are probably typical. According to Henry Fearon, ''these shops are perfectly open, and there is seldom any person in attendance. In the centre, a board is suspended with the notice, 'Ring the Bell.' '' As rents rose in the 1840s, many workshops were forced into ''apartments'' on the upper stories ''of buildings used otherwise for trade and commerce,'' according to the 1865 *Report upon the Sanitary Condition of the City*. Most shops were tiny and cramped. Benjamin McCready, a physician who studied the health of the city's workers in 1837, lamented that ''printing offices are generally too small for the number of men employed, and they are often imperfectly ventilated . . . the offices themselves . . . being situated in the most confined and thickly built streets.'' Small size and poor ventilation made workshops, like homes, subject to what McCready called ''frequent vicissitudes of temperature.'' The Anonymous Cabinetmaker remembered unhappily the exhausting summer heat at the shop where he worked, and Ernest Hagen, a German cabinetmaker, recalled winters during his 1840s' apprenticeship when ''they had only wood stoves in the shops and no steam heat.''[2]

The shops were often dark and dirty. As the city became built up, descriptions grew of workshops like ''dungeons.'' One cordwainer's shop was

1. *Tribune*, 14 August 1845; see also *Tribune*, 9 September 1845, and *Herald*, 11 June 1853. Carl: U.S. Congress, Senate, Committee on Education and Labor, *Report of the Senate Committee upon Relations between Labor and Capital* (Washington, 1885), 1:413–414; see also the *Tribune*, 8 June 1853, and the *Herald*, 25 October 1857. On workers' housing see also Chapter 6 below.

2. Henry Fearon, *Sketches of America* (London, 1819), 24, see also 12–13, 30–31. Council of Hygiene and Public Health, *Report upon the Sanitary Condition of the City* (New York, 1865), 2; see also Eugene P. Moehring, *Public Works and Patterns of Urban Real Estate Growth in Manhattan, 1835–1894* (New York, 1981), 12. Benjamin McCready, *On the Influence of Trades, Professions, and Occupations in the United States in the Production of Disease* (1837; rpt. Baltimore, Md., 1943), 81, 83; ''A Working Man's Recollections of America,'' *Knight's Penny Magazine* 1 (1846), 35; Elizabeth Ingerman, ed., ''Personal Experiences of an Old New York Cabinetmaker,'' *Antiques* 84 (1963), 577.

described by the *Tribune* in 1845 as having a "floor . . . made of rough plank and laid loosely down, and the ceiling is not quite so high as a tall man. The walls are dark and damp. . . . There is no outlet and of course no yard." According to Samuel Gompers, in the 1860s "any kind of old loft served as a cigar shop. If there were enough windows, we had sufficient light for our work; if not, it was apparently no concern of the management." Gompers explained that "factory architecture and industrial sanitation were undeveloped sciences," and messy, disorganized workshops were the rule. James Burn described a Newark workshop in the early 1860s where the hatters were "almost certain . . . to tumble . . . over blocks and pails which were lying about in all directions." A coachmaker's guidebook lamented that in too many establishments, "confusion is written throughout" and pointed out that "much loss is occasioned by want of system in the shop."[3]

Smaller *factories,* such as the capmaker's establishment the *Tribune* described in a "dark back room on a second, third, fourth, or fifth story chamber," or the foundry Frank Roney recalled as "imperfectly lighted, black and dirty," resembled workshops and were probably equally disorganized. However, growing use of division of labor necessitated the inception of "systems" in many city factories. The term *system* referred both to orderly bookkeeping and to a logical arrangement of the work process. By the 1850s a system was considered essential for successful manufacturers, and R. G. Dun's called attention to men like tailor George Landgrebe, who despite "a first rate run of custom . . . lacks system." Factories were increasingly divided into different departments located in separate rooms. At E. Walker's Bookbindery, on Fulton Street, women folded and sewed the sheets together in one room while in the next, men glued the pages into the binding. (This separation of men from women was a general rule.) As employers built upward to minimize real estate costs, factories were subdivided by floors, as at the Morgan Soap factory (see Figure 1). In Singer and Company's huge Mott Street Plant, built in 1857, the sewing machine traveled upward, from the cutting of parts on the second floor to the painting on the fifth.[4]

3. "Dungeons": *Tribune,* 26 September 1845. *Tribune,* 9 September 1845. Samuel Gompers, *Seventy Years of Life and Labor* (1925; rpt. New York, 1967), 1:44; see also "Segar Manufacturing in New York," *United States Economist and Dry Goods Reporter* 2 (1853), 239–240. James Burn, *James Burn; The "Beggar Boy"* (London, 1882), 289; see also McCready, *On the Influence,* 74. *The Coach-Maker's Illustrated Hand-Book* (Philadelphia, 1872), 343, 344.

4. *Tribune,* 19 August 1845; *Frank Roney: An Autobiography,* ed. Ira Cross (1931; rpt. New York, 1976), 180; New York vol. 212, 377, R. G. Dun & Company Collection, Baker Library, Harvard Graduate School of Business Administration; *The Art of Book-Binding* (New York, 1850), 30–31. E. Walker was a medium-sized factory seasonally employing 60–100 workers. Singer: Charles Flint et al., *Eighty Years Progress of the United States* (Chicago, 1864), 422–423, and John C. Gobright, *The New-York Sketch Book and Merchant's Guide* (New York, 1859), 93–95.

FIGURE 18. Forges at the Novelty Works, 1851. From Jacob Abbott, "The Novelty Works," *Harper's Magazine* 2 (1851), 730.

The layout of the interior varied greatly by type of work. Generally, working conditions seem to have been better in factories than in most shops. Inadequate light was perhaps the most serious occupational problem, and larger factories had the capital necessary to preempt the best-lighted parts of buildings and to design their floorplan to take best advantage of windows—as at Haughwout's porcelain factory on upper Broadway, where the employees sat at "long tables . . . located as near as possible to the light." Interiors remained rather messy, but there was some improvement in this regard as well. Stephen Tucker the machinist helped rationalize Hoe and Company's interior in 1851. Previously, tools had been kept "in open racks in care of no one." During a trip to England to set up the company's printing presses,

Tucker observed that the best English factories "were provided with tool rooms," and he fought for, and got, such a room at Hoe and Company. Despite these improvements in organization, however, contemporary illustrations, as of the Novelty Works, the city's largest factory (Figure 18), provide evidence that industrial interiors continued to be messy and cluttered in the 1850s.[5]

Issues related to workplace conditions attracted little protest from employees. Gompers was outraged at the lack of light in his cigar shop, but most workers accepted conditions and said nothing or quit; the compositor Thomas Chamberlain in 1843 "left Trow's [a major printing establishment] on account of having a dark stand." In the shops that dominated New York's industry, the employer shared bad working conditions with his workmen. In addition, before steam power became widespread in the city, serious workplace accidents seem to have been less common than later in the century. Founding and construction were quite dangerous, however, and fatal accidents were common. The immigrant worker's most common complaint was the heat in the shops during the summer, but this was considered inevitable and, except among those who worked outdoors, was viewed as uncomfortable rather than dangerous.[6]

Although the proportion of those working at home grew after 1820, there was generally, with the exception of somewhat better organization, only modest physical change in the city's workplaces; on Manhattan most employees continued to labor in unpowered shops.

THE TONE OF THE WORKPLACE

Diversity was one of the hallmarks of industrialization in the city. With so much complexity over four decades that saw substantial change, is it possible

5. "Art Manufactures: Porcelain," *Putnam's Monthly Magazine* 2 (1853), 403. Described is the old Haughwout plant near Spring Street; the newer building, which still stands on the corner of Broadway and Broome Street, was not built until 1857. Stephen Tucker, "History of R. Hoe and Company," typescript in the Richard Hoe and Company Papers, Rare Book and Manuscript Library, Columbia University, 54.

6. Gompers, *Seventy Years*, 1:44; see also George A. Stevens, *New York Typographical Union No. 6* (Albany, N.Y., 1913), 108. Thomas Chamberlain diary, 10 January 1843, Rare Books and Manuscripts Division, The New York Public Library, Astor, Lenox and Tilden Foundations; see also McCready, *On the Influence*, 74. Dangers in founding: H. F. J. Porter, *The Delameter Iron Works: Cradle of the Modern Navy* (n.p., [c. 1918]), 10–11. Descriptions of typical construction accidents are found in *The Diary of George Templeton Strong*, eds. Allan Nevins and Milton Halsey Thomas (New York, 1952), 348: two Irish laborers crushed to death in an excavation cave-in; and the *Tribune*, 4 December 1850: a scaffolding collapsed, killing one housepainter and seriously injuring two others. Despite high turnover, which usually acts to increase injuries at work, few diaries or letters from the period mention serious accidents, in contrast to accounts from the late nineteenth and early twentieth centuries. See Jerold S. Auerbach, ed., "Pre–World War One—Conditions of Work," in *American Labor: The Twentieth Century* (Indianapolis, 1969), 5–49.

to generalize about the character of the workplace? The answer is yes. Three factors characterized work in New York. The first, and of paramount importance, was the *fast pace of work.*

Immigrant workers were stunned at the rapid manner of working in the city. William Darnley wrote his wife in 1857, "I can assure you I never worked so hard indeed I would not stop in this country if I thought I must work all my life." Lewis Howell Jr. wrote back to Wales in 1845, "Be it remembered that all must work hard; in fact, a man must move at the very top of his speed, if he moves at all—he may not possess the 'steam arm or leg' but he is positively compelled to find the nearest possible approach." This fast pace was general. "Day labor," a New York tinner warned his fellow Norwegian immigrants, "demands a much more strenuous exertion than we are used to." The story was the same in the trades. While bricklayers in Germany laid 1,000 to 1,200 bricks a day, American bricklayers laid 1,500. Charles Steinway, the piano-maker, discouraged his brother from emigrating in 1852, explaining to him that "people here have to work harder" than in Germany. The British Mechanic agreed, noting that "an American ship-yard is a very different spectacle from an English one. Everything about it bears the appearance of the very height of industry; the labour of the individual demands his utmost exertion." Frank Roney, a molder and later a California labor leader, remembered his first view of New York manufacturing in 1867:

> I peered into the semi-darkness and saw men, bare-headed and bare-footed, almost nude, racing back and forth, handling between trips, small wooden tools most dexterously. I asked a bystander what was going on inside, and was told it was a foundry. The information made me gasp. . . . Mechanics, and for that matter all others in the old countries where I had experience, never worked in so exhausting a way as those men did. . . . The American moulders seemed desirous of doing all the work required as if it were the last day of their lives.

When an English proofreader applied at E. O. Jenkins print shop on Frankfort Street he was told: " 'Well, I guess you Englishers are so slow—there's no energy in you; you don't do the quantity of work we Americans do, else I could employ you, I reckon.' "[7]

7. William Darnley, letter to his wife, 31 August 1858, Rare Books and Manuscripts Division, The New York Public Library, Astor, Lennox and Tilden Foundations. Lewis Howell Jr., "to the ed. for the benefit of his acquaintances in the old country," 27 August 1844, in Alan Conway, ed., *The Welsh in America: Letters from the Immigrants* (Minneapolis, 1961), 70. Tinner: "Bishop Jacob Neumann's Word of Admonition to the Peasants [1836]," Gunnar Malmin, ed., *Norwegian-American Historical Association Studies and Records* 1 (1926), 107. Friedrich Pauer, *Die Vereinigten Staaten von Nord-Amerika* (Bremen, 1847), 79–80. Theodore Steinway, *People and Pianos* (New York, 1953), 16; *The British Mechanic's and Labourer's Hand Book* (London, 1840), 230; Roney, *Autobiography,* 179–180; *The Real Experiences of an Emigrant* (London, 187[?]), 83.

Every possible shortcut in working was taken. According to Burn, "there is not a single trade in America, common to both countries, in which there is not a decided difference in the method of manipulation. Every near cut which can be attained by ingenuity or mechanical skill is taken advantage of by all classes of producers." The British Mechanic added that "the American workman has a quick and ridding method of getting through his labour; to use one of his own expressive terms, a 'slick mode' which he invariably practises much to the astonishment . . . of most Europeans." John Kerr wrote to his uncle not to apprentice Kerr's brother in Ireland as a carpenter if the nephew was interested in emigrating, because his Old World craft knowledge "would be of little use to him . . . there is so much difference in the manner of working." It took, another immigrant noted, "five or six weeks' work to learn the method used in this country."[8]

"Dear father, the paving here is very different from Germany," stonecutter Henry Miller (who had changed his name from Heinrich Müller), wrote in 1859. "My paving hammer weighs 11 pounds. While standing you must hold the stone in one hand and the hammer in the other, which requires a good eye." Burn immediately discovered that the British system of "operating upon a single hat at a plank has been superseded by American workmen, who size three, and occasionally four bodies together in a cloth. The secret . . . lies in keeping a roll until the bodies are nearly the required size." Just how different the "slick mode" was from European craftsmanship was discovered by Henry Price, who learned cabinetmaking in New York before ill health forced his return to England in 1849. He began working in a London shop making drawers when the master stopped him:

> It's not exactly the thing, says He I told him I thought they were all right what is the matter with them. With that he brings a piece of silvrd glass and places it behind the Mitres of course the silver could be seen through the joint. . . . he told me I shall not do for London shops, You had better go back to New York. . . . I soon found I had a lot to learn.[9]

8. Burn, *Beggar Boy*, 269–270; see also Theodor Griesinger, *Lebende Bilder aus Amerika* (Stuttgart, 1858), 317–318. *British Mechanic's and Labourer's Hand Book*, 16. John Kerr, letter to James Graham, 5 June 1847, Public Record Office of Northern Ireland (PRONI); see also Alfred Green, letter to his mother, 28 July 1857, British Library of Political and Economic Science, London School of Economics. Sjur Jørgeson Haaeim, "Information on Conditions in North America" (1842), ed., Gunnar Malmin, *Norwegian-American Historical Association Studies and Records* 3 (1928), 9; see also Agnes Bretting, *Soziale Probleme deutscher Einwanderer in New York City, 1800–1860* (Weisbaden, 1981), 94.

9. Henry Miller, letter to his father, 19 October 1859, in Wolfgang Helbich, ed., *"Amerika ist ein freies Land . . ."*: *Auswanderer schreiben nach Deutschland* (Darmstadt, 1985), 89; see also Pauer, *Die Vereingten Staaten*, 78–80. James Burn, *Three Years among the Working-Classes in the United States during the War* (1865; rpt. New York, 1982), 185; "The Diary of Henry Edward Price," in *British Records Relating to America in Microform* (East Ardsley, England, 1963), 53.

The slick mode was especially fitted to American circumstances because, as we have seen, the demand was largely for cheap manufactured goods to be shipped outside the city. A comparison with London is instructive. Like New York, London was a national center for seasonal and fashionable manufacturing, and its industrial structure was similar to New York's. The clothing trade was a major London industry and relied on outwork and division of labor to meet seasonal demand. Furnituremaking was important, and, as in New York, it was subdivided into "fancy," "general," and "slop" work. Workers in both cities specialized in handcrafted and custom-made articles for the elite market. "New York," according to Virginia Penny, "is the depot for everything made in a limited quantity, and for everything new in style." British immigrants were surprised, however, that elite demand in New York was substantially less significant than in London; Fearon was not impressed with the city's shops in 1817, and in 1859 the Anonymous Proofreader remarked on the relative plainness of most Broadway retail stores and noted that "Sarl and Sons on Cornhill could have stocked half the silversmiths in New York."[10]

The 1853 New York Crystal Palace exhibition illuminated this relative weakness in fancy products. In some trades, such as cabinetmaking, the best examples of American art were equal or superior to those of Europe. In most, however, French and English styles set the pattern, and in many (including porcelain, carriages, and bookbinding) America was markedly inferior. Few American bookbinders entered exhibits because "many of [them] . . . deemed it folly to compete with the old and famous houses in Europe, where their vocation has so long attained the dignity of an art." The British Mechanic explained to his readers that "for many businesses of the 'old country' the United States at present are wholly unfitted, particularly such as those connected in any way with the fine arts, or that partake of a fancy nature or character. There is a better chance of employment and better wages given for anything of this kind at home." As John Prentice pointed out to Edinburgh workers, "in a new country like this . . . there is not the demand for the labour of those who work in the fabrication of luxuries as there is for hands to be employed on works of sheer utility. . . . There is not much aristocracy of trade here." Therefore, as the British Mechanic perceived, "excellence is

10. Virginia Penny, *How Women Can Make Money* (1863; rpt. New York, 1971), 446. This description of London's manufacturing comes from E. P. Thompson and Eileen Yeo, eds., *The Unknown Mayhew: Selections from the Morning Chronicle, 1849–1850* (London, 1971), esp. 116–227 and 358–398, and Gareth Stedman Jones, *Outcast London: A Study in the Relationship between Classes in Victorian Society* (1971; rpt. Harmondsworth, England, 1976). Fearon, *Sketches of America*, 10; *Real Experiences of an Emigrant*, 72. Evidence that customized production was more significant in nineteenth-century England is found in Charles Sabel and Jonathan Zeitlin, "Historical Alternatives to Mass Production: Politics, Market and Technology in Nineteenth-Century Industrialization," *Past and Present* 108 (1985), 165–167.

only a secondary consideration . . . a man is principally esteemed for his speed, or, in other words, for the task he can perform.''[11]

Not only was the pace faster, it was more regular than in Britain. Work itself was more seasonal in America, but generally immigrant workers found the pace more constant in the New World. The British Mechanic noted that in most trades in New York, after a wave of strikes in 1835–36, ten hours was the rule. Some shops and factories continued to work twelve hours until the 1840s, but most workers labored from seven in the morning until noon, took one hour for dinner, then worked until six. During working hours, the British Mechanic wrote, ''there is no allowable cessation from labour during any part of this time—no lunching or watering time, or interval of any description; nothing but one round of work without the slightest intermission.'' The Anonymous Proofreader's description is very similar:

> I set to work with a will, but . . . it was almost a matter of impossibility to keep up. . . . This continued all day—and day after day—no intermission, no chance of taking five minutes to rest my weary brain; all hurry, skurry, rush, rush, without cessation until the clock struck six, and I arose from my chair to walk home, with my head aching to distraction, no appetite, and feeling altogether unwell.[12]

Actually, such a fast pace made occasional breaks necessary. The Anonymous Cabinetmaker described how ''after several weeks of real hard work unrelieved by any change'' he quit in the middle of the afternoon for a party ''with wine, brandy, biscuits and cheese.'' In many shops vendors, who followed a regular route, were allowed to sell apples, candy, and nuts. A few workers were like Henry Price who was able to ''filch . . . bits of my working time'' to read Rollin's *Ancient History*. Much more typical, however, were the immigrant watchmaker John Harold, who found that ''my employers have brought me so much work that I have scarced anytime for reading or writing,'' and German saddler Friedrich Jeitt, who learned that in New York there was no talk at all of *blauen Montag*. Immigrant workers were amazed at the steadiness required of them in America.[13]

11. Horace Greeley, ed., *Art and Industry as Represented in the Exhibition at the Crystal Palace New York, 1853–1854* (New York, 1853), 255–256; *British Mechanic's and Labourer's Hand Book*, 201; John Prentice, ''Letter to the Working Classes of the City of Edinburgh,'' *Scotsman*, 16 April 1834. *British Mechanic's and Labourer's Hand Book*, 17; see also *History of Architecture and the Building Trades of Greater New York* (New York, 1899), 1:47.

12. The Brewster coachworks, for instance, did not go to ten hours until 1845; see Census Office, *Tenth Census, 1880, Wages in Manufacturing* (Washington, 1886), XX, 422. *British Mechanic's and Labourer's Hand Book*, 18; *Real Experiences of an Emigrant*, 84; see also Griesinger, *Lebende Bilder*, 316–317.

13. ''A Working Man's Recollections of America,'' 107. Vendors: William Burns, *Life in New York* (New York, 1851), n.p.; Burn, *Beggar Boy*, 268; and George E. McNeil, ed., *The*

"As matters stand the generality of the productive classes have no volun-
tary vacations," wrote James Waddel Alexander, a Princeton professor of
rhetoric, in 1838. "My neighbor the saddler seems to have been at his brisk
employment late and early these ten years. Thus it is with the multitudes of our
mechanics." This was the case in New York. "During the first two years,"
the Anonymous Cabinetmaker recalled, "with the exception of a week's
illness, I was not absent from work for more than a single day. It may be said
that if a man would resolutely pursue such a course in England, he would
hardly find it necessary to emigrate." An anonymous English Workman wrote
in 1859, "few and far between are the holidays of the English workman, but in
the States they are fewer still." In New York in the mid-nineteenth century
there were only three regular holidays a year—Christmas, New Year's, and
the Fourth of July, and sometimes, but not always, Thanksgiving—though
some workers seem to have taken off the week of July Fourth. Even these
holidays were not always observed, as the diary of printer Thomas Chamberlain makes clear: "Dec 25 [1846] Christmas Day—worked till sun-down."
James Burn summed up his view of work in America: "There is no such thing
as shirking labour either in the workshops or the fields. A man must make up
his mind either to work or play, otherwise he will soon find his level." [14]

The rapid pace surely contributed to the growth of labor-intensive manufacturing in the city. Although the tight labor market kept wages high, the true
cost of labor was low because the pace of work was so fast and regular.
American manufacturers were aware of this. "The French weaver," the
*United States Economist and Dry Goods Reporter* told its readers, "lives very
cheap, but he works very slowly. American labor costs more, but is more
productive." The idea that American labor scarcity fostered mechanization
therefore seems dubious, at least in its simplest form, because the real cost of
labor may actually have been cheaper than in Britain. A largely unmechanized

---

*Labor Movement: The Problem of Today* (New York, 1892), 392. Henry Price diary, 28; John
Harold diary, 29 and 30 May, 1832, New-York Historical Society (NYHS). Friedrich Jeitt
letter, 18 January 1862, in Helbich, "*Amerika ist ein freies Land,*" 216; though also see
Theodor Griesinger, *Land und Leute in Amerika* (Stuttgart, 1863), 565. John Petheram wrote in
his diary, "Whilst in England I had been accustomed to study and reading. In America I read
nothing scarcely I had no time whatsoever": Petheram, "Sketches of My Life," 1830, NYHS.
14. James W. Alexander [Charles Quill], *The American Mechanic and Working-Man* (New
York and Philadelphia, 1847), 64; "A Working Man's Recollections of America," 103, this
seems to have been a common immigrant expression, see Griesinger, *Lebende Bilder*, 315.
Thanksgiving was not a holiday at the Delameter Iron Works in the 1850s, see Porter, *Delameter
Iron Works*, 9. Evidence that some workers took off the week of July Fourth comes from the
decline in wages shown in some employment records; see, for example, the "Contractor's
journal, 1815–1820," Rare Books and Manuscripts Division, The New York Public Library,
Astor, Lenox and Tilden Foundations. *London v. New York* "by an English Workman"
(London, 1859), 12; on the few American holidays see also Frederic W. Sawyer, *A Plea for
Amusements* (New York, 1847), 293–296. Thomas Chamberlain diary, 25 December 1846;
Burn, *Beggar Boy*, 282.

setting such as New York City is not a good basis for generalizing about technology, but if some American machinery was more advanced than in England, the youth and low skills of the workforce may provide part of the explanation.[15]

The fast and steady pace was the most striking characteristic of New York's workshops. Time after time immigrants remarked on it as the most distinctive feature of work in the New World. To explain the "railroad pace," as it was sometimes called, we must understand that it was not, in most cases, simply forced on the workers by the bosses, though it was certainly encouraged. "No foreman was needed to urge these men to work to the point of exhaustion. They labored hard of their own volition," wrote Roney. "I have known numerous instances . . . principally in America, where the fast men . . . would have worked all the hours of the natural day if they been allowed," Burn wrote.[16]

Native workers taught immigrants, even those from industrially advanced Britain, their fast and regular method of work. An 1845 *Tribune* article on shoemakers observed, "there is not perhaps a more industrious class in our city than the Germans. They rise early and retire late, and although when arriving on our shores they do not *drive business,* as is a distinguishing characteristic of our native mechanics; yet after some time among us a decided improvement in this respect can be plainly observed." The British Mechanic explained to potential immigrants that

> even a native of Great Britain, accustomed as he is to a quick style of work, at least by comparison with artisans of other countries, falls far short of what he meets with amongst his Transatlantic brethren. . . . This, however, is by no means difficult of attainment; in fact the foreign mechanic in most cases will find himself gradually and imperceptibly, as it were, slide into it.[17]

The relationship of American seasonality to the fast pace is not clear. James Burn believed that the "unsteady nature of business" engendered a "make hay while the sun shines" outlook on the part of many hatters, which certainly seems possible. On the other hand, Carroll Wright discovered in the early

15. *United States Economist and Dry Goods Reporter* n.s. 11 (1857), 103. E. J. Hobsbawm argues that nineteenth-century British employers lacked this understanding of productivity; to them, the longer hours, the more work they believed was being done; Hobsbawm, "Custom, Wages and Work-Load," in Hobsbawm, *Labouring Men: Studies in the History of Labour* (London, 1964), 352. H. J. Habakkuk, *American and British Technology in the Nineteenth Century* (Cambridge, England, 1967).

16. Roney, *Autobiography,* 263; James Dawson Burn, *A Glimpse at the Social Condition of the Working Classes during the Early Part of the Present Century* (London, n.d.), 51–52.

17. *Tribune,* 5 September 1845; *British Mechanic's and Labourer's Hand Book,* 16–17. As the British Mechanic suggests, English journeymen were considerably faster than their Continental counterparts. French workers were notoriously slow, see Charles Manby Smith, *The Working-Man's Way in the World* (New York, 1854), 71, 79.

twentieth century that workers in very seasonal trades tended to stint (that is, work slowly) in order to "make the work go round" by spreading it out. It is likely that seasonality did contribute to the rapid manner of work, but the universality of the railroad pace and its presence even in nonseasonal industries such as founding make it improbable that seasonality was more than a contributing factor. A causal explanation must be sought elsewhere.[18]

Higher wages were the payoff for the fast pace. "Although he [the emigrant] may get better wages, he has to give a much greater amount of labour for his money," the British Mechanic explained. This was especially obvious in trades that paid by the piece, but even in those that paid by the day, such as shipbuilding and construction, the same relationship between harder work and higher wages prevailed. As Chapters 3 and 4 noted, economic motives were prime in the decision to emigrate, and foreign-born workers brought this strong economic orientation to their work. The Anonymous Cabinetmaker often built furniture at home and, when he spent an evening reading, "I will show how far I was possessed by the utilitarian feeling that, on such occasions, I thought on going to bed that I had lost an evening." The compensation for such hard work was the ability to live at a standard higher than in Europe. Indeed, male and supplementary female workers, both native and foreign, discovered for one of the first times in history that common people might live comfortably. As the pro-emigration English *Chartist Circular* put it in 1844, after describing high American living standards, "these are advantages which . . . are within the *reasonable* hopes and expectations of almost all the inferior classes. What a powerful stimulus is not this to industry! What a premium on sobriety and unexceptional conduct!"[19]

Despite this powerful stimulus, it is unlikely the railroad pace could have become so dominant in the city's workshops without a peculiarly American mentality of work. British immigrant workers shared what Edmund Morgan has described as "the assumption that the total amount of work for which society could pay was strictly limited and must be rationed so that everyone could have a little." As Roney put it, "Europeans worked rationally, intelligently, and well, and had some of their work remaining for the next day." To work fast meant to gobble up more than one's fair share of work and to endanger future employment. This "scarcity consciousness," as Selig Perl-

18. Burn, *Three Years*, 186; U.S. Commissioner of Labor, *Eleventh Special Report—Regulation and Restriction of Output*, ed. Carroll Wright (Washington, 1904), 29. Herman Feldman also found "stinting" widespread in seasonal trades, see *The Regularization of Employment* (New York, 1925), 31–32.

19. *British Mechanic's and Labourer's Hand Book*, 107; "A Working Man's Recollections of America," 107. Henry Price also worked in the evening, see Price diary, 28. *Chartist Circular*, 10 July 1841, quoted in Dallas L. Jones III, "The Background and Motives of Scottish Emigration to the United States of America in the Period 1815 to 1861, with Special Reference to Emigrant Correspondence" (diss., University of Edinburgh, 1970), 263, emphasis added.

FIGURE 19. W. S. and C. H. Thomson's Hoop Skirt Manufactory, 1859. From *Harper's Weekly*, 19 February 1859. Photograph courtesy of the Library of Congress.

man called it, what anthropologist George Foster refers to as an "image of limited good," was widespread among British workers. Burn used a food metaphor to explain this view of work: "If a number of people were seated at a common table where there was a certain quantity of food, it would scarcely be accounted fair that the man with the greatest power of mastication would be justified in devouring double the quantity of the slower eaters."[20]

The treatment of apprentices illustrates the difference between American and European views of work. Not only were apprenticeships much easier to obtain in the New World, but the apprentice faced much less hostility from bosses and journeymen. In New York, according to the British Mechanic, "from the very commencement of his [the apprentice's] servitude, he is put to ready and profitable use—nothing is suffered to interfere so as to retard his advancement—no jealousy, no dread that he will learn his trade too quick or too well, and be ultimately injurious to his employer." Nor was there, unlike in Britain, "any desire for keeping him to a distinct branch that he may be made the most of for the time being." Frederick Lockley was apprenticed as a butcher in England, but his master refused to teach Lockley some of the key steps in cutting beef; "his provident idea was that if I learned the business too readily . . . I might take myself off," Lockley wrote. Thomas Mooney expanded on the difference in American attitudes in 1850: "The American mechanics do not object so steadfastly to apprentices as those of the old country do; when there is work enough for all, or nearly so, then will be found less and less restrictions coming from the working men, as to the rights of their fellow-creatures to share in it." Significantly, James Burn was surprised to find that American mechanics were willing to teach him things he did not know about hatting; the implication is that in Britain he might have been "shied the answer." [21]

20.  Edmund Morgan, "The Labor Problem at Jamestown, 1607–1618," *American Historical Review* 76 (1971), 603; Roney, *Autobiography,* 180; Selig Perlman, *A Theory of the Labor Movement* (1928; rpt. Philadelphia, 1979), 239–241. According to Perlman, under conditions of scarcity "free competition becomes a sin against one's fellows, like the self indulgent consumption of the stores of a beleaguered city" (p. 242). George M. Foster, "Peasant Society and the Image of Limited Good," *American Anthropologist* n.s. 67 (1965), 293–315. Burn, *Social Condition of the Working Classes,* 52. This outlook seems to have been widespread among peasant workers. Textile operatives in India in the 1920s "said that . . . there are so many men who want work and cannot get it that it would be unfair if they were to attend more machines." Arno S. Pearse, *The Cotton Industry of India* (Manchester, 1930), 129, quoted in Gregory Clark, "Why Isn't the Whole World Developed? Lessons from the Cotton Mills," *Journal of Economic History* 47 (1987), 168. In Herbert Gutman's classic essay "Work, Culture and Society in Industrializing America, 1815–1919," evidence for "irregular work habits" among artisans often comes from English immigrant workers: "an English cabinetmaker," "immigrant Staffordshire potters," "a British steelworker," "English workmen." The essay appears in Gutman, *Work, Culture and Society in Industrializing America: Essays in American Working Class and Social History* (New York, 1977), 34, 38, 39.

21.  *British Mechanic's and Labourer's Hand Book,* 107, 109; Frederick Lockley, "Memoirs," NYHS, 130. Thomas Mooney, *Nine Years in America* (Dublin, 1850), 149; see also Paul H. Douglas, *American Apprenticeship and Industrial Education* (New York, 1921), 62.

British immigrant workers were therefore *morally* outraged at the speed of American work. Burn was revolted at the pace in New York hat factories; the fast men—"squirtes," Burn called them—have "all the chances of monopolizing more than an equal share of the hats. . . . In the old country, I have never witnessed anything so disgustingly disagreeable as this selfishness of the American hat-makers." Roney was equally offended: "I did not and would not descend to their level if I never worked at moulding. . . . I never hurried and always suppressed any disposition . . . to take work away from others." Irish immigrant laborers loading a cart in 1826 "wanted the job to last as long as possible." But one cartman, native Isaac Anderson, "loaded his cart too quickly. . . ." The Irish carters advised him to " 'work easier,' that is, [he] 'should work slower, like the rest.' " When Anderson refused, he was kicked and beaten. Native workers, raised in a labor-scarce environment, found assumptions about the limited amount of work incomprehensible. In antebellum America the number of tasks to be done seemed boundless, and the idea that workers should "work easier" to save "some of their work remaining for the next day" appeared incredible. Natives thus labored fast and hard without qualms, and immigrants who worked beside them in the workshops learned "gradually and imperceptibly" the railroad pace.[22]

The distinctive age structure of the population in the city facilitated the adoption of the fast pace. As I noted in Chapter 3, the high birthrate and, after the 1840s, the distinctive youth of debarking immigrants gave the city a very young population (see Figure 9). Only 7 percent of the white population in New York in 1850 was over age fifty, while 13 percent of the population was older than that in London in 1851. A youthful workforce was more capable of standing a fast and regular pace, especially as brute force was so often needed in the city's unpowered manufactories. "Physical strength is more in request than scientific acquirements," Prentice reported. At the Hoe Company the ribs for cylinder presses were shaped by a three-foot-long plane. The plane "was drawn forward by a man turning a windlass with the workmen standing on the plane to give it pressure." Work this hard was too much for many older employees. John R. Commons in the early twentieth century pointed to "the strain of excessive speed, which to the men, as they grow older, becomes the greatest of all their grievances." One machine-shop owner explained to

---

Burn, *Beggar Boy*, 268. When one new worker entered a Paris printshop, according to Robert Darnton, the employees "refused to teach him anything. They did not want another journeyman in their overflooded labor pool." Darnton, "Workers Revolt: The Great Cat Massacre of the Rue Saint-Severin," in Darnton, *The Great Cat Massacre and Other Episodes in French Cultural History* (New York, 1984), 89.

22. Burn, *Three Years*, 186; Roney, *Autobiography*, 263; People v. John O'Neil et al., 7 April 1826, New York Court of General Sessions Records, cited in Paul A. Gilje, *The Road to Mobocracy: Popular Disorder in New York City, 1763–1834* (Chapel Hill, N.C., 1987), 137–138.

Carroll Wright, who was collecting information on restriction of production, that "it is the old ones, as a rule, who are the moving spirits in cases of this kind."[23]

In the mid-nineteenth century such older workers were a very small minority, and younger workers who had the speed and endurance needed to "drive business" determined the pace. James Burn was sixty when he came to America, and his age is no doubt responsible, in part, for his sensitivity to the pace of work. He believed fast native workers were "certainly not using the slower class of workmen fairly" and eventually concluded that "no working-man should go to the United States after having passed the prime of life." Immigrant letters repeated this theme. According to Arnold Schrier, "old people were cautioned to stay away from a country where the pace of life and work would be too much for them."[24]

The extraordinarily good American diet, described in Chapter 6 below, helped workers labor at such a rapid pace. It is unlikely the fast manner of working could have been maintained on a European worker's diet. In English families in the 1860s the breadwinner ate "a larger share of the [high-protein] food" than other members to "enable him to perform his labour," according to Dr. Edward Smith. Even in the early twentieth century, meat in most working-class families "figured only in the father's diet and his alone." "Father ate his fill first," Robert Roberts remembered, "to 'keep up his strength.'" When English immigrant Henry Price arrived in New York, he discovered he was too weak to do the work expected of a journeyman cabinetmaker in the city, and he was employed only as a varnisher. "Here I must state," he wrote in his reminiscences, "that I atribute my weakness to the Innsuficient food dole'd out" in the English workhouse where he had been raised.[25]

In the poorer areas of the British Isles, the impact of inadequate diet on work was well-known. "Many of the labourers present" at a hearing of the Irish poor law inquiry in County Galway, "declare that they are fully sensible

23. Census Office, *Seventh Census, 1850, Population* (Washington, 1853), 88–91; *Census of Great Britain, 1851* (London, 1854), II, sec. 1, 1. In the 1980 U.S. census 26 percent of the nation's population was over age fifty. Prentice letter, *Scotsman*, 16 April 1834; Tucker, "History of R. Hoe," 7. Endurance declines more rapidly with age than does strength; see Jacob F. Feldman, "Work Ability of the Aged under Conditions of Improving Mortality," *Milbank Memorial Fund Quarterly: Health and Society* 61 (1983), 430–444. John R. Commons, "Laboring Conditions in Slaughtering and Meat Packing," in Commons, ed., *Trade Unionism and Labor Problems* (Boston, 1905), 241; Wright, *Regulation and Restriction of Output*, 148.

24. Burn, *Three Years*, 186; Burn, *Beggar Boy*, 280; Arnold Schrier, *Ireland and the American Immigration, 1850–1900* (Minneapolis, 1958), 5.

25. Theodore Barker, D. J. Oddy, and John Yudkin, eds., *The Dietary Surveys of Dr. Edward Smith: A New Assessment* (London, 1970), 47; Robert Roberts, *The Classic Slum: Salford Life in the First Quarter of the Century* (1971; rpt. Harmondsworth, England, 1983), 104, 109; Price diary, 64.

that they do not work as well as those who are better fed." "I can speak from my own knowledge," laborer Thomas Lally asserted, "as having seen a man in this parish, about two months ago, (and it was no hard season), fail at his labour from hunger; he had eaten nothing that day; . . . when I went up to him he was sitting on the ground, not able to work from weakness." In Scotland it was widely believed that the lethargy of Highland peasants was due "to the insufficient quality of their food." Such workers often had to rest several times a day to conserve their strength. It took "a week's comfortable feeding" before such malnourished laborers began to work effectively.[26]

The high quality of the New York working-class diet, and especially the large amount of meat protein, made a fast pace possible. I am not arguing that dietary factors *caused* the fast pace; most English workers were not severely malnourished, yet they labored less swiftly than Americans. Nevertheless, it is doubtful that the railroad pace could have been maintained in physically strenuous occupations on an Irish or Highland Scots diet. An Irish-born New York City worker complained to English traveler John White about the pace of American work. White replied, " 'But you all live well here, anyhow.' 'Yes,' " the worker said laughing, " 'the Irishman gets more here than praties and buttermilk—but we need it all, I can tell you, to do the work.' "[27]

The fast pace dominated work in the city, whether in small cabinetmakers' shops on the west side or in the huge East River shipyards. "Work, work, work is the everlasting routine of every day life," Burn wrote. It was so pervasive that it influenced almost every aspect of life in the workplace and, as we shall see, outside it as well. American "celerity," however, should not be considered a "work ethic." There is little evidence that the workers found such hard labor fulfilling or believed it would ensure success. Gompers rhapsodized about how he "loved the touch of soft velvety tobacco and gloried in the deft sureness with which I could make cigars grow in my fingers," but for most workers labor was only instrumental. Charlotte Erickson has noted that in English emigrants' letters, "only rarely does one get a

26. House of Commons, *Parliamentary Papers* XXXI (1836), Poor Inquiry (Ireland), Appendix D, 2, 59; see also Joel Mokyr, *Why Ireland Starved: A Quantitative and Analytical History of the Irish Economy* (London, 1983), 223–226. Ian Levitt and Christopher Smout, *The State of the Scottish Working-Class in 1843* (Edinburgh, 1979), 33. According to a 1962 report by the Food and Agriculture Organization of the United Nations: "One of the most prominent symptoms of prolonged lack of food is the obvious loss of working capacity in its broadest sense. There is an appearance of lethargy and sluggishness; movements are slow, infrequent and interrupted by long pauses; any continuous effort is avoided as far as possible." FAO, "Nutrition and Working Efficiency," *Freedom from Hunger Campaign, Basic Study no. 5* (Rome, 1962), 6, 13. Most of this evidence comes from studies on German miners and steelworkers in World War II. For the issue of malnutrition as a barrier to industrialization see Herman Freudenberger and Gaylord Cumins, "Health, Work, and Leisure before the Industrial Revolution," *Explorations in Economic History* 13 (1976), 1–12. "Comfortable feeding": Henry Colman, *European Agriculture and Rural Economy* (Boston, 1846), 1:50.

27. John White, *Sketches from America* (London, 1870), 370.

glimpse of anything like work for its own sake, or pride in a job well done.'' Few workers had served a thorough apprenticeship or were highly skilled, and most seemed to have regarded labor mainly as a way to make money. Some native workers did take patriotic delight in their ability to work at such a fast pace. Their "great pride . . . is to whip John Bull both in designing and producing. . . . With them there is no halting," Burn wrote. Most immigrants, of course, were like White's Irish worker, who, when reminded he got " 'three times the Irish wages,' replied . . . that he did six times the Irish work.'' They would have preferred higher wages without the faster pace. Generally, though, they seem to have viewed it as an inevitable trade-off, one that many were prepared for by letters before they came to America, and most do not seem particularly resentful.[28]

Though fast pace was the most significant general characteristic, two others can be pointed out. *Division of labor* was to be found, by the late 1840s and 1850s, in almost every area of industry. In 1830 the druggist John Petheram wrote in his diary: "Tried to make the old fool Morrison [his employer John Morrison, a Greenwich Street druggist] believe that by dividing the labour which was not done there as it is in England more work could be done. . . . His answer to me was 'this Sir is a free country we want no one person over another which would be the case if you divided the labour.[']'' But by 1865 James Burn could write, "one thing may be mentioned in connection with the manufacturing industry of the country: division of labour is carried out in all the various branches of skilled labour to the fullest possible extent."[29]

Division of labor so permeated the workplace that it became almost second nature to the workers, especially to immigrants who were young and lacked extensive craft training. In factories, of course, extensive division of labor was built into the industrial design, but even in homes and shops where this was not the case the workers themselves divided the work. Among seamstresses working at home, "two baste and finish off and one operates [a sewing machine].'' When the utopian socialist Wilhelm Weitling worked in the city as a tailor in 1866, he made buttonholes and his wife and sister-in-law made the rest of the vest. In workshops artisans often subdivided work into specialized tasks. At the Harper Brothers printing shop in the 1820s, James

---

28. Burn, *Three Years,* 11; Gompers, *Seventy Years,* 1:56–57. This comment by Gompers probably should not be taken at face value since it so clearly aims to refute the widespread criticism that trade unionism appealed only to incompetent workmen. Charlotte Erickson, *Invisible Immigrants: The Adaptation of English and Scottish Immigrants in Nineteenth-Century America* (1972; rpt. Ithaca, N.Y., 1990), 239; Burn, *Beggar Boy,* 270; White, *Sketches from America* 370. On emigrants' awareness of the fast American pace, note the "Be it remembered" in the Lewis Howell letter, quoted on p. 128 from Conway, *Welsh in America,* 70, which suggests the writer was not telling his Welsh friends anything they did not already know.

29. Petheram, "Sketches of My Life"; Burn, *Three Years,* 178.

dealt with financial matters, Wesley read proof, and Fletcher was in charge of the composing.[30]

The third general characteristic of labor was *rapid turnover*. Sumner Slichter, who studied industrial turnover in the early part of the twentieth century, concluded: "Always when men are scarce and jobs plentiful, workers are prone to change and . . . when men are plentiful and jobs scarce, the opposite is true." The city's tight labor market was largely responsible for the high turnover in this period, and it was the busy season that saw most job changes. According to Burn, "nothing can afford a better proof of the scarcity of working men in the United States than the number of young men who keep flying from one business to another."[31]

The age structure also contributed because, as Slichter noted, "the turnover rate in general is decidedly higher among boys, young men and girls than among workmen in general." These two factors led to a very brisk turnover of labor in the city. Burn pointed out that "when old country mechanics or artisans go to America they are often a good deal surprised at the manner in which numbers of men continue to flit from one workshop to another," a circumstance he attributed both to "the state of trade" and to "the fact that numbers of young men have no taste for vegatating about their homes in cabbage fashion." "When the trade is in a flourishing condition," he continued, "a hat shop in America is not unlike an inn: men come and go as it seems to suit their taste or convenience. This is occasionally so much the case that a man may know his shopmates to-day, while on the morrow he may find himself among strangers."[32]

Burn was exaggerating, but turnover was undoubtedly very rapid. The employment records of one typefoundry—almost certainly Bruce and Company—show that 49 percent of employees in 1859 (when the economy was still somewhat weak) were no longer on the payroll a year later, a figure well above most of the early-twentieth-century rates Slichter calculated (see Table 14). Bruce and Company was not involved in a seasonal trade, but in the many firms that were, the busy season saw the greatest turnover. Although most series of workers' letters and their diaries cover only a short period, they show frequent job changes. John Burke, William Darnley, and the cooper Robert

30. Penny, *How Women Can Make Money,* 112; Carl Wittke, *The Utopian Communist: A Biography of Wilhem Weitling* (Baton Rouge, La., 1950), 310–311; J. Henry Harper, *The House of Harper* (New York, 1921), 22–23. Edward Hazen gives a good idea of the artisanal division of labor in the 1830s in *The Panorama of Professions and Trades* (Philadelphia, 1836), esp. 82–83, 102–103, 227, 230–231.

31. Sumner Slichter, *The Turnover of Factory Labor* (New York, 1919), 32, see also 29–33, 76–84. Burn, *Three Years,* 22.

32. Slichter, *Turnover of Factory Labor,* 76; Burn, *Beggar Boy,* 270, 304; Peter B. Doeringer and Michael Piore, *Internal Labor Markets and Manpower Analysis* (Lexington, Mass., 1971), 166–167.

TABLE 14

Turnover of labor at a New York typecasting firm (probably Bruce and Company), 1859–1863

| Job | Average weekly pay in 1859 | Workforce in January 1859 | Number still working in January | | | |
|---|---|---|---|---|---|---|
| | | | 1860 | 1861 | 1862 | 1863 |
| Dressers (M) | $31.00 | 5 | 4 | 5 | 3 | 2 |
| Jobbers (M) | 23.50 | 13 | 10 | 5 | 4 | 4 |
| Casters (M) | 14.78 | 20 | 12 | 8 | 8 | 6 |
| Rubbers (F) | 7.30 | 18 | 6 | 4 | 4 | 3 |
| Breakers (M) | 5.06 | 11 | 2 | 3 | 2 | 2 |
| Setters (F) | 4.81 | 14 | 7 | 6 | 4 | 4 |
| TOTALS | | 81 | 41 | 32 | 25 | 21 |
| % men still working | | | 57.1 | 42.8 | 34.7 | 28.6 |
| % women still working | | | 40.6 | 31.2 | 25.0 | 21.9 |
| % total still working | | | 50.6 | 39.5 | 30.9 | 25.9 |

*Source:* Day List of New York Typecasting Firm, Typographical Library Papers, Rare Book and Manuscript Library, Columbia University.

Taylor changed jobs often, but the all-time champion was printer Thomas Chamberlain. In a trade where workers were hired for specific orders, Chamberlain changed employers no fewer than ten times during one six-month period in the boom of the mid-1840s without, it seems, being unemployed at all. Such frequent job changes no doubt helped keep wages up.[33]

These three factors—fast pace, extensive division of labor, and rapid turnover—characterized work in the city. Combined with the immigrant background of most workers and an American labor scarcity, they made the American workplace substantially different from that of Britain.

WORKERS AND WORKERS

The way workers got along with one another in workshops was affected in a seemingly paradoxical way by the factors discussed earlier. Workers, both native and immigrant, were highly motivated in economic terms, so they worked hard and made a serious effort to prevent conflicts from interfering

33. Identification of the firm as Bruce is based on a comparison of its workforce as listed in the daybook with the Bruce entry in the 1860 manuscript manufacturing census. The varieties of work in a typefoundry are described in "Inside of a Type Foundry," *Printer* 1 (1858), 116–117. John Burke diary, 1839–1891, NYHS; Darnley letters; Robert Taylor diary, 1846–47, Rare Books and Manuscripts Division, The New York Public Library, Astor, Lenox and Tilden Foundations. Chamberlain diary, 28 September 1845 to 29 March 1846. For other examples of how rapidly city printers changed jobs, see "A Journeyman Printer," *Littell's Living Age* 8 (1846), 626–627; "Sketch of a Typo," *Printer* 4 (1861), 1–2; and James Parton, *The Life of Horace Greeley* (Boston, 1872), 99–103.

with productivity. At the same time the rapid pace and the youth of the workforce seem to have imparted to the workplace a high energy that often found its expression in frolicsome behavior and high jinks. Such high spirits were viewed not as a hindrance to output but as a more or less necessary relief from the pressure of the fast pace.

The workers themselves, propelled by a vision of high wages and a comfortable lifestyle, labored fast and tried to keep work on the shop floor functioning smoothly. The most obvious way they did so involved drink. In nineteenth-century Britain drinking on the job was very common. In New York, however, the story was more complex. In circumstances involving very prolonged or hard labor, where liquor might spur tiring workers, drinking was tolerated, even encouraged. In the shipyards, for example, "often when the sun had set, one of the bosses invited his men to refresh themselves from a pail of brandy and water, and then suggested that some timbers be raised." Indeed, drinking in the shipyards was extraordinarily heavy in the 1830s, and many workers were routinely intoxicated by the afternoon.[34]

However, after the shortening of hours in 1835–36 and the introduction of steam power had diminished the need for really heavy work, drink was viewed as the enemy of productive labor by both bosses and workers. The Washingtonian temperance movement of the early 1840s had thousands of members among the city's workers, and its growth may have marked a turning point away from the heavy drinking of the 1830s toward the moderation of the 1850s. Because of high wages and the low price of liquor in America, consumption of alcohol continued higher than in Britain. Nevertheless, according to the British Mechanic, "the Americans, generally speaking, are not given to intoxication. There exists no comparison in this respect between them and the working class in Great Britain. They are fond of dramming or drinking . . . but . . . to meet with them either in business or in public labouring under the effects of liquor is a very rare occurrence." Drinking was still widespread—in the 1850s printers often imbibed in the high-pressure newspaper branch of the trade, and during the busy season female clothing workers fortified themselves with gin. Alcohol was now acceptable only for its alleged effects as a stimulant, and those who consumed it on the job generally stayed, as the phrase went, "in running order."[35]

34. John Dunlop, *Artificial and Compulsory Drinking Usages of the United Kingdom* (London, 1844); E. P. Thompson, "Time, Work-Discipline and Industrial Capitalism," *Past and Present* 38 (1967), 56–97; G. W. Sheldon, "The Old Ship-Builders of New York," *Harper's Magazine* 65 (1882), 223. "Chips," *Fincher's Trades' Review,* 27 January 1866, contains a description of heavy drinking in the East Side yards in the 1830s.

35. Washingtonian movement: Ian R. Tyrrell, *Sobering Up: From Temperance to Prohibition in Antebellum America* (Westport, Conn., 1979), 159–183, and Sean Wilentz, *Chants Democratic: New York City and the Rise of the American Working Class, 1788–1850* (New York, 1984), 306–314. *British Mechanic's and Labourer's Hand Book,* 19. On the peril of

Although many bosses labored vigorously to prohibit drinking—James P. Allaire erected in his foundry a sign that "Any person that brings or drinks, spiritous liquors . . . will be discharged without pay for a week"—the tight labor market made them hesitate to fire skilled workers who drank; Robert Brownlee, a Scotsman who came to the city in the 1830s, noted that his fellow stonecutters "were in the habit of going four to six times a day to the . . . 'Whiskey-Mill' and . . . the different bosses throughout the town never objected." The most effective sanctions against drinking on the job seem to have come from the workers themselves. In a workplace increasingly dominated by division of labor, one besotted worker threatened the output, and hence the wages, of all. John Kerr, who worked in a hardware store and later as a machinist, wrote to a relative in Ireland in 1847, "when a stranger is seen drinking . . . the first time he is suspected, the second avoided & the third if at a short interval put down as a drinker. Then there is but little confidence placed in him." An 1851 Scottish emigrant's guide explained that "drunkards are not so calmly tolerated as they are at home. The tone and habits of the artisan order are against them; and instead of being supported by their fellow workmen, they are trampled underfoot."[36]

These workplace sanctions, combined with the increasing cost of whiskey, had an effect. When a "pick me up" was needed, by the 1850s it was likely to be coffee. Although drinking remained common, drunkenness on the job became increasingly rare—one boss stonecutter informed visiting Buffalo physician Joel H. Ross that his men were much more sober than formerly, and Abram Hewitt, the New Jersey iron manufacturer and future New York mayor, told an English parliamentary commission of the 1860s that the "habit of intemperance among the artizans was very much greater in America 20 years ago than now."[37]

Another factor threatened workplace harmony: ethnic rivalry. Although city workers were notoriously racist, racial tension in workshops was nonexis-

---

cheap drink to immigrants see Mooney, *Nine Years in America*, 66–67, and Dallas Jones, "Background and Motives," 380–381. Newspaper printers: J. B. Graham, *Handset Reminiscences* (Salt Lake City, Utah, 1915), 71–80. Drinking gin: Wirt Sikes, "Among the Poor Girls," *Putnam's Magazine* n.s. 1 (1868), 440. For other examples of on-the-job drinking, see Burn, *Beggar Boy*, 58, and Henry Brokmeyer, *A Mechanic's Diary* (Washington, 1910), 17. "Running order": "Chips," *Fincher's Trades' Review*, 27 January 1866.

36. James S. Brown, *Allaire's Lost Empire* (Freehold, N.J., 1958), 22; Robert Brownlee, *An American Odyssey: The Autobiography of a 19th-Century Scotsman*, ed. Patricia A. Etter (Fayetteville, Ark., 1986), 20; John Kerr, letter to David Graham, 29 September 1847. *The Emigrant's Manual* (Edinburgh, 1851), 133; see also Christoph Vetter, *Zwei Jahre in New-York* (Hof, 1849), 100, and David A. Jeremy, *Transatlantic Industrial Revolution: The Diffusion of Textile Technologies between Britain and America* (Cambridge, Mass., 1981), 170.

37. Coffee: Brokmeyer, *Mechanic's Diary*, 17. Joel H. Ross, *What I Saw in New-York* (Auburn, N.Y., 1852), 208; House of Commons, *Parliamentary Papers* XXXII (1867), "Second Report of the Commissioners Appointed to Inquire into the Organization and Rules of Trade Unions and Other Associations," 178.

tent—for the simple reason that blacks were almost totally excluded from city manufacturing (see Table 11). Blacks were "nonpersons" to most white workers; in the letters, diaries, and reminiscences I examined, I did not see a single reference to an individual black person. Ethnicity was another matter. Christoph Vetter described the painting establishment where he worked as a "Tower of Babel," with an Italian foreman, four German workers, two Italian workers, two Frenchmen, one Irishman, one Scotsman, and "several" American employees. Other workshops had a similar ethnic diversity, and the workers' differing nationalities and cultures provided a continuing source of tension, especially in the 1850s when immigration began to dissipate the scarcity of labor. Most native and German workers held Irishmen in no high regard, and other ethnic rivalries blossomed as well. In the hat shops where Burn worked, "petty rivalries" often flared between immigrants and native workers, and between the Northerners and the few Southerners in these establishments. The British Mechanic noted that English and American workers, "while together in employment, constantly keeping up a running-fire at each other, respecting their lingual similarities and differences, both satisfied of their correctness." Robert Brownlee, the Scots stonecutter, discovered that his workmates "were ever seeing something in me to laugh at . . . for my Scotch tongue was all I knew, . . . and of course it caused them much merriment."[38]

However, strong workplace sanctions prevented this tension from leading to actual fights, and ethnic humor allowed inevitable strains to be expressed. Disputes over language were "a constant theme of joke and sarcasm," and the British Mechanic recommended that rather than respond to American needling with anger, Britons should instead give "ironical praise and compliment" to conditions in the United States. Burn worked in a Newark hat shop where a long, humorous story about a none-too-bright German worker (who mistakenly believed his wife was in the company of another man but was, in fact, with her dog) was known to almost everyone, and the punchline "Ladies an' shentlemens, stops de ball" became a catch phrase in the shop. In another case an Italian worker

> was giving the Yankees an unmerciful lashing, when several of the persons present asked why the divel he had come among them? He answered with the most provoking composure, that he had committed a very great robbery in his

38. William Otter, Sr., *History of My Own Times* (Emmitsburg, Md., 1835), 82–84, 128–129, boasts of his attacks on blacks and Irishmen early in the century. Vetter, *Zwei Jahre*, 96; for a similar example see "A Workingman's Recollections of America," 103. Hostility toward Irish: Kerby Miller, "Emigrant and Exiles: The Irish Exodus to North America, from Colonial Times to the First World War" (diss., University of California, Berkeley, 1976), 788–789. Burn, *Beggar Boy*, 308–310, 330; *British Mechanic's and Labourer's Hand Book*, 151; Brownlee, *American Odyssey*, 20.

own country, and had been obliged to take wing. "I reflected," he observed, "which of the Old World *contries* I should go to; then I though about America, and I said that is the *contry* for an honest man to succeed in, so I comes here.!"

No doubt such needling sometimes ended with an exchange of blows, but workers were most admired who were adept at badinage and could return one insult with another. In addition to humor, workers used politics and sports as outlets for some of this ethnic tension, a point discussed in Chapter 7 below.[39]

Although workers strove in the workplace to counteract possibly disruptive influences that might threaten their wages, they did not labor with solemnity. In fact, good humor and high spirits were common. Singing in the shop was customary in New York, for example. Female straw sewers "are exceedingly fond of singing," the *Herald* reported; "the whole work-room at times responds to their melody, for they generally sing in chorus." Gompers remembered one worker who sang "song after song" in the Greenwich Street cigar manufactory where Gompers worked, and in one shop there was a song contest between English- and German-speaking workers. There were many nationalities in the hat shops Burn worked, with "the musical gentlemen singing the songs of their native countries in their different languages." Burn was especially surprised to discover that native American workers often sang traditional British ballads.[40]

Pranks and high jinks routinely enlivened the constant pace of work; Burn referred to "those constantly recurring episodes and incidents in which mirth, folly, and not infrequently angry feelings are mingled among large bodies of men, when they are inclined to be playful. Sometimes the butt of the shop would be stirred up for the special amusement of the mischief makers; but which would be enjoyed less or more even by the Solons!" One day a slightly drunk worker bellowed " 'Stops de ball,' " and his fellows dunked him in the tank used for washing hats. "Mine Got, cum an zee de wale," yelled a delighted German hatter. The same levity prevailed in printing, as an account of the scene in the composing room of the *Tribune* in 1869 suggests:

"Proof for No. —!" yells the boy.
Some droll typo[grapher] remarks: "Oh, no, that can't be—must be a mistake somewhere!"
As No. — happens to be a notoriously incorrect compositor, a general laugh follows. No. — retorts with a intimation that the droll typo is suffering from an

39. *British Mechanic's and Labourer's Hand Book*, 151, 150. Burn, *Beggar Boy*, 308, 321; see also Thomas Gunn, *The Physiology of New York Boarding-Houses* (New York, 1857), 83, 244–245.
40. *Herald*, 7 June 1853; Gompers, *Seventy Years*, 1:68, 76. Burn, *Beggar Boy*, 404–405; see also McCready, *On the Influence*, 73, and Thomas Dudgeon, *A Nine Years Residence and a Nine Months Tour on Foot, in the States of New York and Pennsylvania, for the Use of Labourers, Farmers and Emigrants* (Edinburgh, 1841), 9–10.

attack of jim-jams, and a steady stream of jokes and sarcastic allusions follow, until some witty genius says, in a grave voice, "Now we'll have the opening chorus!" accompanying it with a song, usually chanted by a brother typo while on a spree, and another round of laughter follows.

According to Henry Brokmeyer—a German immigrant who worked in New York as a currier and shoemaker and later became a molder—a worker would make "a remark apparently without occasion. It is in a tone of voice a little above the ordinary—courting . . . a challenging reply. Soon you hear peals of laughter, and everyone seems in duty bound to add something to the entertainment. The day closes with the livliest feelings of good fellowship pervading the shop." Pranksterism and joking should not be exaggerated— workers were more likely to recall high jinks than mention days when nothing exciting occurred. Nevertheless, such bantering is much less common in Burn's account of English workshops, and he was surprised to discover that American hat shops "through the whole day . . . [were] filled with singing, shouting, cursing, swearing, fighting, laughing and romping."[41]

Such high spirits can be traced to two factors. Clearly, the youthfulness of the workforce is important. It is also possible that the tight labor market gave a characteristic "high energy" to the entire workshop. The research of environmental psychologist Roger Barker indicates that working in an "undermanned" instead of an "overmanned setting" has demonstrable psychological effects. His evidence suggests that the American labor scarcity may have had a significance beyond ease in getting a job, and it has already been proposed that the labor scarcity led to "abundance consciousness" and a fast pace of work. The labor scarcity may have imparted high energy not only to the workplace but, as Chapter 8 will argue, to working-class life in general. Although high spirits were to some degree a rejection of authority, such exuberance, given the generally strong motivation of most workers, probably enhanced rather than diminished output. When working at a railroad pace, it was necessary occasionally to "let off steam."[42]

The impact of rapid turnover on the relations between employees is less clear. It might be expected that turnover would hinder the development of mutual feelings in the shop; it would be, as the English Workman put it, "every man for himself alone." This, however, was not always the case. A new man was traditionally required to pay a "footing" or "garnish" to buy drinks for shopmates, which served to introduce him to all. The ritual fines

41. Burn, *Beggar Boy*, 307–308; Amos Cummings, "How Newspapers Are Made," *Packard's Monthly* n.s. 1 (1869), 20. "Jim-jams" is delirium tremens. Brokmeyer, *Mechanic's Diary*, 10; Burn, *Beggar Boy*, 287.

42. Roger Barker, *Ecological Psychology* (Stanford, Calif., 1968), esp. 200–202; see also Allan W. Wicker, *An Introduction to Ecological Psychology* (Monterey, Calif., 1979), 70–80, 139–157, esp. 73, 79, 146.

and mock trials under the "Strong Beer Act" (for wearing a dirty shirt or not extinguishing candles, for example) that characterized English artisanal life were absent among New York workers; even paying footing apparently became less common in the 1850s. However, short apprenticeships and the weakness of "the Trade" were probably more responsible than turnover for the erosion of such artisanal traditions.[43]

The regional New York labor market may have helped counteract the effects of turnover. Indeed, turnover was so rapid that new workers routinely found workmates they knew from previous employment. When beginning work with a new employer, both James Burn and Samuel Gompers ran into workers they had known earlier. Probably the high spirits and camaraderie among workers of similar age also served to help unite employees. The English Workman's claim that there is no "good feeling and the helping hand in cases of sickness is there unknown" is belied by numerous accounts such as William Darnley's, of a fellow English worker "who has had very poor health for some time so we made up a Subscription in the shop about 48 dollars the Boss give eight." Workers were extremely generous to their ailing workmates; the *Times* employees raised $500 for an ill Irish journeyman compositor.[44]

## WORKERS AND BOSSES

The factors that influenced relations among workers are also relevant to the boss-worker relationship. However, the situation here was somewhat more complex, with a marked difference between sexes. I describe first the situation in the workplace between men and bosses, then between women and bosses, and conclude with strikes.

The tight labor market posed problems for employers trying to control their male workers. Bosses, for example, could not always pick and choose who to hire. When boss printer John West saw the young Horace Greeley with his illfitting clothes and very pale complexion, he demanded of his foreman: "Did you hire that ———— fool?" "Yes," the foreman replied, "we must have hands, and he's the best I could get." "When work was hurrying, and help

43. *London v. New York*, 9; see also Burn, *Three Years*, 24. Footing: *The Autobiography of Thurlow Weed*, ed. Harriet Weed (Boston, 1883), 1:58; "A Working Man's Recollections," 109; and Burn, *Beggar Boy*, 258. English artisanal rituals: Dunlop, *Artificial and Compulsory Drinking*, esp. 121, 132. Decline of footing: "The Autobiography of Caleb Snug, of Snugtown, Carriage-Maker," *New York Coach-Maker's Magazine* 2 (1859), 44, and 3 (1860), 109.

44. *London v. New York*, 9. William Darnley, letter to his wife, 29 August 1858; see also *Genius Rewarded, or the Story of the Sewing Machine* (New York, 1880), 63. *Printer* 1 (1858), 249.

hard to get, bosses would take all comers,'' shipcarpenter Frank Harley remembered.[45]

Employers were also reluctant to fire workers for disciplinary reasons; one coachmaker was forced to accept an employee's heavy drinking because "it was very difficult to get good trimmers at all." When the *New York Tribune* attempted to measure the output of its compositors in 1852, the workers declared it "incompatible with their dignity as men" and immediately walked out. In the booming economy of the period, these compositors probably had few worries about finding other work, and the paper quickly backed down. (Thomas Chamberlain the printer worked for ten different firms in six months.) George Bruce, the boss typecaster, tried to avoid such problems by reprimanding workers as gently as possible, according to a memoirist. One worker arrived at work "under the influence," and Bruce

> called to him, and said: "Mr. T."—he always commanded the respect of the workman by addressing them as equals—"I observe you have been very irregular in your work for some time, and I speak to you of your habits as much for your own interest as mine . . . for . . . you are losing your time and destroying your health. I wish you to be more attentive hereafter."

Bruce eventually fired the worker, but after an apology Mr. T. was rehired, and Bruce told him, "I did not wish to close the door altogether against you."[46]

The difficulty of "driving" workers minimized the power of the foreman. Far from the authoritarian rulers of the workplace they would become later in the century, most antebellum foremen were simply coordinators of work and had little authority on personnel matters. Except in hatting, foremen usually did not have the power to hire or dismiss employees. Although the use of foremen in the city's industrial establishments is impossible to quantify, it seems clear it grew substantially in the 1840s and 1850s. Since shop size was basically stagnant and workers' conduct generally unexceptionable, the most plausible explanation for this growth is the increasing use of systems that required a more careful timing and organization of work. However, decisions about speed and manner of working remained in the hands of workers themselves. When Samuel Warshinge, a shipwright, was appointed to "superintend" the Fickett and Thomas shipyard in 1835, he did not receive any raise in his $2-a-day wages (though he did enjoy immunity from layoffs during the

45. Parton, *Life of Greeley*, 90; "Chips," *Fincher's Trades' Review*, 27 January 1866.

46. "Autobiography of Caleb Snug," 142; Stevens, *New York Typographical Union*, 386–387; C. C. Savage, "George Bruce, A Sketch of His Life in Connection with Printing," *Printer* 6 (1866), 179. The disciplinary problems employers faced when labor was scarce is discussed in Jonathan Prude, *The Coming of Industrial Order: Town and Factory Life in Rural Massachusetts, 1810–1860* (Cambridge, Mass., 1983), 155–156.

1837 panic and was paid when the shipyard was struck). As time went on, wages for foremen began to diverge from those of workers: by the 1850s foremen received approximately 25 percent more than other employees. The foremen at Steinway, for example, were paid fifty cents a day more than the $2 most workers received in the early 1850s. In most accounts of work by male employees in the city's factories (excluding dockwork, where stevedores were often tyrants), the foreman seems to have had a relatively minor role in labor discipline, especially with the widespread adoption of piecerates in the city.[47]

Overall, male workers were on a more equal footing with the employer in America than in Europe. In England "it is . . . but too common for employers to think that by giving men work they are conferring a favour." But as a Gentleman Lately Arrived in New York noted, American workmen "consider that you are as much obliged to them, as they are to you for your money." Isaac Holmes, an English traveler of the 1820s, noted the same phenomenon and added, "indeed in a country where there is plenty of work, the obligation is the greatest on the part of the employer." John Kerr, the Irish immigrant, decided to become a machinist rather than a clerk because "one thing [is] certain there are no class of working people so independent as mechanics." In the expression frequently repeated in immigrant letters, "Jack is as good as his master." John Parks, an immigrant carpenter who lived on Hudson Street, wrote to a friend in 1827, "workmen here are not afraid of their master; they seem as equals." As labor scarcity diminished, this independence diminished as well, but throughout the antebellum period male American workers and bosses enjoyed an unusual degree of parity.[48]

This new and more equal relationship, so surprising to immigrants, was exemplified in the use of the word "boss." Derived from "baas," the Dutch word for master, it was in use in the city as early as 1817 when Henry Fearon encountered it. Shortly thereafter it spread throughout the country, perhaps because of its use among the work gangs building the Erie Canal. Workers much preferred the term to "master," and its use was considered proof of the

47. On foremen in the late nineteenth century, see Daniel Nelson, "Chapter Three—The Foremen's Empire," *Workers and Managers* (Madison, Wis., 1975), 34–54. Foremen in hatting: Greeley, *Art and Industry*, 142. Samuel Warshinge, Account Book and Personal Notes, August 1835, NYHS. Information on foremen's wages in New York printing and metalworking firms from U.S. Congress, Senate, Committee on Finance, *Report on Wholesale Prices, Wages and Transportation*, "by Mr. Aldrich," 52d Cong., 2d sess., 1893, S. Rept. 1394, pt. 2, 354–392, and pt. 3, 1209–1263. Information on Steinway from pay records reproduced in Census Office, *Tenth Census, 1880, Wages in Manufacturing*, XX, 292; see also 450, 453.

48. Burn, *Social Conditions of the Working Classes*, 52–53. *Scotsman*, 18 April 1828. Isaac Holmes, *An Account of the United States of America* (London, 1823), 375. John Kerr, letter to William Kerr, 5 August 1848. "Jack": John Parks letter, 8 December 1827, in Benjamin Smith, ed., *Twenty-Four Letters from Labourers in America to Their Friends in England* (London, 1829), 37; see also Schrier, *Ireland*, 25; Dallas Jones, "Background and Motives," 275; and Burn, *Social Condition of the Working Classes*, 90. Parks letter quoted in Benjamin Smith, 26.

high status of workers in the New World. Similarly the term "help" was favored over "servant": "If you call them servants they leave you without notice," wrote Fearon.[49]

Fortunately for the bosses, most workers were willing to work quickly and regularly on their own—there was little need to drive workers. Immigrants had come to America to improve their material condition, and most accepted the notion that higher wages required harder work. American wages were indeed, as the *Chartist Circular* put it, "a powerful stimulus . . . to unexceptional conduct." Thus, although the means to enforce labor discipline were relatively weak, the need to use them was, in most cases, also weak. The bosses and the "men" were manual workers and shared the goal of making money, though, as we shall shortly see, the division of this money was bitterly contested. Employers seem usually to have treated workers respectfully, and usually employees labored diligently in return.

The ambience in the city's workshops, given their small size, reflected bosses' personalities. The economic orientation of the workers ensured, however, a permanent division between the person who paid wages and laid off employees and those who received wages and were themselves laid off; despite greater equality the difference in power was still wide. After Henry Walter became a boss manufacturing jeweler, a former employee tried to exploit an alleged friendship with him. Walter set the matter straight: "I knew him as any Employer knows the employees in his shop. He was no companion of mine." Usually relations were civil—in the 1840s Henry Price, for instance, had long discussions about religion with his boss cabinetmaker, who was an atheist. "Ah Henry when you are as old as I am you will think differently," the boss would sigh. But friendships between bosses and workers were rare.[50]

Although employers generally found workers willing to labor at a "railroad pace," both the rise of the factory and outwork posed problems. In these environments bosses found it much more difficult to personally determine how hard employees were working. Therefore payment by the piece, the traditional method of pay in such trades as cabinetmaking, was adapted to these settings. Even in many small shops the growing division of labor often made it more satisfactory to adopt piecework. As late as the 1830s, it seems, most workers were paid by the day, and piecework, though common, was still the exception. By the 1850s piecework was exceedingly widespread, and

49. Fearon, *Sketches of America*, 58. Fearon's use of the word is the earliest recorded in an unambiguously non-Dutch context: see William A. Cragie and James R. Hulbert, eds., *A Dictionary of American English* (Chicago, 1938), 1:228. Holmes, *Account*, 342 is another early example. On the use of the term among workers see William Darnley, letter to his wife, 13 April 1858, and White, *Sketches from America*, 371. Fearon, *Sketches of America*, 80.

50. Henry Walter, "An Autobiography of an English Tramp from 1812 to 1888 inclusive," 48. Price diary, 28; see also Graham, *Handset Reminiscences*, 78.

British workers such as James Burn and Frank Roney commented on its universality.[51]

Employers were aware of the strong economic motivation of most of their workforce and no doubt hoped piecerates would assure them of high output. James Harper, for example, told foremen at his Cliff Street plant that "it is so much easier to draw than push" employees. Employers were usually not disappointed in the results. They uniformly stated that piecerates not only made things easier for them but were favored by the workers as well. Abram Hewitt flatly claimed that "among the larger numbers of mechanics in America there is a preference for piece work." One city capmaker told Penny, "most [pay] by the piece, which is usually most profitable to the worker, and most satisfactory to both parties." The foreman of the *Tribune*'s composing room even believed the 1852 strike was designed to reverse the changes "from piece to week work." Though this evidence comes from employers, protests by workmen against piecework was uncommon, and it may well be that a labor force dominated by immigrants eager for high wages did indeed favor piecework.[52]

Neither workers nor bosses had yet completely "learned the rules" of piecework. By the 1850s some employers were beginning to learn to cut rates when employees speeded up, which workers regarded as a cruel betrayal. However, as David Montgomery has noted, there seems little evidence that workers learned the rationality of stinting before the 1870s. It may be the depression that began in 1873 marked a crucial turning point for American workers, from traditional "abundance consciousness" to the beginnings of "scarcity consciousness"; by the 1880s workers were beginning to fix a limit on work done. In the 1850s and 1860s, however, piecerate workers may have believed it was to their advantage to produce as much as possible. The idea of a "rate buster" seems to have been unknown in the antebellum period.[53]

The most serious threat to efficiency bosses faced from their workforce was not the need to drive reluctant workers but high turnover. "Every store," a

51. *British Mechanic's and Labourer's Hand Book*, 108; Burn, *Beggar Boy*, 287; Roney, *Autobiography*, 180.

52. Eugene Exman, *The House of Harper* (New York, 1967), 7; *Parliamentary Papers* XXXII (1867), 181. Penny, *How Women Can Make Money*, 327; see also the *Coach-Maker's Hand-Book*, 345, and *Tribune*, 5 September 1845. Stevens, *New York Typographical Union*, 385. The city's stonecutters also struck for piecerates (*Workingman's Advocate*, 6 June 1835).

53. For early cases of piecerate reduction in the city, see the *Tribune*, 7 June 1853, and Burn, *Social Condition of the Working Classes*, 51. David Montgomery, *The Fall of the House of Labor: The Workplace, the State and American Labor Activism, 1865–1925* (Cambridge, England, 1987), 22. Evidence on the widespread nature of stinting in the late nineteenth century is given in *Regulation and Restriction of Output*. For evidence of the stint in New York City, see N. I. Stone, "Wages and Regularity of Employment and Standardization of Piece Rates in the Dress and Waist Industry of New York City," *Bulletin of the United States Bureau of Labor Statistics* no. 146 (1914), 35.

corset manufacturer told Virginia Penny, "has its own way of doing business," and Gompers noted that "while cigar making is pretty much the same everywhere, it took some little time to get into the ways of a shop in order to do one's best work." Type cases in the city's printshops were not completely standardized, and so each time a compositor changed employers "he is hindered . . . in his quick and ready way of distributing [type]." The high quit rate among employees kept wages high and was clearly a drag on productivity; it was the most common source of criticism of workers by employers, who bitterly complained that too many workers left without adequate notice. According to the *Coach-Maker's Hand-Book,* the thing a boss liked most in a worker was reliability—the confidence "in seeing him the following day." Too often, employers insisted, this confidence was misplaced. Obviously the polite treatment bosses often accorded workers helped to some extent to reduce turnover, but it failed to prevent workers from seeking better-paying jobs.[54]

More effective was the commonly encountered technique of holding back part of a worker's wages when "the ghost walked," as the expression went for being paid. Clearly the widespread withholding of wages was not done solely to reduce turnover; the use of credit by merchants and a delay of two or three months before manufacturers were paid for their goods left bosses seasonally strapped for cash. Nevertheless, the impact of such withholding upon potentially mobile workers was recognized. The Anonymous Proofreader worked at Trow's on Greene Street in Ward Eight for a week and earned $8.93, "out of which they deducted one dollar ninety-three cents, stating in reply to my remonstrance that they always kept a balance in their own favor." John Burke, the Irish shoemaker, discovered similarly that "all the workmen could draw was $5.00 per week. All else went on their [the employees'] Books and when they wanted to draw what accumulated . . . they would have to give a week or two notice." A worker who quit realized that he might have some difficulty collecting back pay. This practice was one of the most common sources of complaints by laboring men in the city and served, in no small degree, to sour relations between employees and bosses.[55]

Relations between women workers and their employers differed sharply

---

54. Penny, *How Women Can Make Money,* 334; Gompers, *Seventy Years,* 1:63; C. S. Van Winkle, *The Printer's Guide: or, An Introduction to the Art of Printing* (New York, 1836), 123; *Coach-Maker's Hand-Book,* 354.

55. A good example of these delayed payments is found in the Smith and Colgate account books, 1807–1838, Baker Library, Harvard Graduate School of Business Administration: in the spring monthly sales (1817–1820) averaged $650 and receipts $443, whereas in the summer sales were $317 and receipts $923 monthly. *Real Experiences of an Emigrant,* 105–106; John Burke Reminiscences. For complaints by workers, see Weed, *Autobiography,* 57; Mooney, *Nine Years in America,* 80; *Tribune,* 28 May 1853; *Herald,* 7 June 1853; and William Darnley, letter to his wife, 20 July 1858.

from those of male workers. As noted in Chapter 4, many women employees were supplementary workers. Just as these women (estimated at one-half of the female workforce) determined the market for women's labor, so they also influenced the relationship between women and their employers. Because they were only supplementing family income and turned most of their earnings over to their parents, they lacked the commanding economic motivation of men (and nonsupplementary women).

Since supplementary workers lacked this economic stimulation, employers had much more difficulty in getting them to work at the customary railroad pace. The foreman in one city clothing establishment, for instance, found "those [women] that are dependent on the work for a living, do their work better than those that merely do it for pocket money." Complaints by employers about the lack of work discipline among female workers were widespread—"Not more than half of them . . . are steady sober workers," "they make money, and then must have a day or two to rest," "they . . . want a day to go to a picnic, to get ready for a party, or to help their mothers at home," and "are always absent on Monday." In short, "men are considered more reliable . . . and are more easily managed."[56]

Employers could have attempted to restrict hiring to primary female workers but, to return to a point made in Chapter 4, that would have forced them to raise wages to subsistence level. They therefore began to impose a strict labor discipline on the workforce. It was among women workers, not men, that industrial discipline made its most powerful impression in the city, and the relationship between employers and female employees was far different from the relationship between men and their bosses. Employers attempted to regulate strictly the female workforce, to compel the fast and regular style of work they regarded as normal. As early as the 1830s, a systematic attempt was begun to impose order and promptness on female workers in the city's factories. By 1845 female workers in some bookfolding establishments were "not permitted even to speak to each other during" working hours; Brooks Brothers maintained silence among sewers in its inside shop in the late 1850s; and by 1872, in some hoop-skirt manufactories, "the 'silent system' of prisons is rigidly enforced . . . and . . . the windows are closely curtained, so that no girl can look out upon the street." Bruce and Company had a set of "Rules for Employees" that prohibited women workers from going from "[grind]Stone to Stone holding conversations with those who are at work" and directed that "No singing is allowed, nor idle talk" permitted among

56. Penny, *How Women Can Make Money*, 355, 333, 218, 387, 458. Steven Dubnoff, "Gender, the Family and the Problem of Work Motivation in the Transition to Industrial Capitalism," *Journal of Family History* 4 (1979), 121–136, comes to a similar conclusion about female workers, using evidence from a Lowell textile mill. See also Christine Stansell, *City of Women: Sex and Class in New York, 1789–1860* (New York, 1986), 123–125.

"Girls," "by Order of Messrs. Geo. Bruce & Co." It is extremely unlikely that bosses could have enforced, or even would have tried to enforce, such discipline on men. Moreover, the role of the foreman differed. For male workers the foreman was largely a coordinator of production, but where women were employed the foremen and forewomen exercised a great deal of authority and drove employees to increase output.[57]

Such strict disciplinary constraints risked supplementary female workers quitting, and indeed turnover was high (at Bruce and Company the management kept a $1.50 deposit to discourage leaving "if they do not give a week's notice"). But there were always other workers willing to take the place, since there was no labor scarcity for women in most trades. Most women's work was not highly skilled, and hence women workers could be relatively easily replaced, a fact that, with their concentration in seasonal trades, foiled attempts to organize women workers in New York City. Female labor organizing, as Christine Stansell shows, was "short-lived [and] fragile." Working women were unable to sustain unions, despite attempts during the 1830s and the Age of Gold. Relations between women workers and their bosses, then, were quite different from those of males. Discipline was formally and often rigidly enforced as the employers tried hard to compel women to "drive business" the way men did.[58]

## WORKERS AND UNIONS

Male workers were generally treated with respect, and imposed discipline was rarely needed to get them to work hard. (Among women the situation was different, but here I focus primarily on men.) Because the workforce was highly motivated and enjoyed a comparatively high standard of living, it might be guessed that labor relations in the city were cordial. Sometimes, indeed, relations were harmonious, but very often they were not. "What, you say, do strikes occur in America? Yes," wrote the anonymous English Workman. James Burn was also surprised: "I may observe that during the short time I had been in the country I had witnessed more trouble between the

57. *Tribune*, 20 August 1845; Penny, *How Women Can Make Money*, 113. James D. McCabe, *Lights and Shadows of New York Life* (New York, 1872), 827; see also Sikes, "Among the Poor Girls," 441. "Rules for Employees," 6 June 1835, Bruce Papers, Rare Book and Manuscript Library, Columbia University. Foremen: Sikes, 440; article on Douglas and Sherwood's Hoop Skirt Manufactory, *Harper's Weekly* 3 (1859), 68, and *Times*, 2 March 1859. The *Herald*'s 7 June 1853 article on straw sewers, however, reports that forewomen "have very little responsibility resting on them."

58. "Rules for Employees," 6 June 1835, Bruce Papers; Stansell, *City of Women*, quotation 152, 130–154. The difficulties women had in sustaining unions should not be viewed as too sharp a contrast with men; as the next section shows, male workers also had a difficult time creating enduring unions.

men and their employees in the course of half a year than I had experienced in as many years at home."[59]

Although economic motivation made the workforce willing to work hard, it also made it willing to strike, both to raise wages and to keep them up. The vast majority of strikes directly or indirectly involved wages, by far the most salient issue to workers. The best evidence for this proposition is how carefully workers waited for a tight labor market before striking: the greatest strike waves were during the booms of the mid-1830s and the 1850s, and most strikes were in the spring busy season. With one large exception of strikes in the mid-1830s, for shorter hours, wage consciousness of workers was the main cause of labor turmoil in the city, and the importance of economic considerations in the decision to emigrate makes this conclusion no surprise. To many workers, strikes were simply the most logical way of raising wages. "Every employer has a right to get work done as cheaply as he can, and the workingmen have an equal right to get what they can for their labor," one printer explained.[60]

The seasonal nature of Manhattan work no doubt magnified labor unrest. By giving each side its chance—unions in the busy season, bosses in the slack season—the variability of manufacturing heightened labor turmoil. Herman Feldman explained in 1925 "that . . . strikes, and other indicators of friction are more likely to occur in . . . seasonal and irregular occupations." John Britton of Brewster and Company Coachworks complained that "our business is chiefly an order business. When full of orders . . . we [are] . . . always liable to unjust and inopportune demands from the men. Once we came very near a strike; owing to the business undertaken we were forced to yield." Seasonal acrimony was heightened by rapid turnover, which often reduced employers' feelings of responsibility for any individual worker; many bosses "merely treat them as tools." In dull seasons employers quickly laid off workers whom they disliked but had been forced by labor scarcity to retain.[61]

Although seasonality increased strife, it probably also hindered the formation of permanent labor unions. Unions in the city collapsed during the 1837

59. *London v. New York*, 10. Burn, *Beggar Boy*, 297; see also Julius Wesslau, letter to his parents, 28 May 1864, in Helbich, "*Amerika ist ein freies Land*," 87. The hat trade Burn worked in was notoriously conflict-prone; see the *Tribune*, 7 November 1853.

60. The centrality of wage demands is emphasized in Carl Degler, "Labor in the Economy and Politics of New York City, 1850–1860; A Study of the Impact of Early Industrialism" (diss., Columbia University, 1952), 13–15, and Lawrence Costello, "The New York City Labor Movement 1861–1873" (diss., Columbia University, 1967), esp. 65–73. This later period also saw a powerful eight-hour movement. Robert M. Poer quoted in Stevens, *New York Typographical Union*, 289. Thomas Chamberlain described his strike activity in his diary without comment of any sort; Chamberlain diary, 16 May 1853.

61. Virtually all strikes were in the busy season: see the list of strikes in Costello, "New York City Labor," 579. Feldman, *Regularization of Employment*, 32; see also Lloyd Ulman, *The Rise of the National Trade Union* (Cambridge, Mass., 1955), 440–453. *Coach-Maker's Hand-Book*, 354; *New York World*, 31 August 1871.

depression; but business picked up in the mid-1840s, so did union activity. In the 1830s strikes were common, many without previous union organization. Indeed, in the shipyards sometimes "the first notice the bosses get . . . of the strike being our refusal to go to work as the usual hour." More or less spontaneous walkouts continued to be used in response to wage cuts and by unskilled workers, but for skilled workers a pattern had begun to develop by 1850.[62]

Generally, a union would be created, or revived, during the spring busy season in March or April. Meeting in a saloon, or in a rented hall such as Hillenbrand's Mechanics' Hall on Hester Street, the union would elect officers, set dues, and appoint a committee to ascertain wages in the various workshops in the trade. In crafts such as pianoforte making the proceedings were translated into English and German. The clothing industries had separate German and "American," that is, mostly Irish, unions that coordinated actions and tried to prevent bosses from playing them off one against the other.[63]

The union would then debate the increase to be demanded (usually 10 to 15 percent). A committee of workers would be delegated to "wait upon" the employers and inform them of the requested increase. Union demands were presented as a judicious defensive action—a "just rate" or a "fair remuneration" necessary to offset increased living expenses and especially rising rents.

Bosses actually raised wages without a strike fairly often, and the union would pass a motion praising them for their decision. Indeed, in some trades the employers voluntarily raised wages to forestall union organization. More usually, however, some bosses would agree to the wage increase whereas others would refuse. In such cases a strike was accepted as necessary: as one shoemaker explained in 1853, "he was against strikes if there was any other mode for the working men to right themselves, but there was not." The Tailors' Association in 1850 pledged "ourselves to work for no store of any description whatever unless the terms of the bill [of prices] be complied with." Union members would urge nonunion workers to join them in striking "foul" shops and would sometimes parade through the streets to publicize their cause. In March 1860 the *Tribune* explained that "at this season of the year, with the increased demand for labor, the workingman . . . usually expects an increase in the rates of wages. Strikes, and threats to strike, usually occur just about this time."[64]

Strike funds would usually be raised from union members working in

62. "Chips—Early Strikes," *Fincher's Trades' Review*, 10 February 1866.
63. The description of unions and strikes in this and the succeeding paragraphs is taken from the *Herald* and *Tribune*, 1850–1853, 1859. The *Tribune* reported on unions under the headings "City Items" and "Labor Movements." The *Herald* dealt with them under "The Trades." Degler, "Labor in the Economy," 11–69, gives a detailed account of union activities in the 1850s.
64. *Tribune*, 12 April 1853, 5 August 1850, and 31 March 1860.

"fair" shops. Some crafts, among them cordwainers and chairmakers, established union-backed shops where striking employees could continue to work. Most strikes were relatively short—the timing during busy season put pressure on bosses to settle, and the weak organization of many unions was unable to sustain long strikes when employers refused to raise pay. Most strikes were in April, May, and June, though some lasted into July. Generally, by August the spring offensive was over and many unions would hibernate until the following spring.

The boom-and-bust pattern made it difficult for permanent unions, which might have helped stabilize collective bargaining, to survive. In most trades a coterie of union leaders persisted from year to year, but the unions themselves lacked, in Lawrence Costello's words, "an essential ingredient of the modern American labor movement—continuity." The less variable manufacturing of the industrial belt seems to have sustained more enduring unions; on Manhattan, however, "turnouts" were often called by makeshift unions when workers had the advantage. And without permanent unions, as Burn pointed out, "in seasons of dull trade the employers have matters all their own way, and of course are not slow to ring the changes upon the men."[65]

In the 1820s and 1830s the trades in the city held processions to celebrate Independence Day and such major events as the completion of the Erie Canal in 1825. Typically, as Sean Wilentz has described, artisans marched behind banners emblematic of their trade—masters and journeymen paraded together in the 1820s, though by the 1830s the journeymen held a separate celebration. These craft organizations were not devoted only to the economic interests of their members; the regalia (often based on English models) exemplified their pride in, and devotion to, "the Trade." The Society of Shipwrights and Caulkers spent much of its first meeting in 1815 debating how to acquire a banner "for the purpose of walking in the procession on the Fourth of July next." The members later voted to procure "articles Emblematic of our Trade," including a ceremonial caulking hammer.[66]

By the 1850s this Anglo-American artisanal tradition was virtually dead. Unions in the city were economic organizations that waxed and waned with economic conditions; embodying their members' attachment to the trade was no longer significant. Many unions resembled that of the ladies' shoemakers (men who made women's shoes) which, according to the *Tribune*, "shines out for a while, then flickers and remains inert until some other occasion may

65. Costello, "New York City Labor," 7. Burn, *Three Years*, 188.

66. Sean Wilentz, "Artisan Republican Festivals and the Rise of Class Conflict in New York City, 1788–1837," in Michael H. Frisch and Daniel J. Walkowitz, eds., *Working-Class America: Essays in Labor, Community and American Society* (Urbana, Ill., 1983), 37–77. On the Erie Canal Celebration see James Hardie, *The Description of the City of New York* (New York, 1827), 142–144. Minute book, Society of Shipwrights and Caulkers, 29 May and 19 June 1815, Rare Books and Manuscripts Division, The New York Public Library, Astor, Lenox and Tilden Foundations.

demand its action.'' Parades continued to be a major part of urban life until the Civil War, but processions of the 1850s were quite different. The huge 1858 parade to celebrate the completion of the Atlantic Cable illustrates this change. Only two trades marched—the butchers and the New York Typographical Union. The rest of the parade consisted of militia companies, ethnic organizations such as the St. Patrick Society and *turnvereinen,* and wagons representing city factories and displaying their goods—safes, pianofortes, and sewing machines. ''Various lager bier wagons'' made up the tail of the parade, the *Times* reported.[67]

Unions in this period had too ephemeral an existence to have a major impact on workers' daily lives. Industrial belt cities such as Paterson seem to have had a strong base of union support, and unions were a powerful influence on local politics. But matters were much more difficult for unions in the city. Few of the city's unions had their own meeting halls, and before the 1860s social events were rare. Unions lacked the ongoing existence of other major working-class institutions, and even in good times only a minority of workers belonged: in the late 1830s and early 1850s—two periods when New York unions did show significant strength—only about one-quarter of the city's male workers were unionized.[68]

Indeed, it may be the boom and bust of city unions helped increase the attractiveness of cooperatives, land reform, and political action to city workers. Horace Greeley argued that strikes and unions were incapable of permanently raising the living standards of the working class, since any wages increases were temporary and would be rescinded in the slack season. The evidence suggests this criticism had some validity on antebellum Manhattan. In the long run the strike proved its value, whereas independent political action and cooperatives proved less successful. Nevertheless unions, though able to raise wages, were often unable to keep them up.[69]

The age structure of the workforce may also have contributed to the city's

67. Ladies' shoemakers: *Tribune,* 5 September 1845. The Atlantic Cable Parade was reported in the *Times, Tribune,* and *Herald* on 2 September 1858. There was a spontaneous procession on 18 August, the day the cable was completed, by laborers building Central Park. The laborers marched down Broadway with each work gang marching behind a banner emblazoned with the name of their gang boss. They were addressed by the mayor in City Hall Park. See the *Tribune* and the *Herald,* 19 August 1858.

68. Social events: Degler, ''Labor in the Economy,'' 44; and Costello, ''New York City Labor,'' 98–102. On unions' strength in the 1830s see Wilentz, *Chants Democratic,* 220–221, and Maurice Neufeld, ''The Size of the Jacksonian Labor Movement: A Cautionary Account,'' *Labor History* 23 (1982), 599–607. The suggestion of the *New York Post* in 1836, quoted in John R. Commons et al., eds., *Documentary History of American Industrial Society* (Cleveland, 1910), 4:322, that ''two-thirds'' of all workingmen in the city belonged to unions is very likely much too high. For the 1850s, compare the memberships given by Degler, 25, with the total workers in the city compiled by Robert Ernst, *Immigrant Life in New York City, 1825–1863* (1949; rpt. New York, 1979), 214–217.

69. Greeley often criticized strikes: see, for example, the *Tribune,* 24 July 1850 and 12 March 1860.

combative labor relations. Clark Kerr and Abraham Siegel explain that workers with a "regularized family . . . life" are less likely to strike. Occupations such as logging and dockwork—where employees tend to be single and young—have high strike rates. In antebellum New York City single young workers were heavily represented in the workforce. Without family obligations (and also, it should be noted, without family members to aid during a strike), workers in the city may have felt fewer restraints about "turning out."[70]

Though these factors clearly heightened strike activity, strikes involved a bitterness that went beyond a simple expression of workers' economic interests. Strikes in the city were not the routine affairs they would become in the twentieth century; strikers often marched through the streets to mobilize support. High wages were not enough to satisfy employees who felt they were not getting their rightful share from the bosses, especially when times were good and profits high. Although the employer often worked beside his men, power and interests were different, and the separation between them could widen into a chasm. Burn discovered that any worker who attempted to defend an employer during a strike would be branded a "creep," "slave," or "traitor," as well as being made the "butt of ridicule by every fool in the shop." When the Anonymous Cabinetmaker refused to go out on strike in 1836, his fellow workers "resorted to threats, and promised to waylay and 'hammer' me on my way home from work." After a few months in New York in 1858, William Darnley expressed this widely felt acrimony: "the Bosses as they call them they wont call them Master no such thing but they are their masters I can assure you for they reduce their wages without the least resistance."[71]

Workers felt they had a moral right to a "fair remuneration." They labored hard and in return expected high wages. This implicit bargain may have been ratified in the strikes of the mid-1830s for shorter hours—a major exception to workers' singular wage consciousness. Reports of the fast pace predate the strikes of 1835–36 but increase afterward. In shipbuilding the use of division of labor was a direct result of shorter hours, and the traditional craftsmen in that trade gave way to fast-working specialists. In other trades the growth of mass demand put increasing emphasis during these years on rapid production. My focus on 1836 as a year of change is speculative, but clearly workers in

70. Clark Kerr and Abraham Siegel, "The Interindustry Propensity to Strike," in Kerr, *Labor Management in Industrial Society* (Garden City, N.Y., 1964), 115. Michelle Perrot's study of French strikes led her to conclude that "family men rarely take the initiative in making claims against the employer." Perrott, *Workers on Strike: France, 1871–1890*, trans. Chris Turner (New Haven, Conn., 1987), 102.

71. Burn, *Three Years*, 187; "A Working Man's Recollections of America," 108; William Darnley, letter to his wife, 13 April 1858.

general had to give "a much greater amount of labor" to earn "better wages."[72]

When employees did not receive the better wages they felt entitled to, they felt a betrayal of the implicit bargain. This betrayal must have been felt especially keenly by immigrants who had left home and family to come to the New World; they had staked everything on earning better wages in America. Is it any surprise that when they saw their prospects threatened by unfairly low wages, they were infuriated? The whole justification of their decision to emigrate, indeed their lives, were called into question, and the economic orientation of the immigrants was turned against the bosses. It is no wonder that strikes for higher wages, especially when needed to offset higher prices that threatened living standards, were sometimes marked by violence, as in August 1850 when striking German tailors attacked a "foul" shop on 38th Street with stones. The police opened fire, killing two workers.[73]

Hostility seems not to have reached beyond unethical bosses and strike-breakers. There is little evidence that workers found the wage system itself repugnant. Most had come to the city for higher wages and found their status as paid employees unobjectionable, especially since most were apathetic about upward mobility. Workers knew that in labor-scarce America, "Jack is as good as his master." Like the *Tribune* printers who objected to management restrictions as "incompatible with their dignity as men," they meant to keep it that way. Greater economic equality brought with it a respect for the workingman rarely found in the Old World.

72. In one sense, however, shorter hours did involve wages—since daily wages remained unchanged when hours were shortened, hourly wages increased. For evidence of the railroad pace before 1836, see John Harold diary, 29 and 30 May 1832; John Petheram, "Sketches of my Life," and "A Working Man's Recollections of America." John H. Morrison, *History of the New York Ship Yards* (New York, 1909), 94; see also "Chips," *Fincher's Trades' Review*, 10 February 1866. Significantly, in the *British Mechanic's and Labourer's Hand Book* the discussion of the fast and regular pace follows a discussion of the shortening of hours.

73. This is similar to what British sociologists found in a study of Luton, England. "Three-quarters of [the workers] . . . were migrants, most of whom, it would seem, had come to Luton specifically in search of higher wages. . . . Thus . . . the dominant form of aspiration . . . would often be the vindication of important choices made at some earlier stage." John Goldthorpe et al., *The Affluent Worker in the Class Structure* (Cambridge, England, 1969), 78. The striking German tailors achieved a victory when a false fire alarm was sent in and the volunteers "took out the 150 coats to be made at low wages." *Tribune*, 6 August 1850. On labor violence see Gilje, *Mobocracy*, 173–202; Paul O. Weinbaum, *Mobs and Demagogues* (New York, 1979), 77–96; and Degler, "Labor in the Economy," 80–83. Most strikes were nonviolent.

CHAPTER 6

# Consumption

In this chapter and the following ones on residential patterns and institutional life, I shift focus from production to what sociologist Anthony Giddens calls "distributive relationships," paying particular attention to the material conditions of daily life. This chapter examines the workers' standard of living. Because so many workers were immigrants, I compare American material life to that of northwest Europe and describe the development of a common working-class consumption standard. What did the immigrant worker actually gain by coming to America? How did this huge influx of immigrants provide the basis for the development of a working-class material life?[1]

## BUDGETS

Changes over time in the distribution of wealth offer a quantitative approach to the measurement of workers' standards of living. Wealth, such evidence makes clear, was unequally distributed in the antebellum city and becoming more so. However, a mathematical coefficient does little to illuminate the living standards of the city's workers. Workers discussed living standards in concrete terms, and in this chapter I avoid abstraction as much as possible.[2]

The question of working-class budgets is complex. The highly seasonal

1. Anthony Giddens, *The Class Structure of Advanced Societies* (New York, 1975), 109.
2. On the distribution of wealth in New York City, see Edward Pessen, *Riches, Class and Power before the Civil War* (Lexington, Mass., 1973), 33–35, and Lee Soltow, "The Wealth, Income and Social Class of Men in Large Northern Cities in the United States in 1860," in James D. Smith, ed., *The Personal Distribution of Income and Wealth*, NBER Studies in Income and Wealth, vol. 39 (New York, 1975), 234–276.

nature of work in the nineteenth century makes comparisons of daily and weekly wage rates of limited usefulness. In *Three Years among the Working-Classes in the United States,* James Burn criticized the use of wage rates as a measure of standard of living: "Tables of the rates of value of labour in America are very delusive inasmuch as they rest upon the basis of ever-fluctuating quantities." The family economy adds to the complications, since a family with two poorly paid workers could earn more than a family with one well-paid member.[3]

Nevertheless, budgets do offer a useful perspective on working-class spending, and hypothetical working-class budgets were occasionally published in newspapers. In particular, budgets allow us to investigate the seasonal and familial patterns so crucial in the lives of antebellum workers.

The *seasonal* dimension was of prime importance in budgeting. Winter was the worst time for most occupations as outdoor work slowed and trade stagnated. Significant as this decline in earnings was, equally important was the rise in family expenditures as food shipments declined, prices rose, and fuel bills escalated. Horace Greeley remembered the terrible winter of 1832 when a " 'cold snap' . . . closed the Hudson and sent the price of coal at a bound to $16 a ton, while the cost of other necessaries of life took a kindred but less considerable elevation. Our city stood as if beseiged til Spring relieved her; and it was much the same every Winter."[4]

The city's inhabitants recognized the necessity of stocking up on produce and fuel in the fall, before the river froze. "At the approach of winter the 'towboats' that bring down country produce are laden to tenfold degree. . . . It is a common practice among nearly all classes to lay in a stock of such provisions as will keep at the commencement of the cold season," the Anonymous Cabinetmaker noted. Samuel Warshinge, the shipwright, bought his provisions for the winter of 1833 on December 22, including "the best of flour at $6 a barrel." Obviously, to stock up on provisions it was essential that a worker save some money during the summer and fall, and this was, indeed, common practice. Many workers no doubt lacked the space to store reserves of flour and wood; they were forced to buy throughout the winter at inflated prices. Either way it was necessary to have saved some money.[5]

3. James Burn, *Three Years among the Working-Classes in the United States during the War* (1865; rpt. New York, 1982), 308. Information on daily and weekly wages is abundant. The sources on the labor market cited in Chapter 4, note 14, often give wage rates. On prices a standard source is Carl H. Juergens, "Movement of Wholesale Prices in New York City, 1825–1863," *Proceedings of the American Statistical Association* 13 (1911), 544–557.

4. On seasonality in budgeting, see *Tribune,* 31 March 1860. Horace Greeley, *Recollections of a Busy Life* (New York, 1868), 87; see also Andrew Bell, *Men and Things in America* (London, 1838), 230; "A Working Man's Recollections of America," *Knight's Penny Magazine* 1 (1846), 106; and *Tribune,* 8 June 1853.

5. "A Working Man's Recollections of America," 106; see also John J. Sturtevant recollections, Rare Books and Manuscripts Division, The New York Public Library, Astor, Lenox and Tilden Foundations, 54; Carlos Martin, *William E. Dodge* (New York, 1890), 44; and James W.

The British Mechanic wrote that "the working class of the American people . . . are, generally speaking, of saving habits. . . . This perhaps may arise from the very great necessity [in the north] . . . of making provision for a possibly lengthy winter season." Warshinge, whose average savings from 1839 to 1842 are shown in Table 15, gradually built up his savings to an average $75.50 in November before buying supplies. Workers considered these sums not true savings but merely preparation for winter and the dull season. Despite the substantial sum of money ($35.00) on hand in January 1840, Warshinge lamented that "a man that work in New York in a Common Capacity Can not save any of the earning."[6]

Most workers were not able to amass as much as Warshinge, but all tried to save a little. German writer Theodor Griesinger, a Forty-Eighter who lived in the city between 1852 and 1857, believed one had to have enough saved to live for 14 days in order to avoid ruin in Kleindeutschland. Here unskilled workers were at a great disadvantage since the casual nature of their work prevented much counterseasonal saving. Year in, year out, many workers were at the mercy of the weather. If the winter was mild and fuel costs low, their savings would be sufficient. If the winter was severe, destitution threatened. "Mechanics and laborers lived awhile on scanty savings of the preceding Summer and Autumn; then on such credit as they could wring from grocers and landlords, till milder weather brought them work," Greeley explained. During the unusually cold winter of 1833, John Gough, the bookbinder, was reduced to scavenging for wood along roadsides in upper Manhattan to use for fuel. A worker could sell his furniture or pawn his watch and jewelry, but if that was not enough he was forced to try to obtain welfare from the Association for Improving the Conditions of the Poor. It is no exaggeration to say that the principal role of the A.I.C.P. was to provide aid during this "annual season of sorrow and dread." The number of persons relieved during the winter was sixty times that in summer, as Figure 20 illustrates. Although a winter increase in expenditures was expected, the weather determined how severe that increase would be, and it added a yearly random element to the worker's life. Even after seasonality began to decline in the 1850s, A.I.C.P. reports show that it remained a very significant factor in New York City.[7]

Alexander [Charles Quill], *The American Mechanic and Working-Man* (New York and Philadelphia, 1847), 64. Samuel Warshinge account book and personal notes, 22 December 1832, New-York Historical Society (NYHS). A family of four could expect to use six barrels of flour a year.

6. *British Mechanic's and Labourer's Hand Book* (London, 1840), 21; Warshinge account book, January 1840.

7. Theodor Griesinger, *Land und Leute in Amerika* (Stuttgart, 1863), 574; *Tribune,* 16 November 1857; John Gough, *Autobiography and Personal Recollections* (Springfield, Mass., 1870), 70; Greeley, *Recollections,* 87. On furniture see *Annual Report of the A.I.C.P. for the Year 1857,* 70, and James Burn, *James Burn; The "Beggar Boy"* (London, 1882), 325–326.

TABLE 15

Samuel Warshinge's amount of money "on hand in the house every Saturday night," monthly average, 1839–1842

| Month | Dollars | Month | Dollars |
|-------|---------|-------|---------|
| January | 23.75 | July | 30.00 |
| February | 29.75 | August | 63.00 |
| March | 33.75 | September | 53.00 |
| April | 43.25 | October | 56.00 |
| May | 53.00 | November | 75.50 |
| June | 38.50 | December | 39.50 |

*Source:* Samuel Warshinge account book and personal notes, 1839–1842, NYHS.

Economic depressions also added unpredictability, and no amount of saving could help in the severe panics of 1837 and 1857. Prices dropped sharply, but the decline was inadequate to counteract widespread unemployment, especially since secondary workers, crucial to many families' incomes, were so prone to cyclical layoffs. Workers therefore lived at the mercy of random events—an unusually cold winter, a panic, an injury or illness, a fire, all could lead to unemployment and its attendant miseries. In discussions of the workers' standard of living, this unpredictability should be kept in mind.[8]

The *life-cycle* was also important. Changes in the consumer-worker ratio over the life of a family had an impact on living standards. Unmarried male workers, so common in the city, were able to live well when employed. The average male wage of $25 to $30 monthly in the 1850s enabled bachelors to board comfortably. Indeed, the high overall standard of living of the city's working class owed much to the large number of single men. In addition, as noted in Chapter 4, male workers seemed certain that a large family was an economic asset. The British Mechanic explained in a chapter entitled "Advantages to Mechanics of a Family" that children could provide for more than themselves. A larger number of workers also lowered a family's risk; wives and children might be able to keep the family above water during a short period of unemployment for the breadwinner. The most difficult period of the life-cycle for most families was before children entered the labor market.[9]

Gough refused to accept aid because the A.I.C.P. officials "took advantage of their office to insult the children of penury" (Gough, 71). "Annual season": *Five Points Monthly Record* 1 (1854), 167. *Annual Report of the A.I.C.P. for the Year 1857*, 21.

8. Juergens, "Movement of Wholesale Prices," 545–546. Families reduced to poverty by an injury, such as that of a laborer who fell off a scaffold, were common; see the *Annual Report of the Children's Aid Society for 1854* (New York, 1855), 26–28.

9. "Consumer-worker": A. V. Chayanov, *The Theory of Peasant Economy*, ed. Daniel Thorner, Basile Kerblay, and R. E. F. Smith (Homewood, Ill., 1966), 57–60. *British Me-*

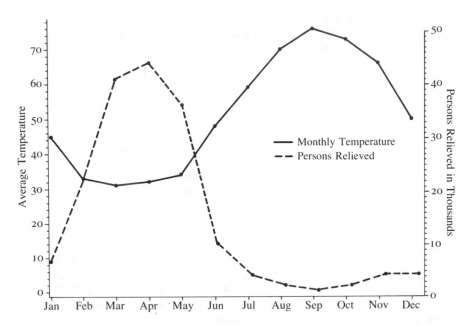

FIGURE 20. Monthly average temperature in New York City, 1850–1863, and persons relieved by the A.I.C.P., 1853–1854.

Changes in income and expenditures over the course of the life-cycle point up the problems involved in drawing up "a working-class budget." Seasonal and familial patterns are missed in the printed budgets of the period. We can, however, make some use of these published budgets by aggregating evidence and comparing it to the budgets of contemporary workers in Europe. This procedure involves some obvious difficulties: budgets were printed for polemical purposes and vary widely by period, occupation, and family size. However, the results reveal what appears to be a genuine pattern. The most striking difference, illustrated in Table 16, was the substantially smaller percentage spent on food in urban America than in Europe and the higher proportion spent on fuel and rent. The percentages spent on clothing and the category "Other" (mainly medical expenses, taxes, and recreation) are nearly the same.[10]

chanic's and Labourer's Hand Book, 101–112. Contemporary evidence is discussed in Chapter 4. Most studies of working-class budgets are based on state and federal government surveys of workers. See Michael Haines, "Industrial Work and the Family Life Cycle, 1889–1890," *Reviews in Economic History* 4 (1979), 289–356; John Modell, "Patterns of Consumption, Acculturation and Family Income Strategies in Late Nineteenth-Century America," in Tamara Hareven and Maris Vinovskis, eds., *Family and Population in Nineteenth-Century America* (Princeton, N.J., 1978), 206–240; and Hareven, *Family Time and Industrial Time* (New York, 1982). Caution should be used in applying these studies to New York, where home ownership, a key expenditure, was rare among workers.

10. The budgets are: "1809 Carpenter's Budget," and "1819 Mason's Budget," in Howard Rock, *Artisans of the New Republic: The Tradesmen of New York City in the Age of Jefferson*

TABLE 16

Nineteenth-century working-class budgets, America and Europe (percentages)

| | N | Food | Rent | Clothes | Other |
|---|---|---|---|---|---|
| LePlay (1842–1853) | | | | | |
|   Continental | 26 | 57.2% | 12.2% | 16.9% | 13.6% |
|   English | 4 | 57.9 | 18.8 | 15.9 | 7.3 |
|   Total | 30 | 57.4 | 13.7 | 16.7 | 12.2 |
| Lees—London workers | | | | | |
|   Street seller (1849) | | 74.2 | 12.8 | 13.0 | |
|   High unskilled (1860) | | 66.7 | 14.6 | 18.7 | |
| New York City workers (1809–1874) | 8 | 48.5 | 23.7 | 15.7 | 12.1 |

*Sources:* F. LePlay, *Les ouvriers européens* (Paris, 1855); Lynn Lees, *Exiles of Erin: Irish Migrants in Victorian London* (Ithaca, N.Y., 1979), 104. Sources of New York City budgets are given in fn. 10.

These results accord with repeated comments in immigrant letters and guidebooks that food was cheaper in New York and that rent was higher. The budgets also show that whether in America or Europe, rent, clothing, and food—the "necessaries of life"—took up about 90 percent of a worker's budget. Because taxes were often greater in Europe, actual New York expenditures on sundries were probably higher. Nevertheless, the main improvement in the standard of living in the United States came *within* the categories of housing, clothing, and food.[11]

These budgets, because of life cycle and seasonal changes as well as differences in the manner of collection and time period, are nothing more than a very rough estimate. They do, however, point up the importance of food in working-class budgets: therefore the lower New World percentage represents a significant difference between Europe and America.

Workers in the city lived under the sway of seasonal and familial factors, and this randomness, and the attempts to counteract it, are important to our

(New York, 1979), 253; "Laborers and Mechanics," *National Trades' Union,* 12 July 1834; "Philadelphia Workingman," *Tribune,* 27 May 1851; "Female Straw Sewer," *Herald,* 7 June 1853; "Mechanic," *Times,* 8 November 1853; "Printer's Budget," *Printer* 5 (1864), 116, reprinted in Richard Cummings, *The American and His Food* (Chicago, 1940), 243; New York worker's budget (1874) in Edward Young, *Labor in Europe and America* (Philadelphia, 1875), 813. On late nineteenth-century workers' budgets, see Daniel Horowitz, *The Morality of Spending: Attitudes toward the Consumer Society in America, 1875–1940* (Baltimore, Md., 1985), 13–19. Horowitz provides a useful compilation of nineteenth- and twentieth-century budgets on pp. 173–176.

11. Similar spending on "necessaries of life" was also noted by Werner Sombart. The American worker's "free income," he wrote, "as a percentage of his total is no higher than is the case with his German colleague, despite the fact that the former's total is so much higher." Sombart, *Why Is There No Socialism in the United States?* (1906), trans. Patricia M. Hocking and C. T. Husbands (White Plains, N.Y., 1976), 102. British and American working-class budgets at the turn of the twentieth century are compared in Peter R. Shergold, *Working-Class Life: The "American Standard" in Comparative Perspective, 1899–1913* (Pittsburgh, 1982).

understanding of working-class life. But a comparison of European and American budgets reveals systematic differences that reflect a real divergence in living standards. The rest of this chapter examines this divergence, focusing on the material life of the city's workers.

## THE WORKING-CLASS MATERIAL STANDARD

*Housing* is an abstraction composed of thousands of individual dwellings, ranging from whitewashed wooden houses to shanties on the northern edge of the city, from brick tenements to dank cellars. To discover "average" workers' housing is impossible. What is possible is to describe general trends in city housing between 1820 and 1860.

Home ownership was out of the question for most workers in New York City; the price of land was too high. In 1819, Howard Rock found, only 1.5 percent of a sample of Eighth Ward journeymen possessed real property. In this period, however, it was still possible for a journeyman to rent all or part of a house. "In the skirts of the town a very small house, one story high, the front rooms of a moderate size, the back less, but suited for a bed, and with one room in the attic story, is from 12*l.* to 14*l.* per annum," Henry Fearon wrote in 1818. Nearer the center of the city, a worker could rent one floor of a two-story house for £18, about $90 a year. Male artisans averaged yearly earnings of around $300, making feasible such residences, essentially smaller versions of middle-class residences, for many workers.[12]

The huge growth of the city starting in the 1820s completely transformed the housing market. In 1824 alone, 1,600 dwellings were built, but even that number failed to keep up with population growth; on completion all were immediately occupied and beds laid out in parlors and dining rooms. The Panic of 1837 slackened the city's population growth, but it also leveled off housing starts, so overcrowding continued. The boom of the 1840s, with a consequent rise in land values and increased immigration, ensured that the building of single-family dwellings would be uneconomic on Manhattan and made three- and four-story residential buildings the norm. In this decade the city's two distinctive working-class residences—the tenement and the boardinghouse—emerged.[13]

---

12. Rock, *Artisans*, 55. Henry Fearon, *Sketches of America* (London, 1819), 40; see also Ward Stafford, *New Missionary Field* (New York, 1817), 6. Betsy Blackmar, "Housing and Property Relations in New York, 1785–1850" (diss., Harvard University, 1980), 292–305. Information on wages is from the *1820 Census of Manufactures;* see Chapter 2.

13. Information on housing from James Hardie, *A Census of New Buildings* (New York, 1825), and I. N. Phelps Stokes, *Iconography of Manhattan Island* (New York, 1897), 3:517; see also Fearon, *Sketches of America*, 40; *Young America*, 7 March 1846; and Blackmar, "Housing and Property," 445.

TABLE 17
Number of families and dwelling size in New
York City, 1859

| No. of families | N | Percentage |
|---|---|---|
| 1 | 20,638 | 13.8 |
| 2 and 3 | 32,542 | 21.8 |
| 4 and 5 | 25,618 | 17.1 |
| 6 and 7 | 23,458 | 15.7 |
| 8–10 | 22,446 | 15.0 |
| 11–15 | 11,089 | 7.4 |
| 16–20 | 10,296 | 6.9 |
| 20+ | 3,289 | 2.2 |
| TOTALS | 149,376 | 99.9 |

*Source:* Compiled from the *Report of the City Inspec-*
*tor for the Year 1860* (New York, 1861), 202.

The first tenement in the city was built, it seems, by the Allaire Works for its
employees in 1833. A *tenement* is a multistory brick structure built especially
to house workers, but within the category there were buildings of various
sizes, materials, and number of living units. In 1845 tenements composed
only a small minority of the city's total housing stock, but the proportion was
growing rapidly. By 1859, as Table 17 shows, only 35.6 percent of the cities'
families, most of them middle-class, shared a dwelling with fewer than three
other family groups. Most tenements were quite small—300–400 square feet
of floor space and two to four rooms (see Figure 21). Samuel Gompers
remembered living in a "typical" three-room tenement apartment on Sheriff
Street (Thirteenth Ward) in the 1860s: "The largest, the front room, was a
combined kitchen, dining room and sitting-room with two front windows.
There were two small bedrooms back, which had windows opening into the
hall." Better-off workers might still hope to share a house with another
family, but tenement life was increasingly the rule.[14]

As the tenement was developing to house workers' families, the boardinghouse became the characteristic place of residence for the city's large numbers
of single men. Boarding was common on Manhattan from the early years of
the century. Arrangements were often rather informal; Thomas Chamberlain,
the printer, in 1835 boarded in "the back room of the first [i.e., second] floor,

14. Charles Haswell, *Reminiscences of an Octogenarian* (New York, 1896), 332. The
diversity encompassed by the term tenement is stressed in Elizabeth C. Cromley, "The Development of the New York Apartment, 1860–1905," (diss., City University of New York, 1982),
esp. 49–50, 58–60. Floor space is estimated from evidence in Council of Hygiene and Public
Health, *Report upon the Sanitary Condition of the City* (New York, 1865), 217, 259–260; see
also I. N. Phelps Stokes, "Appendix," in James Ford, *Slums and Housing* (Cambridge, Mass.,
1936), 2, Plates I, IA, II. Samuel Gompers, *Seventy Years of Life and Labor* (1925; rpt. New
York, 1967), 1:493–449; see also the description in Griesinger, *Land und Leute*, 551–552, 557.

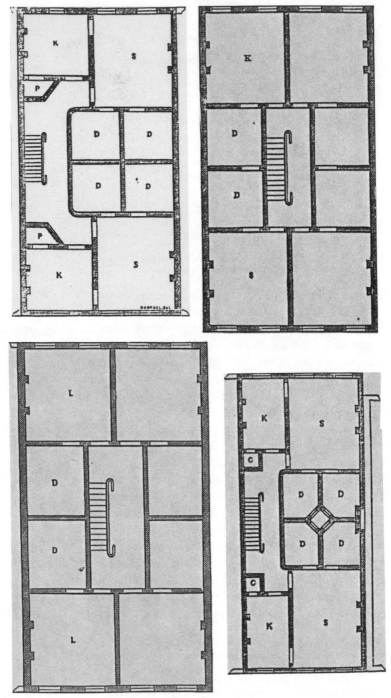

FIGURE 21. Tenement floor plans, 1864. L = living room, S = sitting room, K = kitchen, P = pantry, D = bedroom (i.e., dark room), C = closet. The apartments, clockwise from the upper left, have approximately the following square footage: 380, 480, 300, and 280. From Council of Hygiene and Public Health, *Report upon the Sanitary Condition of the City* (New York, 1865), 217, 259, 260.

it contains two double and two single beds . . . the ground floor of the house is a grocery store.'' As housing became more crowded and single immigrants flooded the city, specialized houses for boarders grew in importance. Usually located in a converted downtown building, the boardinghouse consisted solely of bedrooms for boarders and a common room where meals were taken. ''There are mostly two persons in a bed'' in ''all mechanics' boarding houses'' in the city, the British Mechanic observed in 1840, though single rooms were available at higher rents.[15]

Housing in the city was always expensive, and workers could expect to pay about one-quarter of their budget for rent and fuel. Although this expense remained relatively constant between 1820 and 1860, the accommodations it bought became smaller as the price of land rose and the tenement and the boardinghouse replaced the single- or double-family frame house. Floor plans compiled by I. N. Phelps Stokes show a pre-1850 dwelling with about 640 square feet of floor space, whereas tenements built in the 1850s had 300 to 400 square feet (Figure 21). Apartments where the occupants were engaged in home manufactures must have been especially cramped, and privacy must have been unknown to most workers. Increasing interest in housing conditions, beginning with John Griscom's 1845 report *The Sanitary Condition of the Laboring Population of New York,* suggests a growing awareness of this problem. But although most housing in the city was becoming more crowded, reformers were understandably preoccupied with the city's worst dwellings and neighborhoods; we should be wary of using such reports as evidence of ''typical'' working-class housing. The inhabitants of cellars, who so engaged reformers, were less than 2 percent of the city's population. The dilapidated ''Old Brewery'' in Five Points, and later Gotham Court on Cherry Street in the Seventh Ward, received so much attention not because they were typical but because they were among the poorest residential buildings in the city.[16]

Tenements, though the rooms were small and poorly vented, at least had no garrets and few inhabited cellars, and were usually deemed superior to apartments in converted buildings. Indeed, they may have represented an improvement for many workers; the tuberculosis deathrate declined between 1810 and 1860, though the reduction was not dramatic. Nevertheless, it seems clear that in housing, immigrants to the city saw only a modest improvement over Old

15. In the early decades, the boardinghouse had both workers and middle-class residents. It became distinctively working-class only in the 1850s, as Chapter 8 explains. Chamberlain diary, 26 May 1835, Rare Books and Manuscripts Division, The New York Public Library, Astor, Lenox and Tilden Foundations. *British Mechanic's and Labourer's Hand Book,* 58; see also Thomas Gunn, *The Physiology of New York Boarding-Houses* (New York, 1857).

16. I. N. Phelps Stokes, ''Appendix,'' Plate I; Griesinger, *Land und Leute,* 552, 558; John Griscom, *The Sanitary Condition of the Laboring Population of New York* (New York, 1845). On cellars see *Annual Report of the City Inspector for the Year 1842* (New York, 1843), 163–165, and *Report upon the Sanitary Condition of the City,* 349. On the Old Brewery see Ladies of the Mission, *The Old Brewery and the New Mission House at Five Points* (New York, 1845).

World standards. Yet if the gain was less dramatic in housing than in diet, it was no cause for complaint, though surprise at high rents was common. Griesinger noted that apartments in Kleindeutschland were very small but added that most German immigrants "were little concerned about it." Certainly for Irish peasants, whose dwelling might have been a 10 × 13 feet stone-and-mud hut with a mud floor, no windows, and a roof hole for a chimney, the tenement was an improvement. Even Gompers's East Side tenement apartment, though small, was larger than the Spitalfields apartment (one single large room and a pantry) in which his family had lived before emigrating.[17]

The 1840s and 1850s also saw the growth of such "urban amenities" as indoor plumbing, gaslight, and central heating. By 1860 many upper-class dwellings were equipped with running water, gas, and sometimes even furnaces. The Swedish immigrant Gustav Unonius was awed by the hot and cold running water in his room and the central heating in the "tip-top" boardinghouse where he stayed in 1841. However, these advances were slow to work their way into working-class dwellings. Gompers remembered, "We got water from a common hydrant in the yard . . . the toilet was in the yard also." Only indoor plumbing had made much progress by 1860 and usually was only a single water spigot per floor in newer tenements. Water closets were also beginning to be installed in middle-class apartments, but most workers still used the bedpan and the privy (though now often connected to the sewer). While the middle class could afford the "modern improvements" that made apartment life comfortable, most workers could not. There was a clear divergence between working-class and middle-class dwellings.[18]

It would be a mistake, however, to suggest that workers saw no domestic technological advances between 1820 and 1860. One development—the stove—was responsible for a great improvement in workers' comfort. Al-

17. The annual average tuberculosis deathrate in New York City per thousand dropped by decade as follows: 1810s, 6.3; 1820s, 5.3; 1830s, 5.7; 1840s, 4.8; 1850s, 4.7. John Duffy, *A History of Public Health in New York City, 1625–1866* (New York, 1968), 583–584. On the superiority of tenements to many other residences, see *Annual Report of the A.I.C.P. for the Year 1856*, 18–19. On overcrowding see Benjamin McCready, *On the Influence of Trades, Professions, and Occupations in the United States in the Production of Disease* (1837; rpt. Baltimore, Md., 1943), 42–43; Griesinger, *Land und Leute*, 552–553. Irish huts: House of Commons, *Parliamentary Papers*, XXXI (1836), Poor Inquiry (Ireland), Appendix E, 38–67. Gompers, *Seventy Years*, 1:2, 493.

18. Gustaf Unonius, *A Pioneer in Northwest America* (Minneapolis, 1950), 43–45; Gompers, *Seventy Years*, 1:494. Information on plumbing, gas, and central heating is taken from Haswell, *Reminiscences*, 54, 116, 139; Charles Lockwood, *Manhattan Moves Uptown* (Boston, 1976), 189–197; and *Report upon the Sanitary Condition of the City*, 135; see also *History of Architecture and Building Trades* (New York, 1899), 1:256–258, and Charles Lester, ed., *Glances at the Metropolis* (New York, 1854), 117. On working-class toilet facilities in the 1850s see *London v. New York*, "by an English Workman" (London, 1859), 4; Theodor Griesinger, *Lebende Bilder aus Amerika* (Stuttgart, 1858), 231; and *Annual Report of the City Inspector for the Year 1860*, 53–54.

though the "American stove" was in use in Europe in the late eighteenth century, as late as 1820 many city houses were still heated by fireplaces, which, even with grates, are extremely inefficient. Stoves heated better with less fuel, so workers could be more comfortable and although paying higher lighting costs, paid substantially lower wood or coal costs. Stoves were also easier to cook on. James Burn was especially impressed with American stoves, which he declared "a decided improvement on the common grate" then in use in England.[19]

In furnishings, as in housing, a common working-class standard was emerging. By 1845 "the amount of . . . cheap furniture sold in New-York is incredible. Almost all the dwellings of the laboring class are furnished with it," the *Tribune* reported. By 1854 Hiram Anderson of 99 The Bowery could boast of his "long and successful efforts . . . to bring carpets and floor coverings . . . within the reach of the whole community. *He is the Carpet Merchant of the People."* Since the 1820s some manufacturers had specialized in cheap furniture, but it seems they were producing mostly for export. Workers usually bought less elaborate versions of furnishings purchased by the middle class. Duncan Phyfe, for instance, produced work in a wide range of prices. Cheap stick furniture specifically for working-class customers was something novel and, equally important, of a quality far above what most European immigrants were used to.[20]

Workers did not live luxuriously, but most workers' apartments were decently furnished. Many homes had frame beds, comfortable chairs, and bookcases. William Thomson, a Scottish weaver, noted that American workers "have rocking arm chairs that are a real luxury." Most amazing to immigrants was the presence of rugs in workingmen's apartments. Burn noted in 1865 that the floors "even [of] the poor classes of the people are covered with bits of carpet." Large carpet factories, such as the Higgins Company in Ward 22, produced rugs at modest prices. By the 1880s a New Yorker could write, "I think it was the poorest room I ever was in. There was no carpet on the floor." Rugs, in fact, were more than just furnishings; to many of the city's workers they were a symbolic representation, an icon, of the high American standard of living.[21]

19. Burn, *Three Years*, 298; see also Joseph I. C. Clarke, *My Life and Memories* (New York, 1925), 6; *London v. New York*, 3; Gunn, *Physiology*, 32; and the *Tribune*, 7 December 1855. The Irish did not even have grates; see Poor Inquiry (Ireland), Appendix E, 41.

20. *Tribune*, 11 November 1845. Lester, *Glances*, 99; see also Thomas Mooney, *Nine Years in America* (Dublin, 1850), 150–151. Phyfe: Walter Dyer, *Early American Craftsmen* (New York, 1915), 56–57, 67.

21. Unfortunately, the probate inventories in the New York State Library in Albany are of limited help in assessing workers' physical lifestyle. The number of inventories is small—after 1847 only contested estates were inventoried—and it is usually impossible to tell from the occupation listed ("carpenter," for instance) if the person was a worker or a boss. William Thomson, *A Tradesman's Travels, in the United States and Canada, in the Years 1840, 1841*

In the boardinghouses rugs were common, but bedroom furniture typically consisted of little more than a bed, dresser, and washstand. As a rule, bedroom furnishings were of minor significance in boardinghouses—most rooms were too small to spend much time in. Usually, however, the common room of the boardinghouse was well furnished.[22]

Such furnishings, though well below the standards of the city's middle class, were above what peasants had had in the Old World. In Ireland even privies were rare—most peasants had only a dung pit by the door. Furniture usually consisted of a stool or two, and perhaps a dresser; bedding was chaff and rags with an overcoat used for a blanket. In Gweedore, Donegal, with a population of 9,000 in 1837, there were 93 chairs, 243 stools, and 10 beds. Even poor New Yorkers lived much better. John Morrow, the son of an alcoholic English immigrant, lived with his parents and five brothers and sisters in a single 20 × 30 feet room on 44th Street. The furniture was two beds, a workbench, a table and three chairs, and other "humble articles of furniture." John Maguire described an unskilled laborer's family of seven in 1860 living in two 9 × 12 feet rooms of a tenement apartment with a stove and "no actual want of essential articles of furniture, such as a table and chairs; and the walls were not without one or two pious and patriotic pictures." Their accommodation was substantially smaller than most tenement apartments. To an Irish peasant used to little real furniture at all, however, this probably seemed more than adequate and was above the standard of much of the English working class. Burn summarized the Irish view of American housing: "If they do not get milk and honey in abundance, they are able . . . to exchange . . . their . . . mud cabins and clay floors with fire on the hearth, for clean, comfortable dwellings with warm stoves and 'bits of carpits on their flures.' "[23]

*Clothing* of urban workers was also usually of a high standard. "I wear as good a suit of clothes as any Gentleman in the City of Cork, and twenty dollars' worth of a watch in my pocket," boasted an Irish-born boxmaker in 1852. Clothing was expensive, but most workers dressed well. To a stranger just landed from Europe, "the first objects which attract his attention are [New York's] people, all so neatly and comfortably clad. . . . The stranger is involuntarily led to enquire where are the working classes—the tattered and

---

*and 1842* (Edinburgh, 1842), 34; on rockers see also Sturtevant recollections, 52–53. On apartment furnishings see "A Working Man's Recollections of America," 103. Burn, *Three Years*, 102; see also *Times*, 8 November 1853. "No carpet": Peter Carter, *Peter Carter, 1825–1900* (New York, 1901), 81.

22. Gunn, *Physiology*, 8, 32, 95, and Griesinger, *Lebende Bilder*, 231–232.

23. Poor Inquiry (Ireland), Appendix E, 38–97; "The Memorial of Patrick M'Kye" (1837), in Lord George Hill, *Facts from Gweedore* (Dublin, 1846), 6; John Morrow, *A Voice from the Newsboys* (New York, 1860), 39–40; John Francis Maguire, *The Irish in America* (London, 1868), 232; Burn, *Three Years*, 14–15.

half-fed, miserable-looking starvelings . . . of his native land," wrote the Welsh immigrant Lewis Howell in 1844.[24]

Immigrants were impressed with even the most modest aspects of working-class dress. In Gweedore in 1837, "more than one half of both men and women cannot afford shoes to their feet." Even in England, working-class women often went barefoot. But in America, "I never saw a woman going without shoes," recounted William Thomson. Generally, British workers wore coats and jackets made of heavy, durable material—usually wool or linsey-woolsey—that lasted years. American ready-made clothing was made of lighter cotton, less lasting, but its lower price allowed workers to acquire a wardrobe. American clothing was also brighter than often drab British garments. Particularly notable were the watches and rings American workers wore. Watches were virtually unknown in Ireland (in Gweedore, with its population of 9,000, there were three watches in 1837) and rare in England. But in New York City even seamstresses had timepieces, "acknowledged by all the upper classes . . . to be the most sublime display of plebian effrontery on record."[25]

Indeed, it was often pointed out that unlike in Europe, where workers' clothing was a badge of inferiority, in America "there is very little difference, . . . in the point of appearance, between the young men of most trades and their employers." Work clothes—"everyday clothes"—as contemporary prints and photographs show, were worn on the job, but workers also had "dress-ups" "suitable . . . to be boss or steward," as one upstate worker put it. Single male workers who had a large disposable income were especially able to dress well; the Bowery Boy's bright red shirt, polished boots, and shiny hat were emblematic of the high living standard of this group (see Figure 23). Unmarried working women also dressed "high," wearing jewelry and bright-colored dresses. If in housing the differences between working and middle class were growing, in men's clothing the widespread availability of respectable ready-to-wear clothes may have diminished class differences as

24. Letter to the Society of St. Vincent de Paul, Cork, 3 February 1852, quoted in J. N. Murphy, *Ireland: Industrial, Political and Social* (London, 1870), 180; Lewis Howell Jr., letter "to the ed. for the benefit of his acquaintances in the old country," 27 August 1844, in Alan Conway, ed., *The Welsh in America: Letters from the Immigrants* (Minneapolis, 1961), 69.

25. Hill, *Facts from Gweedore*, 6. Women in English industrial towns sometimes went without shoes, see Friedrich Engels, *The Condition of the Working Class in England* (1844), trans. W. O. Henderson and W. H. Chaloner (New York, 1958), 80. Thomson, *Tradesman's Travels*, 34. British clothing: Joseph Lawson, *Progress in Pudsey* (1887; rpt. Firle, England, 1978), 25–26. Watches in Gweedore: Hill, 6. Among the English working class, "the watch held peculiar eminence"; Robert Roberts, *The Classic Slum: Salford Life in the First Quarter of the Century* (1971; rpt. Harmondsworth, England, 1983), 36. On rings and watches, see also Burn, *Beggar Boy*, 274; Thomson, 36; Kerby Miller, "Emigrants and Exiles: The Irish Exodus to North America from Colonial Times to the First World War" (diss., University of California, Berkeley, 1976), 557. Seamstresses' watches: Cornelius Mathews, *A Pen-and-Ink Panorama of New-York City* (New York, 1853), 116.

"not only the economist, but the man of fashion" began to buy garments off the rack after 1840. A working-class dress did exist for single workers (the Bowery Boy's outfit is discussed in Chapter 8), though it is questionable how many workers actually dressed this way. Other workers' clothing was almost indistinguishable from that of the middle class and served to reinforce the "Jack's as good as his master" egalitarianism of the workplace.[26]

Although the percentage of budget spent on *sundries*—expenditures other than shelter, clothing, and food—seems to have been no larger than in Europe, higher American incomes afforded workers luxuries uncommon in the Old World. New York workers could eat out, they could go to the theatre "without feeling, on the following morning, that they must compensate, by deprivation or extraordinary labour, for their extravagance," and unlike British workers, they were "very careful of their hair," using tonic to style it and having it cut by barbers.[27]

Even more remarkable was the American *diet*. Chapter 3 noted the blandness and inadequacy of the European diet and how immigrants encouraged others to migrate by describing the food available in the New World. In Ireland and Continental Europe, hunger was often a daily fact of life, and the grain-based diet of peasants and workers was always extremely monotonous. Food, which accounted for about 60 percent of most European workers' budgets, was much better and cheaper in the United States. Its quality and availability had an impact on the standard of living of the common people that can only be called revolutionary. "Food is the first thing in the world," wrote iron puddler James J. Davis early in the next century, "cleanliness may be next to godliness, but food is ahead of them all."[28]

It is reasonable, argues Eric Hobsbawm, "to take meat consumption as a criterion of standard of living" of the working class. Grain was the staple food in Europe and meat a luxury rarely indulged in. By contrast, meat was virtually the staple of the American workingman's diet: of the $12 million in sales of produce in the city in 1841, 39 percent was spent on meat, 25 percent on grain, 22 percent on dairy products, and 10 percent on vegetables. Of the meat sold, 53 percent was beef, 22 percent pork. The huge amount of uncleared land in the Midwest suitable for grazing kept beef and pork prices low, and high wages made meat easily affordable. In New York meat was

26. *British Mechanic's and Labourer's Hand Book*, 60. "Dress-ups": *Times*, 8 November 1853. "Man of fashion": *Hunt's Merchants' Magazine* 20 (1849), 116. On ready-made clothing, see the *Tribune*, 15 November 1845, and Egal Feldman, *Fit for Men: A Study of New York's Clothing Trade* (Washington, 1960), 69–78. The upstate worker is quoted in Arnold Schrier, *Ireland and the American Emigration, 1850–1900* (Minneapolis, 1958), 30.

27. Eating out: William Hancock, *An Emigrant's Five Years in the Free States of America* (London, 1860), 77. Theatre: Fearon, *Sketches of America*, 86. Hair: Mooney, *Nine Years*, 135.

28. James J. Davis, *The Iron Puddler* (New York, 1922), 53.

eaten by workers twice, sometimes three times, a day. Afternoon dinner (the main meal of the day) and supper almost always included beef or pork.[29]

The consumption of meat reached extraordinary levels. The 39 percent of 1841 food expenditures devoted to meat compared to 28 percent among highly skilled English artisans and 13 percent among typical Continental workers. Since meat was relatively cheap in America (for beef four to twelve cents a pound depending on cut), this spending purchased a lot. Estimated annual consumption per person in the 1850s and 1860s ranges from 152 to 187 pounds of beef and from 221 to 257 pounds of all meat. On a weekly basis, the figures are 2.9 to 3.6 pounds of beef and 4.2 to 4.9 pounds of meat. (The 1984 American totals are 106 pounds of beef and 176 pounds of meat yearly—2.0 pounds of beef and 3.4 pounds of meat per person per week.) These mid-nineteenth-century figures are so far above current levels as to seem questionable. Since the totals are for the entire population, no doubt they are somewhat greater than working-class averages. Nevertheless, there is no question workers ate a great deal of meat—even the *Tribune*'s 1851 workingman's budget, presented as evidence of the immiseration of urban workers, allowed for 2.8 pounds of "butcher's meat" per person weekly, which comes to 146 pounds per year, approximately equal to American consumption in the mid-1950s.[30]

At a time when average weekly English meat consumption was only 1.8 pounds per person for an average London worker's family in 1841, and 12 to

29. Eric Hobsbawm, "The British Standard of Living, 1790–1850," in *Labouring Men* (Garden City, N.Y., 1964), 111; see also E. P. Thompson, *The Making of the English Working Class* (New York, 1963), 315–316; Standish Meacham, *A Life Apart: The English Working Class, 1890–1914* (Cambridge, 1977), 78; and Jerome Blum, *The End of the Old Order in Rural Europe* (Princeton, N.J., 1978), 178. Statistics on produce sold in the city from *Hunt's Merchants' Magazine* 15 (1842), 185. New Yorkers shared the distaste of the European common people for fish: in 1865 John Hutcheson determined that the city daily consumed only 50 tons of fish but 350 tons of meat. Hutcheson, "The Markets of New York," *Harper's Magazine* 25 (1867), 230–235; see also Gunn, *Physiology*, 94. Generally, Europeans ate very little fish, with the exception of herring; see Hobsbawm, "British Standard of Living," 102; F. LePlay, *Les ouvriers européens* (Paris, 1855), 33; and E. P. Thompson and Eileen Yeo, eds., *The Unknown Mayhew: Selections from the Morning Chronicle, 1849–1850* (London, 1971), 482, 487.

30. LePlay, *Les ouvriers européens*. New York City figures on meat consumption from "Statistics of the Cattle Market," *Tribune*, 1 January 1859; Fitz-Hugh Ludlow, "The American Metropolis," *Atlantic Monthly* 15 (1865), 83; Hutcheson, "Markets of New York," 230; C. W. Elliot, "Life in Great Cities—I," *Putnam's Magazine* n.s. 1 (1868), 92; Solon Robinson, *Facts for Farmers* (New York, 1869), 371. These statistics refer to dressed weights. Of course demand was elastic—when prices were high, less meat was consumed—and no doubt accounts for some variation in the estimates. Some of the meat purchased in the city supplied Brooklyn, so meat sales were divided by the combined population of the two cities. Some meat purchased in the city was shipped to outlying regions, but the writer in the *Tribune*, 1 January 1859 (presumably agricultural correspondent Solon Robinson), believed this was balanced by cattle brought to town and not sold in the regular markets. Some nonquantitative evidence is given in Thomas DeVoe, *The Market Assistant* (New York, 1866). Census Bureau, *Statistical Abstract of the United States* (Washington, 1985), 121; see also Letita Brewster and Michael F. Jacobson, *The Changing American Diet* (Washington, D.C., 1978).

15 ounces in Dr. Edward Smith's national survey of workers' diets in 1863, such meat eating amazed immigrants. "If he [the Irish laboring man] taste meat at all, it is on the two great festivals of the year, when he procures some pork at 2*d*. per lb., or else some inferior beef," Father Thomas Maguire told the Poor Law Commission. Joseph Lawson remembered the diet in Pudsey, England, in the late 1820s: "Flesh Meat [is] looked upon by many as a luxury and fitter for the rich than for them. . . . Oat-cake, brown bread, porridge, pudding, skimmed milk, potatoes and home-brewed beer . . . are the principal articles of food." Even when Europeans ate meat, it was often such inferior cuts as tripe, tongue, or pigs' feet, but in the United States "butcher's meat"—roasts and chops—was the rule. The young John Gough was amazed to discover that "they throw away the hog's inwards" in America, and New York City butchers complained, according to the agricultural editor of the *Tribune,* that "they cannot sell their coarse meat, and 'plates and navels' are a drug upon the market."[31]

Generally, Americans made no attempt to "stretch" meat, except in the winter; it was usually fried on the stove, or the small brazier workers used for summer cooking, and served. The Anonymous Cabinetmaker noted that "to one who had been accustomed to see meat sold, as in England, by ounces . . . the abundance and cheapness of an American market are very gratifying. Instead of buying a chop, wherewith to flavour a large mass of potatoes, he will carry home a quarter of a sheep or lamb, or a solid rib of beef."[32]

Although European workers were most impressed with the amount and quality of meat, they were also delighted with American bread. In Europe, about 80 percent of the caloric intake of the common people was in grain. Meat rivaled grain as a staple in the United States, but bread remained an important part of the working-class diet. And to immigrants, what bread it was! Many immigrants arrived in America accustomed to eating oat, barley, and rye bread. In Ireland even oat bread was considered a luxury, and wheat bread was reserved for Christmas and Easter. Although wheat bread was the rule in England, workers could rarely afford good bread and had to be content with grayish, low-quality wheat bread known as "seconds." In Pudsey, "very little white bread is seen . . . and is not much eaten." One East Anglian remembered that in the 1840s, "a really good piece of bread . . . was

---

31. Hobsbawm, "British Standard of Living," 114, 113. The 1.8 pounds for a London worker is a rather high assessment; see Thompson and Yeo, *Unknown Mayhew,* 482. Theodore Barker, D. J. Oddy, and John Yudkin, *The Dietary Surveys of Dr. Edward Smith: A New Assessment* (London, 1970), 43; Poor Inquiry (Ireland), Appendix E, 4; Lawson, *Progress in Pudsey,* 26; John Gough, letter to his parents, 28 December 1829, quoted in Gough, *Autobiography,* 59; Solon Robinson, *How to Live* (New York, 1860), 308. Thomas DeVoe, a butcher at the Jefferson Market, agreed; DeVoe, *Market Assistant,* 417–418.

32. On the preparation of meat see Hutcheson, "Markets of New York," 230, and Robinson, *How to Live,* 79–81. "A Working Man's Recollections of America," 106.

then a luxury and a treat to the poor—greater than roast beef is to-day.'' Good bread was so revered that in one family a small Sunday loaf of white bread "was cut up and placed between two slices of black bread, and we thought we had luxuries."[33]

Bread in the New World was almost always wheaten. "Not one in a hundred" New Yorkers had even heard of eating oat bread. In addition, it was always first-class wheat bread. Even laborers in the city, according to Solon Robinson, ate "fine flour bread." And, James Burn added, nobody "who has any pretension to be anybody will eat bread a day old; the loaf is therefore fresh, soft and spongy from the oven every morning."[34]

Other dietary luxuries were accepted parts of American working-class diet. Sugar, coffee, and butter—all rare in the European diet—were routinely found on the New York workingman's table. Henry Price, the cabinetmaker who came to New York in 1842, recorded in his diary his pleasure at having "Coffee (the real thing . . .), [and] Bread and Butter a not Bread and Scrape."[35]

Not surprisingly, immigrants were delighted with American food. John Parks, a carpenter, wrote to friends in England in 1827, "You would be surprised to see provisions so cheap; we buy the best of meat for 4p. per pound. . . . The labouring people live by the best of provisions . . . we live on the best of everything here." John Harold recorded in his diary his astonishment at New York boardinghouse fare. The day began with "Beef Steaks, fish, hash, ginger cakes, buckwheat cakes etc such a profusion as I never saw before at the breakfast tables," and dinner was "a greater profusion than breakfast." The Anonymous Proofreader was amazed to be served "hot

33. Ian Levitt and Christopher Smout, *The State of the Scottish Working-Class in 1843* (Edinburgh, 1979), 22–53; see also Barker, Oddy, and Yudkin, *Dietary Surveys,* 29. Poor Inquiry (Ireland), Appendix E, 2. In 1850, 80 percent of England's grain consumption was wheat, see E. J. T. Collins, "Dietary Change and Cereal Consumption in Britain in the Nineteenth Century," *Agricultural History Review* 23 (1975), 111–114. "Seconds": Barker, Oddy, and Yudkin, 27. Lawson, *Progress in Pudsey,* 26. Mrs. Cobden Unwin, *The Hungry Forties* (London, 1904), 94, 248. This last book, essentially a Liberal party campaign document designed to show the glories of free trade, must be used cautiously as evidence on the English standard of living. The letters describing life before the repeal of the Corn Laws, however, seem veracious.

34. Robinson, *How to Live,* 313; Burn, *Beggar Boy,* 314.

35. Evidence on these items in the Old World diet is found in LePlay, *Les ouvriers européens,* Unwin, *Hungry Forties,* and Poor Inquiry (Ireland), Appendix E, 1–37. Evidence on these items in the city diet can be found in the John A. Wolfer (1844–1846) and Charles Dusenberry (1825–1835) grocers' account books, NYHS. The 1851 and 1853 *Times* budgets and the printer's budget listed in fn. 10 all show substantial sugar expenditures. The other five budgets do not break down the category "food." It seems that in general Irish immigrants simply adopted American cuisine, whereas German immigrants created a German-American cuisine that retained some traditional Old World dishes but was much richer; see Christoph Vetter, *Zwei Jahre in New-York* (Hof, 1849), 132. "The Diary of Henry Edward Price," in *British Records Relating to America in Microform* (East Ardsley, England, 1963), 25.

beef-steaks (cut from the ribs), mutton chops, fish, fried potatoes, boiled potatoes, huckleberries and sugar . . . fresh butter, [and] new bread'' three times a day. A Scotch gilder told Virginia Penny in 1860, ''the accommodations in Scotland are far superior in an intellectual point of view; but so far as pies and doughnuts go, American boardinghouses have the advantage.'' The immigrant view was summed up in the famous story of the Irishman who wrote home that he had meat twice a week. ''When his employer happened to see the letter and indignantly pointed out that the Irishman had meat three times a day the Irishman replied, 'Faith . . . my friends would disbelieve all I have said, if I told them that.' ''36

Irish immigrants on arriving in America sometimes overate to the point of sickness. Despite the bounteous American fare, native workers were moderate eaters who took small portions of the array served, and it took some time for immigrants to learn to take modest helpings. The Shamrock Society of New York warned the arriving Irishman about the dangers of ''an abundance of animal food to which he was unaccustomed.'' The Irishmen's ''bewildered minds revel in epicurean feasts, but diarrhoea [and] sickness,'' Burn wrote, ''frequently throw them on the broad of their backs in the middle of their luxurious mode of living.''37

The high dietary standard also led to excessive drinking, an even more serious danger to health. Frederic LePlay noted in 1851 that alcohol consumption ''is one of the most reliable indices to which one can resort to estimate the poverty or well-being of a family.'' As a rule, though substantial variations existed, the standard of living among European workers—and here England was a clear exception—was too low to permit drink to be consumed on a regular basis. Despite widespread drinking in Irish towns, the Irish peasantry rarely consumed alcohol except at fairs. ''Labourers have not the means of drinking,'' an informant told the Poor Law Commission. When asked about drinking among Armagh peasants like himself, an incredulous Pat Campbell responded, ''after supporting a wife and family out of a day's wages, what remains for whiskey? What nonsense you talk!''38

In New York, however, ''finding themselves in possession of large wages,

36. John Parks letter, 8 December 1827, in Benjamin Smith, ed., *Twenty-Four Letters from Labourers in America to Their Friends in England* (London, 1829), 26. John Harold diary, 25 October 1832, NYHS; *Real Experiences of an Emigrant,* 70. Such praise of American food was surely enhanced by the meager diet immigrants endured on shipboard during the journey to America. But there is no doubt Americans ate much better than most Europeans. Virginia Penny, *How Women Can Make Money* (1863; rpt. New York, 1971), 249. The story about the Irishman is quoted from *Counsel for Emigrants* (Aberdeen, 1834), 5.

37. Vetter, *Zwei Jahre,* 130; *Hints to Emigrants from Europe* ''by the Shamrock Society of New York'' (London, 1817), 8; Burn, *Beggar Boy,* 315.

38. LePlay, *Les ouvriers européens,* 35; Blum, *End of the Old Order,* 185. Poor Inquiry (Ireland), Appendix E, 106, 108; pages 102–109 make it clear how rare was drinking—except during fairs, few Irishmen even tasted liquor. See also Appendix D, 103, 106. The same was true in Scotland; see Levitt and Smout, *State of the Scottish Working Class,* 136–137.

and the means of intoxication cheap, [immigrants] run to excesses," according to one Scottish visitor. Henry Price's grandfather "finding that spirits [in America] were as cheap as the Ale at home gave way to it, and it soon finish'd Him." Most observers believed that although drunkenness was rarer, liquor consumption was much higher in America than in Europe, and the ability to consume alcohol regularly was considered additional evidence of high American living standards. C. Hermitage, an immigrant from Wiltshire, cited the fact that "now I can have a glass of wine or two every day" as proof of the New World's advantages.[39]

Can we detect significant change in workers' diet during this period of rapid industrialization and immigration? The answer, perhaps surprisingly, is no. Even with the decline in labor scarcity associated with the huge immigration of the 1840s and 1850s, diet seems to have remained good. Transport improvements and especially the rail link to Lake Erie in 1851 allowed easy shipment of cattle from the west to New York and kept meat prices low. Immigrant letters mention the superiority of the American diet right through the 1860s, and Fitz-Hugh Ludlow, an *Atlantic Monthly* reporter, discovered that sales of meat in the city had almost exactly mirrored population growth in the dozen years before 1863 despite immigration and the economic downturns of the late 1850s.[40]

Two European luxuries, meat and drink, were thus aspects of everyday life in New York. To immigrants used to a diet of bread, beans, and potatoes it was, indeed, "very satisfying," and the American diet played a large part in the decision to emigrate. Native American workers took a good diet for granted; one labor paper in the city described a typical native worker's family eating a breakfast of smoked fish, "good home baked bread and capital butter." Thomas Mooney's comment that the "food of the American farmer, mechanic, or labourer, is the best, I believe enjoyed by any similar classes in the whole world," seems justified.[41]

## THE HEALTH OF THE WORKING CLASS

How did New York City life affect workers' health? Generally, city life had a positive effect, but there were negatives. Overeating and drinking were minor

39. Scottish visitor quoted in Dallas L. Jones III, "The Background and Motives of Scottish Emigration to the United States of America in the Period 1815–1861, with Special Reference to Emigrant Correspondence" (diss., University of Edinburgh, 1970), 381; Price Diary, 16. Grocers' account books (cited in note 35) show numerous liquor purchases. C. Hermitage letter, 4 October 1832, in G. Poulet Scrope, *Extracts of Letters from Poor Persons* (London, 1832), 21.
40. Edward Spann, *The New Metropolis: New York City, 1840–1857* (New York, 1981), 121–122; Juergens, "Movement of Wholesale Prices," Table 2. Ludlow, "American Metropolis," 83; see *Tribune*, 1 January 1859, for a similar conclusion.
41. *Young America*, 7 March 1846; Mooney, *Nine Years*, 21.

problems compared to congested housing, which was becoming recognized as the city's most serious health hazard. Two additional factors may have increased illness in New York. One was the fast pace of work. European immigrants, like the Anonymous Proofreader quoted in the last chapter on the railroad pace of work, became physically ill after a few weeks in the country. William Darnley wrote to his wife in 1860: "The store that I work for the[y] expect us to do such a quantity of work in a day that any man following it for a few years it will injure himself verry much." It was widely believed that "exhaustion [and] . . . premature decay" were common among native workers who labored at the railroad pace, and the characteristic thinness of Americans, so often noted by travelers, was the inevitable result. Second, the fast pace was carried on in a climate that was, by European standards, exceedingly changeable. Immigrants routinely attributed their maladies to American weather. Samuel Fogarty, a carpenter, wrote his brother in 1839 that he had been ill for three weeks, "this Climate is very variable. We often have great heat and extreme cold in the same day, which renders a stranger very susceptible of taking cold."[42]

As in all cities in the first half of the nineteenth century, the deathrate in New York was high. Mortality was especially high in the late 1840s and early 1850s because of the influx of famine immigrants who arrived in a weakened condition and brought infectious diseases into the city. (Note in Figure 22 how closely the upsurges in immigration and deaths coincide.) According to Kerby Miller, "a significant minority of famine arrivals were permanently incapacitated . . . from malnutrition and associated diseases from the potato blight. . . . Thousands so afflicted perished shortly after disembarking." When the number of immigrants declined in the late 1850s, the adult deathrate dropped. However, the infant mortality rate remained high in that decade, probably reflecting the effects of the city's increasingly crowded housing (see Appendix D). Generally, the waxing and waning of the total deathrate in response to immigration limits the usefulness of mortality as an index of the general health of the city's adult population.[43]

Civil War draft records give a useful insight into the physical condition of

42. On housing see Duffy, *History of Public Health*, 405–418, 522–532, and Spann, *New Metropolis*, 131–138. William Darnley letter, 17 July 1860; *British Mechanic's and Labourer's Hand Book*, 19; Samuel N. Fogarty, letter to Joseph Fogarty, 4 March 1839, Schrier Collection.

43. Correlations of social statistics in 1855 are given in Table 23. Though there are significant positive correlations of the deathrate with the percentage of foreign-born and the child/woman ratio, there is no statistically valid correlation between the deathrate and wealth. The Tenth Ward, which had one of the lowest personal per capita wealth figures in the city, was also one of the healthiest. Kerby Miller, *Emigrants and Exiles: Ireland and the Irish Exodus to North America* (New York, 1985), 296. Robert Higgs's quantitative study discovered that "short-term variations in the rate of immigration were strongly associated with corresponding variations in the rate of mortality"; Higgs, "Cycles and Trends in Mortality in 18 Large American Cities, 1871–1900," *Explorations in Economic History* 16 (1979), 402. The city deathrate is given in Appendix D.

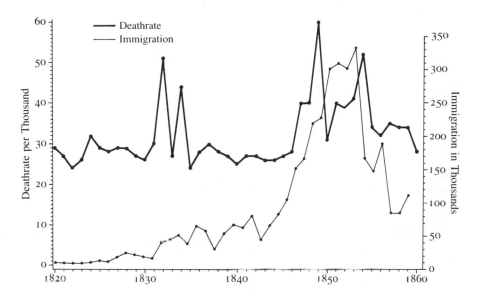

FIGURE 22. Immigration and deathrate, New York, 1820–1860. From John Duffy, *A History of Public Health in New York City, 1625–1866* (New York, 1968), 576–577.

New York's residents. These records clearly cannot be used as an absolute indicator of physical status. Aliens were excluded, and the records, of course, apply only to men. In addition, despite elaborate guidelines, different examining physicians used different categories and criteria for rejection. There is even evidence that New York City, because of its strong pro-Democratic political sentiment, was given a larger quota than Republican districts. Despite these problems, draft statistics do offer an otherwise unavailable glimpse of the general health of the city's adult male population.[44]

As Table 18 illustrates, draftees were deferred for physical reasons less often in the city than in the country as a whole. The rate of tuberculosis was high, as were circulatory disorders including heart disease. On the other hand, deferments for digestive problems and injuries were low—comparison with upstate figures suggests that industrial work in this period may have been less dangerous than agricultural work. Table 19 treats deferments by the city's congressional districts. These statistics generally substantiate the A.I.C.P. reports on ward health conditions. The very small number of deferments in lower Manhattan (the Fourth Congressional District) is surprising—the rate of rejection is even lower than in the largely middle-class Sixth District. Perhaps

44. Grounds for rejection are given in J. H. Baxter, ed., *Medical Statistics of the Provost Marshall's General Bureau* (Washington, D.C., 1875), 1:li–lxi. Larger quotas: Basil Leo Lee, *Discontent in New York City, 1861–1865* (Washington, D.C., 1943), 112–118.

TABLE 18
Rejection rates per thousand draftees, 1863–1864

| Reasons for rejection | New York City | Upstate New York | Total U.S. |
|---|---|---|---|
| General | 52.2 | 38.6 | 29.5 |
| Tuberculosis and respiratory | (43.3) | (28.8) | (29.7) |
| Syphilis | (4.3) | (2.9) | (1.6) |
| Eye | 20.6 | 19.6 | 6.4 |
| Ear | 5.7 | 7.7 | 6.7 |
| Circulatory | 34.1 | 20.7 | 17.7 |
| Heart | (23.1) | (13.2) | (14.2) |
| Nervous | 8.9 | 19.5 | 16.2 |
| Digestive | 43.1 | 68.9 | 59.2 |
| Hernia | (28.1) | (27.2) | (31.6) |
| Urinary | 5.4 | 4.1 | 2.7 |
| Generative | 5.2 | 6.6 | 5.0 |
| Locomotive | 26.1 | 38.9 | 33.6 |
| Miscellaneous | 28.7 | 36.2 | — |
| General debility | (25.1) | (36.2) | (—) |
| Injuries | 18.0 | 38.2 | 33.1 |
| Unclassified | 8.4 | 6.3 | — |
| TOTALS | 249.2 | 311.5 | 282.8 |

N = New York City = 13,031; Upstate New York = 82,545; Total United States = 501,002
(includes draftees and recruits).

*Source:* Compiled from J. H. Baxter, ed., *Medical Statistics of the Provost Marshall's General Bureau* (Washington, D.C., 1875), 2:524–542.

examining doctors were more rigorous with the large bachelor population of the lower wards.[45]

Additional evidence on native workers' health is provided by figures on height in the draft records. Stature is related very closely to diet because inadequate food intake retards physical growth. The average American-born New Yorker was 66.9 inches tall, slightly shorter than the national average of 67.7. Since most native workers were in-migrants, it is possible that poorer (and less-well-fed) farmers migrated to the city. The work of Robert Fogel and others from the manuscript draft records has shown, however, that even city-born workers were slightly shorter than the national population. Robert Margo and Richard Steckel suggest that "the relative shortness of the urban born need not imply a lower level of food intake: the body's surplus of growth may have been reduced by an increased intensity of work." Though the effect of work intensity on stature has not been established, the fast pace in the city's workshops makes it a possibility.[46]

45. During the war single men were discharged before married men; Lee, *Discontent,* 11.
46. Evidence of the impact of diet on stature is given in J. M. Tanner, "The Potential of Auxological Data for Monitoring Economic and Social Well-Being," *Social Science History* 6

TABLE 19

Rejection rates per thousand draftees by area of New York City, 1863–1864

| Congressional District | Wards | Respiratory ailments | General debility | Total | N |
|---|---|---|---|---|---|
| 4 | 1–6, 8 | 41.5 | 2.3 | 131.9 | 1,736 |
| 5 | 7, 10, 13, 14 | 50.9 | 28.4 | 310.1 | 2,077 |
| 6 | 9, 15, 16 | 30.4 | 36.4 | 247.1 | 2,363 |
| 7 | 11, 17 | 47.8 | 24.2 | 289.4 | 2,239 |
| 8 | 18, 20, 21 | 26.8 | 38.2 | 200.7 | 2,197 |
| 9 | 12, 19, 22 | 56.6 | 16.5 | 289.8 | 2,419 |
| TOTALS | | 43.3 | 25.1 | 249.2 | 13,031 |

*Source:* Baxter, *Medical Statistics*, 2:534–542.

Only W. H. Thomson, the examining physician of the city's outer wards (19, 22, and 12), felt urban life exerted an unfavorable influence, especially on the "better classes" within his jurisdiction. Doctors in the other districts felt residents' health was generally good, and C. Roberts, physician for the partly German Seventh District, was amazed at the *turnverein*-developed physiques of many of the workers. The large number of laborers among the foreign-born population especially impressed Thomson, since this occupation demanded good health and a powerful physique.[47]

Generally, physicians were impressed with the health of city residents. The physician Benjamin McCready, though warning of overcrowded housing, was relieved that in 1837 the city was free of the "disease and deformity which . . . could only be found in the over-grown towns of Europe." Another doctor in the 1860s scrutinized the draft records expressly to gauge the city's health. Discovering those drafted for military service were notably fit, he attributed their condition "to the diffused blessings of meat and drink." There is little doubt the high quality of the workers' diet was most responsible for their good health. Though many native New Yorkers regarded immigrants, especially the Irish, as simian brutes, there is no objective evidence of a physically degenerated working class.[48]

---

(1982), 571–581. Heights by congressional district were (in inches) 4, 66.6; 5, 65.7; 6, 67.4; 7, 66.9; 8, 67.4; 9, 66.0. There were 2,575 men measured; Baxter, *Medical Statistics*, 2:29. Robert W. Fogel et al., *Changes in American and British Stature since the Mid-Nineteenth Century*, NBER Working Paper no. 890 (Cambridge, Mass., 1982). Robert A. Margo and Richard H. Steckel, "Heights of Native-Born Whites during the Antebellum Period," *Journal of Economic History* 63 (1983), 173; see also Fogel et al., 31.

47. Baxter, *Medical Statistics*, 1:252, 251, 255. Note also the low deferment rates for laborers in Baxter, 1: Chart xxxiv.

48. McCready, *On the Influence*, 118; Lewis Evans Jackson, *Walks about New York* (New York, 1865), 18. Christine Stansell notes that some of the "investigations" of the city's workers by reformers did little more than repeat the formulas of sensational Victorian urban fiction. Stansell, *City of Women: Sex and Class in New York, 1789–1860* (New York, 1986), 200–203.

Overall, it is clear that the standard of life was far higher in New York than in the Old World. "The fact is," James Burn remarked, "the generality of the working people in the United States live more sumptuously than most middle-class people in England."[49]

## "WORKERS" AND "THE POOR" IN THE ANTEBELLUM CITY

Between 1820 and 1860 a working-class standard of living began to develop. The skill level of the city's workforce was probably declining, but the size of the workforce was growing enormously. The rapid growth of the urban working population, with the influx of hundreds of thousands of immigrants of similar skills and age, was the basis of the growth in working-class demand. Because of their similar economic status, workers most likely had a similar living standard for a long time, but only after 1840 did production expressly for mass consumer demand become widespread. The tenement and the boardinghouse emerged as distinctly working-class housing, and stick furniture was widely produced. While the city's fashionable stores were on Broadway, Chatham Street and the Bowery became a working-class shopping district; both streets were lined with clothing, furniture, and hardware stores. Workers could "purchase any conceivable article, . . . [they] may stand in need of," wrote *Tribune* reporter George "Gaslight" Foster. "Cheapness is its strongest recommendation," and the price of the articles sold was well below that of Broadway stores. In meeting this mass demand, retailers created a standard of living separate from that of the middle class.[50]

To speak of working-class living standards does not mean, of course, that all workers lived the same way. Obviously, single women had few chances to escape poverty, and skilled native workers lived better than their less skilled immigrant counterparts. In America, according to Frank Roney, "mechanics thought themselves superior to laborers . . . [and] it was to a measure recognized by both sides." Foreigners did occupy worse housing than natives—if natives had been forced to live the way many Irish and Germans did, they would surely have been resentful. But usually the higher wages of the natives

49. Burn, *Beggar Boy*, 314.
50. George Foster, *New York in Slices* (New York, 1849), 16, 121. Descriptions of Chatham Street and its Jewish clothiers were a staple in literary descriptions of the city; see, for example, Mathews, *Pen-and-Ink Panorama*, 161–169, and Griesinger, *Lebende Bilder*, 142–147. Even in food, which is to a large extent an exception since both middle- and working-class residents ate well, there was a divergence. Workers in the 1850s were buying bread from bakeries and purchasing canned pickles and vegetables at groceries at a time when servants did almost all the baking and canning for the middle class. Baking: Thomson, *A Tradesman's Travels*, 36; Robinson, *Facts for Farmers*, 327–328; Mooney, *Nine Years*, 136; and Penny, *How Women Can Make Money*, 166. Note also the low index for bakers in the wealthy wards in Table 20. Canning: Fearon, *Sketches of America*, 32, and Penny, 68–69.

bought them better housing, whereas immigrants continued to compare their standard of living with the Old World. Massive immigration in the 1840s marked a crucial change in workers' "frame of reference," from the past—the standard by which natives had judged living conditions—to the Old World. Low European standards usually made the comparison favorable to the United States.[51]

Although a segmented workforce was beginning to develop, in most industries bifurcation had not advanced far enough to create permanent divisions among skilled workers. Michael Piore suggests that segmentation occurs "when portions of the labor force begin to be insulated from uncertainty and variability in demand." But in the mid-nineteenth century, most work, even in the industrial belt, was inconstant. There were some exceptions such as newspaper printers, but few employees could count on steady wages. Laboring was only *more* variable than skilled work; almost no worker was immune.[52]

Though fundamentally higher than the Old World standard, then, the American standard was extremely precarious, and this precariousness most clearly distinguished working-class life from that of the middle-class. Workers who boasted about eating meat three times a day were staging a traditional grain riot in 1837 and mobbing bread carts in Tompkins Square in 1857. Indeed, furniture and the watches and jewelry that were a hallmark of the city's working class were probably in part a form of insurance that could be cashed in easily, and pawnshops were common and did a good business. It is striking how many workers who generally praised American living standards—John Doyle, the Anonymous Cabinetmaker, John Gough, William Darnley—were at one time or another in desperate straits, living from day to day. The demand for labor was highly variable, and a panic, a bad winter, or illness could demolish high standards in a flash. The large number of single workers increased the precarious quality of working-class life—they had no familial "safety net" to rely on when they were out of work. "Journeymen live well or ill, according as they have or not, permanent situations," the *Tribune* blandly noted in 1845.[53]

Although descent into poverty was a real fear for all workers, it burdened

51. *Frank Roney: An Autobiography*, ed. Ira Cross (1931; rpt. New York, 1976), 350. On America-homeland comparisons among New York City workers, see Dorothee Schneider, " 'For Whom Are All the Good Things in Life?' German-American Housewives Discuss Their Budgets," in Harmut Keil and John B. Jentz, eds., *German Workers in Industrial Chicago, 1850–1910: A Comparative Perspective* (DeKalb, Ill., 1983), 145–160.

52. Michael Piore, "The Technological Foundations of Dualism and Discontinuity," in Suzanne Berger and Piore, eds., *Dualism and Discontinuity in Industrial Societies* (Cambridge, England, 1980), 24.

53. 1837: Joel T. Headley, *Great Riots of New York* (1873; rpt. Miami, Fla., 1969), 97–110. 1857: *Herald*, 12 November 1857. Pawnshops: Matthew Carey, *Miscellaneous Essays* (Philadelphia, 1830), 160–161; see also Foster, *New York in Slices*, 30–33. *Tribune*, 11 September 1845.

English immigrant workers more than either Irish or natives. Irish peasants were used to seasonality and economic insecurity, and native workers also accepted such uncertainty as an integral part of urban life. " 'Come easy, go easy' seems to be the maxim by which nearly all classes of [American] working-men . . . regulate their conduct," Burn believed. The notion that a diligent worker might insulate himself against serious economic difficulties through savings was viewed (correctly, it seems) as a fantasy. English workers, however, were often distressed by American unpredictability. New York working-class life may have been no more uncertain than that of English cities—Burn noted that pawnshops were less numerous than in European cities. However, higher New World standards meant further to fall, and, as noted, serious economic unpredictability called into question the decision to emigrate.[54]

Any worker could become poor and many single women and unskilled workers faced enduring poverty, but "worker" and "poor" were not synonymous in antebellum New York City. There were thousands of poor in the city in the middle of the nineteenth century, and a great deal has been written about them, both by nineteenth-century reformers and by twentieth-century historians. The degradation and misery they recount is dismal. However, the A.I.C.P. reports of starving seamstresses and tubercular workers living in cellars cannot be taken as typical of the city's working class. The poor were only a part of the working class. Perhaps the most knowledgeable of antebellum writers on New York City was George Foster of the *Tribune*. His graphic accounts of the misery of the city's needy are a landmark in urban journalism, but Foster never equated "the poor" with "the working classes." In his writings he described three representative areas of New York—Broadway (the elite), the Bowery (workers), and Five Points in Ward Six (the poor). The Bowery was the domain of Mose and Lize, the archetypal city workers discussed in Chapters 8 and 9, while Five Points had been the symbol of city poverty since Charles Dickens published *American Notes for General Circulation* in 1842.[55]

54. Burn, *Beggar Boy,* 337. Dallas Jones also notes the resilience of native workers: "Americans facing situations that would have ruined anyone in Britain, simply turned their heads and built up again from scratch," Jones, "Background and Motives," 185. The only group of workers who seemed really afflicted by such uncertainty was printers—one of the few occupations that had become partly accustomed to permanent employment. When printers saw their wages drop they became "dissipated and unsettled" (*Tribune*, 7 November 1845). Burn, *Beggar Boy,* 280.

55. Spann, *New Metropolis,* chap. 4, "Poverty," describes the city's poor and attempts to ameliorate their condition. Stuart M. Blumin, "Explaining the New Metropolis: Perception, Depiction, and Analysis in Mid-Nineteenth Century New York City," *Journal of Urban History* 11 (1984), 23–24, explains Foster's social geography. Both Foster's *New York in Slices* (New York, 1849), and *New York by Gas-Light* (New York, 1850) use this typology. "The Bowery" as a metaphor for the city's workers is discussed in Peter George Buckley, "To the Opera House: Culture and Society in New York City, 1820–1860," (diss., SUNY at Stony Brook, 1984), 317–353.

Although not poor, most workingmen apparently did not aspire to middle-class status; they were not "consumers" in the twentieth-century meaning of the word. Newspaper printers were described as "select in associations" and desirous of "*genteel accommodations*," but they were unique because of their year-round employment. Despite a clear divergence between middle- and working-class consumption patterns, most workers seem to have had little desire to match bourgeois standards. "The miserable ambition to be accounted 'genteel' . . . [is] not among the national characteristics," wrote English visitor William Hancock in 1860. After studying English immigrants' letters, Charlotte Erickson concluded that "a desire to display one's economic success through fine dress . . . or lavish furnishings" was quite rare. Material objects such as furniture were desired simply because they were more comfortable and convenient. "The houses in their internal fittings generally evince a degree of thrift seldom seen in the dwellings of the same class in Great Britain," Burn wrote approvingly. Most immigrants came to the United States with modest expectations and were not unhappy as workers.[56]

This satisfaction was especially true because the material life of the working class was better in the New World than the Old. "There are a number of destitute poor [in New York City] . . . but none of the real actual poverty and distress which is in all parts of Ireland," wrote printer John Doyle. Joseph I. C. Clarke, who arrived in the city in 1868, fifty years after Doyle, had a similar reaction: "I saw no slums, no exhibition of the brutalized poverty to be found a-plenty in the richest capitals of Europe," except in Five Points. One immigrant tailor to New Jersey told English traveler Isaac Holmes, "the corroding anxiety of not knowing whether I could maintain myself is removed; and this more than recompenses me for coming hither." Few workers expected to get rich, and simply to be "undisturbed by pinching want," as Scottish visitor John Prentice put it, was enough for them to consider themselves successful. To be well-housed, clothed, and fed, and in generally good health, was "very gratifying" to workers.[57]

There is evidence that this high standard eroded in the late 1850s. The unsettled state of the national economy and the huge influx of immigrants combined to make housing overcrowded. Kerby Miller notices a subtle decrease in the optimism of Irish immigrant letters written during good times in the 1850s, and in New York City permanent beggars—a group whose scarcity had long amazed European visitors—appeared in the streets. The decline in

56. *Tribune*, 11 September 1845; Hancock, *Emigrant's Five Years*, 86; Charlotte Erickson, *Invisible Immigrants: The Adaptation of English and Scottish Immigrants in Nineteenth-Century America* (1972; rpt. Ithaca, N.Y., 1990), 239; Burn, *Three Years*, 103.

57. "Letter of John Doyle," *Journal of the American-Irish Historical Society* 12 (1913), 203; Clarke, *My Life*, 78; Isaac Holmes, *An Account of the United States of America* (London, 1823), 128–129; John Prentice, "Letter to the Working Classes of Edinburgh," *Scotsman*, 16 April 1834.

standards seems to have been limited mostly to housing, however, and the American diet held up well.[58]

Time and again immigrants returned to the subject of American food. "You get so used to better living that you finally think potato soup tasted better in Germany than the daily roast here," Charles Steinway wrote to his brother in 1852. Among immigrants who returned to England, "the American daily bill of fare [was] . . . not forgotten," and many, Burn claimed, soon came back to the United States. America was probably the first country to offer the mass of its population the opportunity to eat well most of the time. To European immigrants, who for generations had made the pursuit of sufficient bread to eat the center of their lives, the opportunity to eat meat twice daily was a revelation. William McLurg no doubt spoke for many when he wrote to his parents, "there is nothing I regret so much as not coming here . . . sooner."[59]

58. Kerby Miller, "Emigrants and Exiles," 391–392. On beggars in New York see Burn, *Beggar Boy,* 337.

59. Charles Steinway quoted in Theodore Steinway, *People and Pianos* (New York, 1953), 16; Burn, *Beggar Boy,* 353; William McLurg letter to his father David McLurg, 5 July 1833, McClorg Correspondence, PRONI.

CHAPTER 7

# Working-Class Neighborhoods

Urban residential patterns mirrored the divergence between working-class and middle-class consumption. New York's industries were not scattered randomly throughout the city, and neither were its people. The development of a working-class area of the city was, with the experience in the city's workshops and in material life, a precondition for the development of the working-class institutions described in the next chapter. Residential patterns, and especially the clustering of single men in the city's lower wards, were especially important in shaping the boardinghouse and saloon, at the heart of working-class culture.

## THE RESIDENTIAL GEOGRAPHY OF THE METROPOLIS

New York in 1820 already contained significant geographical divisions by wealth. Even in colonial times there had existed distinct residential neighborhoods of differing economic rank, though such areas were more residentially heterogeneous than they would later become. In one way, however, New York in 1820 still conformed to a preindustrial urban pattern—the city's wealthier residents tended to concentrate in the core area, Wards One, Two, and Three. Lower Broadway, Bowling Green, and Pearl, Cliff, Greenwich, and Chambers streets all contained fashionable dwellings intermixed with offices and shops.[1]

1. Carl Abbott, "The Neighborhoods of New York, 1760–1775," *New York History* 60 (1974), 35–53; Edward Pessen, *Riches, Class and Power before the Civil War* (Lexington,

Beginning in the late 1830s and gaining speed in the 1840s, the growth of commerce and manufacturing began to force population out of the lower wards. The New York State Assembly's 1857 report described the process: "As our wharves become crowded with warehouses, and encompassed with bustle and noise, the wealthier citizens, who peopled old 'Knickerbocker' mansions near the bay, transferred their residence to streets beyond the din; compensating for remoteness . . . [with] the advantages of increased quiet and luxury." The booming economy made it possible for builders to pay huge sums for the conversions of dwellings to commercial purposes. Philip Hone was reluctant to dispose of his mansion on Broadway opposite City Hall Park "to be converted into shops" in 1836, but he eventually concluded that "$60,000 is a great deal of money" and sold.[2]

As the elite moved out of the lower wards, they consciously set themselves off from other city residents. Although wealthy residents continued to live in every ward, mingling was no longer the general pattern; new fashionable neighborhoods developed in the northern areas of the city and in Brooklyn. The residents of these wealthy areas had to make a daily journey from their homes to the lower wards, where they transacted the city's commercial, legal, and financial business. Such residential dispersion required an urban transit system. One contemporary observer described the significance of omnibuses to the city's geography:

> At that time [1830] the omnibus system commenced running. By that plan coaches pass every five minutes through the principal avenues, carrying businessmen to their homes at night, and to their offices in the morning. This immediately permitted an expansion of the surface occupied by dwellings, and houses multiplied rapidly in the upper part of the city.

By 1833 the price of the most widely used of the several horse-drawn bus lines was "6 Tickets for 50 Cts from Wall St to the upper part of Bdway" according to John Pintard.[3]

An estimated seventy-thousand people commuted in 1855 to the city from suburbs as distant as Flushing by omnibuses, ferries, and later horse-drawn

---

Mass., 1973), 172–176; Charles Lockwood, *Manhattan Moves Uptown: An Illustrated History* (Boston, 1976), 32–47.

2. The number of people resident in the lower three wards dropped from 29,133 in 1830 to 23,637 in 1860. *Documents of the Assembly of the State of New York*, 80th sess., 1857, III, no. 205, 11. *The Diary of Philip Hone*, ed., Alan Nevins (New York, 1927), 2:201 (8 March 1836).

3. Thomas Kettel, "Internal Transportation," *Democratic Review* 27 (1850), quoted in Bayrd Still, *Urban America: A History with Documents* (Boston, 1974), 85; "Letters from John Pintard to His Daughter," *Collections of the New-York Historical Society* 72 (1941), 4:130. A complete list of omnibus routes is in D. T. Valentine, ed., *Manual of the Corporation of the City of New York*, annual, beginning in 1841. In addition, frequent ferry service (with boats leaving every five minutes during rush hours) linked lower Manhattan with Brooklyn and Jersey City.

railcars. This transit system permitted a rapid dispersal of the city's upper-class population. By 1865 only two of the 1,348 stockbrokers in the city lived in Ward One, where Wall Street was located. The most important of the new fashionable commuter neighborhoods was Washington Square in the Fifteenth Ward. In 1849 one city guide explained to its readers, "The NORTHERN PART OF THE CITY is the fashionable quarter, where the residences of the wealthy are located," and the term "above Bleecker" meant expensive housing. Brooklyn Heights also became an exclusive residential suburb in this period.[4]

By setting themselves off from the city in fashionable neighborhoods and suburbs, the upper classes ensured the development of working-class residential areas. Like the elite, workers, of course, had to get from their homes to their work. But the emerging omnibus system was too expensive for most to use regularly: at six cents for a one-way trip, the weekly total of 72 cents would be 11 percent of an average worker's weekly wages of $6.70 in 1860—way above the 2 or 3 percent a person of median income would spend on subway fares today in New York. So workers, as they had for decades, continued to walk to their employment. Obviously, workers preferred to live near their jobs. Employees at the Novelty Works, for example, "all . . . reside in the streets surrounding the works," and John Harold, who worked in the lower wards, wrote in his diary in 1832, "seeking about for a new lodging my present one [on Canal Street] not suiting on account of the distance from my employment."[5]

The concentration of industrial jobs in the lower wards has already been described: in 1860 Wards Two and Three had 31,215 manufacturing jobs

4. The 70,000 estimate is in "Great Cities," *Putnam's Monthly Magazine* 5 (1855), 261; it may be too high. The 1865 New York State census asked for the "Usual Place of Employment, if out of the city or town where the family resides." Franklin B. Hough, ed., *Statistics of the Population of the City and County of New York as Shown by the State Census* (New York, 1866), 133, indicates that 23,281 residents of nearby counties worked in the city. The 1865 census was not particularly accurate, and the total, of course, does not include those commuting from New Jersey. It does suggest, however, that 70,000 is not a low estimate. Brokers: Hough, 246. Kenneth Jackson's research shows that in 1825, 1.1 percent of a sample of New York City attorneys lived outside Manhattan; by 1865, 35.7 percent had their homes elsewhere; Jackson, "Urban Decentralization in the Nineteenth Century: A Statistical Inquiry," in Leo Schnore, ed., *The New Urban History* (Princeton, N.J., 1975), 138. The journey-to-work evidence compiled by Allan Pred in *The Spatial Dynamics of U.S. Urban-Industrial Growth, 1800–1914* (Cambridge, Mass., 1966), pertains largely to masters. The 300 machinists Pred (p. 159) finds in the 1840 *Longworth's Almanac* are a fraction of the 1,409 listed in the 1840 census. Lockwood, *Manhattan Moves Uptown*, 60–64; Andrews & Company, *Stranger's Guide in the City of New-York* (New York, 1849), 2. The chapter "Escape to Suburbia" in Edward Spann, *The New Metropolis: New York, 1840–1857* (New York, 1981), describes the process in detail.

5. Wirt Sikes, "Among the Poor Girls," *Putnam's Magazine* n.s. 1 (1868), 441, notes that horse cars were too expensive for women workers. The six-cent rate on most omnibuses is noted in *The Real Experiences of an Emigrant* (London, 187?), 73–74. Jacob Abbott, "The Novelty Works," *Harper's Magazine* 2 (1851), 724; John Harold diary, 23 October 1832, New-York Historical Society (NYHS).

(including outworkers) and only 6,264 residents. Map 3 suggests the relationship between manufacturing jobs and residence. Clearly there was a large daily movement of workers into these lower wards from nearby, but where did most of these workers live? Since the East River was the major port area (though the Hudson was gaining fast in the 1850s), wealthier residents preferred the less congested West Side as the city grew, leaving the area east of Fifth Avenue mainly to workers. Some better-paid workers, especially native-born ones, lived in Wards Five, Eight, and Nine, but the areas today known as the Lower East Side and East Village became heavily working-class. This section of the city had contained some workers' homes since the first decade of the century, but only after 1840 did the huge growth of the city create a densely populated residential area. Many workers in this section found employment in the East River shipyards and foundries, but for thousands of others a one- or two-mile walk from East Side tenements to the city's lower wards was unavoidable.[6]

The development of class areas in the city is illustrated in Table 20. Based on information drawn from the 1865 census, the table shows consistently high concentrations of manual occupations in East Side wards. Merchants and professional people were concentrated in Wards Fifteen, Eighteen, Nineteen, and Twenty-One but were rare in the eastern wards. The distribution of servants is perhaps the best indicator of a ward's class nature, though Wards Two and Three also had a high proportion of servants because of their many boardinghouses. Table 21 suggests it was the wealthy who set themselves off from the workers, not vice versa: the general population correlations for physicians, merchants, servants, lawyers, and brokers were low—among manual occupations only maritime trades were more concentrated.

The focus on the East Side should not lead us to ignore the tens of thousands of workers who lived elsewhere in the city. The growth of the Hudson River waterfront brought to the West Side many workers, such as the employees of the Higgins Carpet Company who "sought residences nearby" in Wards Sixteen, Twenty, and Twenty-Two. Note in Table 20 the very high concentration of (carpet) weavers in those wards. Indeed, the development of the Hudson in the late 1850s and 1860s caused a reversal of the wealthy–West Side, worker–East Side pattern above 14th Street, with many well-off New Yorkers now choosing to live on the quieter East Side in Wards Eighteen and Twenty-One.[7]

6. Manufacturing figures from Census Office, *Eighth Census, 1860, Manufacturing*, Manuscript; population figures from Census Office, *Eighth Census, 1860, Population*. On native-born workers in Wards Five and Eight see Council of Hygiene and Public Health, *Report upon the Sanitary Condition of the City* (New York, 1865), 24, 37. On the development of the East Side working-class area see Elizabeth Blackmar, "Housing and Property Relations in New York City, 1785–1850" (diss., Harvard University, 1980), 292. Two mile walks: Sikes, "Among the Poor Girls," 439, 441. Griesinger noted that "most" Kleindeutschland residents worked in the city's lower wards; Theodor Griesinger, *Land und Leute in Amerika* (Stuttgart, 1863), 554–555.

7. Higgins carpet: Ortho Cartwright, *The Middle West Side* (New York, 1912), 35.

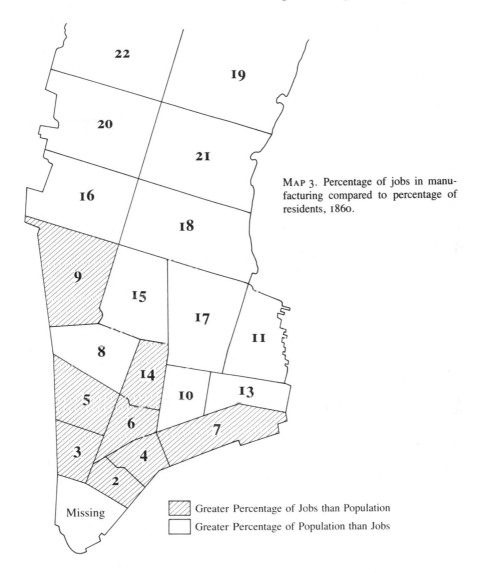

MAP 3. Percentage of jobs in manufacturing compared to percentage of residents, 1860.

Missing

Greater Percentage of Jobs than Population

Greater Percentage of Population than Jobs

The ability of upper- and middle-class residents to use omnibuses and railroads allowed a greater spatial separation of economic groups than heretofore. Between 1843 and 1856, as the city moved out of the 1837 depression and into the Age of Gold, the three richest wards in the city increased annual average per capita income by $300 (from $281 to $581) while in the three poorest wards it increased by only $41 (from $21 to $62). Table 22 illustrates the increasing differentiation of wealth. While the city's richest wards increased their concentration of wealth, the poorest stayed about the same and the middle wards lost ground. The increase in the wealth/population ratio in the richest wards may be largely due to recovery from the depression, but the

TABLE 20
Occupations by ward, 1865 (index numbers)

This table is an index that compares the percentage of the population living in a ward with the percentage of employees in each occupation living in the ward. The formula is Pct. Employees in an Occupation living in the Ward / Pct. Total Population living in the Ward × 100. An index of 100 means the percentages of employees and population are equal. Ward Twelve was the area of the city above 86th Street. The categories Carter, Construction trades, Furniture, Milliner, Printer, and Shipbuilder are compiled from subcategories in the 1865 census. Some of the returns for Ward Fourteen are imcomplete.

| Ward | Men 20–35 | Native-born | German-born | Irish-born | Barkeepers | Boarding-housekeepers | Bakers | Blacksmiths | Brokers | Butchers | Carters |
|---|---|---|---|---|---|---|---|---|---|---|---|
| 1 | 119 | 76 | 75 | 186 | 359 | 594 | 83 | 48 | 11 | 69 | 133 |
| 2 | 106 | 125 | 64 | 160 | 810 | 657 | 118 | 46 | — | — | 470 |
| 3 | 152 | 78 | 94 | 157 | 539 | 148 | 109 | 49 | 144 | 26 | 225 |
| 4 | 108 | 77 | 80 | 171 | 213 | 337 | 132 | 48 | 28 | 53 | 125 |
| 5 | 126 | 92 | 92 | 109 | 188 | 270 | 87 | 59 | 27 | 51 | 212 |
| 6 | 106 | 75 | 74 | 164 | 125 | 177 | 81 | 79 | 22 | 58 | 139 |
| 7 | 115 | 91 | 59 | 141 | 71 | 156 | 104 | 90 | 44 | 36 | 130 |
| 8 | 112 | 108 | 84 | 76 | 186 | 171 | 70 | 68 | 64 | 53 | 131 |
| 9 | 110 | 123 | 44 | 74 | 59 | 50 | 83 | 87 | 134 | 103 | 242 |
| 10 | 122 | 88 | 229 | 45 | 282 | 100 | 159 | 55 | 44 | 96 | 105 |
| 11 | 90 | 95 | 204 | 54 | 72 | 32 | 128 | 196 | 11 | 111 | 83 |
| 12 | 80 | 117 | 47 | 94 | 52 | 13 | 63 | 82 | 151 | 47 | — |
| 13 | 102 | 103 | 134 | 73 | 89 | 22 | 100 | 148 | 18 | 143 | 147 |
| 14 | 115 | 82 | 87 | 140 | 116 | 98 | 112 | 128 | 23 | 85 | 88 |
| 15 | 118 | 106 | 37 | 106 | 85 | 491 | 50 | 36 | 427 | 38 | 53 |
| 16 | 79 | 107 | 42 | 109 | 44 | 53 | 77 | 88 | 82 | 66 | 152 |
| 17 | 99 | 89 | 206 | 68 | 111 | 50 | 147 | 93 | 45 | 225 | 89 |
| 18 | 93 | 97 | 54 | 142 | 55 | 87 | 90 | 103 | 226 | 62 | 77 |
| 19 | 88 | 105 | 61 | 116 | 55 | 20 | 69 | 106 | 117 | 92 | 28 |
| 20 | 93 | 106 | 69 | 107 | 71 | 40 | 115 | 122 | 75 | 111 | 91 |
| 21 | 87 | 108 | 37 | 122 | 35 | 64 | 63 | 76 | 309 | 82 | 40 |
| 22 | 87 | 116 | 97 | 75 | 67 | 30 | 89 | 117 | 97 | 148 | 46 |
| N | 84,993 | 407,312 | 107,269 | 161,334 | 3,074 | 1,018 | 2,572 | 3,672 | 1,348 | 3,998 | 7,405 |

TABLE 20—continued

| Ward | Clergymen | Clerks | Construction trades | Coopers | Furniture makers | Jewelers | Laborers | Laundresses | Lawyers | Merchants | Metal-workers |
|---|---|---|---|---|---|---|---|---|---|---|---|
| 1 | 69 | 58 | 22 | 316 | 24 | 40 | 334 | 160 | 12 | 20 | 66 |
| 2 | — | 256 | 9 | 217 | — | 66 | 34 | 68 | 49 | 468 | 352 |
| 3 | 201 | 226 | 38 | 77 | 32 | 117 | 104 | 150 | 88 | 105 | 488 |
| 4 | 20 | 90 | 59 | 206 | 41 | 68 | 184 | 195 | 7 | 29 | 178 |
| 5 | 56 | 180 | 44 | 122 | 34 | 116 | 167 | 213 | 39 | 153 | 210 |
| 6 | 51 | 91 | 87 | 139 | 42 | 143 | 195 | 162 | 12 | 54 | 164 |
| 7 | 128 | 118 | 69 | 389 | 49 | 81 | 134 | 88 | 43 | 62 | 46 |
| 8 | 45 | 92 | 82 | 124 | 137 | 177 | 83 | 9 | 18 | 65 | 94 |
| 9 | 132 | 173 | 106 | 141 | 67 | 128 | 53 | 56 | 115 | 134 | 112 |
| 10 | 38 | 123 | 94 | 136 | 169 | 239 | 27 | 83 | 39 | 53 | 150 |
| 11 | 37 | 45 | 98 | 116 | 112 | 93 | 89 | 65 | 24 | 29 | 114 |
| 12 | 138 | 82 | 95 | 22 | 65 | 44 | 133 | 44 | 154 | 123 | 80 |
| 13 | 58 | 82 | 86 | 173 | 160 | 104 | 84 | 69 | 40 | 38 | 107 |
| 14 | 65 | 79 | 56 | 80 | 141 | 114 | 100 | 183 | 25 | 16 | 448 |
| 15 | 146 | 196 | 44 | 18 | 79 | 178 | 23 | 125 | 427 | 303 | 33 |
| 16 | 149 | 122 | 113 | 61 | 52 | 52 | 86 | 154 | 121 | 145 | 59 |
| 17 | 94 | 94 | 111 | 70 | 198 | 128 | 65 | 75 | 63 | 71 | 47 |
| 18 | 136 | 94 | 111 | 35 | 74 | 53 | 106 | 131 | 219 | 192 | 187 |
| 19 | 123 | 101 | 118 | 53 | 70 | 79 | 116 | 84 | 130 | 79 | 65 |
| 20 | 107 | 83 | 165 | 52 | 115 | 74 | 112 | 155 | 71 | 74 | 74 |
| 21 | 184 | 88 | 109 | 25 | 83 | 87 | 86 | 39 | 270 | 236 | 80 |
| 22 | 107 | 64 | 117 | 46 | 80 | 45 | 122 | 37 | 93 | 86 | 50 |
| N | 2,084 | 17,620 | 14,223 | 1,401 | 3,429 | 925 | 21,231 | 3,590 | 1,232 | 5,978 | 5,517 |

TABLE 20—continued

| Ward | Milliners | Physicians | Plumbers | Printers | Sailors | Seam-stresses | Servants | Ship-builders | Shoe-makers | Tailors | Teachers | Weavers |
|---|---|---|---|---|---|---|---|---|---|---|---|---|
| 1 | 87 | 17 | 53 | 53 | 439 | 129 | 97 | 22 | 77 | 33 | 39 | 26 |
| 2 | — | 0 | 109 | 290 | 11 | 26 | 369 | — | 77 | 94 | — | — |
| 3 | 102 | 85 | 19 | 109 | 157 | 34 | 391 | 0 | 99 | 49 | 14 | 75 |
| 4 | 102 | 36 | 116 | 281 | 507 | 154 | 69 | 73 | 132 | 104 | 87 | 51 |
| 5 | 177 | 123 | 25 | 115 | 195 | 106 | 86 | 34 | 121 | 84 | 48 | 14 |
| 6 | 255 | 29 | 174 | 205 | 103 | 157 | 56 | 24 | 138 | 204 | 91 | 96 |
| 7 | 130 | 68 | 79 | 184 | 555 | 130 | 70 | 552 | 86 | 74 | 122 | 10 |
| 8 | 92 | 78 | 91 | 98 | 131 | 61 | 81 | 29 | 110 | 89 | 55 | 17 |
| 9 | 171 | 77 | 147 | 184 | 65 | 97 | 78 | 31 | 79 | 58 | 139 | 23 |
| 10 | 111 | 98 | 91 | 213 | 121 | 111 | 43 | 77 | 175 | 198 | 71 | 40 |
| 11 | 93 | 29 | 69 | 79 | 59 | 91 | 19 | 462 | 131 | 163 | 72 | 62 |
| 12 | 30 | 77 | 71 | ND | 30 | 57 | 119 | 14 | 66 | 27 | 26 | 9 |
| 13 | 85 | 80 | 64 | 180 | 127 | 71 | 24 | 255 | 92 | 139 | 68 | 34 |
| 14 | 79 | 169 | 169 | 153 | 92 | 105 | 55 | 32 | 140 | 186 | 100 | 38 |
| 15 | 165 | 448 | 71 | 65 | 46 | 98 | 313 | 15 | 62 | 55 | 155 | 5 |
| 16 | 131 | 91 | 138 | 57 | 35 | 106 | 147 | 14 | 77 | 64 | 119 | 127 |
| 17 | 98 | 134 | 98 | 94 | 34 | 103 | 62 | 55 | 175 | 188 | 121 | 40 |
| 18 | 88 | 92 | 108 | 69 | 31 | 150 | 247 | 30 | 74 | 69 | 79 | 40 |
| 19 | 45 | 67 | 91 | 62 | 36 | 64 | 82 | 21 | 31 | 32 | 155 | 29 |
| 20 | 122 | 81 | 131 | 46 | 38 | 143 | 70 | 18 | 88 | 71 | 134 | 352 |
| 21 | 34 | 155 | 79 | 45 | 21 | 61 | 215 | 5 | 48 | 25 | 105 | 20 |
| 22 | 30 | 44 | 86 | 43 | 26 | 47 | 75 | 24 | 66 | 73 | 90 | 576 |
| N | 1,689 | 1,269 | 1,108 | 3,672 | 3,291 | 9,501 | 33,282 | 1,651 | 6,307 | 9,734 | 1,598 | 582 |

Source: Franklin B. Hough, ed., Statistics of Population of the City and County of New York as Shown by the State Census (New York, 1866).

TABLE 21

Correlation of selected trades and nationalities with general population, by wards, 1865

| Group | Correlation |
| --- | --- |
| Native-born | .98 |
| Construction trades | .94 |
| Men 20 to 35 | .93 |
| Bakers | .91 |
| Teachers | .89 |
| Plumbers | .87 |
| Blacksmiths | .87 |
| Seamstresses | .86 |
| Butchers | .85 |
| Furnituremakers | .84 |
| Shoemakers | .81 |
| Clergymen | .79 |
| Clerks | .77 |
| Irish-born | .77 |
| German-born | .76 |
| Tailors | .75 |
| Laborers | .74 |
| Milliners | .73 |
| Jewelers | .72 |
| Laundresses | .66 |
| Carters | .62 |
| Physicians | .59 |
| Merchants | .54 |
| Printers | .49 |
| Saloonkeepers | .46 |
| Weavers | .46 |
| Servants | .45 |
| Lawyers | .45 |
| Brokers | .36 |
| Shipbuilders | .35 |
| Coopers | .34 |
| Metalworkers | .34 |
| Sailors | .02 |
| Boardinghousekeepers | −.06 |

*Note:* The totals are given in Table 20. This is a Pearson correlation, by wards.
*Source:* See Table 20.

TABLE 22

Spatial distribution of personal wealth by ward, 1843 and 1856

| | 1843 | | | | 1856 | | | | |
|---|---|---|---|---|---|---|---|---|---|
| | A | B | C | D | A | B | C | E | F |
| Richest Ward | 1 | 3.3 | 41.4 | 12.55 | 1 | 2.1 | 41.3 | 19.66 | 1.57 |
| 2nd " Ward | 3 | 3.2 | 9.1 | 2.84 | 2 | .5 | 3.0 | 6.00 | 2.11 |
| 3rd " Ward | 15 | 5.2 | 13.4 | 2.58 | 15 | 3.8 | 15.0 | 3.95 | 1.53 |
| 4th " Ward | 2 | 1.9 | 3.0 | 1.58 | 3 | 1.3 | 1.2 | .92 | .58 |
| 5th " Ward | 7 | 6.9 | 7.3 | 1.06 | 16 | 24.5 | 20.2 | .82 | .77 |
| 6th " Ward | 5 | 5.5 | 4.4 | .80 | 5 | 3.4 | 1.8 | .53 | .66 |
| 7th " Ward | 12 | 3.6 | 2.7 | .75 | 17 | 9.5 | 4.2 | .49 | .65 |
| 8th " Ward | 6 | 5.2 | 2.8 | .54 | 7 | 5.5 | 2.5 | .45 | .83 |
| 9th " Ward | 4 | 5.7 | 2.9 | .51 | 14 | 3.9 | 1.7 | .44 | .86 |
| 10th " Ward | 14 | 5.7 | 2.8 | .49 | 9 | 6.3 | 2.2 | .35 | .71 |
| 11th " Ward | 8 | 8.3 | 3.2 | .39 | 4 | 3.6 | 1.1 | .31 | .79 |
| 12th " Ward | 17 | 7.3 | 2.2 | .30 | 8 | 5.4 | 1.7 | .31 | 1.03 |
| 13th " Ward | 9 | 8.3 | 1.8 | .22 | 6 | 4.1 | 0.9 | .23 | 1.05 |
| 14th " Ward | 10 | 5.7 | 1.1 | .19 | 12 | 9.2 | 1.8 | .20 | 1.05 |
| 15th " Ward | 16 | 10.9 | 1.1 | .10 | 10 | 4.2 | 0.7 | .16 | 1.60 |
| 16th " Ward | 13 | 6.0 | 0.5 | .08 | 13 | 4.3 | 0.3 | .07 | .88 |
| Poorest Ward | 11 | 7.3 | 0.1 | .01 | 11 | 8.4 | 0.4 | .04 | 4.00 |

A = Ward number (new wards added 1843–56 are incorporated in seventeen wards in existence in 1843)
B = Percent population, 1845 and 1855
C = Percent wealth, 1843 and 1856
D = B/C 1843
E = B/C 1856
F = E/D

Sources: *Census of the State of New York, 1845* (Albany, 1846); *Census of the State of New York, 1855* (Albany, 1857); Moses Beach, *Wealth and Pedigree of the Wealthy Citizens of New York City* (New York, 1842), 24; William Boyd, ed., *New York City Tax-Book* (New York, 1857), viii.

decline in the ratio of the middle wards between 1843 and 1856 is less easily explained by cyclical economic changes. Edward Pessen has shown that wealth was becoming more unequally distributed; it seems increasingly to have become spatially differentiated as well.[8]

This spatial divergence of economic groups is made clear by looking at the occupations of the residents of Fourth Street in Ward Eleven, the "Dry Dock Ward." The weak working-class demand for transit ensured that East Side omnibus service would be limited, forcing nonworkers with jobs in the ward such as bosses, ministers, physicians, and clerks to live there. In the 1850s Thomas Stillman, the proprietor of the Novelty Works, for instance, lived

8. Figures on ward personal wealth compiled from Moses Beach, *Wealth and Pedigree of the Wealthy Citizens of New York City* (New York, 1842), and William Boyd, *New York City Tax-Book* (New York, 1857). These are tax assessment figures and, as such, substantially understate the true amount of personal wealth. Their only value is comparative; see Pessen, *Riches, Class and Power*, 14–15, 33–35.

nearby on Seventh Street in the heart of Ward Seventeen. Nevertheless, the predominance of manual occupations among Fourth Street's residents is striking—348 of 407 inhabitants were workers, mostly in metals, shipbuilding, and construction. There were no merchants or lawyers at all (see Appendix E). Most areas on the East Side were less occupationally homogenous than Fourth Street, as Table 20 shows. However, there were now large areas of the city where middle- and upper-class presence was faint.[9]

By the 1850s public awareness of geographical class regions in the city was widespread, and the East Side was recognized as *the* working-class area. For the first time in the city's history, large areas were inhabited overwhelmingly by workers, unknown and faintly frightening to middle-class observers. George Foster, the *Tribune* reporter, described the streams of workers at 6 P.M. quitting time "all forming a continuous procession which fills Nassau Street, and turning away up Chatham and the Bowery loses itself gradually in the innumerable side-streets leading whence into the unknown regions of Proletareism in the East End." Dr. J. T. Kennedy, in *Report upon the Sanitary Condition of the City,* pointed out that "the east end of the city is a *'terra incognita'* to most of the inhabitants of the west end." Cornelius Mathews, another writer on the city, noted that "there are thousands in the western part of the city . . . who couldn't find their way to the Bowery without a guide" and "have expressed a belief that the people of that whole section of the city lying east of Broadway are composed of different material from the settlers about Fifth Avenue and Union Square; that they are an essentially distinct and inferior race."[10]

## THE WORKING-CLASS CITY

Though to middle-class observers a vast undifferentiated working-class area, the East Side was, in fact, patterned in several ways. One pattern was *economic*—workers were differentiated by income. In antebellum New York a dwelling "near enough the business part of the city to be convenient," as *Young America* put it, was every worker's goal. Although a short walk to work was desirable, real estate became more expensive the nearer one got to the "business part" of the city. William Darnley, for instance, noted that the family he boarded with in 1858 "have two small bedrooms and living place on

9. See Appendix E. Evidence from *Doggett's New York City Directory* (New York, 1851)—a "reverse directory" giving name by location of residence. Stillman's address is from the 1851 *Rode's City Directory.*

10. George Foster, *New York by Gas-Light* (New York, 1850), 107; *Report upon the Sanitary Condition of the City,* 107; Cornelius Mathews, *A Pen-and-Ink Panorama of New-York City* (New York, 1853), 129.

the second storey. The[y] pay 4 shillings British per week and it is a long way out of town [15th Street] otherwise it would be 7 or 8 per week.''[11]

A witness before the Senate Committee on the Relations between Labor and Capital explained later in the century that, in a period when few workers used transit, ''workers whose employment was regular and at one place generally contrived to get apartments as near their work as possible, so they could go home to dinner, while those whose work was irregular . . . usually selected their apartments with a reference to cheapness.'' However, builders constructed five- and six-story tenements on relatively expensive land near the lower wards; workers who wanted less crowded housing could find it only in the upper wards. Nevertheless, it was generally true that a desire for proximity to work tended to cause better-paid workers to preempt housing close to work, especially near the East River shipyards and foundries.[12]

Living near work was especially important because the main meal of the day was noontime dinner, which workers preferred to eat at home or at the boardinghouse. Commuting by omnibus made it impossible for the middle class to eat at home, and the growth of an omnibus system was accompanied by an ''eating-house revolution'' and the ''institution of eating downtown.'' Many middle-class New Yorkers now favored a light meal at noon and the day's major meal at home after work: ''Lunch is a very modern word, so far as New York is concerned,'' wrote Abram Dayton in 1880. However, workers who had nearby accommodations returned home at noon, while those who were unable to find convenient housing brought their meal in a dinnerpail.[13]

As builders put up tenements on the East Side, the wards near manufacturing areas became overcrowded. The Council on Hygiene and Public Health noted of the Eleventh Ward that shipyards and foundries on the East River ''give employment to many thousand hands to whom a residence near is a great necessity. Hence the excessive crowding in this locality.'' The ratio of persons per room, shown in Map 4, effectively depicts the East Side working-class tenement area.[14]

There were differences even within blocks and buildings on the East Side. The cheapest housing in working-class districts was in rear dwellings built inside blocks of buildings and in cellars. There was a vertical differentiation

---

11. *Young America,* 7 March 1846; William Darnley, letter to his wife, 16 March 1858, Darnley family letters, Rare Books and Manuscripts Division, The New York Public Library, Astor, Lenox and Tilden Foundations; see also Joh. Frei, *Drei Monate in New-York* (Zurich, 1869), 130–131.

12. Edward Pratt, *Industrial Causes of Congestion of Population in New York City* (1911; rpt. New York, 1968), 116–188; U.S. Congress, Senate, Committee on Education and Labor, *Relations between Labor and Capital* (Washington, 1885), 1:97.

13. ''Eating-house revolution'': James Parton, *The Life of Horace Greeley* (Boston, 1872), 97. Abram C. Dayton, *Last Days of Knickerbocker Life in New York* (New York, 1880), 46–47; Thomas Gunn, *The Physiology of New York Boarding-Houses* (New York, 1857), 36, 258.

14. *Report upon the Sanitary Condition of the City,* 174.

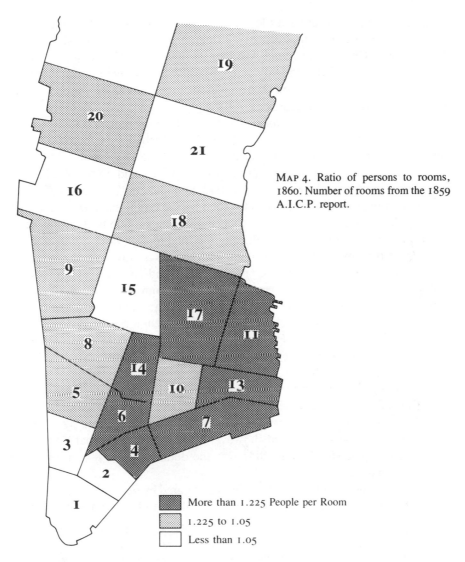

MAP 4. Ratio of persons to rooms, 1860. Number of rooms from the 1859 A.I.C.P. report.

More than 1.225 People per Room

1.225 to 1.05

Less than 1.05

also, with cheaper apartments on upper floors; in one Third Street tenement, for example, a second floor apartment in 1853 cost $5 monthly, the third floor $4.50, the fourth floor $4. Any particular block, therefore, contained a wide variation in rent.[15]

The East Side was patterned by *ethnicity* in this period. The vast majority of immigrants were workers, and it is no coincidence that the city's immigrant neighborhoods were within the "whole section of the city lying East of Broadway." On the East Side was Little Germany—Kleindeutschland—

15. Ibid.; see also Blackmar, "Housing and Property," 573. *Tribune*, 2 December 1853.

centered around the Tenth and Eleventh wards, where thousands of Germans lived and the major institutions of German immigrant life (most notably St. Nicholas' Church on Second Avenue) were located. The Irish neighborhood centered around the "bloody ould" Sixth Ward. Native-born workers, a minority in the 1850s, had their own area in the Fifth and Eighth wards, one of only a few working-class areas west of Broadway (see Map 5). There seems to be no convincing ecological explanation for the location of these ethnic areas; as Griesinger says, "it just happened." Both the Irish and the German areas had begun to form by the 1820s and survived until the 1880s and 1890s.[16]

Curiously, the massive immigration of the 1840s and 1850s weakened rather than reinforced the city's ethnic residential pattern. The huge influx of immigrants proved too great to be absorbed by the traditional ethnic areas of the city. David Ward has discovered that central concentrations of immigrants in the city housed only about one-third of the total foreign-born population in 1860, and the correlation of the main immigrant groups with the general population was relatively high—.77 for the Irish and .76 for the Germans in Table 21. In 1855 the *lowest* percentage of foreign-born (all children of immigrants are counted natives) in any ward was 34, and no ward had fewer than 13 percent Irish-born (see Appendix F). This figure is misleading: the high Irish population in the Fifteenth Ward reflects the number of servants employed there rather than the existence of an Irish community. Nevertheless, the city had no areas where a strong ethnic presence was absent.[17]

Despite the relatively low level of ethnic segregation on the ward level, ethnic residential patterns were important, especially on a small scale. Blocks, tenements, and boardinghouses flourished which were dominated by a single ethnic group. Most workers did, however, live in the wards that were ethnically heterogeneous; the East Side was the domain of *workers,* no matter what their nationality.[18]

The city's working-class area was also configured by *age* and by *sex*. Map 6 shows that persons age 20 to 35 were more likely to be found in the lower

16. On the native working-class area see Blackmar, "Housing and Property," 316. There were regional differences within these major concentrations of immigrants. In Little Germany could be found concentrations of immigrants from Hesse, Nassau, Hannover, and Bavaria. In the Sixth Ward, Corkonians lived on Mulberry Street, Kerryonians on Baxter Street. Stanley Nadel, "Kleindeutschland: New York City's Germans, 1845–1880" (diss., Columbia University, 1981), 73–75; Carol Pernicone, "The 'Bloody Ould Sixth': A Social Analysis of a New York City Working-Class Community in the Mid-Nineteenth Century" (diss., University of Rochester, 1973), 63–65; Griesinger, *Land und Leute*, 554.

17. David Ward, "The Internal Spatial Differentiation of Immigrant Residential Districts," *Special Publications* no. 3, Dept. of Geography, Northwestern University (Evanston, Ill., 1970), 27–29. The .76 figure understates the concentration of Germans in Kleindeutschland. Because Germans were located in the city's most populous wards, the correlation is misleading.

18. Interestingly, in the late nineteenth century ethnic segregation again increased. See David Ward, "The Internal Spatial Structure of Immigrant Residential Districts in the Late Nineteenth Century," *Economic Geography* 42 (1966), 337–353.

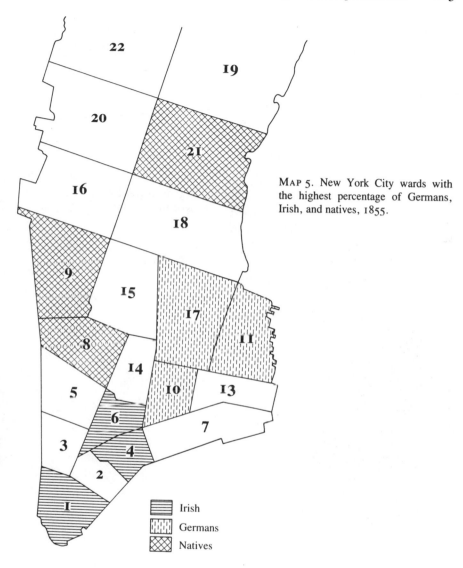

MAP 5. New York City wards with the highest percentage of Germans, Irish, and natives, 1855.

Irish
Germans
Natives

wards; in Ward Two, 48 percent were aged 20 to 35, and in Ward Three 44 percent, compared to 30 percent in northern Ward Twenty-Two. (Ward totals used for Maps 6, 7, and 8 and Table 23 are given in Appendix G.) Why? Many young workers were single, and, according to the British Mechanic, "it is the universal practice with the unmarried of all classes, male and female," to live in boardinghouses. In Table 23 the negative correlations (−.771, −.394) between number of boardinghouses in a ward and the child/man and child/women ratio illustrate the British Mechanic's statement. Boardinghouses were disproportionately located in lower wards—note the .699 correlation

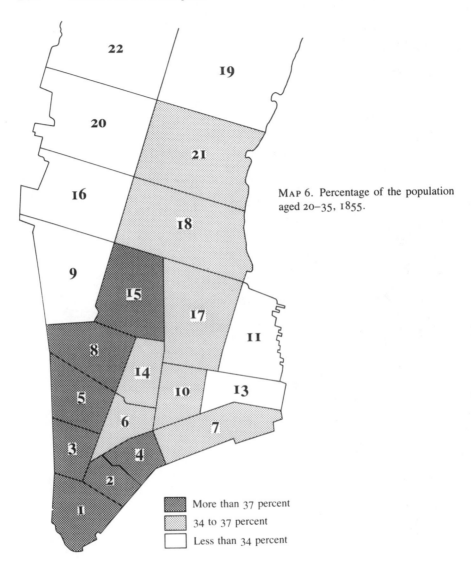

MAP 6. Percentage of the population aged 20–35, 1855.

More than 37 percent
34 to 37 percent
Less than 34 percent

between boardinghouses and proximity to City Hall. Moreover, boarding-houses were economically feasible on downtown land too expensive for family dwellings, as the .470 correlation between real estate wealth and boardinghouses suggests. Single workers who boarded, then, could afford to live near the lower wards, where so many of them worked, and conveniently walk to their job and home for dinner. Such young, unmarried workers were the boardinghouses' most loyal patrons (.657 correlation between age 20–35

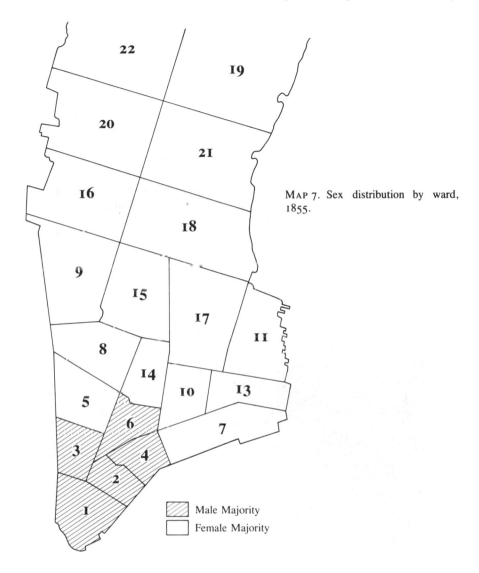

MAP 7. Sex distribution by ward, 1855.

Male Majority
Female Majority

and boardinghouses), and the lower wards therefore were disproportionately young.[19]

The lower wards were not only young but also, as Table 23 shows, had a slight male majority. Despite the female majority in the city overall, these

19. If single persons could be ascertained from the printed census, the differences by ward would likely be considerably greater. *British Mechanic's and Labourer's Hand Book* (London, 1840), 47.

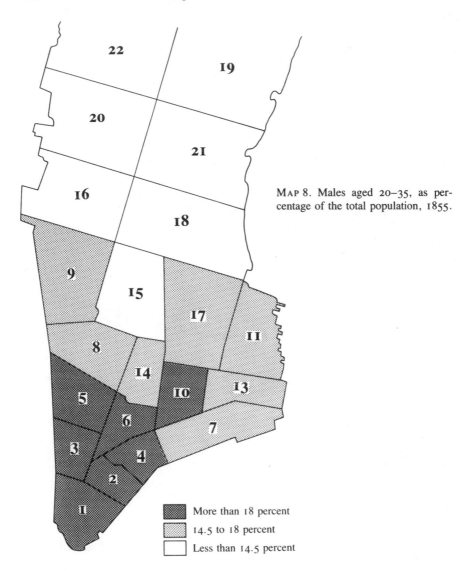

MAP 8. Males aged 20–35, as percentage of the total population, 1855.

More than 18 percent
14.5 to 18 percent
Less than 14.5 percent

wards had more men than women. Many of the single women in the city were servants who lived with their employers in upper wards; it is no surprise that the Fifteenth Ward, the richest in the city, also had the largest majority of women—56.6 percent. However, Map 7 shows that women were a majority even in the East Side working-class areas. Many worked in Wards Two and Three, so why did they not, like men, live in boardinghouses near their work? So many women were supplementary workers, it seems, and lived with their

TABLE 23

Correlations of New York social statistics by wards, c. 1855

| | C/W | AGE | FB | PERS | REAL | PROX | DEATH | BH |
|---|---|---|---|---|---|---|---|---|
| C/M | .728 | −.697 | (−.073) | −.483 | −.516 | −.845 | (.143) | −.771 |
| C/W | | (−.295) | (.341) | −.545 | −.605 | −.470 | .527 | −.394 |
| AGE | | | (.356) | (.164) | (.027) | .902 | (.019) | .657 |
| FB | | | | (−.108) | (−.086) | (−.063) | .539 | (.253) |
| PERS | | | | | .649 | (.323) | (−.245) | (.356) |
| REAL | | | | | | (.272) | (−.045) | .470 |
| PROX | | | | | | | (−.020) | .699 |
| DEATH | | | | | | | | (.178) |

N = 21 Spearman Rank Order (not significant at .05)
*Sources:* C/M    = Children 1–5 per 1000 men 20–45 (1855 NYS census)
    C/W    = Children 1–5 per 1000 women 20–45 (1855 NYS census)
    AGE    = Pct. persons aged 20–35 (1855 NYS census)
    FB    = Pct. foreign-born, 1855 (Ernst, *Immigrant Life in New York City*, p. 193)
    PERS    = Per capita personal wealth, 1856–57 (Boyd's *New York City Tax Book*, p. viii)
    REAL    = Per capita real wealth (Boyd's *NYC Tax Book*, p. viii)
    PROX    = Proximity of ward center to City Hall
    DEATH    = Deathrate per 1000 (1858 A.I.C.P. Report)
    BH    = Modeled No. of Boardinghouses, 1854 (Scherzer, "The Unbounded Community,"
      272). My thanks to Prof. Scherzer for allowing me to use this information.
The raw data on which these correlations are based are given in Appendix G.

families, so it was the job location of the husband or father that determined residence. According to the *Tribune*, women "almost universally bring dinner with them" since they usually did not live near their jobs.[20]

While the city's young unmarried males were disproportionately represented in the lower wards (see Map 8 and also note the high correlation of young people and proximity in Table 23), married New Yorkers tended to dominate in the upper ones. The lower six wards in 1855 had 39,020 men, and 34,082 women; 39.4 percent of the population was age 20–35 compared with 34.1 percent in the upper wards; and there were 217 children (age 1 to 5) per thousand adults (age 15 to 40) in the lower wards in contrast to a ratio of 273 in the rest of the city. One area was characterized by boardinghouses and single men, the other by tenements and families.

Like ethnic residential patterns, this demographic-spatial pattern was only a tendency. Thousands of single men lived in upper wards as boarders with working-class families. The pattern was real, however, and may have tended to counteract the seeming randomness of the city's population turnover. A

20. Note the high correlation of seamstresses with the general population in Table 21. If this statement is true it reverses the twentieth-century pattern in which women generally live closer than men to their jobs; see Janice Fanning Madden, "Why Women Work Closer to Home," *Urban Studies* 18 (1981), 181–194. *Tribune*, 20 August 1845.

married man and his wife and children were extremely unlikely to move from Ward Twenty-Two to Ward Four. Despite the visible mobility on May First, New York's traditional moving day—"First of May, clear the way"—moves were not haphazard, they were related to the life-cycle. The raising of a family was typically accompanied by a northerly move, or a series of northerly moves, up Manhattan Island. This point should not be overstated; transiency was a fact of working-class life. However, residential mobility in the city was channeled by demographic and economic factors.[21]

This patterning of geographic mobility did much to further the development of a strong neighborhood localism in the city, a tendency reinforced by the proximity of home and job for many workingmen. As groceries replaced the city's public markets as the main place to buy food and fuel, so there was less reason to leave the neighborhood. The ward became a matter of passionate identification, and man could proudly proclaim "I am a first-warder yet." No doubt ward loyalty also reflected the importance of politics in city life, but an extreme localism also existed for often nonpolitical reasons.[22]

Many workers did have a fair knowledge of the city's geography since recreational walks about town were a common habit among immigrants. Brown Thurston, a printer from upstate New York, for example, spent his free days "roaming about . . . every place in the city." As Christine Stansell has noted,"walking out," given the sexual segregation of the city's saloons and theatres, was one way for single men and women to mingle. But generally, workers lived, labored, shopped, and were entertained on the lower East Side. There is no evidence, for example, that workers frequented Broadway department stores or theaters; most working-class purchasing was done in the cheap retail shops of Chatham Street, and workers were much more likely to frequent a Bowery than a Broadway theatre.[23]

The development of a working-class area of the city was a precondition for the development of working-class institutional life. The areas were workers' own "space"—during the Draft Riots of 1863, barricades were set up along First and Third avenues, and to the east was the workers' terrain. It was here that workers created and fostered the associational life described in the next

21. The nonrandom quality of moves by city workers is discussed in William N. Black, "The Union Society of Journeymen House Carpenters: A Test of Residential Mobility in Antebellum New York City" (thesis, Columbia University, 1975).
22. Groceries: James D. McCabe, *Lights and Shadows of New York Life* (Philadelphia, 1872), 489. "First warder": *Relations between Labor and Capital,* 94. To some degree, localism was part of the reason politics was so significant; see Chapter 8.
23. Brown Thurston, "Reminiscences of the Early Life of Brown Thurston," in the Brown Thurston journal, 1834–1893, American Antiquarian Society; Christine Stansell, *City of Women: Sex and Class in New York, 1789–1860* (New York, 1986), 86. Stewart's Department Store did boast "Every class of customers equally favored," but none of the workers' letters or diaries mentions shopping at it or any other Broadway shop. Such stores were probably too expensive. *Stranger's Guide,* 34.

chapter. Especially significant was the lower-ward area of single men, which served as a crucible for these institutional forms and gave them a certain flavor. It was no coincidence that the Bowery became the symbol of working-class life in the city.[24]

24. Iver Charles Bernstein, ''The New York City Draft Riots of 1863 and Class Relations on the Eve of Industrial Capitalism'' (diss., Yale University, 1985), 75.

# CHAPTER 8

# Working-Class
# Institutions

The creation in the city of a geographical area dominated by workers made it easier to shape new institutions in accord with workers' experience. The massive immigration of the 1840s and 1850s undermined the traditional, artisan-based institutional life of the early nineteenth century, and immigrants altered established American usages or modified the European customs they brought with them. Like the Jacks-of-all-trades guidebooks suggested they should become, the immigrants drew on what they had known in Europe and on existing American institutions but reworked them into something new.

There is some continuity between the immigrant working-class institutions of the 1850s and the native artisanal institutions of the 1820s, but more striking are the differences. Immigrants had a common workplace experience, demographic profile, motives for emigrating, and consumption patterns. The institutions they created reflected this commonality, which differed from that of the artisan of the 1820s. In every institution discussed in this chapter, there is substantial, often transforming, change after the 1830s.

Despite middle-class disapproval, workers' institutions developed largely unhindered by outside authorities. Gordon Wood has remarked of the period 1820–1860, "Americans in that era of individualism, institutional weakness, and boundlessness experienced 'freedom' as they rarely have since; power, whether expressed economically, socially, or politically, was as fragmented and diffused as at any time in our history." This freedom was especially strong in New York because of the city's growth and spatial reorganization. The increasing size of the city and widening residential segregation, for example, broke down the paternalistic private relief system. The A.I.C.P.'s visitor programs to the city's poor workers became increasingly ineffective, and efforts were focused only on those poor people who happened to live near the city's wealthy neighborhoods.[1]

The city's police force in this period was small and poorly organized. A series of larger-than-usual brawls in the Sixth Ward in 1857 revealed ignorance and confusion on the part of the police and press about the causes or even about what was occurring. Except during moments of crisis, such as the Astor Place and Draft riots, most middle-class New Yorkers knew little and cared less about the city's working class—it truly was *terra incognita*. And, it seems, many workers felt similarly about the middle class. Although workers insisted on equality with the middle class, working-class institutions and culture were, in Roy Rosenzweig's terms, more "alternative" than "oppositional." Obviously workers did not have complete autonomy to shape their institutional life, but the weakness of municipal government gave them greater latitude in the antebellum city than later in the century.[2]

The lower wards served as a crucible in which was forged this new institutional life and culture, and the Bowery came to symbolize working-class life in the city. In this small area lived and worked large numbers of single young men with relatively high disposable incomes. It was they who provided "critical mass" for this "Bowery milieu," as Christine Stansell calls it, and working-class associational life reflects the youthfulness of this part of the city. Although this male-dominated section of the working-class area contained only a small minority of city workers, it was here, upon arrival in the city, that workers usually first stayed, and many male workers who lived elsewhere were employed there, reinforcing its character as a male area. Indeed, one of the most striking features of workers' institutions is their masculine quality—women were excluded from almost all of them. Most working-class associational life was for men only, and this chapter therefore has a masculine focus. The relationship of women to this male world, and gender relations more generally, are discussed in the final chapter.[3]

1. Gordon Wood, *History Book Club Review* (1975), quoted in Samuel P. Huntington, "American Ideals versus American Institutions," *Political Science Quarterly* 97 (1982), 4. During the terrible winter of 1854–55 relief committees were formed in only twelve of twenty-two wards, by no means the poorest ones; Paul O. Weinbaum, *Mobs and Demagogues: The New York Response to Collective Violence in the Early Nineteenth Century* (Ann Arbor, Mich., 1979), 144–145.

2. Joshua Brown, "The 'Dead Rabbit'–Bowery Boy Riot: An Analysis of the Antebellum New York Gang" (Master's essay, Columbia University, 1976), 45, 54, 59, 70. On the police see Paul O. Weinbaum, "Temperance, Politics, and the New York City Riots of 1857," *New York History* 59 (1975), 246–270, and James Richardson, *The New York Police: Colonial Times to 1901* (New York, 1970), 109–111. Roy Rosenzweig, *Eight Hours for What We Will: Workers and Leisure in an Industrializing City, 1870–1920* (Cambridge, England, 1983), 64.

3. Christine Stansell, *City of Women: Sex and Class in New York, 1789–1860* (New York, 1986), 89–101. The census showed many women employed in the lower wards, but as Chapter 1 showed, they were mainly outworkers.

Associational life did not create working-class culture; the development of working-class institutions reflected working-class mentality. But the working-class culture of the 1850s did not spring full-formed from daily life—homogenous material circumstances do not spontaneously generate consciousness. This new culture developed over time, and it was in the boardinghouse, the saloon, the firehouse, the theatre, and at the polls that it was clarified and refined. A working-class way of life—and that is what it had become by the 1860s—is quite different from common working-class environmental conditions. The new institutions did much to shape it.

The most significant underlying environmental factor was the high energy level. "Abundance consciousness" and fast pace in the workshops, combined with a youthful age structure and a good diet and health, gave the city worker a distinctively vigorous way of life. "Work hard, play hard," might have been their motto. A high energy level had existed among native workers for years, but only when the working class began to acquire a demographic similarity and geographic cohesion—critical mass—was this impulse infused into working-class life generally. This energy level is clearly reflected in working-class institutions, but the development of these institutions also served to embed this environmental factor into a more precise form that, by the 1850s, we can call a culture. Chapter 9 analyzes the content of this culture and the meaning of this associational life. This chapter focuses on the genesis of the working-class institutions that created and refined this culture, by looking at the boardinghouse, the saloon, the firehouse, the theatre, prizefighting, and politics.

THE BOARDINGHOUSE

The institutions that touched most directly on the lives of workers were the boardinghouse and the saloon. Although most city boarders probably lived with families, the boardinghouse had been common in New York City since the 1790s and housed thousands of single men and couples without children. In the first three decades of the nineteenth century, all classes of New Yorkers boarded, rich as well as poor. Beginning in the 1850s, however, two developments began to weaken the boardinghouse's all-class nature. The first was the building of "French flats," as apartments were originally called, which "induced people of moderate means" to live in them, according to *Appleton's Directory*, "and abandon boardinghouses and hotels."[4]

4. Bayrd Still, *Mirror for Gotham* (New York, 1956), 66–68, gives travelers' accounts of the city's early boardinghouses. *Appleton's Directory of New York City* (1880), quoted in Kenneth Alan Scherzer, "The Unbounded Community: Neighborhood Life and Social Structure in New York, 1830–1875" (diss., Harvard University, 1982), 297–298.

The boardinghouse was far from exclusively working-class in the 1850s—note the high index of boardinghouse keepers in the Fifteenth Ward in Table 20. Walt Whitman wrote that the city's boardinghouses "are of various grades," and since living in a boardinghouse was more expensive than boarding with a family, clerks and other single middle-class males were more likely than workers to board. However, as the British Mechanic noted, "the unmarried of all classes" tended to live in boardinghouses, and the sheer numbers of single workers on Manhattan ensured that most boardinghouses were dominated by workers.[5]

Table 20 showed that keepers of boardinghouses, and presumably boardinghouses themselves, were very heavily concentrated in the lower wards; so concentrated was the boardinghouse district that there is actually a *negative* correlation with the general population in Table 21. The residents were mostly single men: a sample of forty-five boardinghouses in Wards Two, Four, and Seven from the 1850 population schedules shows that 533 of 698 residents were unmarried men. Among these men 372 were skilled workers, 49 unskilled and semiskilled workers (these groups were more likely to save money by boarding with families), 94 were clerks, merchants, or "gentlemen" (18 were unclassifiable). There were 104 women in the sample, many of them servants.[6]

Boardinghouses were usually based on language: it was highly unusual for Germans to mix with Americans and Irish. French-speakers likewise kept separate, whereas English-speakers, whether native, Irish, Scottish, or Canadian, boarded together. It was to a boardinghouse the male migrant first went, and it was there he experienced his often traumatic introduction to urban life; immigrant guidebooks constantly warned readers to be on guard for "sharp" keepers, or even other tenants, who might try to take advantage of the neophyte city dweller.

Boardinghouses, however, did not provide just a temporary place to stay. Kenneth Scherzer sampled the 1855 state census and discovered that 292 of 573 boarders had lived in New York more than five years. Because they were young and without families, boardinghouse residents fashioned a kind of

5. Scherzer, "Unbounded Community," 285. My thanks to Prof. Scherzer for permission to cite this evidence. *Walt Whitman of the New York Aurora*, ed. Joseph Rubin and Charles Brown (State College, Pa., 1950), 23. Middle-class reformers warned of the dangers of the unsupervised life young clerks led in boardinghouses, and the founding of the Y.M.C.A. in 1852 was an attempt to control this evil; see Allan Horlick, *Country Boys and Merchant Princes: The Social Control of Young Men in New York* (Lewisburg, Pa., 1975), 226–243. *British Mechanic's and Labourer's Hand Book* (London, 1840), 47.

6. On the propensity of semiskilled and unskilled workers to board with families, see Carol Pernicone, "The 'Bloody Ould Sixth': A Social Analysis of a New York Working-Class Community in the Mid-Nineteenth Century" (diss., University of Rochester, 1973), 63. The evidence in Scherzer, "Unbounded Community," 227–292, basically confirms this profile of boarders.

community. Living with a roommate or two, eating three meals a day, and sharing such activities as indulging "in beer and short pipes" on the roof in the summer helped generate, despite very high turnover, strong feelings of camaraderie. Thomas Gunn, in his humorous work *The Physiology of New York Boarding-Houses*, published in 1857, described the strong friendships (and antipathies) that boardinghouse life produced. Boarders shared stories over meals and joked about boardinghouse conditions, such as the "awful legend current among the boarders" at one place Gunn described, that a resident's "watch had been broken by an elderly bed-bug tumbling upon it!"[7]

Out of this atmosphere arose what we might call a "boardinghouse ethos." The large number of young, energetic males living together created an atmosphere not unlike that of a college dormitory. One boardinghouse in Columbia Street in Ward Thirteen was the "headquarters of considerable jocularity," and at night residents often "went out on a festive expedition . . . changing sign-boards in modern collegiate fashion." At another boardinghouse south of Bleecker Street, "some of the young men" stayed home Sunday afternoon and 'carried on' extensively in their chambers; beating each other with pillows and struggling upon the beds." High jinks of this sort were similar to those in the shop and, no doubt, helped relieve tensions caused by the crowding of boardinghouse life.[8]

Staying in one's room was an unpleasant prospect, however, because of the small size of rooms and cramped conditions. And the "common room" in most boardinghouses was not large enough to accommodate all the boarders. "Boarding houses were merely shelters not homes," Henry Walter remembered. Therefore, especially after the shortening of working hours in the 1830s, a boarder would find himself with several hours to kill after supper. In the summer, according to Virginia Penny, "people live . . . mostly out of doors. Their crowded apartments and the high price of rent account for it." But for much of the year the street was not an option, and the British Mechanic made the situation plain to his readers: "The mechanic has very little choice left him in the matter. He must go to a tavern or drinking-house, or to theatres or other places of amusement."[9]

7. Scherzer, "Unbounded Community," 280; Thomas Gunn, *The Physiology of New York Boarding-Houses* (New York, 1857), 56. Turnover: *British Mechanic's and Labourer's Hand Book*, 49; Gunn, *Physiology*, 52.

8. Mark Peel, "On the Margin: Lodgers and Boarders in Boston, 1860–1900," *Journal of American History* 72 (1986), 813, carefully distinguishes between boarding and lodging. What Peel calls the "lodging subculture" resembles what I call the "boardinghouse ethos." G. W. Sheldon, "The Old Ship-Builders of New York," *Harper's Magazine* 65 (1882), 234; Gunn, *Physiology*, 72. Boardinghouse keepers seem to have regarded this sort of behavior as inevitable; see Fannie Benedict, "Boarding-House Experiences in New York," *Packard's Monthly* n.s. 1 (1869), 103.

9. Henry Walter, "Autobiography of an English Tramp, from 1812 to 1888 inclusive," 23; see also Theodor Griesinger, *Lebende Bilder aus Amerika* (Stuttgart, 1858), 231–232. Virginia Penny, *How Women Can Make Money* (1863; rpt. New York, 1971), 317; *British Mechanic's and Labourer's Hand Book*, 63.

THE SALOON

The saloon was immensely important in the lives of workers and became the characteristic working-class institution. Both boardinghouse residents and those who boarded with families had few options but to spend most evenings in the saloon. Here the change from the traditional artisanal culture is quite clear. In 1817 Henry Fearon mentioned the city's "retail . . . spirit shops" and "taverns and porter-houses . . . similar to our second-rate public houses." "Bar-rooms in my early time were conducted on the Plan of the English Ale-house, . . . fitted up with tables and chairs" with a small bar, and centered around a large fireplace, remembered John Sturtevant. Ale, porter, and brandy were the common drinks. The widespread use of traditional English tavern names in New York, many of them centuries old—the Bull's Head, the Hole-in-the-Wall, the Black Horse Inn, the Green Dragon, and the famous Pewter Mug—highlights this continuity.[10]

In England in the 1830s, the tavern was changing into the pub. But the pub, with its typically horseshoe-shaped bar, seats, internal partitions, and multiple exits, was quite different from the saloon, and English immigrants often commented on the difference. The British Mechanic proclaimed in 1840 "the mode and manner" of the city's barrooms "in every respect perfectly different" from those of England. "There is no public houses the same as London," brushmaker Alfred Green complained in 1857.[11]

The city's traditional taverns had been completely transformed by the early 1840s. Apparently borrowing much from Irish rural drinking places, and serving German lager beer as the principal drink, the barroom—or "saloon" as it was coming to be called in the 1850s—emerged as a new and distinctive institution in New York. Located in a single long room on a corner or in a cellar, the saloon bore little physical resemblance to the tavern. A long, straight bar along one wall was the dominant feature, and, according to English traveler William Hancock, there were only a few chairs: "no sitting accommodation is provided at these resorts." "No chairs or lounges, or seats of any kind" in most barrooms, Matthew P. Breen remembered. Traditional

10. Henry Fearon, *Sketches of America* (London, 1819), 28; John J. Sturtevant recollections, Rare Books and Manuscripts Division, The New York Public Library, Astor, Lenox and Tilden Foundations, 19. The ambience of one of the city's most famous taverns in the 1820s, the Bull's Head, is described in *The Book of Daniel Drew*, ed. Bouck White (New York, 1901), 73–77; see also Alvin F. Harlow, *Old Bowery Days: The Chronicle of a Famous Street* (New York, 1931), 109–114. Thomas DeVoe also noted how saloons differed from traditional taverns in *The Market Assistant* (New York, 1867), 46.

11. See Brian Harrison, "Pubs," in H. J. Dyos and Michael Wolf, eds., *The Victorian City: Images and Realities* (London, 1973), esp. 169–171, and Mark Girouard, *Victorian Pubs* (London, 1975), esp. 27–28, 40–42, 56–59. *British Mechanic's and Labourer's Hand Book*, 63. Alfred Green letter, 28 July 1857, British Library of Political and Economic Science, London School of Economics; see also William Hancock, *An Emigrant's Five Years in the Free States of America* (London, 1860), 75–76.

names disappeared, and most bars were simply named after their owners. A few "Old Country" public houses, such as the House of Commons and the Brown Jug Tavern, survived in the city. Here an English immigrant could take his ale seated "and perfectly free from the critical remarks which these peculiarities would subject him to elsewhere."[12]

The emergence of the barroom coincided with the increase in immigration in the 1840s. Located mostly in the lower wards (Table 20), saloons both reflected and enhanced the lifestyle of young, male workers. Table 24 shows that the number of licensed liquor establishments correlated with single, young men in the city in 1855, and that most barrooms were concentrated in the boardinghouse area.[13]

The barroom was designed to suit its vigorous young customers. The Anonymous English Workman described New York drinking habits in 1859: "John Bull sits leisurely down and makes a night of it: *Jonathan can't keep still,* but rushes first to the bar-room of the hotel where he had dined, has a drink, thence to the confectioner's saloon, then to a cigar ditto, next to an oyster ditto, and . . . most likely 'smiles' at each of them." James Burn noticed the same thing: "Instead of sitting in tap-rooms and bar-parlours, as is the case in many of the English towns, the Americans take their drinks at the counter and are off." Chairs, according to Matthew Breen, would "promote lethargy. . . . None of that slow, lazy, stupid process of imbibition which is nurtured by chairs." The high-energy environment seems apparent here, and the good wages workers made allowed them to visit several bars in an evening. The idea of the saloon as a place, like the tavern, where a patron could spend a quiet, relaxed evening seems almost totally absent in New York. Immigrants such as Henry Price and Alfred Green were at first surprised but learned to accustom themselves to American drinking establishments.[14]

Just as the active ways of the barroom mirrored the fast pace of the workshop, so they mirrored the workshop's turnover, and the "vogue" of visiting several barrooms in the course of an evening allowed newcomers to meet new people and learn the neighborhood. Chairs, Breen explained, allow men to sit for hours "without mixing up with the general crowd of drinkers," but at a bar a stranger could fit right in. The elaborate ritual of "treating" in

12. Irish influence on saloons: Charles Haswell, *Reminiscences of an Octogenarian* (New York, 1896), 379. Hancock, *Emigrant's Five Years*, 76; Matthew P. Breen, *Thirty Years of New York Politics Up-to-Date* (New York, 1899), 252; *British Mechanic's and Labourer's Hand Book*, 64.

13. The relationship of the saloon to young, single males is emphasized in Jon M. Kingsdale, "The Poor Man's Club: Social Functions of the Urban Working Class Saloon, 1890–1920," *American Quarterly* 25 (1973), 472–489.

14. *London v. New York* "by an English Workman" (London, 1859), 51–52, emphasis added; James Dawson Burn, *James Burn; The "Beggar Boy"* (London, 1882), 276; Breen, *Thirty Years,* 252; "Diary of Henry Edward Price," in *British Records Relating to America in Microform* (East Ardsley, England, 1963), 26; Alfred Green letter.

Table 24
Correlation of number of liquor establishments with other social statistics by wards, 1855

|  | *C/M* | *C/W* | *AGE* | *FB* | *PERS* | *REAL* | *PROX* | *DEATH* | *BH* |
|---|---|---|---|---|---|---|---|---|---|
| M/LIQ | −.714 | (−.312) | .723 | .489 | (.182) | .409 | .666 | (.215) | .775 |

N = 20.   Spearman Rank Order (not significant at .05)

| | |
|---|---|
| M/LIQ | = No. of men per licensed liquor establishment |
| C/M | = Children 1–5 per 1000 men 20–45 |
| C/W | = Children 1–5 per 1000 women 20–45 |
| AGE | = Percent persons age 20–35 |
| FB | = Percent foreign-born |
| PERS | = Per capita personal wealth |
| REAL | = Per capita real wealth |
| PROX | = Proximity of ward center to City Hall |
| DEATH | = Deathrate per 1000 |
| BH | = Modeled number of boardinghouses |

*Source.* Number of licensed liquor establishments is from *Manual of the Corporation of the City of New York for 1855,* ed. D. T. Valentine (New York, 1855), 336. Ward Nine is missing. Sources for other statistics are given in Table 23.

barrooms facilitated this mingling. Rather than each individual buying his own drinks, a common procedure was to treat " 'good fellows' when we meet them, and receiving treats from *good fellows* in return," explained Thomas Mooney. The reciprocity involved in this traditional Irish custom served to increase the communal atmosphere of the city's barrooms.[15]

This frenetic activity did not mean throwing aside all restraint and discipline. The saloon as a center for leisure did little to interfere with work. As early as 1810 Tench Coxe had noted "a peculiar taste for lively or foaming beer" in America. However, beer brewed by the top-fermenting English process was not highly carbonated and often spoiled in summer. In 1848 Ferdinand and Maximilian Schaefer popularized lager beer in the city. Using German bottom-fermenting yeasts, they created a product that could be served all year round. Lager was lighter than ales and porters and, with the high carbonation that quickly came to mark American lager, sated the thirst for a "lively" product. Lager beer quickly became a fad. "New Yorkers ran mad after it, and nothing was spoken of or drunk but LAGER," the Anonymous Proofreader reported. Sales boomed, and poetry extolling the virtues of lager became a minor genre:

> Twas drank in "fader land" first,
> But now we drink it here,

15. Breen, *Thirty Years,* 252. Thomas Mooney, *Nine Years in America* (Dublin, 1850), 65; see also James Dawson Burn, *Three Years among the Working-Classes in the United States during the War* (London, 1865), 49. Treating was common in Ireland and probably spread from there to America. On this point, and for a general analysis of treating, see Rosenzweig, *Eight Hours,* 59–61.

>   Then drink it boys! Drink freely!
>   Three rounds for lager bier!

Lager, indeed, became something of a symbol of the city's remade working class.[16]

Significantly, lager was less intoxicating than ale—"too tonic," some said. Lager beer was (and is) usually about 4 to 4.5 percent alcohol compared to 5 to 7 percent for ale, stout, and porter. It was widely believed that it was impossible to become drunk on lager: "The smallness of the quantity [of alcohol] . . . renders it . . . ineffective on the brain," the *Scientific American* explained. A patron could stand around drinking lager for several hours and still remain sober, and in most New York saloons drunkards were rare. The British Mechanic described "the general practice" in saloons as going to the bar to get a beer and then "to enter into conversation, or read the papers, both of which are usually done in a standing position." The general ambience was orderly, and the common term "regulars" exemplifies the barroom's disciplined, if energetic, atmosphere. The physical layout of the saloon was also integrated with the work process. The absence of seats made it easier to accommodate rushes of customers at dinnertime (i.e., noon) and after work. The geographic expansion of the city and the decline of the dinner taken at home led saloons in New York to begin serving in the 1850s "a liberal lunch, of soup and meats daily . . . *gratis* to those purchasing beer," according to William Hancock.[17]

Saloons also provided recreation for their clients: bowling, billiards, and shuffleboard were all very popular. Bowling, introduced by Germans, was adopted widely in the city in the late 1840s. Billiards became a fad in the same period, publicized by a series of high-stakes matches involving New Yorker Michael Phelan—by 1851 the number of tables in the city had grown to a thousand. Phelan believed that in America, "where the population is dispro-

16. Tench Coxe, *A Statement of the Arts and Manufactures of the United States of America for the Year 1810* (Philadelphia, 1814), ix. George Gillig in 1844 was the first New York brewer of lager. The Schaefer brothers began brewing four years later; see *One Hundred Years of Brewing* (Chicago and New York, 1903), 209, 213, and John Siebel and Anton Schwartz, *History of the Brewing Industry and Brewing Science in America* (Chicago, 1933), 192–196. Theodor Griesinger exhaustively catalogues American drinking habits in his chapter "Wie trinkt man im Lande der Yankees?" in *Land und Leute in Amerika* (Stuttgart, 1863), 685–707. *Real Experiences of an Emigrant*, 86–87. "Lager bier song": *Porter's Spirit of the Times* 1 (1856), 141. For further examples of lager beer poems and songs, see William Harmon, ed., *The Oxford Book of Light American Verse* (New York, 1979), 124–126, 129–135.

17. "Lager Beer": *Scientific American* n.s. 1 (1859), 35; see also F. W. Salem, *Beer, Its History and Economic Value* (Hartford, Conn., 1880), and Junius H. Browne, *The Great Metropolis: A Mirror of New-York City* (Hartford, Conn., 1872), 761. Unruly customers were quickly ejected by the bouncer; see Breen, *Thirty Years*, 151–152. *British Mechanic's and Labourer's Hand Book*, 66; Hancock, *Emigrant's Five Years*, 76.

portionately small . . . in a new and undeveloped country . . . , in such a condition of society toil raises to an unnatural importance," and he hoped billiards would serve as needed recreation. Known as the Young Man's Game, billiards was especially popular among the city's Germans, and Phelan's 1859 four-ball challenge match against John Seeriter in Detroit, for stakes of $15,000, spurred enormous interest. An 1865 match involving Phelan's cousin Dudley Kavanaugh "aroused more interest in the mind of many a young man than all other items of news."[18]

The saloon, then, was the communal institution for young men. Gunn captures well the atmosphere: "Men clustering in front of the bar; men sitting, spitting, drinking and smoking, . . . men bending over the bagatelle table." Saloons, of course, were not all physically alike, nor did they serve identical clienteles. In some, various ethnic groups or—like the sailors' barroom Gunn describes—occupational groups predominated. In Kleindeutschland, of course, the clientele was mostly German. But even there the saloon retained its popularity: "Biersalon! Biersalon! nicht als biersalon!" exclaimed Griesinger in his 1863 description of Little Germany. Smaller than the beer hall, the biersalon seems quite similar to saloons elsewhere in the city. However, Kleindeutschland also had the "lokal" or "respectable drinking house" that had seats and catered to a family trade.[19]

Outside Kleindeutschland, the saloon's patrons probably reflected the diversity of the city's immigrant population. There were German, native, and Irish saloons, but the lower ward barroom described by Gunn, where the patrons were of various occupations and the "language used being as various as the speakers," was probably typical, and the "stand up" saloon predominated everywhere. The 5,550 liquor establishments in the city in 1855 attest to the barroom's enormous popularity. Saloons became the center of working-

18. Billiards and bowling: *British Mechanic's and Labourer's Hand Book,* 67–68; George Foster, *New York by Gas-Light* (New York, 1850), 18–25; and T. H. Green, *Report on Gambling in New York* (New York, 1851), 77–80. Recreational activity in saloons shows amazing continuity—a 1975 study of a Wisconsin barroom found bowling, shuffleboard, and pool part of the establishment's "very rich" social life; E. E. LeMasters, *Blue Collar Aristocrats* (Madison, Wisc., 1975), 126–127. Number of tables: Green, 80; see also Michael Phelan, *Billiards without a Master* (New York, 1850), 122, quoted in Leonard Ellis, "Men among Men: An Exploration of All-Male Relationships in Victorian America" (diss., Columbia University, 1982), 86–87. Michael Phelan, *The Game of Billiards* (New York, 1857), 14; Melvin Adelman, *A Sporting Time: New York City and the Rise of Modern Athletics, 1820–1870* (Urbana, Ill., 1986), 220–229. The best source on the significance of nineteenth-century billiards is Ellis, 62–125. Charles Dawson Shanly, "Germany in New York," *Atlantic Monthly* 19 (1867), 560. Kavanaugh: "The Billiard Mania," *The Round Table* n.s. 1 (1865), 89. Billiards was, according to Ned Polsky, "the exact center" of a "bachelor subculture . . .—heterosexual but all male"; Polsky, *Hustlers, Beats and Others* (Chicago, 1967), 31.

19. Gunn, *Physiology,* 112. Griesinger, *Land und Leute,* 563; see also Griesinger, *Lebende Bilder,* 56–64, and Stanley Nadel, "Kleindeutschland: New York City's Germans, 1845–1880" (diss., Columbia University, 1981), 215–220.

class life in the city, and it is not surprising that the state's attempt to enforce its Sunday Closing Law on barrooms in 1857 was violently resisted.[20]

The boardinghouse and the barroom were the centers of working-class life in the city. The associational life of workers, however, was not restricted to them alone. Four other working-class institutions—the theatre, fire companies, prizefighting, and politics—were also important. In each case the influx of immigrants in the 1840s created something original or transformed existing customs into something new that both reflected and served to shape working-class life.

THE THEATRE

The theatre was enormously popular among workers. Theatrical critic William Northall doubted in 1851 "if there be a city in the world of the same size and population which can exhibit a theatrical prosperity equal to New York," a situation he, like the British Mechanic, attributed to "our boarding-house system of living" that threw city residents "on their own resources for amusement." The goods wages of many workers made theatregoing routine, and workers such as Thomas Chamberlain, John Petheram, and Brewster Maverick refer constantly in their diaries to plays they attended. John Gough the bookbinder acted in small parts, experience that stood him in good stead during his later career as a temperance lecturer.[21]

In the 1820s and 1830s theatre in New York was dominated by what David Grimsted has called the "Good Old Plays"—mostly Shakespeare and Restoration comedies. Few were American. There was also, as Peter Buckley has shown, no class theatre in the city. Indeed, the theatre audience was commonly called "the town," which suggests the way rich and poor, merchants and journeymen, attended performances together. In the 1830s began what Buckley calls the "bifurcation" of theatre culture. Walt Whitman remembered the significance of the change fifty years later. After describing the old Bowery of the 1830s, "pack'd . . . with . . . American-born mechanics," Whitman noted the transformation:

> Awhile after 1840 the character of the Bowery . . . completely changed. . . .
> Not that there was more or less rankness in the crowd even then. For types of

---

20. Gunn, *Physiology*, 112. On the predominance of the "stand up" saloon in every American city and almost every neighborhood later in the century, see Raymond Calkins, *Substitutes for the Saloon* (Cambridge, Mass., 1901), esp. 7, 19–21. Gunn, 278–279. On the closing law see below.

21. William Northall, *Before and Behind the Curtain* (New York, 1851), 6, 7. This point was echoed by the *British Mechanic's and Labourer's Hand Book*, 63. Brewster Maverick diary, 1847, NYHS. John Gough, *Autobiography and Personal Recollections* (Springfield, Mass., 1870), 80.

sectional New York . . .—the streets East of the Bowery, that intersect Division, Grand, and up to Third Avenue—types that have never found their Dickens, Hogarth, or Balzac . . .—the young shipbuilders, cartmen, butchers, firemen, they too, were always to be seen in these audiences, racy of the East River and the Dry Dock.[22]

A key event in the creation of working-class theatre was Benjamin Baker's 1848 play *A Glance at New York*. The play does not seem to have been written originally for a working-class audience. Indeed, it may have been intended to show middle-class New Yorkers a way of life and part of the city they knew little about. After the play opened, however, workers took the hero, Mose, for their own. Baker had earlier written a short sketch that introduced "Mose, the fire b'hoy." A young actor, Frank Chanfrau (the son of French immigrants and a former ship carpenter), played the part so realistically that it created a sensation among workers. Dressed as a volunteer fireman (see Figure 23), Chanfrau walked briskly to center stage, "taking the cigar stump from his mouth and turning half way around to spit he said: 'I ain't a goin' to run with dat mercheen no more!' Instantly there arose a yell of recognition as had never before been heard in the little house"—the city's young male workers had found themselves on stage. So authentic was Chanfrau's portrayal that a legend quickly arose that he had based it on a real volunteer fireman, Moses Humphrey, who had been bested by Frank Chanfrau's brother in a brawl.[23]

The sketch was so popular that Baker immediately expanded it into a full play, lengthening favorite parts and adding Mose's girlfriend Lize, played by Bowery favorite Mary Taylor, "charming Miss Taylor," one admirer, printer Thomas Chamberlain, called her. The result—*A Glance at New York*—was, according to George C. D. Odell, "one of the greatest successes ever known in the history of the New York Stage." The plot was amusing but hackneyed: Mose's efforts to prevent a "verdant" country visitor from being victimized by sharpers. It was Chanfrau's characterization of Mose, the Bowery B'hoy, complete with red fireman's jacket, tight trousers, shiny hat, and "soap-

---

22. David Grimsted, *Melodrama Unveiled: American Theatre and Culture, 1800–1850* (1968; rpt. Berkeley, Calif., 1987), 111–136, 249–261; Peter George Buckley, "To the Opera House: Culture and Society in New York City, 1820–1860" (diss., SUNY at Stony Brook, 1984), 102–161; see also Lawrence W. Levine, *Highbrow/Lowbrow: The Emergence of Cultural Hierarchy in America* (Cambridge, Mass., 1988), 13–81. Walt Whitman, "The Old Bowery," in *Prose Works 1892*, ed. Floyd Stovall (New York, 1964), 2:595.

23. The background of *A Glance at New York* is well described in Buckley, "To the Opera House," 388–399. The best primary source on the creation of the play is the *Clipper*, 6 April 1878. Quote: Undated letter from T. Allston Brown in the *Times*, Frank Chanfrau File, Harvard Theatre Collection. A Moses Humphrey is listed in the city directories between 1827 and 1842 as a morocco worker, living on Mulberry Street. For the legend see the T. Allston Brown letter and Fred Mathers, *My Angling Friends* (New York, 1901), 58, which has Chanfrau spending "weeks" studying Humphrey. However, Baker always insisted Mose was based on a *type*, not a particular individual; see his interview in the *Clipper*, 6 April 1878.

"SYKESY TAKE DE BUTT"
M͞r. F. S. CHANFRAU AS "MOSE."
IN M͞r BAKER'S PIECE ENTITLED "A GLANCE AT NEW YORK."

Published by H. Long & Bro. 32 Ann St N.Y.

FIGURE 23. Frank Chanfrau as Mose in *A Glance at New York in 1848*. Photograph courtesy of the Harvard Theatre Collection.

224

locked'' hair, that made the play such a sensation. Mose was the archetypal *b'hoy*—a term first recorded in 1846 and increasingly applied to young male workers. Mose was a native worker in the play, but his appeal was more as a new urban type than as the representative of any national group. Although a comic caricature, Mose embodied some of the virtues the city's workers attached to themselves. Mose held ''Broadway in such contempt that . . . [he] could'n even be persuaded to cross it''; was a loyal volunteer fireman— ''I love that ingine better than my dinner''; and was always looking for a brawl—''if I don't have a muss soon I'll spile.''[24]

The play was so popular that Chanfrau at one point was playing Mose at the Olympic, in a later show at the Chatham on the Bowery, and then traveling by coach and boat to play Mose a final time the same evening at Newark. Many Mose sequels followed: *New York As It Is, Mose's Visit to Philadelphia, The Mysteries and Miseries of New York, Mose in California,* and *Mose in France,* among others. Although, as Peter Buckley shows, the brawling side of Mose was toned down after the Astor Place Riot in 1849, Chanfrau toured widely as Mose (indeed, his close identification with Mose made it hard for him to get other parts), and the plays continued to be performed throughout the 1850s. With the abolition of the volunteer fire department in 1865 the Mose plays passed from popularity, but the b'hoy remained a stock character in melodramas about New York City.[25]

Soon, ''Mose, instead of appearing on stage, was in the pit, the boxes and the gallery,'' and theatres such as the Bowery, National, and Chatham were the province, as William Bobo put it, of ''the democracy'' and specialized in boisterous, high-spirited, working-class fare. Popular actors such as Edwin Forrest, an outspoken Democrat in politics, were working-class heroes, and it is evidence of the importance of theatre that a rivalry between Forrest and English actor William Macready became the basis of the bloody 1849 Astor Place Riot. The theatre provided the working class with inexpensive entertainment created, of course, by professionals, but workers' responses helped shape this theatre according to their preferences. Middle-class observers might sneer at sketches about ''ruffians, housebreakers and highwaymen,'' but the ''violent shouts and clapping of hands among the 'boys' of the pit and

24. *Clipper,* 6 April 1878. Thomas Chamberlain diary, 23 May 1843, Rare Books and Manuscripts Division, The New York Public Library, Astor, Lenox and Tilden Foundations; according to Abram Dayton, her ''rough admirers'' called her ''Our Mary''; Dayton, *Last Days of Knickerbocker Life in New York* (New York, 1897), 302–303. George C. D. Odell, *Annals of the New York Stage* (New York, 1931), 5:373. Unidentified clipping, ''Early Struggles of Prominent Actors—F. S. Chanfrau,'' in Chanfrau File, Harvard Theatre Collection. ''B'hoy'': Richard H. Thorton, *An American Glossary* (London, 1912), 1:58–60. Benjamin A. Baker, *A Glance at New York* (New York, 1857), 10, 24, 15.

25. Richard Dorson, ''Mose, the Far-Famed and World-Renowned,'' *American Literature* 15 (1943), 288–300, details the history of the Mose plays. Buckley, ''To the Opera House,'' 396–399.

gallery'' showed that workers enjoyed such entertainment, and so theatres kept presenting it. Mose became the representation of the young male worker and hastened public awareness of the development of a working-class lifestyle in New York.[26]

> Mose he went to college—he said he was a poet,
> And whilst he's young he's bound to blaze and says he
> means to go it,
> He goes wid a rush, my boys, no matter what befalls
> him—
> He's de fust man to de engine-house, whenever duty
> calls him.
>
> *Chorus*
> Wake up, Mose wake up, Mose!
> Wake up, Mose! de Fire am burning;
> Round de corner de smoke am curling.
> Wake up, Mose! the engine's coming;
> Take de rope and keep a running!

So sang Wood's Minstrels in 1852. New York was "the birthplace of the minstrel show . . . [and] its greatest stronghold," and it is perhaps not surprising that Mose worked his way into minstrelsy. Although performances in blackface by such entertainers as New York–born Thomas "Daddy" Rice had been standard fare for years, the first real minstrel troupe emerged from a chance meeting of four musicians in a Catherine Street boardinghouse in 1843. Led by William Whitlock, a former compositor on the *Herald,* and Dan Emmett, the Virginia Minstrels became a smash hit in the city.[27]

The first generation of minstrels, as Alexander Saxton has pointed out, were predominantly Northern and urban, and for "the minstrels . . . the city was the focal experience of life." Minstrelsy had a "vitality, exuberance, and rapid-fire pace previously unknown on the American stage. . . . *They could*

26. Northall, *Before and Behind the Curtain,* 92; William Bobo, *Glimpses of New-York City* (New York, 1852), 26; *Tribune,* 16 July 1853. On the Astor Place Riot, see Buckley, "To the Opera House," and Bruce A. McConachie, "'The Theatre of the Mob': Melodrama and Preindustrial Riots in Antebellum New York," in McConachie and Daniel Friedman, eds., *Theatre for Working Class Audiences in the United States, 1830–1980* (Westport, Conn., 1985).

27. *Wood's Minstrel Songs,* ed. M. Campbell (New York, 1855), 25. Henry Wood, the promoter of the enormously popular Wood's Minstrels, was the brother of Fernando, the charismatic Democratic mayor of the city in the late 1850s; see Alexander Saxton, "Blackface Minstrelsy and Jacksonian Ideology," *American Quarterly* 27 (1975), 15. "Wake Up, Mose" was an "old favorite" in the nineteenth century according to Jon Newsome, "The Music," liner notes for *Where Home Is: Life in Nineteenth Century Cincinnati* (New World Records NW251, 1977). This evidence on the creation of minstrelsy is from Hans Nathan, *Dan Emmett and the Rise of Early Negro Minstrelsy* (Norman, Okla., 1962), 113–119, and Robert Toll, *Blacking Up: The Minstrel Show in Nineteenth-Century America* (New York, 1974), 30–36. Minstrel tunes were often sung by boarders according to Gunn, *Physiology,* 73.

*not stay still for an instant.''* Crude and often vulgar, minstrelsy was, in origin, working-class entertainment: the *Literary World* derided minstrelsy in 1849 as having ''returned to its original haunts; there to convulse the b'hoys.'' However, the highly ritualized combination of song, dance, and drama proved popular with almost all Americans, not just workers. A somewhat softened version emerged in the 1850s that would enjoy national popularity until the twentieth century.[28]

''Built primarily on elements of blackface minstrelsy,'' variety (so called because of the variety of the performances) or vaudeville, as it came to be called, emerged in the late 1850s as the most characteristic and enduring form of working-class entertainment. Informal singing performances in saloons, known as ''free and easies,'' had been popular for years, and sometime in the early 1850s (the exact date is unclear) the first ''concert saloon'' in the city opened. The concert saloon was simply a large saloon ''filled with men and boys . . ., odors of a spiritous nature, and smoke'' in which a stage show was presented. In 1861 Tony Pastor, the son of Eighth Ward Italian immigrants, opened a regular ''music hall'' at 444 Broadway, that starred Pastor—''one of the greatest local favorites ever seen in the city''—and other polished performers.[29]

The variety bills, according to Parker Zellers, ''were hearty robust affairs seasoned well to the particular tastes of the east side.'' ''Patronized,'' in Pastor's words, ''almost entirely by men,'' the show consisted of acts— singers, dancers, comedians, circus performers—climaxed by an afterpiece, often a ''hearty burlesque on a popular or classic play,'' that allowed performers to reprise their specialties. Blackface was common, ''and the performers were a cosmopolitan array. France, Germany, Italy, Ireland, and ''the land of the free and the home of the brave'' were all represented, recounted a disapproving *Harper'*s reporter in 1859.[30]

It was also in the 1850s that the popular German-language *Volkstheatre* became popular in Kleindeutschland. Singers and bands had long been popular in the beer halls, and in 1854 the Stadttheatre opened on the Bowery. It

28. Saxton, ''Blackface Minstrelsy and Jacksonian Ideology,'' 8. ''Vitality'': Toll, *Blacking Up,* 32, 36, emphasis added; *Literary World* 127 (1849), 1.

29. Concert saloons: Parker Zellers, ''The Cradle of Variety: The Concert Saloon,'' *Educational Theatre Journal* 20 (1968), 578–585, and George C. D. Odell, *Annals of the New York Stage* (New York, 1931), 6:589–593. ''Filled with men'': ''Sketches of People Who Oppose our Sunday Laws—A Sunday Afternoon Sacred Concert,'' *Harper's Weekly* 3 (1859), 641–642 (the word ''sacred'' is a joke as such concerts were anything but). Parker Zellers, *Tony Pastor: Dean of the Vaudeville Stage* (Ypsilanti, Mich., 1971), esp. xiii–xix, 2–33, and Myron Matlaw, ''Tony the Trouper: Pastor's Early Years,'' *Theatre Annual* 34 (1968), 70–90. ''Greatest Local Favorites'': *Clipper,* 17 September 1864.

30. Zellers, *Tony Pastor,* xvii, 33. Pastor quoted in ibid., 42. Zellers, ''Cradle of Variety,'' 583. As variety evolved into vaudeville later in the century, the afterpiece was dropped. *Harper's Weekly* 3 (1859), 641; see also Kenneth Rossman, ''The Irish in American Drama in the Mid-Nineteenth Century,'' *New York History* 21 (1940), 39–53.

specialized, to the disgust of Little Germany's intellectuals, in farces and melodramas, some of which were translated versions of popular American sketches and plays. Beerhall entertainment itself seems in the 1850s to have been quite similar to variety: there were musical acts, clowns, and comedians with their "ribald songs."[31]

The variety shows "tended to be boisterous and unsophisticated; the comedy was low [and] robust." It was entertainment fitted to the city's large population of young males. Such Pastor favorites as "The Streets of New York," "What Are You Going to Stand?" (on treating in saloons), "The Single Young Man Lodger," and "Go It While You're Young"—"Go it while you're young, / Go to ebery rebel; / Go to ebery ball and show; / Go it like de debbel"—touched directly on the daily experience of variety's customers. The influence of youthful customers is evidenced by "the demonstrations of physical prowess" that "East Siders took delight in." A favorite vaudeville performer was Daniel Rice (né McLaren). "A New Yorker born and bred," the son of a Mulberry Street grocer and a former worker at Lorillard's tobacco factory, this onetime prizefighter was known as the "young American Hercules" because of his magnificent physique. His act consisted of sparring exhibitions and feats of strength, during which he sang and told jokes.[32]

The potential of this dynamic form of entertainment was only partly developed until the 1870s, when actor Ned Harrigan, a former Seventh Ward ship caulker, created "Dan Mulligan," a character supposedly based on a real Sixth Ward grocer Harrigan had known. A protégé of Pastor, Harrigan drew on *A Glance at New York* ("Mose," according to Richard Moody, "could have served as a model for Dan Mulligan"), minstrelsy, and variety in creating his brilliant and enormously popular Mulligan sketches. Setting the action mainly in the tenement where the pugnacious Mulligan and his family lived, and in the corner saloon where the Mulligan Guards (a militia company) met, Harrigan chronicled virtually every colorful and humorous facet of the city's working class. The plots usually revolved around the Mulligans' relations with their neighbor, Gustavus Lochmuller, a German butcher, and his family. Harrigan and his partner Tony Hart treated serious issues such as ethnic rivalry with humor and understanding in a "knockdown and slambang" style, interspersing sketches with such popular Harrigan songs as "My

31. Griesinger, *Land und Leute*, 572–573; Joh. Frei, *Drei Monate in New-York* (Zurich, 1869), 105–106; Foster, *New York by Gas-Light*, 88–89; Fritz Leuchs, *The Early German Theatre in New York, 1840–1872* (New York, 1928), 200–221; Nadel, "Kleindeutschland," 217–222.

32. Zellers, *Tony Pastor*, 35. Tony Pastor, *Tony Pastor's Complete Budget of Comic Songs* (New York, 1864[?]). Maria Ward Brown, *The Life of Dan Rice* (Long Branch, N.J., 1901), 2–79. This is partly autobiographical. Dan Rice should not be confused with Thomas "Daddy" Rice, the blackface singer and comedian of the 1830s and 1840s.

Dad's Dinner Pail," "I Never Drink behind the Bar (But I Will Take a Mild Cigar)," and the famous "Mulligan Guards March."[33]


FIRE COMPANIES

The Mulligan Guards were fictional, but dozens of real guard companies were associated with the volunteer fire companies. "Run with a Hook and Ladder Truck to an alarm of Fire from Hudson to Greene St," wrote Thomas Chamberlain in his diary on June 22, 1835, less than one month after his arrival from England. New York, like most American cities, relied on volunteers to battle the fires that were such a common part of urban life in the nineteenth century. Early in the century the volunteers were dominated by merchants and masters, but by the 1820s and 1830s artisans gained increasing influence, and in the late 1840s immigrants began to enter the companies in large numbers. Charles Mackay, an English writer, described the firemen in 1857 as "mostly youths engaged during the day in various handicrafts and mechanical trades."[34]

With four thousand official members in 1854 and thousands more "runners" unofficially attached to the various companies, the volunteers were a vital part of nineteenth-century urban society. Fire companies became social organizations for workers, and the firehouses, clubhouses. Like so many aspects of working class life, the companies were divided along ethnic lines. The M. T. Brennan Hose in the Sixth Ward was a gathering place for Irish workers of the area, the Howard Engine Company on the West Side a club for native workers. Some young firemen even bunked in the firehouses. To members "the engine house was their sanctuary," wrote department historian Augustine Costello.[35]

City workers loved a "frolic" or "spree," and "target excursions" were enormously popular social events sponsored by fire and guard companies— "every company of firemen has its annual [target] excursion," according to

33. Richard Moody, *Ned Harrigan: From Corlear's Hook to Herald Square* (Chicago, 1980), 13; see also E. J. Kahn, *The Merry Partners: The Art and Stage of Harrigan and Hart* (New York, 1955). Actually, the differences between the Mose of *A Glance at New York* and Dan Mulligan are almost as significant as the similarities; see below. *The Mulligan Guard Ball* (1879), the most popular and apparently only surviving Mulligan sketch, is reprinted in Richard Moody, ed., *Dramas from the American Theatre, 1762–1909* (Cleveland and New York, 1966), 549–565.

34. Chamberlain diary. On elite membership see Augustine Costello, *Our Firemen* (New York, 1887), 145; Stephen F. Ginsberg, "Fire Protection in New York City, 1800–1842" (diss., New York University, 1968), 44–47; and Richard Boyd Calhoun, "From Community to Metropolis: Fire Protection in New York City, 1790–1875" (diss., Columbia University, 1973), 117–118. Charles Mackay, *Life and Liberty in America* (New York, 1857), 35.

35. James Tyler, *Reminiscences of the V.F.D.* (Bay Ridge, N.Y., 1878), 6–7; Costello, *Our Firemen*, 165.

Thomas L. Nichols. When the weather was good, members would convene at a saloon to "wet their necks" and then march to the ferry to Staten Island or "Jersey," their boisterous comportment on route irritating middle-class New Yorkers. After a picnic dinner, the target shooting commenced. The Anonymous Proofreader described a typical excursion: "The firing went on all afternoon without intermission, and there was considerable expenditure of ball and powder, not one shot of fifty going anywhere near the mark." When, "after long-continued firing," someone "lodged a ball in the target . . . the spectators gave three cheers, and a prize was awarded to the fortunate rifleman. . . . These affairs generally ended by every man gaining a prize." This camaraderie, and the shared dangers of firefighting, created among members, in George Foster's words, a "great devotion and attachment to each other."[36]

The fire companies reflected the youthful energy of city workers. The engine and hose carts were pulled by hand to fires, and races between companies on their way to a blaze (or to a false alarm sent in as an excuse for racing) were common. "No 2 Engine stood for us we came out and ran away from them as usual" is a typical entry in the Lady Washington Engine Company Number 40's minute book for 1859. In an era when organized sports were in their infancy, these runs were welcome exercise to youthful members, and races often ended with brawls between the highly competitive companies. The volunteer fireman Mose "spiling" for a fight was grounded in reality, and in many companies the best fighter was named foreman.[37]

No doubt the fighting was also an attempt to establish "turf" by the companies and their attached youth gangs, the runners. Gangs were nothing new in the city—there are references to them as early as 1728, and by 1800 they were common. It does seem, however, that gangs became more aggressive with the immigration of the 1840s and 1850s, and groups such as the Bowery Boys and the so-called Dead Rabbits became widely known. Territorial brawling between fire companies and gangs clearly reflected the intense localism of working-class life.[38]

The destruction and injuries that occurred during these brawls should not

36. "Annual excursion": Thomas L. Nichols, *Forty Years of American Life* (London, 1864), 2:230. *Real Experiences of an Emigrant*, 91–92. When none of the Mulligan Guards hit the target, a carpenter member drilled holes in the target before returning to the city; *Illustrated History of the Mulligan Guard* (New York, 1874), quoted in Moody, *Ned Harrigan*, 50. George Foster, *New York Naked* (New York, n.d.), 130; see also J. Frank Kernan, *Reminiscences of the Old Fire Laddies* (New York, 1885), 42, 54, and Christoph Vetter, *Zwei Jahre in New-York* (Hof, 1849), 104–105.

37. Lady Washington Engine Company Minute book quoted in Kenneth Dunshee, *As You Pass By* (New York, 1952), 34.

38. Early gangs: William Duer, *Reminiscences of an Old Yorker* (New York, 1867), 31, and David Bruce, "Autobiography of David Bruce," NYHS. On gangs see Brown, "The 'Dead Rabbit'–Bowery Boy Riot," and Paul A. Gilje, *The Road to Mobocracy: Popular Disorder in New York City, 1763–1834* (Chapel Hill, N.C., 1987), 260–264.

obscure the element of play in them. Brawling and even rioting were rough forms of sport for male workers, and combatants were cheered on by crowds of spectators watching from windows and rooftops. In both England and Ireland deadly brawling, though increasingly suppressed by authorities, was common. The freedom that workers enjoyed in America allowed the city's youthful population to engage in this pastime with surprising impunity.[39]

Fists, sticks, and bottles were used, rarely knives or pistols. Women did not take part in donnybrooks but were allowed to bring stones to those engaged. "Even in the worst of times," George Foster explained, "when the spanners [wrenches used to connect firehouses] and brickbats fly thick as hail . . . there is as much fun as ferocity, and the whole affair is regarded as a frolic rather than a riot." Deaths and crippling injuries were unusual but did happen. When the battles ended, combatants often shook hands. Such fighting between the volunteer companies was hardly conducive to effective fire protection and was a main reason the volunteer force was disbanded in 1865.[40]

PUGILISM

Nothing so excited antebellum New York as a prizefight. Virtually unknown in America in the 1820s, pugilism by the 1850s was a working-class passion. Fights between local champions at fairs in England and Ireland were an established practice that immigrants brought to America. The intense localism of city life was reflected in a large number of "rough-and-tumble" fights between neighborhood champions, which sometimes ended with brawls among spectators. The most famous rough-and-tumble fight of the period was "Butcher Bill" Poole's victory (despite receiving a bite in the early going) over John Morrissey in 1854 on the Amos Street Dock.[41]

*Pugilism* included both rough-and-tumble fighting and prizefighting, and the line between the two was vague—Bill Poole, although he never took part in a prizefight, was regarded as one of the very best, if not the best, boxers in

39. See Patrick O'Donnell, *The Irish Faction Fighters of the 19th Century* (Dublin, 1975). In a "faction fight" parishes typically battled with sticks and stones "merely for the diversion of fighting." For England see Christina Hole, *English Sports and Pastimes* (London, 1949), 51–57.

40. Role of women: Brown, "The 'Dead Rabbit'–Bowery Boy Riot," 50–51. George Foster, *New York in Slices* (New York, 1849), 69; see also Costello, *Our Firemen*, 126. Shook hands: Brown, 134–135.

41. Elliott J. Gorn, *The Manly Art: Bare-Knuckle Prize Fighting in America* (Ithaca, N.Y., 1986). English fights: Joseph Lawson, *Progress in Pudsey* (1887; rpt. Firle, England, 1978), 76–77. The most complete account of the Poole-Morrissey fight is by Theodore "The" Allen in Edward Van Every, *Sins of New York as "Exposed" by the Police Gazette* (New York, 1930), 76–79. Allen's account dates from 1880; see also William E. Harding, *John Morrissey—His Life, Battles and Wrangles* (New York, 1881), 16–19.

the city. However, a series of heavily publicized matches involving large stakes impressed the public: "In the year 1840," according to the *Herald,* "the fighting spirit took a sudden start." Because prizefighting was illegal in most places, matches were held secretly. When a championship fight was about to take place, the city was gripped by intense excitement.[42]

The match between Tom Hyer, a New York butcher, and "Yankee" Sullivan (also a New Yorker), which "came off" on February 7, 1849, on the shores of Chesapeake Bay, created a "perfect frenzy of excitement." The *Herald* (the "appropriate organ of such disgraceful recitals," grumbled Philip Hone) noted the "vast interest which was felt by the great floating population of this city. . . . Nothing has been heard of or talked about for several days past but the fight." "Urchins in school," it reported, "could not be kept at their lessons, but insisted upon their right to talk of what the whole town talked about. They became impatient of rule, were flogged for their disobedience, and returned to their seats, but to renew the forbidden conversation." Only the "rigidly righteous, the pious, the saints, and the puritans remained uninvolved." When the victorious Hyer returned to New York, "excitement . . . raged in the city . . . all down town was in a swarm, like so many bees."[43]

John Morrissey's 1858 victory over John Heenan, "the Benicia Boy" from Benicia, California, also attracted great enthusiasm. Morrissey was born in Ireland in 1831 and emigrated with his family to Troy, New York. Known as "Old Smoke" for having been pushed against a stove in an early brawl, Morrissey had come as a teenager to New York, where his extraordinary toughness in combat made him a hero to the city's Irish workers (see Figure 24). Throughout the country intense enthusiasm greeted the news that both fighters had left the city and the match was about to "come off." Reported the *Herald,*

> Since the formation of this match . . . this fight has been the theme of conversation throughout the country, among all classes of men, more particularly among the youth, who, in all pursuits of life, from the schoolhouse to the workshop, seemed to have thought of nothing else than the fight for the championship. . . . To the barrooms it has been a source of great profit, for there it was that the merits of the men were principally discussed and much of the betting done.

Interest in New York reached almost hysterical levels. "From an early hour in the evening until past midnight the spirit of the prizering was prevalent in every bar room, bowling alley and billiard saloon in the city." Large crowds

---

42. *The American Fistiana* (New York, 1873), 10–11; *Herald,* 9 February 1849.

43. Gorn, *Manly Art,* 85–96; *Life and Battles of Yankee Sullivan* (Philadelphia, 1854), 34; *Herald,* 8 and 9 February 1849; *The Diary of Philip Hone,* ed. Alan Nevins (New York, 1927), 2:861 (9 February 1849); *Life and Battles of Yankee Sullivan,* 62–63.

FIGURE 24. John Morrissey, in an 1860 Currier & Ives lithograph. Photograph courtesy of the Library of Congress.

gathered outside newspaper offices in an "intense state of excitement" awaiting word of the outcome. Morrissey's victory made him acknowledged American champion.[44]

The great international match of 1861 between Heenan and 150-pound English champion Thomas Sayers may have attracted more popular interest than any other sporting event in the nineteenth century. Excitement built as the outcome was awaited from London. When news came that the fight had ended in a disputed draw (both fighters were later given championship belts), it

44. *Herald*, 22 and 21 October 1858; Gorn, *Manly Art*, 116–122.

provoked a controversy that lasted for months and a popular ballad, "Heenan and Sayers," that was sung in saloons into the twentieth century. Heenan-Sayers was the last great championship match until the 1880s, for the sport was discredited in the late 1860s by several allegedly fixed fights (one involving Heenan himself). In New York, however, pugilism continued to enjoy popularity in the form of legal "exhibition" matches. Originally held in lower ward saloons such as Florence's at Broadway and Houston, by the 1860s these bouts were shifted to theatres to accommodate larger crowds.[45]

Both rough-and-tumble fighting and prizefighting under London Rules were extremely brutal, and the sport was sporadically suppressed by the authorities. Nevertheless, in the late 1840s and 1850s it attracted amazing enthusiasm. The thousands of young, single males in the city found it especially to their taste. According to George Foster, what attracted them was "the fierce excitement of human battle—the blood, the bravoes, the ambition, the dauntless courage and contempt for pain and danger, and even life, which make up the elements of the prize fight." Reported in the *Herald, Clipper,* and *Spirit of the Times* (it was widely believed that "a report of a prize-fight will sell a newspaper more widely than the news of a presidential election"), boxing and the wagers placed on fights were prime topics of conversation among workers. When volunteer firemen got together, according to Foster, "points of great pith and moment in the science of the Ring are definitively settled." Boxing's significance was heightened by its role as symbolic competition between ethnic groups (a role understood by all concerned). The notion that a fight was between two individuals, one of whom might happen to be Irish and the other American, was alien to the nineteenth century. When Irish-born "Yankee" Sullivan (a nickname he got while fighting in England for a short time before returning to America) beat Thomas Secor in 1842, American-born New Yorkers "cast their eyes round about the pugilistic circle to find a man capable of holding up the honor of the Stars and Stripes against the encroachments of the Green Flag of the Emerald Isle"—Sullivan was not just an Irishman but Ireland.[46]

Boxing reflected neighborhood feeling, but "mills" (as fights were sometimes called) could lend working-class life a citywide and even national importance. The most obvious example was the Heenan-Sayers fight. In this case Heenan, much like Edwin Forrest in the Astor Place Riot, united both the

45. The Heenan-Sayers match is the subject of Alan Lloyd, *The Great Prizefight* (New York, 1977), esp. 158–159; see also Gorn, *Manly Art,* 148–157. "Ballad of Heenan and Sayers": Frank Shay, ed., *The Pious Friends and Drunken Companions* (New York, 1936), 46–47. On "exhibitions" see *Clipper,* 26 April 1856, and *The Night Side of New York* (New York, 1868), 82–83. Florence's Saloon: Charles Townsend Harris, *Memories of Manhattan in the Sixties and Seventies* (New York, 1928), 28.

46. *Harper's Weekly* 2 (1858), 690; Foster, *New York in Slices,* 47, 69; *Life and Battles of Yankee Sullivan,* 22.

Irish and the Americans against England. To the common people, the *Herald* reported, "this fight will settle the question of the national superiority as between England and the United States." No wonder the fight caused such tremendous excitement.[47]

## POLITICAL PARTIES

No discussion of working-class life would be complete without an account of political parties. Much has been written on working-class politics in New York; my purpose here is to suggest how political parties and elections fit within the developing framework of working-class institutional life. My emphasis on politics as a struggle for neighborhood control and patronage, and as an arena for ethnic rivalry, does not mean to suggest these were the only functions of working-class politics. The city Democratic party advertised itself as "the true home of the working classes" and acted strongly to defend their interests when the saloon was threatened or, during the 1857 panic, when Tammany proposed public works projects in the city. It does seem, however, that the intense interest surrounding elections was due in large part to the ways politics was embedded in the daily life of the neighborhood. With such a large foreign-born population, only half of New York's adult males could legally vote in 1855; nevertheless, politics attracted a great deal of interest. Female straw sewers, during their noon dinner, the *Herald* reported, "advocate with no slight zeal the claims of rival candidates," and James Burn discovered that "three topics . . . form the stock in trade of both men and women in the workshops. These are country, politics and religion."[48]

Political discourse in the city in the 1820s and 1830s was dominated by artisan republicanism that, in Sean Wilentz's words, "fused craft pride and resentment of deference and fear of dependence into a republican celebration of the trades." The Working Men's party of the 1830s opposed "the aristocracy of privilege and monied corruption" that artisans saw emerging in the city. The Working Men's party proved short-lived, and by the 1850s artisan republicanism began to wane. This republicanism's roots stretched back to eighteenth-century England and earlier; the causes of its decline are complex, but one significant factor was certainly the influx of immigrants. Irish and

47. *Herald*, 25 April 1860, quoted in Melvin Adelman, "The Development of Modern Athletics: Sport in New York City, 1820–1870" (diss., University of Illinois, 1980), 567.

48. On working-class politics see Amy Bridges, *A City in the Republic: Antebellum New York and the Origin of Machine Politics* (Cambridge, England, 1984). Fifty-three percent of adult males could legally vote in 1855: 166,531 males over age twenty-one and 88,817 voters, native and naturalized, according to data in New York Secretary of State, *Census of the State of New York, 1855* (Albany, 1857), 8. Tammany's opponents were convinced that many aliens voted despite the legal prohibition. *Herald*, 7 June 1853; Burn, *Three Years*, 24–25.

German peasants were not attuned to its meaning and significance in the way native workers were. The American Revolution could hardly have the same resonance for immigrants it did for natives, and the language of "corruption" and "virtue" must have sounded alien to those not steeped in republican discourse.[49]

A new and distinctively working-class style of politics began to emerge in the 1840s and 1850s. Related to changes taking place in working-class life, it paid attention less to ideology than to the personal qualities of political leaders. At the same time pugilists came to dominate working-class politics in the city, and elections themselves became stormy, brawling affairs. At the same time, also, the saloon emerged as central to the city's political life.

Mike Walsh was the crucial transition figure. Born in Ireland in 1810, he and his family migrated to New York when Mike was a child. A journalist by trade, Walsh became involved in Democratic politics. In his speeches, he remained firmly within the artisan republican tradition: ancient Greece, Walsh explained in 1842 to an audience of workers, was destroyed when "all love and virtue and honesty were entirely lost" because of a love for "Asiatic luxury." Walsh argued that the working class was the home of rectitude in political life. At the same time, however, Walsh's speeches were delivered in a bombastic, high-spirited style unlike any heard in the city. Speaking in working-class dialect, the bejeweled Walsh was by turns profane, sarcastically humorous, and vitriolic—"vulture," "grub-worm," "booby," and "cur" were among his favorite epithets. Walsh also formed his own political gang, "the Spartan Band," in 1840. Though nothing new in politics, Walsh's gang was the most effective the city had seen. Walsh used this group of young workers to literally strong-arm his way into Tammany politics and eventually Congress.[50]

Few doubted that Walsh, though a relentless self-promoter, was truly devoted to the city's workers. The same could not be said about Captain Isaiah Rynders. Native-born, Rynders had earned the title "captain" by commanding a sloop on the Hudson. He had a political gang in the 1840s, the Empire Club, much better organized than the Spartan Band ever was. Rynders was, according to Matthew Breen, "as practical and persistent as Walsh was the reverse." A Democrat, Rynders had little interest in political issues and used his brawlers mostly as Tammany directed; the Empire Club took special delight in breaking up abolitionist meetings.[51]

49. Sean Wilentz, *Chants Democratic: New York City and the Rise of the American Working Class, 1788–1850* (New York, 1984), 94, 219, and Bridges, *City in the Republic*.

50. On Walsh see Robert Ernst, "The One and Only Mike Walsh," *New-York Historical Society Quarterly* 36 (1952), 43–65, and Wilentz, *Chants Democratic*, 326–335. Mike Walsh, *Sketches of the Speeches and Writing of Mike Walsh* (New York, 1843), 31. Dialect: Breen, *Thirty Years*, 303.

51. On Rynders see Thomas L. Nichols, *Forty Years of American Life* (London, 1864), 2:159–164; Breen, *Thirty Years*, 303; and M. R. Werner, *Tammany Hall* (Garden City, N.Y., 1928), 64–67.

Rynders was the prototype of the new professional working-class politician who would dominate the city into the twentieth century: the boss. To call Rynder a boss is not to suggest he was *the* boss of Democratic politics; working-class life was too localized for a single individual to control more than a neighborhood or at most a ward. By the 1850s the city had numerous local bosses, each with personal followings from their own neighborhood ethnic group. It was difficult to unite these ethnically heterogeneous local bosses into a citywide governing coalition—even Tammany was but one faction of the party, and Tweed did little more than bribe a handful of officials to create his "ring." Only with the ascendancy of John Kelly in the 1870s did there appear a measure of party discipline and organization.[52]

These local bosses were a far cry from the artisan political leaders of the 1830s. According to Breen, the boss was "in politics as a matter of business. . . . He laughs to scorn those who sanctimoniously publish to the world . . . that the sole object of their existence on earth is to see . . . the citizen upheld in all his inalienable rights. Such declarations he regards (and justly in most cases) as the merest sham."[53]

Local issues began to surpass national issues in New York politics, and ethnicity became a crucial factor in almost every election. Displaced from workshop to elections, city politics came to be based heavily on national origin. Burn described this dimension:

> After I had been in New York a short time, I felt a good deal interested in hearing my shopmates talking of whom they would vote for during the municipal elections, and discussing the merits of the respective candidates. It was not a little amusing to learn upon what conditions the preference for some of their favourite candidates was based; among these, *country* and *religion* were prominent.

The Irish and Germans supported the Democrats, whereas native workers often favored the Whig party, which had its own brawlers, including Tom Hyer, organized in the Knickerbocker Club.[54]

By the 1850s the politics that mattered most to workers was centered on neighborhood control and patronage. It is a mistake to view brawling as a part of politics—for many young men both were part of a struggle, also carried on by fire companies, for neighborhood control. The politician with the best fighters ruled the ward: Con Donaho deposed Rynders as Sixth Ward political leader by defeating the Empire Club in a brawl at the ward nominating

52. Martin Shefter, "The Emergence of the Political Machine," in Willis Hawley et al., eds., *Theoretical Perspectives on Urban Politics* (Englewood Cliffs, N.J., 1976), 21–33; Werner, *Tammany Hall*, 282–286.

53. Breen, *Thirty Years*, 233.

54. Bridges, *City in the Republic*; Burn, *Three Years*, 250. Knickerbocker Club: James O'Meara, *Broderick and Gwin* (San Francisco, Calif., 1881), 16–17.

convention. "How they would crow over each other for weeks after, if their side won," J. Franklin Kernan remembered. "Regularity in the Old Sixth was oftimes only won by black eyes, torn coats and dilapidated hats. . . . Knowing politicians of the ward never went well dressed to a caucus meeting." "Elections nowadays are sissy affairs," complained labor racketeer Richard "Big Dick" Butler in the twentieth century; "nobody gets killed any more and the ambulances and patrol wagons stay in their garages." For European immigrants, politics may have served some of the purposes of carnivals, with the pageantry and agitation that surrounded many elections giving workers festive excitement and a feeling of personal importance. The torchlight parades, rallies, hoopla, and brawls were exhilarating.[55]

This new style of politics was firmly embedded in working-class life. The best evidence is the importance of prizefighters and saloons in mid-nineteenth-century urban politics. Pugilists were working-class heroes; they were also useful in the brawls that accompanied nominations and elections. It was nearly impossible for a man to succeed in East Side politics in the mid-nineteenth century unless he was good with his fists. "To be a challenger at the polls you had to be a nifty boxer," remembered Butler. It was essential for working-class political leaders to display manly courage in combat.[56]

The most famous working-class politician was the flamboyant Morrissey, who parlayed his American heavyweight championship into a career that included two terms in the 1860s as a Democratic congressman from the Fifth District. Sullivan and Heenan were also active as Democrats, Hyer and Poole important in the Whig party. "The prizefighters of this country are to be its governing class in due course of time, if they are not so already," the *Clipper* suggested in 1857. Virtually every major Tammany politician in the nineteenth century was described as a good fighter: Tweed had no superior in "fistic prowess"; John Kelly was a man of "Herculean strength" whose early life was "divided between hard work and fighting"; Richard Croker defeated prizefighter "Dickie" Lynch by knocking out most of Lynch's teeth; Charles Murphy "became a leader among his associates because of his physical strength." The success of pugilists in politics illustrates the significance of the youthful, brawling element in working-class life. This style, rather than support for a particular party, distinguished working-class politics.[57]

55. Donahue-Rynders: Breen, *Thirty Years*, 518–519, and Kernan, *Reminiscences*, 52–54. "Crow": Kernan, 49. Richard J. Butler and Joseph Driscoll, *Dock Walloper: The Story of "Big Dick" Butler* (New York, 1933), 65. On the carnival element in American politics, see Charlotte Erickson, *Invisible Immigrants: The Adaptation of English and Scottish Immigrants in Nineteenth-Century America* (1972; rpt. Ithaca, N.Y., 1990), 259.

56. Butler and Driscoll, *Dock Walloper*, 65.

57. Morrissey: Harding, *John Morrissey*, and Breen, *Thirty Years*, 525–542. Poole: William L. Knapp, *I Die a True American; The True Life of William Poole* (New York, 1855). Hyer: O'Meara, *Broderick and Gwin*, 16; *Clipper*, 14 February 1857, quoted in Adelman, *A Sporting*

Working-class politics centered on the saloons, which were, in Mike Walsh's words, "the homes and nurseries of Democracy." There were few other institutions in most working-class areas, and barrooms were the center of East Side life—it is no surprise that local bosses looked to the saloons to consolidate their power. Similarly, volunteer fire companies were deeply involved in politics; Tweed created his first power base among firemen, and cartoonist Thomas Nast used Americus Engine Number Six's emblem of a tiger to symbolize Tammany.[58]

The saloonkeeper was in a position to influence the opinion of regular customers. Politics was a major topic of conversation, and a saloonkeeper's praise of the local boss was significant. Indeed, ward captains often made their headquarters in saloons. "As a labor leader and politician, it was inevitable for me to go into the saloon business," Butler explained. Fifteen percent of all Democratic officeseekers in 1858 were engaged in the liquor trade, and one joke held that the fastest way to empty the Common Council Chamber was to shout, "Mister, your saloon's on fire."[59]

The saloon was useful as a forum in which the boss could show his generosity. In return for votes, the boss was expected to aid "genuine cases of distress" in the neighborhood, and political leaders lacking in charity were likely to face a challenge in the next primary. The saloon was a place where the boss could openly display his liberality, especially by treating customers. "Boys, step up, and take something," Matthew Breen's "Dan Breezy" would call out. "Big Dick" Butler's mentor, Bill Devery, ran for district leader in the Hell's Kitchen area later in the nineteenth century on the slogan "Everybody have a drink on me."[60]

The importance of the saloon in Democratic politics helped spur the temperance crusade of the 1850s. Temperance sentiment was widespread long before then, of course, but the huge immigration of the 1850s gave it new impetus. In New York State, upstate Whigs pushed for a Maine Law, hoping that crippling the saloons would weaken their political rivals. A temperance law was

*Time*, 236. Tweed: Denis Tilden Lynch, *"Boss" Tweed* (New York, 1927), 34. J. Fairfax McLaughlin, *The Life and Times of John Kelly, Tribune of the People* (New York, 1885), 17, 26. Croker: Lothrop Stoddard, *Master of Manhattan: The Life of Richard Croker* (New York, 1931), 29. Murphy: Werner, *Tammany Hall*, 483–484. The links between Tammany and prizefighting later in the century are analyzed by Steven A. Reiss, "Sports and Machine Politics in New York City, 1870–1920," in Raymond A. Mohl, ed., *The Making of Urban America* (Wilmington, Del., 1988), 100–106.

58. Walsh: *Times*, 2 December 1859. Tiger: Leo Hershkowitz, *Tweed's New York* (Garden City, N.Y., 1972), 12.

59. Butler and Driscoll, *Dock Walloper*, 84. On saloonkeepers in politics, see Breen, *Thirty Years*, esp. 249–257; the joke is on p. 250. Fifteen percent: W. J. Rorabaugh, "Rising Democratic Spirits: Immigrants, Temperance, and Tammany Hall, 1854–1860," *Civil War History* 22 (1976), 155.

60. "Distress": Breen, *Thirty Years*, 231–232. "Dan Breezy": Breen, 235. Butler and Driscoll, *Dock Walloper*, 75.

enacted in 1855, but city mayor Fernando Wood refused to enforce it, and the law was eventually declared unconstitutional by the state Court of Appeals. Republicans and Know-Nothings made a new, twofold effort in 1855: a temperance law that limited saloon licenses and banned Sunday liquor sales, and a law creating a metropolitan police force with commissioners appointed by the governor. This second law aimed to deprive New York's mayor of control of the city police, in part because Republicans believed that Wood would try to undermine the new temperance law. Wood's opinion may not have mattered; it is doubtful that the city police, closely tied to Tammany and the local bosses, would have made a serious effort at enforcement.[61]

If ever a law was guaranteed to outrage city workers, it was the temperance legislation of 1857. The Sunday closing provision was especially repugnant; workers labored hard six days a week, and now temperance advocates were proposing to close the saloons the workers' only day off. No wonder the East Side reacted with ferocity: metropolitan police were attacked in the streets and pelted with rocks. Attempts to enforce Sunday closing led to major riots in the "bloody ould" Sixth and heavily German Seventeenth wards. Even with the metropolitan force, the legislation proved virtually unenforceable. And by associating themselves with temperance, the Whigs, and later the Republicans, did much to unite workers—natives, Irish, and German—behind the Democrats, the traditional laissez-faire party.[62]

## RELIGION

It is difficult to gauge the importance of religion for city workers. Revivals in the city in the 1830s and 1840s attracted some working-class support. The immigration of the 1840s ensured that Catholicism would be the predominant religion among workers and weakened, if it did not eliminate, the possibility of widespread religious revivals among working people. Although a substantial Protestant minority remained, most workers in the 1850s were at least nominally Catholic; however, it is difficult to measure the importance their religion held for them.[63]

61. The best account of the temperance struggle, police reform, and the subsequent turmoil is Brown, "The 'Dead Rabbit'–Bowery Boy Riot"; see also Edward Spann, *The New Metropolis: New York City, 1840–1857* (New York, 1981), 386–394; Paul O. Weinbaum, "Temperance, Politics, and the New York City Riots of 1857," *New-York Historical Society Quarterly* 59 (1975), 246–270; and Rorabaugh, "Rising Democratic Spirits."

62. See Rorabaugh, "Rising Democratic Spirits," 142–144, and Brown, "The 'Dead Rabbit'–Bowery Boy Riot."

63. Revivals: Wilentz, *Chants Democratic,* 145–153. In 1855 New York, with a population of 629,924, had only 138,678 church members, of whom 78,488 were Catholic; see *Census of the State of New York, 1855,* 445–476.

The primary significance of religion among workers was, it would seem, social. About 40 to 50 percent of Catholics in the city attended mass regularly, and to thousands of immigrants, Sunday services served both as a way of meeting people and as a way of maintaining links with their previous experience. For all the enormous changes in their lives, religion offered stability and continuity. For many, as for Henry Price, the church was "my best and only friend . . . when far away in a strange land."[64]

Less clear is the significance of religious beliefs to workers. Thomas Chamberlain, the printer, was a Catholic, yet he often went to Protestant services, and Sunday comments in his diary mostly concern church music and people he met at services. Middle-class complaints about working-class irreligiosity were standard in the nineteenth century, and New York was no exception; according to one divine, "the religious destitution of New York is greater than that of Pekin." Thomas Dudgeon, a British traveler, found secular singing the rule in New York on Sundays, and hymnsinging "you must . . . put down as a novelty." The perception of religion's weakness among workers was strengthened by the number of churches that closed as the wealthy left lower Manhattan. By 1855, twenty-eight houses of worship in the lower seven wards had shut down. According to historian Edward Spann, in the late 1850s the "Uptown of Progress and Protestanism" appeared to many to face the "Lower City" of "foreigners, . . . infidels, and Roman Catholics." Such laments, despite their anti-Catholic nature, are common enough that it is hard to dismiss them. Indeed, Catholic priests were quite pessimistic: one referred to the "religious indifference" of the city's Irish Catholics, another claimed that the city's Germans had "lost all sense of religion."[65]

For many of the city's younger workers, it does seem, customary beliefs withered. These workers were at an age at which, in the twentieth century at least, religious enthusiasm is typically low. And certainly the world of the boardinghouse, barroom, and prizering did not encourage reverence. In Thomas Gunn's *Physiology of New York Boarding-Houses*, devout residents are invariably ridiculed by other boarders. Among "disagreeable boarders"

64. Jay Dolan, *The Immigrant Church: New York's Irish and German Catholics, 1815–1865* (Baltimore, Md., 1975), 57; Price diary, 27.

65. "Religious destitution": C. W. Eliot, "Life in Great Cities—I," *Putnam's Magazine* n.s. 1 (1868), 94. Thomas Dudgeon, *A Nine Years Residence, and a Nine Months Tour on Foot, in the States of New York and Pennsylvania, for the Use of Labourers, Farmers and Emigrants* (Edinburgh, 1841), 10; see also William Thomson, *A Tradesman's Travels in the United States and Canada in the Years 1840, 1841 and 1842* (Edinburgh, 1842), 35, and *Real Experiences of an Emigrant*, 81. Spann, *New Metropolis*, 274, 273; Dolan, *Immigrant Church*, 56, 84. "*Kleindeutschland* was basically a secular community where religion played a far from central role," according to its historian, Nadel, "Kleindeutschland," 213; see also Agnes Bretting, *Soziale Probleme deutscher Einwanderer in New York City, 1800–1860* (Weisbaden, 1981), 121–127, and Shanly, "Germany in New York," 561.

Gunn listed "unmitigated pious people who will have 'grace' said before meals . . . and look eternal sulphur-and-pitchforks at you if you talk of theatres."[66]

Clearly for many workers, among them Chamberlain and Price, a Baptist who was "Imers'd" in the East River ("after the ice had been broken"), religion was important. However, few working-class diaries or reminiscences pay it special attention. Religion was not strong enough to challenge the Bowery milieu. Indeed, the very dichotomy is probably false. A scrupulous Protestantism was part of the process by which the middle class defined itself in the antebellum period, and while genteel New Yorkers might view piety and the Bowery as opposed, some religious workers saw nothing incongruous about it at all. Henry Price's diary complains about the lack of seats in saloons as well as recounting his baptism in the East River; there is no evidence Price believed churchgoing meant he should avoid the barroom. Similarly, Thomas Chamberlain's diary consists largely of accounts of the printers he worked for, plays and minstrel shows he saw, fires he ran to, and church services and temperance meetings he attended.[67]

## A WORKING-CLASS LIFE

Within the working-class areas of the city, boardinghouses, barrooms, fire companies, and theatres flourished. The saloon was the most significant of these institutions, but all were interconnected in a way that gave emergent working-class life a logic and unity that defined working-class experience for men. When Tom Hyer fought "Yankee" Sullivan in 1849, he battled not only as a prizefighter but as a native-born American, a Whig, a Seventeenth Warder, and a member of Tompkins Engine Company Number 30. Boarding-house jokes were a staple in the theatre; a chronicle of American prizefighting recorded Mike Walsh's death; minstrelsy was oriented toward the Democratic party; prizefighters owned saloons; Haverly's Minstrels burlesqued the paid fire department after the volunteer department had been disbanded.[68]

66. On the decline in religious activity in the young adult period, see Michael Argyle and Benjamin Beit-Hallahrni, *The Social Psychology of Religion* (London and Boston, 1975), 65–67. Gunn, *Physiology*, 290, see also 69–70, 83, 148, 286–287.

67. Price diary, 26–27; see also Breen, *Thirty Years*, 313. Chamberlain diary, *passim*. See also Peter Bailey, " 'Will the Real Bill Banks Please Stand Up?' Towards a Role Analysis of Mid-Victorian Working-Class Respectability," *Journal of Social History* 12 (1979), 336–353.

68. *Life and Battles of Yankee Sullivan*, 34. Boardinghouse jokes: see, for example, "Rules of our New Boarding House" ("De soups good . . . dey take a quart ob water an boil it to a point to make it strong"), in C. H. Fox, *Charley Fox's Sable Songster* (New York, 1859), 41; also Toll, *Blacking Up*, 181, and Harry B. Weiss, "A Brief History of American Jest Books," *NYPL Bulletin* 47 (1943), 285–286. *American Fistiana*, 74. Democratic orientation of minstrelsy: Saxton, "Blackface Minstrelsy," 16–18; Dunshee, *As You Pass By*, 242.

These interconnected institutions reflected the high energy of working-class life. Pillowfights in boardinghouses, "stand up" saloons, races between fire companies, minstrelsy, brawls between political gangs—almost no aspect of working-class life was unaffected. Even sleep was kept to near a biological minimum: "We have often heard," the Artisan's Department of *Fincher's Trades' Review* recounted, "young men remark that four or five hours sleep was all they wanted."[69]

All of these institutions faced varying degrees of hostility from "respectable" opinion. The boardinghouse was regarded as an invitation to licentiousness. The evils of the saloon were endlessly condemned—especially saloons that stayed open on the Sabbath and violated, as *Harper's* put it, "*our* Sunday laws." Billiards was "positively disgraceful . . . it draws young men away from the home circle." New York clerics held thanksgiving services after theatre fires. A theatre, if not in itself evil, Grant Thorburn explained, was a danger because saloons "sprung up around it" almost immediately. Volunteer firemen "became proud of vices, and popular with their fellows because they possess them." "Bunkers" in fire stations were a special danger because they were cut off "from all home or virtuous female influence." Prizefighting was "brutal, barbarous, cruel, a disgrace to human nature and to our nation's name." (This last description many middle-class New Yorkers would have found equally applicable to the Democratic party under Fernando Wood.)[70]

Indeed, it is probable that the emphasis in the literature of the period on the boisterous, violent side of working-class life stems in part from the hostility it aroused among the city's middle classes. The b'hoy was most visible and fearsome when brawling on the streets, and for some urban writers, such as Benjamin Baker and Cornelius Mathews, b'hoys were defined by physical aggression. The thousands of workers who spent uneventful evenings in saloons or tenement apartments did not attract attention, but a dozen brawlers on the Brooklyn Ferry did. Middle-class accounts certainly helped spread the image of the brawling worker; however, we should not conclude that he was merely a literary construct. The evidence on pugilists and fire companies makes it clear that brawling was an integral part of life for male workers—it was, after all, workers themselves who elected John Morrissey to the House of Representatives.

These workers' institutions were divided by ethnic group and by language.

69. *Fincher's Trades' Review*, 15 August 1863.
70. Boardinghouse: Horlick, *Country Boys*, 232. *Harper's Weekly* ran a series in 1859 titled "Sketches of the People Who Oppose Our Sunday Laws"; see 3 (1859), 641–642, 657–658, 673–674, 707–708, 739–740, emphasis added. Theatre fires: Kahn, *Merry Partners*, 225–226. Grant Thorburn, *Life and Writing of Grant Thorburn* (New York, 1852), 183. Billiards: *Round Table* n.s. 1 (1865), 89. *Report of the Police Commissioners* (1865) and an unidentified newspaper quoted in Costello, *Our Firemen*, 796, 798. *Harper's Weekly* 3 (1859), 659, emphasis added. On hostility to Wood, see Spann, *New Metropolis*, 378–385.

There was a clear division between the Irish and the Americans—the Irish had their own saloons, prizefighters, and political bosses, and the native-born had their equivalents. Despite the sometimes violent nature of the native-Irish rivalry, however, from the institutional point of view the Germans were most often "odd man out." Their status can be attributed largely to language—this more than anything caused the creation of German boardinghouses and the German theatre. Despite the popularity of Irish actors, and Irish sketches and plays, there was no distinctive Irish theatre in the city. Generally, the Germans lacked the native and Irish enthusiasm for fire companies and pugilism. German interest in politics, though significant, was not as deep as that of the Irish, and though Tammany successfully recruited Kleindeutschland saloon-keepers, the city had few major German bosses.[71]

Neither were Germans divorced from this life. They lived in boarding-houses and frequented theatres and saloons. And, if Germans lacked enthusiasm for brawling and pugilism, they shared a love for guard and target companies, and *Schutzenverein* were common in Kleindeutschland. Since shooting societies were popular in Germany, Germans may even have introduced the idea to America. Generally, therefore, it is clear that the city's working class was divided, linguistically and ethnically. But although divisions existed, they did so to a large degree within a common institutional framework, a framework that reflected the shared demographic, motivational, workplace, budgetary, and dietary experience of the city's workers. Irish, native, and German workers usually lived in separate boardinghouses and drank in separate saloons. But it is perhaps more significant that they all lived in boardinghouses and drank in saloons.[72]

This significance is illuminated by the murder of Bill Poole. Butcher Bill was a famous native rough-and-tumble fighter, Eighth Ward Whig leader, saloon keeper, and member of Howard Engine Company Number 15. He had, according to the *Times,* "a great many friends among the class to which he belonged—comprising not only fighting men and rowdies of the City, but the butchers, mechanics, and working men at large." Butcher Bill was a bitter rival of John Morrissey, and the two men had been involved in a brutal rough and tumble in 1854. A fierce drunken argument took place between them in a saloon in February 1855. Morrissey called Poole a "G–d d–d American son of a b–h"; Poole replied by labeling Morrissey a "d–d lying, Irish son of a b–h." Later that evening Poole was murdered in the Stanwix Hall barroom on

71. Costello, *Our Firemen,* 592–593, 689. Brawls among Germans were not unknown, only less common than among the Irish. For a major brawl among German workers in a Duane Street saloon, see the *Tribune,* 12 September 1851. Breen discusses German involvement in politics in a rather patronizing way; Breen, *Thirty Years,* 252–277; see also Bretting, *Soziale Probleme,* 152–162, esp. 155.

72. *Schutzenverein:* Griesinger, *Lebende Bilder,* 300–308; Nadel, "Kleindeutschland," 233–236; and Bretting, *Soziale Probleme,* 203.

Broadway by a Morrissey crony, Lew Baker. After lingering for several weeks Poole expired, his last words allegedly being "I die a true American." He immediately became a nativist martyr—a hundred thousand people lined the streets of the city to watch Poole's funeral procession, and a play based on his life and death was rushed on stage. Obviously his death illustrates ethnic rivalry at its most violent, but the episode also reflects common working-class institutions, as it occurs within the saloon–fire company–theatre–boxing–politics nexus. Ethnic divisions among male workers existed, to a large extent, within a broad framework of mutual institutions.[73]

The same cannot be said about female workers—they were mostly excluded from this working-class associational life. Few women lived in boardinghouses, they were barred from most saloons and many theatres, and, despite their interest in politics, they could not vote. This is not to suggest they were completely excluded from working-class social life: women attended church, they were invited to fire company balls, and in numerous dance halls and oyster houses on the Bowery they could meet single men. They also took part with men in the popular Sunday "frolics"—the summer picnic excursions to Hoboken or Long Island. Especially popular with both sexes was the "water frolic" aboard a Hudson River steamer.[74]

Christine Stansell argues that the creation of the Bowery milieu in the 1840s brought with it more respect for working women from their male peers. Yet she also notes that, to a degree, women remained outsiders in this milieu. Indeed, one of the conclusions that emerges most strongly from an examination of working-class life in the city is the sharp difference in the daily life experience of men and women. Women's working experience was different from men's—wages for single women were usually too low to allow them to live independently except in poverty. It was single men who provided the critical mass for the Bowery, and the associational life they created was basically masculine, offering women only a marginal role.[75]

By the 1850s New York offered men an attractive and powerful working-class institutional life. It was basically a youth culture, but in the 1850s a very large proportion of the city's working class was young, and these institutions helped alleviate the boredom and loneliness of male immigrants to the city. It is important, however, not to overstate this point. Recently arrived immi-

73. *Times* quoted in the *Life of William Poole, with a Full Account of the Terrible Affray in Which He Received His Death Wound* (New York, 1855), 61. Insults: transcript of the inquest in Knapp, *I Die a True American*, 10, 31. For a detailed account of this incident and its significance, see Elliott J. Gorn, " 'Good-Bye Boys, I die a true American': Homicide, Nativism, and Working-Class Culture in Antebellum New York City," *Journal of American History* 74 (1987), 388–410.

74. Unlike in England few saloons admitted women, see Burn, *Beggar Boy*, 276, 337. Dance halls: Griesinger, *Lebende Bilder*, 237–244; *British Mechanic's and Labourer's Hand Book*, 73, and Foster, *New York by Gas-Light*, 72–81.

75. Stansell, *City of Women*, 95–96.

grants did often feel isolated. If they knew what things would be like "the first six months after leaving home . . . they would never come here," printer John Doyle wrote.[76]

After male workers had become accustomed to American conditions, high wages allowed them to live quite independently in good times, but the cooperation forced by Old World scarcity was less common. This was the negative side of high American living standards. Workers still faced seasonal adversity, but those workingmen who were recently arrived or felt shy and uneasy in the backslapping camaraderie of the saloon found themselves cut off from the working-class mainstream and had no guarantee of aid when out of work or sick. In 1848, new from England, immigrant Frederick Lockley found little help when unemployed. He did not find it surprising: "We had drifted away from our community and had not been taken up by the other community." As a common maxim about American social life in British immigrant letters held, "It is a free country if you have no shoes you can go without no one will trouble themselves about you doeing so." Among Germans the saying went that if you asked someone for help in America the response would be, as one immigrant put it, "Help Youself."[77]

Evidence of generosity and fellowship among workers indicates, however, that such opinions, though widespread, were not universal. Many male immigrants, like Thomas Chamberlain, who ran with a fire company within four weeks of his arrival in the city, fit rather quickly into working-class life. Working-class institutions were, after all, being created largely by the immigrants themselves and reflected their backgrounds and motives.

By the early 1850s, then, a coherent and satisfying institutional life had grown up in the city's working-class neighborhoods and found public expression in the Bowery. The totality of experiences—life in a boardinghouse, trips to barrooms and theatres, major boxing matches and political races—comes across in the extraordinarily nostalgic reminiscences of the city's volunteer firemen, collected by Augustine Costello in 1897. *Our Firemen* is imbued with an almost palpable sense of loss; Costello's interviews suggest that for many men, their service as volunteers was the most exciting and rewarding period of their lives.[78]

76. "Letter of John Doyle," 25 January 1818, in *Journal of the American Irish Historical Society* 12 (1913), 204.

77. Frederick Lockley memoirs, NYHS, 226. "No shoes": William Darnley, letter to his wife, 16 March 1858; see also Dallas L. Jones III, "The Background and Motives of Scottish Emigration to the United States of America in the Period 1815–1861, with Special Reference to Emigrant Correspondence" (diss., University of Edinburgh, 1970), 289, 292, and Mathews, *Pen-and-Ink Panorama*, 128–129. "Help Youself": Vetter, *Zwei Jahre*, 160; and Pankratz Settele, letter to his brother Franz, 20 November 1854, in Wolfgang Helbich, ed., "*Amerika ist ein freises Land . . .*": *Auswanderer schreiben nach Deutschland* (Darmstadt, 1985), 193.

78. Chamberlain diary, 22 June 1835. Costello, *Our Firemen*, especially 145–197. Tyler, *Reminiscences of the V.F.D.*, is also very nostalgic.

# CHAPTER 9

# Culture

The creation of Mose in 1848 was more than a landmark in the city's theatrical history. It symbolized a cultural change: the 1840s and 1850s saw the beginnings of a distinctive working-class culture. A precise description of this culture is impossible; the process of cultural change was of bewildering complexity, and the surviving evidence is often filtered through middle-class perceptions and consists of such diverse elements as speech patterns, songs, and jokes. But the subject is significant, and it is possible to illuminate some of the important characteristics of this new, class culture.

This culture differed not only from that of the middle class but also from that of the native artisan of the early part of the century. Howard Rock and Sean Wilentz have described the political culture of native, Protestant craftsmen, "self-reliant, respectable men" wedded to their trade and to the maintenance of virtue in the nation's political life. This native artisan culture resembled that of respectable London artisans; indeed, John Jentz labels it "Anglo-America" and points out the importance of the tavern and Blue Monday on both sides of the Atlantic in the 1830s. The artisan's parades described by Wilentz were based on English models, and Tom Paine was a hero in both London and New York taverns. However, though we know far less about early-nineteenth-century popular culture than about popular politics, it seems clear that artisanal life in the New World was always somewhat different from life in the Old. Labor scarcity eroded the traditional apprenticeship system; even in the colonial period many journeymen had not been formally apprenticed, limiting their loyalty to "the Trade." In addition Blue Monday was far from a universal practice in labor-scarce American cities.

These differences are considerable. Nonetheless, they do not invalidate the generalization that American artisanal culture was in some key ways similar to the English.[1]

New York's artisanal culture was undermined by changes I have described in earlier chapters, and especially by immigration. There was some continuity; labor scarcity, with the consequent fast pace and "abundance consciousness," certainly predate the 1840s. But there was also change. Immigrants adapted New World artisanal customs, modified Old World popular culture, and created new cultural forms appropriate to the changing conditions of urban life.

The changes transforming New York's manufacturing were part of a broad process of industrialization that occurred in both America and Europe. What was emerging in the city bore some resemblance to mid-nineteenth-century English working-class culture. The separation of work from residence, for instance, created separate male and female worlds not only among New York workers but within the British working class as well. But unlike English cities, New York had a tight labor market dominated by overseas immigrants with a distinctive age structure.[2]

Within the city there had long been a youth subculture among apprentices, unmarried journeymen, and especially sailors. Indeed, the sailors' subculture of the eighteenth and early nineteenth centuries and the working-class culture of the 1850s resemble each other in interesting ways. Sailors were mainly young males, and the significance of profanity and drinking among them, along with the unimportance of religion, corresponds closely with the life of the b'hoy. Evidence of direct linkages is scarce, but the Bowery dialect did include nautical terms—Mose "blowed" into saloons, for example.[3]

1. Sean Wilentz, *Chants Democratic: New York City and the Rise of the American Working Class, 1788–1850* (New York, 1984), 53–60; Howard Rock, *Artisans of the New Republic: The Tradesmen of New York City in the Age of Jefferson* (New York, 1979), 295–319; John Barkley Jentz, "Artisans, Evangelicals and the City: A Short History of Labor Reform in Jacksonian New York" (diss., City University of New York, 1977), 112–136. Apprenticeship: Samuel McKee, Jr., *Labor in Colonial New York, 1664–1776* (New York, 1935), 21–23, 85–88. On the weakness of Blue Monday, see Gary B. Nash, *The Urban Crucible: Social Change, Political Consciousness, and the Origins of the American Revolution* (Cambridge, Mass., 1979), 12.

2. Sexual separation between men and women in the English working class is discussed in Ellen Ross, " 'Fierce Questions and Taunts': Married Life in Working Class London, 1870–1914," *Feminist Studies* 8 (1982), 575–602; see also Paul Willis, *Learning to Labour: How Working Class Kids Get Working Class Jobs* (1977; rpt. New York, 1981), 43–47. Herbert Gans argues for the existence of a multinational working-class culture in *The Urban Villagers: Group and Class in the Life of Italian-Americans* (New York, 1962).

3. On sailors' subculture see Marcus Rediker, *Between the Devil and the Deep Blue Sea: Merchant Seamen, Pirates, and the Anglo-American Maritime World, 1700–1750* (Cambridge, Mass., 1987). For a fascinating account of the city's youth subculture early in the century, see William Otter, Sr., *History of My Own Times* (Emmitsburg, Md., 1835), 83–107. On sailors in New York, see Paul A. Gilje, "On the Waterfront: The World of Sailors and Stevedores in New York City, 1783–1834," paper delivered at the Organization of American Historians, 12 April

Only in the late 1840s, with the rapid increase in immigration and the growth of a working-class area of the city, did young males become peculiarly influential in working-class life. Large numbers of foreign-born workers in the labor force at this crucial period of industrialization ensured that American working-class culture would diverge significantly from that of other industrializing nations. Paradoxically, the influx of immigrants was creating something peculiarly American.

Similar conditions did not automatically create working-class culture. The precise creative process is obscure, but it seems probable that working-class institutions, especially the saloon and theatre, helped transmute environmental factors into a recognizable culture. Mose was the central symbol of this new culture; the dialogue between Baker, Chanfrau, and the audience created a symbolic representation of the young male worker. Mose simplified diverse elements and brought them into a whole; he explained to workers the logic and consistency of their world. "Never was there such a theatrical hit as Mose has made," the *Herald* reported, "the boys in the street have caught his sayings. . . . We were quite amused to see a squad of youngsters enacting 'New York as it is' on their own account."[4]

It is possible to describe some salient features of this emerging culture, despite its complex, protean nature. I divide the analysis, somewhat arbitrarily, into two parts. The first focuses on several diverse areas I call "style." The second part concentrates specifically on working-class speech.

## STYLE

The term "style" is vague, but basically it focuses on those qualities workers most admired, those they deemed most worthy of praise. Some evidence is contradictory, but such working-class heroes as Mose, Bill Poole, and John Morrissey had attributed to them enough similar qualities that we can discern a common cluster of values.

Abundance consciousness and the high-energy environment underlay the development of working-class style. James Burn was rather surprised when American workers openly taught him aspects of hatting he did not know. In Europe, employees tended to view their fellows as rivals for scarce resources, such as work. This slight undercurrent of suspicion in the Old World stemmed

---

1986, New York City, and Horace Lane, *The Wandering Boy, Careless Sailor and Result of Inconsideration* (Skaneateles, N.Y., 1839), esp. 103–107. Many volunteer fire companies had nautical names, among them *Black Joke* [a War of 1812 privateer] Engine Company No. 33 and *Oceana* Hose Company No. 15.

4. *Herald*, 26 April 1848; see also *Theatrical Biography of Eminent Actors and Authors* (New York, n.d.), cited in Walter J. Meserve, *Heralds of Promise: The Drama of the American People during the Age of Jackson, 1829–1849* (New York, 1986), 122.

from an awareness that workers were competitors, a view, in anthropologist George Foster's words, that one "can only progress at the expense of another."[5]

Such suspicion was absent in antebellum America. Almost everything about America was plentiful compared to Europe. One odd example of abundance consciousness concerns how whiskey was served in American saloons. According to Matthew P. Breen,

> when a man in London . . . or any other part of Great Britain or Ireland, steps up to the bar and asks for a drink of whiskey, the attendant keeps the bottle containing the stimulant in his or her own custody (you have lady bar-tenders), carefully pours out the drink from a regulation pewter measure, as if every drop of it was an extract from the golden fruits of the Hesperides; while in New York, and in every city, town, and village and hamlet in the United States, the bartender (never a woman) fearlessly, and with perfect confidence in human nature, delivers the bottle to the personal custody of the customer who, without let or hindrance, refreshes himself as suits his own taste and capacity.[6]

However, scarcity did create a unity among European workers—the way English workers cooperated to slow the pace of work is one example. Conditions of scarcity made necessary an interdependence of both workmates and neighbors—losing the benefits of community goodwill put a person in hazard. It made sense to aid others in need in the expectation that you would be aided when needy in turn. In such a situation, reciprocity and mutuality were in workers' self-interest; European workers were knit together by necessity.[7]

The situation in the New World was less clear. Prosperity did, to some degree, erode this interdependence; healthy male workers could live as individualists, and some certainly did—"Help Youself." Nevertheless, their high living standard was extremely precarious, and few workers could expect to go through life without a period or season of serious difficulty. It was certainly prudent to help others, and American workers did; Thomas Gunn described the "rough, careless, hardworking men" in a lower ward saloon as "always willing to assist one another when the occasion calls for it." But can such behavior be reduced to self-interest? It may well be that generosity was so highly regarded by New York workers precisely because it was less

5. George Foster, "Peasant Society and the Image of Limited Good," *American Anthropologist* n.s. 67 (1965), 294–295. American abundance consciousness seems related to what John Higham calls "boundlessness," see *From Boundlessness to Consolidation* (Ann Arbor, Mich., 1969).

6. Matthew P. Breen, *Thirty Years of New York Politics Up-to-Date* (New York, 1899), 255.

7. Michael Anderson, *Family Structure in Nineteenth-Century Lancashire* (Cambridge, England, 1971), 136–161; see also James C. Scott, *The Moral Economy of the Peasant: Rebellion and Subsistence in Southeast Asia* (New Haven, Conn., 1976), 26–28.

instrumental; almost nothing would have seemed more noble to economically minded immigrants than disinterested liberality. Biographies of working-class politicians often mention their generosity; in particular, Bill Poole was eulogized as "lavish with money" and "free and generous to friends." Dan Rice, the actor, although "rough in his manner and language," was "warm of heart. . . . No one who asked him for aid was refused."[8]

The ideal worker was vigorous as well as generous. Given the high energy level of working-class life, nothing would have seemed more out of place than a sedentary worker. Mose is portrayed in *A Glance at New York* as constantly on the move—running to fires, brawling, on a spree with Lize. Even his work involves perambulating the city with his butcher's cart. As described by Cornelius Mathews, "the b'hoys on a Sunday outing were always in a wonderful state of commotion . . . pushing and pulling each other freely and indulging in a good deal of vigorous horse-play." When they began dancing, "there is more muscle expended in one shuffle than in a whole evening of a fashionable party."[9]

Another quality deemed laudable was being "rowdy" or "rough." Of course there were "respectable" workers in the city. But in the 1850s young, often single, workers were demographically dominant, and their energy and rowdiness dominated working-class culture. Some evidence suggests that this situation changed as the remade working class matured. Dan Mulligan, though a brawler, was in other ways quite different from Mose: Mulligan was married, and the sketches were set in a tenement neighborhood rather than the lower wards.

Rowdiness partly reflects a youthful workforce, but it was also a *cultural* statement: it signified adherence to the working-class way of life and hence a form of egalitarianism. Workers felt no inferiority to "respectable persons" and thus saw no reason to conform to bourgeois standards of comportment. Pugilists held heroic status among workers, in part, because prizefighting rejected propriety so brutally.[10]

Rowdyism was perhaps even magnified, as a signal to outsiders that b'hoys did not recognize any superiority in middle-class standards of refinement. The b'hoy, George Foster wrote, "exaggerates the feeling of self-reliance so much to appear, on the surface, rude and boorish." In *A Glance at New York* one scene is set in a "female bowling saloon" whose members include "fifty ladies of the first families in New York." When Mose entered, disguised as a

8. Thomas Gunn, *The Physiology of New York Boarding-Houses* (New York, 1857), 114; *The Life of William Poole, with a Full Account of the Terrible Affray in Which He Received His Death Wound* (New York, 1855), 61, 66; unidentified clipping in the Dan Rice File, Harvard Theatre Collection.

9. Cornelius Mathews, *A Pen-and-Ink Panorama of New-York City* (New York, 1853), 88–89, 137–140; see also George Foster, *New York by Gas-Light* (New York, 1850), 74.

10. George Foster, *New York in Slices* (New York, 1849), 43.

woman, the audience gleefully anticipated he would not long respect the decorum of the establishment. Significantly, Mose *intentionally* reveals his identity:

> *Mrs. M.* You appear to be a stranger in our saloon, and I had no idea there were others.
>
> *Mose.* There's a lots ov 'em in de Bowery, beside a whole load ov 'em in Broadway.
>
> *Mrs. M.* I thought they were for gentlemen?
>
> *Mose.* Ov course dey are. [*Aside.*] I almost let de cat out ov de bag. [*Aloud.*] As I wus a sayin', I've seen de signs a hangin' out: dat's de way I cum to know 'em.
>
> *Mrs. M.* . . . What sort of a game do you play?
>
> *Mose.* Why, a fair game, ov course. Jest look a-here!
>
> [*Takes her around the waist and kisses her.*—MRS. MORTON *screams and shouts,* "A man!"—WOMEN *all scream*—HARRY *and* GEORGE *come forward.*]
>
> Yes, sir-ree, I am a man, and no mistake—one of de b'hoys at dat! [*Squares off.*][11]

The egalitarian strain in rowdiness is exemplified in the importance of a "fair fight." No one was more admired than a good fighter, no one more scorned than a fighter who tried for an unfair advantage. To gang up on someone or use a knife or gun was a clear breach of working-class ethics. Bill Poole's murder, while shocking in itself, was especially dastardly because Lew Baker violated fair play by using a gun. Poole himself, so the story went, allegedly adhered to the code by throwing away his gun during a brawl earlier in the evening and challenging Morrissey's lieutenant Mark Maguire, "the King of the Newsboys," to a fair fight.[12]

Workers themselves took great pains to ensure fairness. In fireman's brawls, "the boys of both companies stood by to see fair play." When the young John Kelly fought with another foundry worker during dinnertime, "the hands of the establishment finding the boys meant to fight undertook to secure fair play in the encounter," and fighting was not allowed while either of the boys was on the ground. Even theatre audiences got into the act— spectators sitting onstage halted the action of a New York production of

11. Foster, *New York by Gas-Light,* 105; Benjamin A. Baker, *A Glance at New York* (New York, 1857), 12.

12. William L. Knapp, *I Die a True American: The True Life of William Poole* (New York, 1855). Elliott J. Gorn, " 'Good-Bye Boys, I die a true American': Homicide, Nativism and Working Class Culture in Antebellum New York City," *Journal of American History* 74 (1987), 388–410, shows that this was a legend. The folkloric Mose would never use a knife or pistol; see Augustine Costello, *Our Firemen* (New York, 1887), 699.

*Othello* to ensure a fair fight. Only victory man-to-man, using fists (and occasionally teeth, elbows, and knees), brought honor.[13]

This egalitarianism, with its rowdyism and emphasis on a fair fight, suggests the strongly masculine nature of working-class culture—there was no mistake that Mose was a man. Peasant societies exhibit a clear gender division, and conditions in the city reinforced this traditional division among immigrant workers. In New York the separation was especially pronounced, because of the concentration of young males living and working in the lower wards. Male peer groups flourished, and loyalty to one's fellows became of paramount importance. Mose's loyalty to his friend Syksey is a constant theme of *A Glance at New York,* and the play ends with Mose's apologies for leaving, apologies he was confident his audience would understand: "Don't be down on me 'cause I'm goin' to leave you—but Sykesy's got in a muss, and I'm bound to see him righted, 'cause he runs wid our machine, you know." William Thomson, who visited New York in the 1840s, discovered that "amongst the working classes it is common, when about the same age, to call each other brother."[14]

This masculine quality is highlighted by the fascination California held for men in the city. California in 1850 had 85,580 men and 7,017 women, 45,144 of the men were between ages twenty and thirty. Like the city's lower wards, Gold Rush California was a male world (indeed, much more so), and as such it held a profound attraction. Alexander Saxton has noted this "dual relationship of city and frontier"; George Foster believed that the b'hoy's "contempt" of all things aristocratic made him indistinguishable from "the trapper of the Rocky Mountains and the gold hunter of California, . . . an unpracticed hand could not distinguish one from the other." "Oh! California! That's the land for me! / I'm going to Sacramento, / With my wash-bowl on my knee," sang Mose in *Mose in California,* second in popularity among the Mose plays only to *A Glance at New York.* Real-life working-class heroes from the city also made the trip. Not surprisingly, prizefighting was tremendously popular in California, and Hyer, "Yankee" Sullivan, and Morrissey all visited the West Coast.[15]

13. J. Frank Kernan, *Reminiscences of the Old Fire Laddies* (New York, 1885), 54; J. Fairfax McLaughlin, *The Life and Times of John Kelly, Tribune of the People* (New York, 1885), 17. The prohibition on fighting while down was part of London Rules. Lawrence W. Levine, *Highbrow/Lowbrow: The Emergence of Cultural Hierarchy in America* (Cambridge, Mass., 1988), 30.

14. On gender divisions among Irish peasants see Hasia Diner, *Erin's Daughters in America: Irish Immigrant Women in the Nineteenth Century* (Baltimore, Md., 1983), 19–25. Baker, *Glance,* 32; see also Foster, *New York in Slices,* 44. William Thomson, *A Tradesman's Travels in the United States and Canada in the Years 1840, 1841, and 1842* (Edinburgh, 1842), 32.

15. *Seventh Census, 1850, Statistics* (Washington, D.C., 1853), 966–969. By 1860 California had 259,923 males (86,340 aged 20 to 30) and 98,187 females; *Eighth Census, 1860,*

David C. Broderick was one of the "rudest, roughest, most aggressive and truculent" young men in New York City in the 1840s. A Ninth Warder, by age twenty Broderick, a stonecutter, was foreman of Howard Engine Company No. 15. Extremely intelligent and well-read, Broderick was a friend of Bill Poole, an excellent fighter in his own right, and owned a popular saloon. In 1846 he "threw his hat in the ring" (a prizefighting expression that came to be applied to politics), and became at age twenty-six the Tammany candidate for Congress from the Fifth District. Though he lost the election (in part because an "aristocratic Democrat" ran and split the vote), it was clear that by working-class standards Broderick "had it all." Yet in 1849 he sold his saloon and journeyed to California. The decision quickly paid off—he was extremely popular in California and achieved even greater success there than in the city. By 1851 Broderick was president of the California State Senate and by 1857 a United States senator. He was killed fighting a duel in 1859.[16]

Mose's close relationship with Syksey symbolizes the extremely strong bonds the world of the boardinghouse, saloon, firehouse, and workshop created among young men. Masculinity required an assertive heterosexuality—Mose's attentions to Lize are exemplary, and success with women was admired. "But," as Elliott Gorn has noted, "maleness seemed most emphatically confirmed in the company not of women, but of other men." Indeed, for many males, it seems, their deepest emotional attachments were to other men. An 1857 letter to the *Clipper* indicates the devotion volunteer firemen had for their fellows:

> There is no purer feeling kindled upon the altar of human affections, than a fireman's pure, uncontaminated love for his brother fireman. It is unlike all other affections: so disconnected with selfish sensuality; so great in its developments; so dignified, and yet so fond, so devoted, nothing can alter it, *nothing can surpass it.*[17]

Surviving letters between young male workers are very rare, but some of the existing examples reveal the depth of fondness men felt toward one another. The Henry Price diary contains two letters he preserved from George Birmingham, a bookbinder who had left New York to work in Buffalo. Birmingham tells Henry repeatedly how much he misses him and praises

---

Population (Washington, D.C., 1864), 592–593. Alexander Saxton, "Blackface Minstrelsy and Jacksonian Ideology," *American Quarterly* 27 (1975), 13; Foster, *New York by Gas-Light*, 101. Song "Mose's Farewell" quoted in Richard M. Dorson, "Mose, the Far-Famed and World-Renowned," *American Literature* 15 (1943), 291. Elliott J. Gorn, *The Manly Art: Bare-Knuckle Prize Fighting in America* (Ithaca, N.Y., 1986), 104–105.

16. Jeremiah Lynch, *A Senator of the Fifties: David C. Broderick of California* (San Francisco, 1911), 29. On Broderick see David A. Williams, *David C. Broderick: A Political Portrait* (San Marino, Calif., 1969), and James O'Meara, *Broderick and Gwin* (San Francisco, 1881).

17. Gorn, *Manly Art*, 142; George Fenner, Philadelphia, letter in the *Clipper*, 18 April 1857.

Henry's "Kind and benevolent, and I may say forebearing heart . . . I have been so used to talk our troubles and release our minds . . . [that] I find my selfe thinking about you half of my time." "Henry, I shall never forget you, and I can allways bring you to mind when I think of your kindness. I think of you every day." When George Foster was a journeyman printer, his letters to the young Edwin Griswold (later a noted editor) were similarly effusive: "I have never felt towards any human being—man or women—so strong and absorbing an affection as I bear you . . . I scarcely know what else to add— except that which you do or should already know—that my love, my *devotion* (we may both I trust use the word), is unaltered and unalterable."[18]

Such emotional attachments help explain the homoerotic element in working-class culture, and especially the interest in male physique. Elliott Gorn notes the extraordinary attention that mid-nineteenth-century prizefighting accounts pay to physique—extremely detailed descriptions of the combatants' bodies were virtually always provided. "Men perceived men as creatures of beauty," Gorn concludes, "because they focused so much attention on one another." Boxing involved strength and stamina, and so the attention commanded by the builds of Hyer, Poole, and Morrissey may not seem completely surprising. It is more difficult to find a logical reason for the public fascination with the physiques of Tammany Hall politicians. Tweed "possessed the physique of a young gladiator," John Kelly had "the thews and sinews of a young Hercules," Croker "a tremendously sturdy body, massive shoulders, deep chest, and powerful arms shaggy with black hair." Indeed, as this recital suggests, a fine build may have been a prerequisite for success in working-class politics.[19]

Intense same-sex friendships, attention to physique, and the lively horse-play of grabbing and slapping raise the question whether homosexuality was common among workers. Alexander Saxton has discovered veiled references to homosexuality in minstrel songs, but no other evidence speaks to this point. What is clear is that male workers focused intense emotional attention on one another, and many found their deepest sense of companionship among fellow

18. George Birmingham, letters to Henry Price, 28 September 1847 and 7 March 1846, "The Diary of Henry Edward Price," in *British Records Relating to America in Microform* (East Ardsley, England, 1963), 41; George A. Foster to Rufus Griswold, 30 September 1834, in Joy Bayless, *Rufus Wilmot Griswold* (Nashville, Tenn., 1943), 10, quoted in W. J. Rorabaugh, *The Craft Apprentice: From Franklin to the Machine Age in America* (New York, 1986), 104. These intense same-sex friendships between working-class men strongly resemble those among middle-class women described in Carroll Smith-Rosenberg, "The Female World of Love and Ritual: Relations between Women in Nineteenth Century America," in Smith-Rosenberg, *Disorderly Conduct: Visions of Gender in Victorian America* (New York, 1986), 53–89.

19. Gorn, *Manly Art*, 116–117; Dennis Tilden Lynch, *"Boss" Tweed* (New York, 1927), 33; McLaughlin, *Life and Times of John Kelly*, 17; Lothrop Stoddard, *Master of Manhattan: The Life of Richard Croker* (New York, 1931), 28. It is also possible, of course, that these physiques were attributed to politicians after they became successful.

males, as Augustine Costello's nostalgic reminiscences of volunteer firemen suggest.[20]

Masculinity was an essential part of working-class culture; indeed, working-class culture *was* basically male. The fellowship and strong bonds between workers created by the boardinghouse and saloon were sources of great strength. They were also, by excluding women, working-class culture's greatest weakness; it is no accident that the word "workingman" was the preferred term in the antebellum period. Despite this obvious limitation, however, "manliness" gave workers' egalitarianism a tangible edge. The camaraderie of the peer group could easily and naturally be turned against outsiders— "foo-foos," as Mose called them.

Loyalty of male peers, along with rowdiness and generosity, helped define the style of the ideal worker. Mose, Poole, and Morrissey embodied those traits and thus became folk heroes whose exploits passed into legend. Writer Herbert Asbury was able to collect Mose stories in New York early in the twentieth century. Twenty years after Poole's death, the *Saloon Keeper's Companion and Book of Reference* lauded him as "the champion exponent of native vigor and courage." Morrissey was celebrated in a ballad popular into the twentieth century, "Jack Morrisy and the Russian Sailor," in which the prizefighting hero triumphs over allcomers. Another song, "The Days of '49"—in which an "old timer" recalls his fellow goldminers—was popularized by California minstrels and also survived in the oral tradition into this century. The song seems to combine Mose with the tragic ends of Poole and Broderick to create an archetypal city worker:

> There was New York Jake, the butcher boy,
> So fond of getting tight;
> And whenever Jake got on a spree
> He was sp'iling for a fight,
> One day he ran agin' a knife,
> In the hands of Old Bob Cline;
> So over Jake we held a wake,
> In the days of Forty-nine.[21]

20. Saxton, "Blackface Minstrelsy," 11–13. On Costello see Chapter 8.

21. On the folkloric Mose see Dorson, "Mose," 298, which summarizes a letter from Herbert Asbury, and Asbury, *The Gangs of New York: An Informal History of the Underworld* (New York, 1928), 34. For another example of Mose folklore, see below. A. V. Newton, *Saloon Keeper's Companion and Book of Reference* (Worcester, Mass., 1875), 82. "Morrisy and the Russian Sailor": Gorn, *Manly Art*, 122–123. "Days of '49": *The Great Emerson New Popular Songster* (San Francisco, 1872), 53, quoted in William L. Alderson, " 'The Days of '49,' Reprise," *Northwest Folklore* I (1965), 7. This song passed from the minstrel stage into the oral tradition. In 1941 John and Alan Lomax recorded an almost identical version from John Galusha in upstate New York; see Lomax and Lomax, eds., *Folk Song U.S.A.* (1947; rpt. New York, 1975), 235. The song has been widely collected in the twentieth century.

SPEECH

This manly, egalitarian style was central to working-class culture and found its most distinctive embodiment in speech. The speech of workers differed from that of the middle class in a way that expressed fundamental values of working-class culture. I begin with an examination of New York dialect and slang and then explore the meaning of the way working-class speech was used.

Perhaps the most striking aspect of *A Glance at New York* is Mose's speech—he talks in what is clearly an urban working-class dialect. Chanfrau was widely praised for the verisimilitude with which he reproduced the b'hoy's speech. It is impossible, of course, to hear the dialect as used by Chanfrau. Instead, we have to rely on Baker's printed version of the play and other written versions of the dialect, the accuracy of which is hard to evaluate. Despite the difficulties, however, it is possible to discern the development of a working-class dialect in antebellum New York.[22]

A New York City dialect had existed since early in the century, if not before, and in 1840 the British Mechanic noted some "peculiarities of dialect" in New York, Boston, and Philadelphia; New York speech was "distinct in its character from all [other cities]." The context suggests he was probably referring to an urban rather than a class dialect. E. H. Babbitt, a student of the city's late-nineteenth-century speech, noted that the dialect was "most marked in the lower classes," so to some extent New York speech probably was a class dialect. In any case, in the 1840s there emerged a widespread comprehension that workers spoke with an accent distinct from that of middle-class New Yorkers.[23]

Early attempts to capture this vernacular depict it as either an Irish accent (as in Asa Greene's *A Glance at New York,* 1837) or simply "common" American speech—"knockin' down," "afore" (as in Cornelius Mathew's *The Career of Puffer Hopkins,* 1842). The literary portrayal of working-class dialect emerged as a minor genre in the late 1840s—examples include F. A. Durivage's popular poem "Love in the Bowery" in 1846, Baker's play *A Glance at New York* in 1849, George Foster's *New York in Slices* (which contains several examples) also in 1849, and *The Mysteries and Miseries of New York* by Edward Z. C. Judson ("Ned Buntline") in 1851. Unfortunately, though the timing of the appearance of dialect in published sources is precise,

22. On the accuracy of Chanfrau's performance see William K. Northall, *Before and Behind the Curtain* (New York, 1851), 90–91.

23. William Cullen Bryant, "Dictionary of the New York Dialect of the English Tongue [c. 1820]," *American Speech* 58 (1941), 157–158; *The British Mechanic's and Labourer's Hand Book* (London, 1840), 153; E. H. Babbitt, "The English of the Lower Classes in New York City and Vicinity," *Dialect Notes* 1 (1896), 459.

what the dialect actually sounded like is uncertain. Literary depiction of American dialect was in its infancy, and the evidence from these writers is confusing and sometimes contradictory.[24]

It is clear this dialect was presented as an *American* form of speech. The literature and the theatre of the period drew on American popular speech—especially that of the Yankee and the backwoodsman—and the speech of the b'hoy is depicted as a version of national speech. Mose's "seys," "goin'," "No, sir-ree," "just look a-here," and "How are you, old hoss?" mark him as a distinctively American character. Given the connection between the city and frontier, such language accurately captured Mose's affinity with men of the American West. However, Mose was also recognized as the product of a particular area of the city, and Mose's dialect is distinguishable from the frontiersman's, and from that of middle-class New Yorkers, as well: this was clearly a class dialect. Harry Gordon, a schoolmate of Mose in *A Glance at New York,* is a native New Yorker and wise in the ways of the city, but Gordon is not a worker and does not have a trace of an accent.

What did East Side dialect sound like? The literary evidence is ambiguous, but some distinctiveness can be detected. The speech of city workers was loud and fast; the *Clipper* mentioned the b'hoy "clipping his words and running them into one another." More distinctive was the dialect itself. Chanfrau's Mose, as transcribed by Baker, tended to pronounce /oi/ as /i/ as in "spile" or "bile" and usually substituted /d/ for /th/—"de," "wid," "dat." Other pronunciations are distinctive: for example, "fust" for "first" and "ingine" for "engine."[25]

There was, however, no great consistency in the characterization of city dialect. Indeed, without knowing the context it is sometimes difficult to

24. Asa Greene, *A Glance at New York* (New York, 1837), 171–172. Greene's New Yorkers also sometimes use common speech, e.g., "nothin'," see pp. 167–168. Cornelius Mathews, *The Career of Puffer Hopkins* (New York, 1842), 233; F. A. Durivage and George P. Burnham, *Stray Subjects Arrested and Bound* (Philadelphia, 1849), 107–108. This very popular poem was widely reprinted and even appears as a sidebar to the story of the Hyer-Sullivan fight under the title "Tom Hyer, in his Youthful Days," in the *Herald,* 9 February 1849. Foster, *New York in Slices:* on the background of this work see George Rogers Taylor, " 'Gaslight' Foster: A New York 'Journeyman Journalist' at Mid-Century," *New York History* 58 (1977), 302–303. Edward Z. C. Judson, *The Mysteries and Miseries of New York: A Story of Real Life* (New York, 1851). Judson began publishing this work (based on Eugène Sue's popular *Mysteries of Paris*) in installments in early 1848. *A Glance at New York* opened in February; Judson wrote Mose into the later episodes. When the installments were collected in 1851, the book sold a hundred thousand copies and acquainted Americans with Bowery Speech; see Peter George Buckley, "To the Opera House: Culture and Society in New York City, 1820–1860" (diss., SUNY at Stony Brook, 1984), 431–447; also Jay Monaghan, *The Great Rascal: The Life and Adventures of Ned Buntline* (Boston, 1952). Also, numerous examples of dialect are scattered through newspapers and magazines of the period.

25. Loud: Mathews, *Pen-and-Ink Panorama,* 138–139. Fast: "The Bowery and the Bowery Boy," *Clipper,* 12 May 1866. *A Glance at New York* was not published until 1857, so Foster and Judson could not have drawn on the printed version of the play.

determine in antebellum publications, on the basis of the language alone, if the speaker is black, German, or b'hoy. Baker made a consistent effort to capture Chanfrau's vernacular, but Judson's Mose, with the trouble he has pronouncing his /v/s—"wisit" for "visit" and "gi's" for "gives"—seems drawn more from Dickens's novels than the streets of New York. Twentieth-century New York dialect is marked by a high degree of variation between individual speakers, so literary inconsistency may reflect real diversity. More probably it reflects the absense of conventions to depict oral speech. However, the tendency of Baker's Mose to pronounce /th/ as /d/ or /t/ is significant, since it is an early example of part of the New York accent described by later investigators. According to linguist William Labov the /d/ or /t/ substitution for /th/ has "entered into folk mythology" as the hallmark of "working class and lower class speech."[26]

Babbitt attributes this characteristic pronunciation to a large foreign-born population that lacked the /th/ interdental in their native languages. Indeed, it does sound a bit German—*the* was sometimes spelled "der" in city dialect. Yet in this period the Irish were the largest immigrant group, and some of Mose's other pronunciations—"spile" for "spoil," for example—sound Irish. With a huge Irish-born population in the city, working-class speech must have had Celtic influences. Other than /d/ for /th/ substitution the continuity between Mose and the twentieth century seems rather limited. One principal part of later speech, the tendency to drop the postvocalic /r/—"New Yawk"—is absent from written versions of the dialect. Nevertheless, observers widely agreed in the 1840s that a new mode of speech was appearing, a mode distinctively working-class.[27]

Working-class idiom included not only a distinctive accent but also a large number of slang usages and terms. We are on firmer ground here since we do not need to rely on confusing phonetic spellings. Many of the slang terms used by city workers were used by New Yorkers generally, including adaptations of such Dutch words as "boss," "loafer," and "hunk" (safe and sound). But other slang terms were popularized largely by workers.[28]

Perhaps the most distinctive word to originate among the b'hoys was "gallus." Derived from the word "gallouses," suspenders (an important part

26. Variation: William Labov, *The Social Stratification of English in New York City* (Washington, D.C., 1966), 47–59. On the substitution of /d/ for /th/ see Babbitt, "English of the Lower Classes," 464; Alan Forbes Hubbell, *The Pronunciation of English in New York City* (New York, 1950), 34–38; and Labov, 28.

27. Babbitt, "English of the Lower Classes," 462–463. The spelling "b'hoy" may well indicate an Irish influence, but the original spelling was "bo-hoy"; see *The Knickerbocker* 27 (1846), 60.

28. The best sources for slang etymology are John Russell Bartlett, *Dictionary of Americanisms* (Boston, 1860), and William Craige and James R. Hurlbert, *A Dictionary of American English on Historical Principles* (Chicago, 1938–1944). "Hunk": from the Dutch word *honk* meaning home, especially as in home base in tag, Mathews, *Pen-and-Ink Panorama*, 208.

of a fireman's costume), it meant energetic or exciting. *"Mose.* Say Lize, you're a gallus gal, anyhow. *Lize.* I ain't nothin' else.'' Other slang terms have unclear derivations. "Foo-foos" are defined by Mose:

> *Mose.* [*To* HARRY, *pointing after* LOAFERS.] Them's foo-foos!
>
> *George.* What's foo-foos?
>
> *Mose.* Why, foo-foos is outsiders, and outsiders is foo-foos.
>
> *George.* I'm as wise now as ever.
>
> *Mose.* Well, as you're a greenhorn, I'll enlightin' you. A foo-foo, or outsider, is a chap wot can't come de big figure.
>
> *George.* What's the big figure?
>
> *Mose.* The big figure here, is three cents for a glass of grog and a night's lodging.

Mose was always looking for a "muss" (brawl), Lize's song was "slap up," while a coward was "spooney." Such terms were limited to New York City (the standard historical dictionaries give only city references). Though the use of these terms was not limited to workers, such words were regarded, as Mose and Lize attest, as characteristically working-class.[29]

By the 1840s, then, there was an increasing awareness of distinctive working-class speech. Though many older Irish and German immigrants continued to speak with a foreign accent (and some Germans did not learn English at all), Babbitt's research suggests that younger immigrants quickly learned to speak in a city accent and adopted slang terms, spurred on, no doubt, by the ribbing foreign accents received. Dialect and slang set off workers linguistically, just as the city's spatial reorganization set them off geographically. Indeed, it seems likely that the development of the East Side working-class area was a precondition for the emergence of this dialect. Working-class idiom testified to the separation of working-class experience from that of other New Yorkers. By differentiating workers from foos-foos, dialect increased workers' sense of distinctiveness and perhaps their solidarity.[30]

This discussion of dialect and slang does little, however, to enlighten us about how speech was *used,* about the content of working-class culture and its

---

29. Baker, *Glance,* 21, 16. Both "gallus" and "foo-foos" were apparently not used in print before *A Glance at New York,* see Bartlett, *Dictionary of Americanisms,* 166, 158. "Muss" was first printed in 1838 in the *New York Advertiser and Express,* Craige and Hulbert, *Dictionary of American English,* 1573. Both "muss" and "loafer" appear in the list of "American terms" in the Thomas Chamberlain diary, 18 June 1840, Rare Books and Manuscripts Division, The New York Public Library, Astor, Lenox and Tilden Foundations.

30. Babbitt, "English of the Lower Classes," 459. Theodor Griesinger notes that young German immigrants learned English easily, older ones did not; Griesinger, *Land und Leute in Amerika* (Stuttgart, 1863), 556.

meaning. We need to go beyond the mere existence of working-class speech and look at the way speech expressed a system of values.

At the heart of working-class speech was profanity and coarse humor. Norman Mailer has written that no one who has proclaimed the virtue of the American common man has ''ever mentioned that noble common man was as obscene as an old goat, and his obscenity was what saved him. The sanity of said democratic man was in his humor, his humor was in his obscenity. And his philosophy as well—a reductive philosophy which looked to restore the hard edge of proportion to . . . overblown values.'' Profanity was not exactly unknown in the Old World, but in the male world of the workshop and saloon profanity flourished to a degree that astonished observers.[31]

One surprised Irish immigrant described American cities in the 1860s as ''the most wicked place[s] I ever saw for Cursing Blasphemy.'' James Burn noted the same thing: ''One of the worst features in American society is the almost universal habit of using profane language.'' According to Burn, ''if a man wishes to give force to an expression, whether the subject of conversation be grave or gay, he is sure to fix it upon the attention of the listener with some foul phrase culled from the vocabulary of Billingsgate.''[32]

That immigrants found profanity more common in New York than in Europe is clear. But how was it used? Profanity, according to Leo Marx, represents the triumph of ''the earthy facts of everyday life over affected sentiment.'' Working-class discourse was largely oral, and unfortunately, but not surprisingly, surviving examples of profane speech are rare. Among them is evidence that supports the Mailer-Marx interpretation of profanity. Bill Poole's last words, as reported in the press, were ''I die a true American.'' Patriotic Poole no doubt was, but no true b'hoy would have expired with such melodramatic pathos. According to Charles Haswell, the word on the street was that Poole really said ''By ———, boys, I'm a goner!'' In one popular story, a stranger demanded of Mose, '' 'I want to go to the Astor House.' 'Well,' said Mose, without taking the 'Long Nine' cigar from between his lips, 'why in ——— don't you go.' ''[33]

31. Norman Mailer, *The Armies of the Night: History as a Novel, the Novel as History* (New York, 1968), 61. Mailer's argument is brilliantly elaborated by Leo Marx, ''The Uncivil Response of American Writers to Civil Religion in America,'' in Russell E. Richey and Donald G. Jones, eds., *American Civil Religion* (New York, 1974), 222–251.

32. Maurice Wolfe, Washington, D.C., letter to his uncle, 25 September 1863, quoted in Kerby Miller, ''Emigrants and Exiles: The Irish Exodus to North America, From Colonial Times to the First World War'' (diss., University of California, Berkeley, 1976), 811. James Burn, *James Burn; The ''Beggar Boy''* (London, 1882), 275. Burn, *Three Years among the Working-Classes of the United States during the War* (1865; rpt. New York, 1982), 69. William Thomson and Griesinger also noted workers' use of profanity, see Thomson, *Tradesman's Travels,* 33, and Griesinger, *Land und Leute,* 556.

33. Marx, ''Uncivil Response,'' 242; Charles Haswell, *Reminiscences of an Octogenarian* (New York, 1896), 498; J. Franklin Kernan, *Reminiscences of the Old Fire Laddies* (New York,

Profanity, when jocular, was a way of letting down barriers and strengthening camaraderie. More important, swearing was a way of deflating pretension. Workers insisted on, and expected, social equality. "The b'hoy can stand anything but affectation—on that he has no mercy," Foster wrote. Jack *was* as good as his master. This egalitarianism is exemplified by the popularity among workers of Robert Burns's poem "A Man's a Man for a' That." The last stanza summarizes Burns's theme:

> Then let us pray that come it may,
>     As come it will for a' that,
> That Sense and Worth o'er a' the earth
>     Shall bear the gree, and a' that.
> For a' that, and a' that,
>     It's coming yet for a' that
> That Man to Man the world o'er,
>     Shall brothers be for a' that.

This song was widely sung and the verses recited in saloons throughout the nineteenth century. It was also popular in the theatre—Dan Rice recited "Capital vs. Labor," a poem extolling the virtues of the working man and ending with "A Man's a Man for a' That," while Tony Pastor adapted Burns to the daily life of the city in his very popular song "Don't Despise a Man Because He Wears a Ragged Coat." Later in the century "John Henry," the "steel drivin' man," expressed the same sentiment in the vernacular, when in the famous folk song he tells the boss "a man ain't nothin' but a man."[34]

When genteel Victorian culture was at its height in America, profanity and humor were weapons to attack gentility and aggressively assert equality; as in ethnic humor, any assertion of superiority was ridiculed. Surviving examples of profanity are rare, but nonprofane examples exhibit the tendency to use humor to attack pretense:

A lady lately come out from England, in calling on a friend in New York, enquired of an Irish servant whether "his mistress was at home." Of course, no American dares speak of the "master" or "mistress" of a household. . . . No wonder the Irishman was indignant; but he speedily saw his way to revenge. "No ma'am," he replied, very courteously, "the fact is, *I don't keep one at present.*"

---

1885), 64. The Astor House was the most expensive hotel in the city. This joke is not in *A Glance at New York;* for another example of the anecdote, one that diminishes the class aspect by having the stranger want to go to Brooklyn, see *The Knickerbocker* 39 (1852), 95–96.

34. Foster, *New York by Gas-Light,* 105. The poem is included in virtually all Burns anthologies; the standard scholarly edition is James Kinsley, ed., *The Poems and Songs of Robert Burns,* 3 vols. (Oxford, 1968). "Bear the gree" means "win out." George Ade, *The Old-Time Saloon* (New York, 1931), 130; Maria Ward Brown, *The Life of Dan Rice* (Long Branch, N.J., 1901), 302–303; Tony Pastor, *Tony Pastor's Comic Songster,* (n.p., 1864[?]). On "John Henry" see Louis W. Chappell, *John Henry: A Folk-Lore Study* (Jena, 1933).

Affectation was attacked by reinterpreting context to focus on the concrete and palpable: "A richly-dressed lady stopped a boy trudging along with a basket, and asked: 'My little boy, have you got religion?' 'No, ma'am,' said the innocent, 'I've got potatoes.'" Both protagonists in these jokes begin their response politely, appearing to adhere to genteel discourse and thereby heightening the effect when, in Leo Marx's terms, "the earthy facts of everyday life" (literally so in the latter story) deflate pomposity.[35]

Food metaphors were often used by workers. Not only was food symbolic of a tangible, down-to-earth working-class outlook, but the high level of the American diet and its large amounts of meat, traditionally associated with masculinity, was emblematic of equality.

> *Mose.* Bring me a plate of pork and beans.
> [WAITER *is going.*] Say, a large piece of pork, and don't stop to count de beans.

This, one of the most famous lines in *A Glance at New York*, captures Mose's confidence and American abundance. Dan Rice once found himself in an informal acting contest with W. F. Wallett, an English comic actor who had "attracted the attention of the elite." After Wallett brilliantly and eloquently recited Shakespeare, Rice responded with

> Is that a beefsteak I see before me?
> With the burnt side toward my hand?
> Let me clutch thee! I have thee not,
> And yet I see thee still in form as palpable
> As that I ate for breakfast this morning.

When the Bowery Theatre manager asked an unruly, vegetable-throwing audience demanding the firing of an English actor in 1837 what the crowd wanted, he was greeted with the cry "Roast beef rare! No gravy."[36]

In their stalls at market or pulling a cart through the streets, butchers were among the most visible members of the working class. Their association with meat and the shedding of blood helped make the butcher the symbol of the New York worker: Poole was a butcher, and Baker made Mose a butcher in *A Glance at New York*. By shedding blood—not only in the market but also, as in the cases of Hyer and Poole, in the ring—butchers placed themselves totally outside respectable, genteel society. "*Mose:* What! yer don't know where de slaughter-house is yet? Well, drive up Chrystie Street till you smell blood, and dere stop." Mose in his bloodstained apron—a "little raw," he

---

35. John White, *Sketches from America* (London, 1871), 371; Newton, *Saloon Keeper's Companion*, 23.

36. Baker, *Glance*, 30; Brown, *Life of Dan Rice*, 172; see also Levine, *Highbrow/Lowbrow*, 14. "Roast beef rare!": Buckley, "To the Opera House," 188.

described himself—sitting down to "a large piece of pork" was an ideal symbol of the urban workers.[37]

It is even possible that, as Paul Willis has suggested for twentieth-century English workers, manual work itself took on a masculine connotation. Work in the city's shops and docks was hard, dirty, and sweaty, and American workingmen prided themselves on being able to do such work at the customary railroad pace. Mose's toughness stemmed from his ability to do the work itself as well as from shedding blood. Laboring with one's hands in a job too tough for women or genteel men may have infused manual work with masculinity. Unfortunately, the participant observation that Willis used is not available to historians, and given the absence of evidence this manual work–masculinity association must remain a hypothesis. It does, however, suggest the possibility that given the middle-class valuation of mental labor—"head work"—physical labor symbolized a manly rejection of white-collar values. Manual work might have been not a stigma or evidence of oppression but a kind of affirmation.[38]

The masculine, profane, tangible working-class outlook obviously constituted rejection of what David S. Reynolds calls genteel, "Conventional" sensibility that "valorized the home, good works . . . and Christian virtues." The main weapon was humor—"sarcastic, bitter, withering, relentless" humor. The main target of this rude wit was genteel sentimentality; such humor was not only unsentimental but *anti*sentimental, cynical, and often cruel. According to Ann Douglas the "archetypical . . . scene" of American Victorian culture was Little Eva's death in *Uncle Tom's Cabin*—pale Little Eva dies a lingering death, to the end a model of piety. Not surprisingly, this scene was relentlessly parodied—"What Kind ob cake is Little Eva?" Wood's Minstrels asked; "Angel Cake!" The cultural distance between Little Eva and Bill Poole dying with a curse on his lips could hardly have been greater. Even a novel like Solon Robinson's *Hot Corn* (1854), despite its urban working-class setting, is clearly within the Victorian tradition; it is unrelentingly serious and sentimental, and various young angelic heroines die lingering deaths.[39]

37. Baker, *Glance*, 22. According to Jacques Le Goff, the blood taboo made butchering in medieval times an illicit trade. Le Goff, "Licit and Illicit Trades in the Medieval West," in Le Goff, *Time, Work and Culture in the Middle Ages*, trans. Arthur Goldhammer (Chicago, 1980), 58–70.

38. See Willis, *Learning to Labour*, 145–152. Burn, *Three Years*, 11. On the middle-class valuation of head work and scorn for manual work in the nineteenth century, see Stuart Blumin, *The Emergence of the Middle Class: Social Experience in the Industrializing American City* (forthcoming).

39. David S. Reynolds, *Beneath the American Renaissance: The Subversive Imagination in the Age of Emerson and Melville* (New York, 1988), 182. "Sarcastic": Junius Henri Browne, "Printers—Their Character and Characteristics," *Packard's Monthly* 1 (1869), 67. Ann Douglas, *The Feminization of American Culture* (New York, 1977), 1–3. Wood's Minstrels

This unsentimental attitude is evident in working-class patriotism. Workers were extremely patriotic: the Fourth of July was the year's biggest holiday, and flags were commonly displayed in workshops and saloons. Female straw sewers, according to the *Herald,* were "exceedingly national and patriotic. . . . If the question of the annexation of Canada or Cuba were to be decided by them, it would not long remain unsettled." An Irish New York City policeman told English traveler John White how much the Irish loved America: "And why wouldn't they be pleased, I wonder," White continued. "Isn't it a country where there's equal laws for all, and a man may get a good living for good work." "A good living" was a major reason why America was so popular—"You can't be patriotic," explained twentieth-century Tammany leader George Washington Plunkitt, "on a salary that just keeps the wolf from the door. . . . When a man has a good fat salary, he finds himself hummin' 'Hail, Columbia' all unconscious. . . .'" This patriotism was unsentimental; few workers could have believed Poole really said "I die a true American." The sentimental variety was fair game: Dan Mulligan, on spying a statue of Washington, says "That's the man—when he was a boy [he] said to his father, 'Take back the meat ax I can't tell a lie. I broke the window with a brick.' ''[40]

Songs provide some of the best evidence of how workers used language and humor. Music was enormously popular among all classes in the nineteenth century. The reigning song tradition was genteel. Beloved examples are Thomas Moore's "The Last Rose of Summer" and "Oft, in the Stilly Night," Henry Russell's "Woodman, Spare That Tree," Samuel Woodworth's "The Old Oaken Bucket," Henry Bishop's "Home, Sweet Home" (perhaps the most popular song of the nineteenth century), and the songs of Stephen Foster. The most popular genre of "parlor songs," according to Nicholas E. Tawa, were love songs which depict a woman who is "pious, gentle, pure, sweet and graceful. . . . But regrettably her health is often poor," and she typically dies young, leaving the "loyal lover to lament nostalgically over her passing." By the 1850s such sentimental songs even made their way into minstrelsy, such as in the popular "Annie Lisle":

> Raise me in your arms, dear mother,
> Let me once more look,

quoted in Robert C. Toll, *Blacking Up: The Minstrel Show in Nineteenth Century America* (New York, 1974), 94. Solon Robinson, *Hot Corn: Life Scenes of New York Illustrated* (New York, 1854).

40. Flags: William Hancock, *An Emigrant's Five Years* (London, 1860), 61, and Andrew Bell, *Men and Things in America* (London, 1838), 31. *Herald,* 7 June 1853; White, *Sketches from America,* 371; William L. Riordan, *Plunkitt of Tammany Hall* (1905; rpt. New York, 1963), 56; Ned Harrigan, *Down Broadway,* quoted in Richard Moody, *Ned Harrigan: From Corlear's Hook to Herald Square* (Chicago, 1980), 52.

On the green and waving willows,
    And the flowing brook:
Hark, those strains of angel music
    From the choir above;
Dearest mother, I am going,
    Truly "God is love."

*Chorus*
Wave willows, murmur water,
    Golden sunbeams smile;
Earthly music cannot waken
    Lovely Annie Lisle.[41]

The songs most popular with New York's workers were very different. Sold as broadsides strung along the palings of City Hall Park, this musical tradition was described in 1867 by George Wakeman, in the magazine *The Galaxy*. The "love of the grotesque," according to Wakeman,

is illustrated especially in wild and astounding forms in the kind of literature to which I shall call your attention. It is a kind of literature, of which, perhaps, many of our scholars, clergymen, and cultured men, ensconced in classic halls, petrified in stately parsonages, or snugly housed in country villas, scarcely know the existence. It is co-ordinate with the language of slang, and it ramifies, with a wonderful circulation, all these channels of amusement patronized more especially by the lower classes of cities, and which are the peculiar delight of newsboys and bootblacks. . . . You will come across this sort of literature in "free and easys," at negro minstrel halls, and in publications under the title of "popular songs."

Wakeman then describes this type of comic grotesque song in some detail. Though the scene "will probably be laid in the city, yet there must be some reference to Hoboken, Jersey City, Communipaw, Weehawken, Staten Island, Coney Island, Gowanus or, at least, Brooklyn." The songs were extremely formulaic, and the theme usually "that sort of love the course of which runs exceedingly rough and tends to tragic terminations. . . . Suicide is the most common *dénouement,* and the different methods of suicide would furnish the sensation novelists with abundant material." One young man

41. A good survey of popular music is Charles Hamm, *Yesterdays: Popular Songs in America* (New York, 1979). The importance and diversity of music in the city's cultural life is emphasized in Vera Brodsky Lawrence, *Strong on Music: The New York Musical Scene in the Days of George Templeton Strong, 1836–1875,* vol. 1: *Resonances* (New York, 1988). Nicholas E. Tawa, *Sweet Songs for Gentle Americans: The Parlor Song in America, 1790–1860* (Bowling Green, Ohio, 1980), quotation 129. The text of "Annie Lisle" is in E. Byron Christy and William E. Christy, eds., *Christy's New Songster and Black Joker* (New York, 1863), 5–6. The rather mournful tune was later adopted for "Far above Cayuga's Waters."

stabbed himself with a boiled carrot, another shot himself with a codfish ball, a woman burned herself to death with a red pickled cabbage.[42]

"The writers of songs of this character," observes Wakeman, "take many liberties with our language." Interestingly, some of the liberties Wakeman notes are conventions of traditional broadside balladry: the "come all ye" introduction, the use of "for to" and other unneeded words to retain the meter, and formulaic adjectives: "briny sea," "gay young man," and so forth. In addition, the songs contained "all sorts of queer phrases" and were often written in a city dialect. "Blow me if I live long arter" one hero exclaims before cutting his throat with a piece of chalk. The "Peanut Stand" (Figure 25) was a popular example of this genre.[43]

Such songs were completely outside the genteel tradition. The topics were resolutely mundane—"The Gay Conducter on the City Railway Car," "The Soap Fat Man" ("who lived in Bowery Street near Grand"), "The Man who Set up the Whitewashing Business in a Cellar." But more than that, they consciously rejected and parodied the genteel song. The last stanza of the "Peanut Stand" is typical. It appears to follow the standard "lover dies of heartbreak" formula with the two ghosts hand-in-hand, but the last line demolishes incipient sentimentality with the ghost of the peanut stand. Like the jokes noted earlier, it appears to conform to gentility in order more sharply to undercut it. One Tony Pastor song starts with the conventional sentimentality of the popular Irish ballads of Moore and others: "Should e'er the Ould Sod be forgot? / Tho distant many a mile." The next two lines, however, use daily life to counter sentiment: "The nate pig-sty, the mud-built cot, / All in the rare ould style?"[44]

"My Helen is the Fairest Flower" became Pastor's "My Mary has the Longest Nose," and there are numerous other examples of such parodies. Temperance was almost always the subject of ridicule. "Woodman, Spare That Tree" became the minstrel ballad "Niggar, Put Down That Jug" (because it belongs to the singer), and the didactic "You Never Miss Your Water

42. George Wakeman, "Grotesque Songs," *Galaxy* 4 (1867), 789–791.

43. Ibid., 792–796. Numerous examples of this type of song appear in the minstrel and vaudeville songbooks of the 1860s, many of which were published by the New York firm of Dick and Fitzgerald. See, for example, *George Christy's Essence of Old Kentucky* (New York, 186[?]); *Bob Hart's Plantation Songster* (New York, 1862); and *Frank Converse's "Old Cremora" Songster* (New York, 1862).

44. Pastor, *Tony Pastor's New Comic Irish Songster* (N.p., 1864[?]), 8. Buckley discusses the importance of parody in the theatre and minstrelsy; "To the Opera House," 380–385. The most able theatrical parodist of the period was probably Irish-American playwright John Brougham. By the middle of the century his burlesque of *Metamora* had become more popular than the original Forrest vehicle. In *Po-ca-hon-tas; or, The Gentle Savage* (New York, 1855), Brougham included references to, among other things, lager beer, target excursions, Tom Hyer, and running "wid de machine" to ridicule the then-popular genre of sentimental melodramas about American Indians.

# The Peanut Stand.

Sung by L. Simmons, Ethiopian Comedian.

Air—"Joe Bowers."

Come listen to me, white folks, while I rehearse a ditty,
It's all about a nice young gal, she lived in Jersey City·
She fell in love with a gay young man, he was wealthy
    once in his time,
He was *chief engineer of a shoemaker's shop* and his name
    was Conny O'Ryan.

Now Biddy Magee was a handsome gal and known both
    near and far,
She kept a peanut stand in Jersey City and supplied the
    railroad cars;
But when her mother she heard of Conny, she swore
    vengeance against his clan,
She said if her daughter kept company with him she'd
    bust up her peanut stand.

Now Conny O'Ryan was a man of fame, and noted far and
    near,
He'd beat Saint Patrick at "forty-fives" a playing for
    lager bier;
He got in with a parcel of Jersey "roughs," they led him
    around like a toy,
So he joined the New York Fire Zoo-Zoo's and he went for
    a sojer boy.

When Biddy Magee she heard of this she took right to
    her bed,
The peanut stand went up the spout, and the gal she died
    right dead;
The news took effect on Conny himself, so he never could
    march to time,
So out of the camp in a very short time they drummed
    poor Conny O'Ryan.

The old woman's house is haunted now, at night about
    twelve o'clock,
She sees the most horrible sort of a sight, which gives her
    a terrible shock;
The ghosts of Conny and Biddy Magee come walking in
    hand and hand,
While right behind them comes marching along the ghost
    of the peanut stand.

FIGURE 25. "The Peanut Stand." From R. Byron Christy and William E. Christy, *Christy's New Songster and Practical Joker* (New York, 1863), 25–26. "Forty-fives" is a version of faro. The "Fire Zoo-Zoos" were a Zouave regiment raised from the city's volunteer firemen during the Civil War.

Till the Well Runs Dry'' was parodied with ''You Never Miss de Lager Till de Keg Runs Dry''; the line ''Waste not, want not is a maxim I would teach'' became ''Drust not, Jacob or you never vill get paid.'' Hymns were also the targets of parodies. ''There is a Happy Land, Far, Far Away'' became

> There is a boarding house
>   Right across the way;
> Where they have ham and eggs
>   Three times a day.
> Oh, how the boarders yell
>   When they hear the dinner Bell;
> Oh, how the eggs do smell,
>   Three times a day.[45]

This emphasis on parodies, oaths, food metaphors, and ''grotesque laughter'' resembles traditional European popular culture—there is a carnivalesque element here, a tendency perhaps strengthened by the traditional connection of carnival with meat. It may well be that the city's large numbers of immigrants drew upon Old World popular culture in the formative period of working-class culture in the 1840s and 1850s. Significantly, the *charivari* was used by city workers to protest poor boardinghouse food and abrasive boarders. It is difficult, however, to point to direct links or borrowing, only to a broad thematic similarity.[46]

Although the idea that popular European culture played a role is speculative, the evidence does suggest an emerging working-class culture. I do not suggest this new culture was entirely, or even largely, autonomous; the popularity of parodies shows a high level of awareness of mainstream culture. Similarly, Wakeman noted that grotesque songs, ''when presented in less questionable shapes, [are] often much relished by those who move in higher

---

45. Pastor, *Pastor's New Comic Irish Songster*, 12; Saxton, ''Blackface Minstrelsy,'' 11; *Gus Williams' Olympic Songster* (New York, 1857), 13. ''There Is a Boarding House'' quoted in Herbert Asbury, *Ye Olde Fire Laddies* (New York, 1930), 164. Asbury describes this as ''a famous, and very old, boarding house song.''

46. On European popular culture see Peter Burke, *Popular Culture in Early Modern Europe* (New York, 1978), and Mikhail Bakhtin, *Rabelais and His World,* trans. Helene Iswolsky (1968; rpt. Bloomington, Ind., 1984). It should, however, be noted that in Ireland, the source of New York's largest immigrant group, the carnival was not particularly strong. For examples of the *charivari* in New York see *British Mechanic's and Labourer's Hand Book,* 55–57, and Gunn, *Physiology,* 99–100, in which a boarder is serenaded with minstrel songs ''interspersed with howls.'' The *charivari* was also used during the Draft Riots, see Iver Charles Bernstein, ''The New York City Draft Riots of 1863 and Class Relations on the Eve of Industrial Capitalism'' (diss., Yale University, 1985), 53–54. Although direct links are rare, the popularity in New York of the English music hall favorite ''The Rat Catcher's Daughter'' suggests that grotesque songs found favor in this period with workers on both sides of the Atlantic; see Wakeman, ''Grotesque Songs,'' 790, and Olive Anderson, *Suicide in Victorian and Edwardian England* (Oxford, 1987), 207–211.

circles and possess refined and cultivated tastes.'' Surely, many workers blinked back a tear listening to ''Woodman, Spare That Tree'' and many ''respectable'' people chuckled at ''Niggar, Put Down That Jug.'' And workers certainly had no monopoly on profanity. But if it is mistaken to see impermeable boundaries between working-class and genteel discourse, it is also mistaken to suggest that profane, unsentimental humor was as characteristic of the middle class as of the working class.[47]

## MALE AND FEMALE

Neither urban working-class nor genteel culture should be studied in isolation. The antebellum period saw the coalescence not only of working-class culture but also of bourgeois culture. Perhaps working-class culture can be called masculine; certainly Ann Douglas labels the tenets of genteel Victorian culture ''feminine.'' In the emerging ''cult of domesticity'' the role of women was to remain in the home and raise children. The home thus became ''woman's sphere,'' and the definition of domestic ethical conduct her responsibility. Writers such as Catherine Beecher, Lydia Maria Child, and Horace Bushnell, and publications such as *Godey's Ladies' Book,* helped define genteel behavior and morality in the 1830s and 1840s. With other writers, such as Sarah Josepha Hale and the popular Lydia Sigourney, they were striving to create a distinctively middle-class sensibility.[48]

If this culture was not only middle-class but also ''feminine,'' then class conflict was also, to some degree, a gender conflict. Note again two jokes cited earlier—in one the target is a ''*lady* lately come out from England,'' in the other ''a richly dressed *lady*.'' Making women the butt of these jokes situated the target more clearly within the middle class. The working-class emphasis on manliness partly resulted from its conditions of existence, but the ''feminization'' of middle-class culture made masculinity an explicit class statement.

A masculine working-class culture and a feminine middle-class culture left working-class women and middle-class men in a liminal position. To suggest that working-class males and middle-class females experienced no cultural class-gender contradiction is not to argue that all individuals in those groups

47. Wakeman, ''Grotesque Songs,'' 789.
48. The standard sources on domesticity, besides Douglas's *Feminization of American Culture,* are Barbara Welter, ''The Cult of True Womanhood: 1820–1860,'' *American Quarterly* 18 (1966), 151–174; Kathryn Kish Sklar, *Catherine Beecher: A Study in American Domesticity* (New Haven, Conn., 1973); and Nancy Cott, *The Bonds of Womanhood: ''Women's Sphere'' in New England, 1780–1835* (New Haven, Conn., 1977). I am not suggesting that America was divided into working-class and middle-class cultures in the antebellum period. This was, after all, a predominantly *rural* country—what I discuss here is an urban phenomenon.

felt contented. Many women felt imprisoned by the cult of domesticity and tried to find ways to take part in public activities outside the home. Similarly, many working-class men, especially those who were ambitious, were repelled by the swaggering style and profane language of the boardinghouse and saloon. Yet the large number of intense same-sex friendships between middle-class women, and between working-class men, suggests that many in these groups may have found their lifestyle so attractive they had difficulty relating to outsiders.[49]

Working-class women were in a culturally ambiguous situation. A culture that stressed being "manly" as one of its highest attributes could hardly expect to receive undivided loyalty from working women. Women were usually separated from men at work and in most working-class social organizations, so there are strong reasons why women did not find this culture completely congenial. There is evidence, for example, to suggest women did not use profane language as often as men did. Virginia Penny noted that "some men . . . do not like to have women work in the same room where they are. They feel under more restraint, and not so free to say what they please. Such a restraint may be a wholesome one. Many women make the same objection in regard to working with men." It is unclear if Penny refers specifically to profanity, but she does point to differences in male and female speech.[50]

Women did use many of the same slang words men did. Lize pronounced things "prime," talked about "fellers," and declared Mose "gallus." However, Baker does not have her consistently use /d/ for /th/, and Lize seems to use fewer colloquial expressions. Since Mose himself sometimes says "the" and "they," this is not conclusive evidence that Lize's working-class dialect was less strong than Mose's. Yet this evidence, inconclusive as it is, fits with William Labov's research on twentieth-century New York City speech. Labov discovered that, though women talk in city dialect, they do not pronounce /th/ as /d/ as commonly as men. According to Labov, "the sexes are opposed in their personal attitudes toward the speech of the city, with men favoring it slightly, and women heavily against. . . . The masculine values associated with the working class speech pattern used by men do not seem counterbalanced by any similar positive values with which women endow their native speech pattern."[51]

Working women thus found limited attractions in masculine working-class culture. Significantly, Lize is a minor figure compared to Mose, and she does

49. Horace Greeley, for example, had little to do with the saloons and theatres and, according to James Parton, spent his evenings reading. James Parton, *The Life of Horace Greeley* (Boston, 1872), 89–98. See also the evidence on Robert Bonner below.

50. Virginia Penny, *How Women Can Make Money* (1863; rpt. New York, 1971), 372.

51. On women's use of dialect see *The Real Experiences of an Emigrant* (London, 187[?]), 78. Baker, *Glance;* Labov, *Social Stratification,* 310–313, 495.

not seem to have passed into the oral tradition. According to Christine Stansell, a workingwomen's subculture was beginning to develop, and later in the century, a single female worker's "world" of dance halls and other amusements and meeting places would grow up in New York. In the mid-nineteenth century, however, women were largely isolated in cultural terms. Grant Thorburn believed that among immigrants, most men were pleased with Ameria, but "it is very rare that . . . a *woman* ever got reconciled to or was happy in America." The improvement in living standards was pleasant, but culturally the situation was much less agreeable for working-class women. Some may have been attracted to feminine genteel culture; they attempted to culturally define themselves as women, not as workers. Burn believed "that there is more snobbishness among the various grades of females in America than there is among the same class in England." However, both limited incomes and status as workers outside the home made it virtually impossible for such women culturally to join the middle class.[52]

Their position was mirrored by that of middle-class men. In wealth and power, of course, such men dominated American society. Yet they also faced a cultural ambiguity. It seems unlikely most men could have found much amusement or interest in Fanny Fern or Lydia Sigourney. Many had lived in boardinghouses when single and were surely attracted to the masculine lower ward world that large numbers of single workers had created. They too saw the appeal of cultural gender solidarity. Advice manuals often warned respectable young men to resist the temptation: "The enticer will . . . take you . . . to the beer shop, and the oyster-seller. By degrees he leads you on till you find yourself in the billiard room, then the theatre, and probably next entering the door of her whose house is the gateway to hell." Despite the genteel disdain for saloons, theatres, and especially prizefighting, many middle-class men, and not just single ones, found these attractive, and middle-class wives had to struggle constantly to "domesticate" their husbands.[53]

In both working and middle class, men and women brought to marriage enormous differences in perception and expectation. The cultural separation between male and female workers was bound to cause misunderstandings, even incomprehension, after marriage; young men were torn between the home and the masculine world of the peer group and saloon. A single woman

52. Stansell, *City of Women*, 92–94. Kathy Peiss, *Cheap Amusements: Working Women and Leisure in Turn-of-the-Century New York City* (Philadelphia, 1986) describes the "homosocial world of working class amusements" and the later "emergence of a female audience," see esp. 142–145. Burn, *Beggar Boy*, 320; Grant Thorburn, *Life and Writings of Grant Thorburn* (New York, 1852), 195.

53. John Todd, *The Young Man* (New York, 1844), 133–134, quoted in Buckley, "To the Opera House," 333. Cott notes the "psychological distance placed between the sexes by sex-role stereotyping," *Bonds of Womanhood*, 190. Blumin, *Emergence of the Middle Class*, describes this struggle as an ongoing "battle to be won."

like Lize might enjoy a night on the Bowery and offer to hold Mose's coat when a brawl began, but after marriage and with a family things were different. When Anthony Street and Leonard Street Irishmen had a Sunday afternoon brawl, "a small army of women came in quick procession up Leonard Street, forced themselves in the midst of the belligerents and each seizing her man, dragged him from the crowd, and . . . succeeded in getting them fairly started toward their homes." The sense of longing many men felt for their days as firemen has been noted; often, it seems, marriage was unable to match the emotional intensity and excitement of unmarried life—many must have sympathized with Tony Pastor's lament "I'm not a single man."[54]

In the middle class the distance was also great. An 1856 play, *My Wife's Mirror,* by Edward G. P. Wilkins, playfully makes fun of the sexual gulf. Mr. Racket—the husband—is clearly middle-class, yet he obviously lived in an urban, masculine world before marriage and yearns for the "great times" of the club and enginehouse. His new wife he describes as "so etherial—a sort of crinoline angel." Mrs. Racket describes her husband as "poetic as the editor of the *Home Journal.*" The servant brings breakfast.

> *Mrs. Rac.* I had such a splendid chat [at a literary soiree] with that beautiful Graphnapkinzen. . . . He was exiled for his . . . attachment to the popular cause, and he seeks . . . a foreign land . . . where he hopes to taste ——
>
> *Rac.* Sausages!
>
> *Mrs. Rac.* Don't you like the German type of character, my dear? . . . If there had been no Germany we should have no Goethe.
>
> *Rac.* No lager beer. . . .
>
> *Mrs. Rac.* No Carl Von Weber.
>
> *Rac.* No symphonies in XX minor.

After breakfast Mr. Racket begins to read a cookbook. When Mrs. Racket asks what he is reading, Mr. Racket lies and tells her he is reading Longfellow. "*Mrs. Rac.* I thought so! You choose the delicate, heavenly aspirations of the American Tennyson. . . . Read to me a little of Endymion."

> *Rac.* [*Aside.*] Well, if I must . . . I think I remember a bit of Endymion.
> [*Opens the book and pretends to read.*]

> The Rising moon has hid the stars,
> Her level rays, like golden bars,
> Lie on the landscape green

54. Stansell, *City of Women,* 76–101, describes the relations between working class men and women. Baker, *Glance,* 31; *Workingman's Advocate,* 4 October 1834; Pastor, *Pastor's New Comic Irish Songster,* 14–15.

With shadows brown between
And silver-white the river gleams.
As if Diana-Diana-Di-Di-

[*Aside.*] Dem, di's! [*Closes book.*] Excuse me my love, I'm a little hoarse.
*Mrs. Rac.* Oh, no; your voice is so pure, so tender—it is absolutely tearful!
*Rac.* As if Diana-Diana—[*opens book very much confused*]—to make beef-
steaks with mushroom sauce!

Again we see the confrontation of gentility with daily life represented by food,
though this passage lacks the cutting edge of working-class humor—here the
man is as ridiculous as the woman. Mr. Racket believes the distance between
husband and wife is inevitable: "You take etherials and I take the solids—you
send me venison-steaks, and I will allow you to feed continually on Charlotte
of Russia." The scene ends in a formulaic "Grand tableau of reconciliation."
In the end the wife is victorious—the husband agrees to abandon his obsession
with eating—identifying the play with middle-class sensibility. The play
obviously is not meant to be a realistic comedy—both husband and wife are
absurdly exaggerated stereotypes. But it does suggest the distance between
gentility and the manly culture of the saloon.[55]

Despite complexity and ambiguity, then, there was a comprehension of
cultural difference between the city's working and middle classes. Cornelius
Mathews framed the issue this way: "Is human life, take it altogether,
happiest in Broadway or the Bowery? on the Aristocratic or Democratic side
of New York?"

In the one it's short-cake—substantial, but perhaps a little lumpish; in the other,
fancy tea-cake, with all sorts of caraway-seeds and dainty frost-work. . . . The
one looks to the useful—the other ornamental. The one is especially careful to
fill his belly—the other to illuminate his back. Light goods, of more show than
substance, are for Broadway wear—heavy, with a strong tendency to coarse-
ness for the Bowery. The one thinks more of homely virtues—the other of
elegant accomplishments.[56]

Although most in the Bowery seemed happy being workers, those who desired
upward mobility found that a cultural change was necessary to enter fully the
middle class. The sense of cultural difference is illustrated in an 1868 sketch
of Robert Bonner, the editor of the enormously popular *New York Ledger*.
While a journeyman, though his fellow printers "smoked and chewed and

55. Edward G. P. Wilkins, *My Wife's Mirror* (New York, 1856). "XX" is the classification
of strong beer.
56. Mathews, *Pen-and-Ink Panorama*, 130–131.

drank; he did not smoke, nor chew, nor drink. They went to the theatre, and spent their leisure time in idleness . . . ; he went to the prayer meeting, and spent his leisure time in solid study. . . . On the Sabbath they went on excursions to Hoboken, or roamed the city streets, having a 'jolly time'; while he attended church or read his Bible at home.'' Though Bonner was a journeyman, he was not a workingman; culturally he was middle-class, which no doubt helps explain his success.[57]

This cultural definition of class points again to the significance of the 1850s. It is not a coincidence that Walt Whitman, perhaps the nineteenth-century author who stood farthest outside the genteel tradition, emerged from the New York City of that period. David Reynolds has argued that Whitman (and other writers of the American Renaissance) used the "subversive humor" and "grotesque posture" (Reynolds's terms) of working-class discourse as a weapon against the oppressive literary influence of staid, genteel "Conventionalism." Reynolds, indeed, entitles one section "Walt Whitman, One of the B'hoys."[58]

Whitman extensively reshaped this discourse in his poetry, as Reynolds shows, and most city workers would have found the mystical, stylized *Leaves of Grass* a bit puzzling. Still, if Whitman was not "one of the roughs," as he famously claimed, he was at home in boardinghouses, saloons, and theatres. His celebration of the city's concrete daily life, and his homoeroticism and egalitarianism, touch on key aspects of working-class culture, and the distinctive voice that emerged in the 1850s stands in sharp contrast to the popular genteel poets of the day.[59]

The enormous changes that industrialization caused in New York combined with massive immigration to remake the city's working class in the fifteen years before the Civil War. The development of a working-class area on Manhattan, the core of an industrial region, had allowed workers to create a culture that differed from both the native artisans of the 1820s and 1830s and

57. Olive Dyer, ''Robert Bonner and the New York Ledger,'' *Packard's Monthly* 1 (1868), 17. George W. Swartz, a carpenter in Brooklyn in the late 1840s, was another worker who adhered to genteel standards and, like Bonner, was rewarded. Swartz became a boss and, though his success was far more modest than Bonner's, proudly informed readers of his autobiography that ''I have been all my life a strict temperance man . . . [and] I have never been to the theatre but once''; Swartz, *Autobiography of an American Mechanic* (Philadelphia, 1895), 60.

58. Reynolds, *Beneath the American Renaissance,* 508–516. I am skeptical of Reynolds's argument that Whitman was trying to ''rescue'' the b'hoy from ''becoming simply a frolicsome character in American humor,'' but Reynolds does show how Whitman drew in his work on popular humor.

59. George Santayana called Whitman ''the one American writer who has left the genteel tradition entirely behind.'' Santayana, ''The Genteel Tradition in American Philosophy,'' in Douglas Wilson, ed., *The Genteel Tradition: Nine Essays by George Santayana* (Cambridge, Mass., 1976), 52.

the middle class. Mose symbolized this emergence. The theatrical character soon faded from the city's stages, but his culture's memory proved longer-lived. Walt Whitman's poetry captures something of that cultural significance in "Song of the Broad Axe" (1856):

> Where no monuments exist to heroes,
> but in common words and deeds. . . ,
> There the Great City stands.

# Appendixes

# *Appendix A*

# Workers' First-Person Accounts of Antebellum New York Life

This book is based in part on the letters, diaries, and reminiscences of antebellum New York City workers. A complete list of these sources appears at the end of this appendix; it does not include immigrant guidebooks (unless combined with a first-person account) or travelers' accounts of the city.

The most common type of account I used is the published reminiscence.

| | |
|---|---|
| Published reminiscences | 22 |
| Letters, series | 19 |
| Unpublished reminiscences | 9 |
| Diaries | 6 |

Published reminiscences vary enormously in usefulness. Many are the narratives of emigrants who returned to England, such as James Burn and the English Workman. Wilbur Shepperson, who has studied many of these accounts, suggests they were a minor literary genre, a subfield of the vast travel literature. There is little evidence, however, that they influenced one another; they seem to be genuine first-person accounts. Because most were written by returnees, these accounts, like travelers' narratives generally, are usually not particularly favorable to life and work in America. Nevertheless, only the English Workman wrote specifically to discourage emigration, and even his book is not completely negative. Many writers seem to have written their articles and books simply as a way of making a few pounds after returning to Britain. They often contrast English and American working-class life.[1]

1. Wilbur Shepperson, *Emigration and Disenchantment* (Norman, Okla., 1965).

The next most common source is letters. The Darnley and Kerr collections contain numerous letters, but most have only a single item. The veracity of these letters is discussed in Chapter 3—contrary to popular belief, they do not invariably portray America as the Promised Land. Letters from Irish immigrants proved the best source on that immigrant group, since Irishmen so seldom published reminiscences.

The next most numerous evidence is diaries. About 90 percent of diary entries deal with the weather and personal affairs that matter little to social historians. The other 10 percent is quite useful, often giving information on the writer's work and sometimes on housing and diet. I also found nine unpublished reminiscences, often written for family and children. Unlike their published counterparts, they were often written many years after the experiences they recount.

What trades were the writers employed in?

| | |
|---|---|
| Printing | 10 |
| Building | 9 |
| Metals | 4 |
| Cabinetmaking | 4 |
| Clothing | 3 |
| Shipbuilding | 3 |
| Other | 22 |
| Unknown | 1 |

Printers were clearly overrepresented among the documents I had. Printers' autobiographies were a well-established genre, of which Benjamin Franklin's is the most famous example. In addition, a printer who returned to Britain was in a position to get his account published. Unskilled workers are clearly underrepresented—there are only two laborers (and the identification of one is uncertain). There are also relatively few clothing workers, largely because I could find so few women's accounts—only 3 out of 56. For the same reason, there are only two servants. Although unskilled workers are clearly underrepresented, most workers were not unskilled, and the city's largest crafts are all represented. Printing was one of the bigger occupational groups, as were metals and the building trades.

What were their nationalities?

| | |
|---|---|
| English | 20 |
| Irish | 13 |
| Native-born | 13 |
| German | 7 |
| Unknown | 2 |
| Scottish | 1 |

English workers predominate in published narratives, while the Irish are strongest in the letters. Native workers' accounts, despite a strong numerical showing, are often rather disappointing. Many were written years later, and of course, they could not make the sharp Old World–New World contrasts that make immigrants' accounts so interesting. One important question concerns the literacy of the immigrants. Might the relative scarcity of first-person accounts from Irish immigrants be because few could read and write? Apparently not—the overwhelming majority of Irish immigrants were literate. Arnold Schrier estimates that about 70 percent of the Irish population in the 1850s could read and write, and the 1855 New York State Census shows illiteracy rates below 10 percent for Irishmen, though a somewhat higher rate for Irishwomen. However, most of the letters I have seen are rather well-written, which reinforces the impression that poorer and less-educated workers are rarely to be found writing first-person accounts.[2]

What period do the narratives and letters focus on?

| | |
|---|---|
| 1810s | 5 |
| 1820s | 4 |
| 1830s | 14 |
| 1840s | 13 |
| 1850s | 15 |
| 1860s | 5 |

Despite the huge increase in immigration and city population in the 1840s and 1850s, my sample favors the 1830s, mainly because published accounts, which are more accessible, were more numerous in earlier years. As emigration swelled and letters from immigrants increased, accounts of America became less novel and hence, perhaps, less worthy of publication. Letters from emigrants published in the *Scotsman* (Edinburgh) seem to appear almost in inverse proportion to numbers leaving.

Perhaps the two most useful sources are James Burn and the British Mechanic. Burn's 1882 revision of his autobiography, *James Burn; The "Beggar Boy"* (first published in 1855), is very interesting, more so than *Three Years among the Working-Classes in the United States during the War* (1865). "*Beggar Boy*" discusses the workplace in much more detail, and Burn's view of America seems rather more favorable in 1882 than 1865; the earlier work perhaps reflects the tension in British-American relations during the Civil War. In 1981, the 1855 version of "*Beggar Boy*" was republished with an introduction by David Vincent. Vincent, though of the opinion that the 1855 edition is superior to that of 1882, finds Burn an accurate observer. "*Beggar*

---

2. Arnold Schrier, *Ireland and the American Emigration* (Minneapolis, 1958), 22.

*Boy*," Vincent believes, is the most consistently interesting of all nineteenth-century English working-class autobiographies.[3]

*The British Mechanic's and Labourer's Hand Book* (1840) is also very valuable. Though it is a treatment of general American conditions, the author admits the "observations apply more to the city and state of New York, and the manufacturing places in its vicinity, than to other parts of the union." He defends this focus by arguing that New York's "modes, opinions, and general management materially influence the whole of the Union." The British Mechanic treats working-class life in some detail; barrooms and boardinghouses are each given a chapter. He even explains how to meet girls in 1830s' New York (go to a dance hall). His eight chapters on the status of trades in the city are helpful, though possibly optimistic even if we take into account that the bulk of the information was compiled before the Panic of 1837. His own trade is unclear, but the extraordinary detail in his description of American lithography suggests he may have been employed in that craft.

This brief survey of the evidence makes it clear that the worker who left a written record, or at least a written record I could find, was not typical: he was likely to be skilled, English, and male. Workers nevertheless wrote these reminiscences, letters, and diaries, and this is their value. I obviously wanted more letters from Irish laborers and servants, but a researcher interested in the everyday life of working people in antebellum America has to take what he or she can get. What I had is atypical, and I made a special effort to pay attention to women workers and laborers. Nevertheless, the basic outlook presented in the first-person evidence I found is, inevitably, that of the skilled, male worker.

3. David Vincent, "Introduction," in James Burn, *The Autobiography of a Beggar Boy* (1855; rpt. London, 1981), 1–33.

TABLE 25

Reminiscences, diaries, and letters of immigrant workers (in chronological order)

| Name | Nationality | Type of Document | Period* | Occupation |
|---|---|---|---|---|
| David Bruce | N | UR | 1810–30 | Typecaster |
| Elisha Blossom | ? | D | 1811–18 | Shipwright |
| Thurlow Weed | N | PR | 1810s | Printer |
| John Ford | E | L | 1816–23 | Blockmaker |
| John Doyle | I | L | 1818 | Printer |
| "Caleb Snug" | N | PR | 1820s | Carriagemaker |
| Robert Taylor | N | D | 1815–46 | Cooper |
| John Parks | E | L | 1827 | Carpenter |
| William McLurg | I | L | 1827–36 | Sawyer |
| Benjamin Tilt | E | L | 1830 | Weaver |
| John Petheram | E | UR | 1830–31 | Chemist |
| C. Hermitage | E | L | 1832 | Laborer |
| John Harold | E | D | 1832–33 | Watchmaker |

TABLE 25—*continued*

| Name | Nationality | Type of Document | Period* | Occupation |
|---|---|---|---|---|
| Brown Thurston | N | UR | 1834 | Printer |
| Robert Brownlee | S | UR | 1836 | Stonecutter |
| Samuel Warshinge | N | D | 1832–42 | Shipwright |
| John Gough | E | PR | 1830s | Bookbinder |
| Horace Greeley | N | PR | 1830s | Printer |
| "Frank Harley" | N | PR | 1830s | Shipbuilder |
| Henry Walter | E | UR | 1830s | Man. jeweler |
| Anonymous Cabinetmaker | E | PR | 1830s | Cabinetmaker |
| "British Mechanic" | E | PR | 1830s | Lithographer? |
| Samuel Fogarty | I | L | 1839 | Carpenter |
| Stephen Tucker | ? | UR | 1840s | Machinist |
| Thomas Chamberlain | I | D | 1835–53 | Printer |
| William Thomson | E | PR | 1840–42 | Carpetweaver |
| Henry Price | E | UR | 1840s | Varnisher |
| Christoph Vetter | G | PR | 1840s | Teacher, Painter |
| James Toal | I | L | 1845 | Baker? |
| Brewster Maverick | N | D | 1847 | Printer |
| John Kerr | I | L | 1847–48 | Machinist |
| John Burke | I | UR | 1847–90 | Shoemaker |
| Thomas Garry | I | L | 1848 | Laborer? |
| Frederick Lockley | E | UR | 1848 | Butcher |
| Eliza Quin | I | L | 1848 | Servant? |
| George Swartz | N | PR | 1848–50 | Carpenter |
| Margaret MCarthy | I | L | 1850 | Servant |
| Charles Steinway | G | L | 1852 | Pianomaker |
| "New Yorker" | I | L | 1852 | Boxmaker |
| Ernest Hagen | G | PR | 1850s | Cabinetmaker |
| Alfred Green | E | L | 1857 | Brushmaker |
| John Morrow | N | PR | 1850s | Furnituremaker |
| Charles Porter | N | PR | 1850s | Machinist |
| Henry Brokmeyer | G | PR | 1850s | Currier |
| "English Workman" | E | PR | 1850s | ? |
| William Darnley | E | L | 1857–63 | Housepainter |
| J. B. Graham | N | PR | 1858–60 | Printer |
| Anonymous Proofreader | E | PR | 1859 | Proofreader |
| Henry Miller | G | L | 1859 | Stonecutter |
| Mary Brown | I | L | 1859 | Dressmaker? |
| Conrad Carl | G | PR | 1850s | Tailor |
| James Burn | E | PR | 1862–64 | Hatter |
| Friedrich Jeitt | G | L | 1862 | Saddler |
| Robert Crowe | E | PR | 1860s | Tailor |
| Samuel Gompers | E | PR | 1860s | Cigarmaker |
| Frank Roney | I | PR | 1860s | Molder |

E = English, I = Irish, N = Native, G = German, S = Scottish
PR = Published reminiscence, UR = Unpublished reminiscence (or not intended for publication), D = Diary, L = Letter(s)
*The period in the document in which the author lived in New York City.

*Appendix B*

New York City manufacturing, by ward, 1850 and 1860

| Ward | No. of Firms | No. of Workers | Avg. Firm Size | Avg. Capital per Firm in $ | Avg. Capital per Worker in $ | Value added per Worker in $ |
|---|---|---|---|---|---|---|
| | | | **1850** | | | |
| 1 | 137 | 9,976 | 73 | 7,200 | 99 | 188 |
| 2 | 854 | 36,671 | 43 | 12,800 | 298 | 426 |
| 4 | 191 | 2,802 | 15 | 8,800 | 602 | 731 |
| 5 | 82 | 2,204 | 27 | 15,100 | 561 | 636 |
| 6 | 157 | 3,724 | 24 | 7,500 | 316 | 672 |
| 7 | 422 | 5,924 | 14 | 3,900 | 280 | 527 |
| 8 | 232 | 2,793 | 12 | 3,900 | 325 | 693 |
| 9 | 189 | 2,434 | 13 | 4,200 | 328 | 732 |
| 10 | 97 | 1,035 | 11 | 3,200 | 299 | 713 |
| 11 | 150 | 4,446 | 30 | 14,400 | 484 | 654 |
| 13 | 172 | 1,291 | 8 | 3,200 | 428 | 711 |
| 14 | 72 | 1,527 | 21 | 14,300 | 672 | 1,023 |
| 15 | 93 | 1,176 | 13 | 11,200 | 889 | 793 |
| 16 | 129 | 2,654 | 21 | 10,700 | 521 | 794 |
| 17 | 140 | 1,435 | 10 | 9,600 | 937 | 508 |
| 18 | 198 | 2,720 | 14 | 6,100 | 446 | 647 |
| 19 | 42 | 668 | 16 | 10,300 | 650 | 610 |
| TOTALS | 3,364 | 83,480 | 25 | 8,900 | 359 | 503 |
| | | | **1860** | | | |
| 2 | 847 | 18,883 | 22 | 13,900 | 622 | 681 |
| 3 | 130 | 11,642 | 90 | 30,200 | 337 | 410 |
| 4 | 75 | 2,743 | 36 | 47,100 | 1,228 | 1,718 |
| 5 | 80 | 2,584 | 32 | 30,700 | 949 | 1,397 |
| 6 | 175 | 5,483 | 31 | 13,500 | 431 | 526 |
| 7 | 387 | 4,937 | 13 | 9,400 | 741 | 983 |
| 8 | 396 | 6,014 | 15 | 10,600 | 698 | 897 |
| 9 | 253 | 3,501 | 14 | 10,300 | 762 | 984 |
| 10 | 98 | 1,025 | 10 | 6,400 | 612 | 875 |
| 11 | 260 | 3,704 | 14 | 12,700 | 890 | 872 |
| 13 | 150 | 1,911 | 13 | 9,800 | 772 | 811 |
| 14 | 318 | 7,596 | 24 | 13,400 | 563 | 722 |
| 15 | 90 | 1,591 | 18 | 6,100 | 345 | 829 |
| 16 | 163 | 2,428 | 15 | 10,800 | 725 | 1,037 |
| 17 | 127 | 1,984 | 16 | 17,300 | 1,107 | 891 |
| 18 | 179 | 4,276 | 24 | 28,800 | 1,207 | 847 |
| 19 | 58 | 930 | 16 | 19,300 | 1,205 | 1,051 |
| 20 | 273 | 3,208 | 12 | 8,300 | 713 | 867 |
| 21 | 105 | 1,443 | 14 | 8,200 | 595 | 769 |
| 22 | 71 | 2,049 | 29 | 20,700 | 716 | 487 |
| TOTALS | 4,355 | 89,485 | 21 | 14,900 | 679 | 759 |

*Note:* In both years Ward Twelve was excluded since it consisted of the portion of New York County outside the city. In 1850 Ward Three was missing. In 1860 Ward One was missing and Ward Nineteen was incomplete.

*Sources:* Census Office, *Seventh Census, Manufactures, 1850,* Manuscript; Census Office, *Eighth Census, 1860, Manufactures.*

*Appendix C*

Immigration to the United States, 1821 to 1860

| Year | N | To New York City (percent) | Irish (percent) | German (percent) |
|------|------|------|------|------|
| 1821 | 11,664 | 34.7% | 25.6% | 6.6% |
| 1822 | 8,549 | 48.1 | 51.3 | 3.3 |
| 1823 | 8,265 | 54.1 | 47.5 | 4.6 |
| 1824 | 9,637 | 50.8 | 47.2 | 4.6 |
| 1825 | 12,858 | 59.6 | 57.2 | 5.3 |
| 1826 | 13,908 | 49.7 | 55.5 | 5.2 |
| 1827 | 21,777 | 57.9 | 58.4 | 2.6 |
| 1828 | 30,184 | 65.8 | 50.5 | 7.5 |
| 1829 | 24,513 | 60.4 | 59.2 | 4.8 |
| 1830 | 24,837 | 55.4 | 37.7 | 27.4 |
| 1831 | 23,880 | 45.0 | 44.3 | 18.5 |
| 1832 | 54,351 | 53.2 | 36.4 | 29.8 |
| 1833 | 59,925 | — | 29.7 | 24.0 |
| 1834 | 67,948 | 65.8 | 42.6 | 30.8 |
| 1835 | 48,716 | 67.8 | 49.8 | 19.8 |
| 1836 | 80,972 | 67.1 | 43.4 | 29.4 |
| 1837 | 84,959 | 60.8 | 40.1 | 33.4 |
| 1838 | 45,159 | 55.2 | 37.1 | 34.3 |
| 1839 | 74,666 | 63.8 | 37.4 | 32.8 |
| 1840 | 92,207 | 65.7 | 49.2 | 37.1 |
| 1841 | 87,805 | 63.6 | 49.6 | 20.1 |
| 1842 | 110,980 | 66.7 | 51.4 | 20.4 |
| 1843 | 56,529 | 68.9 | 40.1 | 29.5 |
| 1844 | 84,764 | 70.5 | 44.8 | 27.7 |
| 1845 | 119,896 | 63.8 | 41.0 | 31.4 |
| 1846 | 158,649 | 62.3 | 35.4 | 39.3 |
| 1847 | 239,482 | 60.9 | 46.1 | 32.4 |
| 1848 | 229,483 | 70.2 | 51.8 | 26.8 |
| 1849 | 229,683 | 71.3 | 55.6 | 21.0 |
| 1850 | 315,334 | 58.6 | 53.2 | 25.6 |
| 1851 | 408,828 | 72.0 | 59.9 | 19.6 |
| 1852 | 397,343 | 76.3 | 44.0 | 40.3 |
| 1853 | 400,982 | 73.5 | 45.0 | 39.3 |
| 1854 | 460,474 | 71.2 | 25.0 | 53.0 |
| 1855 | 230,476 | 70.0 | 26.4 | 38.3 |
| 1856 | 200,346 | 70.8 | 29.2 | 38.1 |
| 1857 | 251,306 | 73.1 | 25.1 | 42.4 |
| 1858 | 123,126 | 63.8 | 24.1 | 40.7 |
| 1859 | 121,282 | 65.4 | 31.7 | 37.7 |
| 1860 | 153,640 | 68.4 | 34.4 | 38.7 |

*Sources:* Numbers landing between 1821 and 1855 from William Bromwell, *History of Immigration to the United States* (New York, 1856); numbers landing 1856 to 1860 from Bureau of the Census, *Historical Statistics of the United States, Colonial Times to 1970* (Washington, D.C., 1975). Percentage landing in New York 1821 to 1855 in Bromwell, 1856 to 1860 in Robert Ernst, *Immigrant Life in New York City, 1825–1863* (1949; rpt. New York, 1979), 198. Percentage Irish and German from *Historical Statistics of the United States.*

*Appendix D*

Deathrate per thousand in New York City, 1820 to 1864

| Year | Avg. No. of Deaths per Year | Deathrate per Thousand | | |
|---|---|---|---|---|
| | | < 5 Years | > 5 Years | Total |
| 1820–24 | 3,406 | 71.6 | 16.8 | 27.1 |
| 1825–29 | 4,783 | 76.7 | 17.8 | 28.8 |
| 1830–34 | 7,022 | 102.4 | 20.9 | 35.6 |
| 1835–39 | 7,437 | 93.4 | 14.1 | 27.6 |
| 1840–44 | 8,197 | 85.5 | 13.3 | 26.2 |
| 1845–49 | 14,579 | 119.3 | 21.8 | 39.3 |
| 1850–54 | 20,968 | 165.8 | 19.4 | 40.7 |
| 1855–59 | 21,439 | 140.7 | 14.1 | 34.0 |
| 1860–64 | 23,626 | 102.9 | 14.1 | 29.7 |

Source: Compiled from John Duffy, *A History of Public Health in New York City, 1825–1866* (New York, 1968), 575–579.

*Appendix E*

Occupations of residents of Fourth Street in the Eleventh Ward of New York City, 1851

| Occupation | N | Occupation | N |
|---|---|---|---|
| Shipbuilding trades | 61 | Cooper | 8 |
| Metal trades | 49 | Jeweler | 8 |
| Construction trades | 39 | Peddler | 7 |
| Clothing | 36 | Physician | 6 |
| Carter | 31 | Saloonkeeper | 5 |
| Laborer | 24 | Cigarmaker | 5 |
| Furnituremaker | 20 | Pianomaker | 4 |
| No occupation listed | 20 | Policeman | 4 |
| Food processing | 18 | Engineer | 4 |
| Boot and shoemaker | 15 | Seaman | 3 |
| Grocer | 12 | Agent | 3 |
| Clerk | 10 | Captain | 3 |

2 each: Printer, Scavenger, Teacher, Musician, Barber, Hardware, Clergyman, Collector, Waiter

1 each: Toymaker, Miller, Soapmaker, Missionary, Factor, Foreman, Court Crier, Architect, Author, Saddler, Bookkeeper, Corkmaker, Combmaker, Brushmaker

Source: *Doggett's New York City Street Directory for 1851* (New York, 1851).

*Appendix F*
Nativity of New York's population by wards, 1855

| Ward | Population | Foreign-born (percent) | Irish (percent) | German (percent) |
|------|-----------|------------------------|-----------------|------------------|
| 1 | 13,486 | 68.4% | 46.0% | 14.8% |
| 2 | 3,249 | 60.9 | 35.8 | 10.6 |
| 3 | 7,909 | 48.0 | 28.9 | 9.2 |
| 4 | 22,895 | 70.0 | 45.6 | 4.4 |
| 5 | 21,617 | 47.6 | 22.5 | 12.5 |
| 6 | 34,422 | 70.0 | 42.4 | 14.9 |
| 7 | 34,052 | 50.8 | 34.0 | 9.0 |
| 8 | 39,982 | 43.7 | 21.2 | 11.2 |
| 9 | 26,378 | 34.2 | 19.7 | 6.1 |
| 10 | 52,979 | 50.9 | 13.0 | 30.3 |
| 11 | 17,656 | 55.7 | 17.5 | 33.6 |
| 12 | 26,597 | 52.7 | 33.0 | 12.2 |
| 13 | 24,597 | 47.3 | 18.7 | 22.6 |
| 14 | 24,754 | 57.4 | 36.2 | 13.3 |
| 15 | 24,046 | 41.3 | 26.1 | 4.5 |
| 16 | 39,823 | 45.9 | 39.0 | 5.9 |
| 17 | 59,548 | 57.8 | 24.9 | 27.3 |
| 18 | 39,509 | 53.1 | 37.1 | 9.0 |
| 19 | 17,866 | 53.8 | 35.4 | 10.0 |
| 20 | 40,075 | 61.2 | 27.3 | 16.8 |
| 21 | 27,914 | 41.3 | 29.7 | 5.4 |
| 22 | 22,605 | 54.0 | 25.4 | 21.0 |
| TOTALS | 622,924 | 52.3 | 28.2 | 15.7 |

*Source:* Ernst, *Immigrant Life in New York,* 193.

*Appendix G*
Selected social statistics, c. 1855

| Ward | A | B | C | D | E | F | G | H | I | J | K |
|------|-----|-----|----|-----|-----|-----|----|----|----|-----|------|
| 1 | 508 | 552 | 38 | 482 | 276 | .6 | 46 | 52 | 20 | 18 | 89 |
| 2 | 163 | 277 | 48 | 145 | 702 | .3 | 29 | 61 | 30 | 12 | 21 |
| 3 | 148 | 268 | 44 | 24 | 415 | .3 | 21 | 62 | 33 | 21 | 24 |
| 4 | 441 | 475 | 40 | 8 | 41 | .4 | 37 | 52 | 20 | 22 | 82 |
| 5 | 438 | 414 | 39 | 13 | 66 | .5 | 44 | 49 | 19 | 34 | 81 |
| 6 | 503 | 516 | 36 | 6 | 37 | .2 | 47 | 51 | 18 | 25 | 16 |
| 7 | 604 | 536 | 35 | 15 | 37 | 1.0 | 35 | 48 | 16 | 50 | 0 |
| 8 | 516 | 432 | 37 | 8 | 48 | .9 | 29 | 47 | 17 | 48 | 41 |
| 9 | 588 | 464 | 34 | 9 | 34 | 1.5 | 26 | 46 | 15 | — | 17 |
| 10 | 501 | 489 | 37 | 4 | 32 | .8 | 27 | 49 | 19 | 70 | −2 |
| 11 | 677 | 635 | 32 | 1 | 14 | 1.7 | 38 | 49 | 16 | 95 | −53 |
| 13 | 587 | 572 | 33 | 2 | 19 | 1.2 | 37 | 49 | 16 | 62 | −11 |
| 14 | 533 | 481 | 36 | 10 | 41 | .7 | 31 | 48 | 17 | 34 | −3 |
| 15 | 401 | 249 | 37 | 98 | 107 | 1.4 | 28 | 42 | 14 | 70 | 15 |
| 16 | 670 | 507 | 33 | 9 | 39 | 2.1 | 29 | 46 | 14 | 264 | −18 |
| 17 | 623 | 537 | 35 | 11 | 27 | 1.5 | 31 | 48 | 16 | 72 | −48 |
| 18 | 662 | 445 | 35 | 46 | 84 | 2.0 | 35 | 44 | 13 | 318 | −26 |
| 19 | 582 | 498 | 32 | 5 | 45 | 3.3 | 43 | 50 | 14 | 48 | — |
| 20 | 760 | 649 | 32 | 3 | 36 | 2.7 | 36 | 48 | 14 | 58 | −43 |
| 21 | 678 | 504 | 35 | 31 | 75 | 2.7 | 34 | 46 | 14 | 95 | −149 |
| 22 | 762 | 675 | 30 | 3 | 45 | 3.5 | 41 | 49 | 14 | 46 | — |

A = Children 1–5 per 1000 men 20–45
B = Children 1–5 per 1000 women 20–45
C = Pct. persons aged 20–35
D = Per capita personal wealth in $100s
E = Per capita real wealth in $100s
F = Distance of ward center from City Hall in miles
G = Deathrate per 1000
H = Pct. men
I = Pct. men 20–35
J = Men per licensed liquor establishment
K = Deviation from modeled norm for boardinghouses
Ward 12 is excluded in these calculations since it began at 86th Street, beyond the built-up area of the city.
    The source of most of this information is given in Table 23; other statistics are from the 1855 New York State Census.

# Index

*Library of Congress Cataloging-in-Publication Data*

Stott, Richard Briggs.
    Workers in the metropolis: class, ethnicity, and youth in
  antebellum New York City / Richard B. Stott.
      p.   cm.
    Includes bibliographical references.
    ISBN 0-8014-2067-9 (alk. paper)
      1. Working class—New York (N.Y.)—History—19th century.
    2. Alien labor—New York (N.Y.)—History—19th century.   I. Title.
    HD8085.N53S76   1989
    305.5'62'09747109034—dc20

                                                        89-42890